THE TELEGRAPH

THE TELEGRAPH

A History of Morse's Invention
and Its Predecessors
in the United States

by

Lewis Coe

McFarland & Company, Inc., Publishers
Jefferson, North Carolina, and London

To the men and women of the telegraph

Frontispiece: S. F. B. Morse at age 75 (photo by
Mathew Brady, 1866; courtesy of Library of Congress).

British Library Cataloguing-in-Publication data are available

Library of Congress Cataloguing-in-Publication Data

Coe, Lewis, 1911–
    The telegraph : a history of Morse's invention and its predecessors
in the United States / by Lewis Coe.
        p. cm.
    Includes bibliographical references and index.
    ISBN 0-89950-736-0 (lib. bdg. : 50# alk. paper) ∞
    1. Telegraph–United States–History. 2. Morse, Samuel Finley
Breese, 1791–1872. 3. Inventors–United States–Biography.
I. Title.
TK5115.C54 1993
621.383–dc20   92-53597
                                                              CIP

Manufactured in the United States of America

McFarland & Company, Inc., Publishers
  Box 611, Jefferson, North Carolina 28640

Contents

Acknowledgments

I am greatly indebted to my brother telegraphers in the Morse Telegraph Club, whose many contributions to the club quarterly, *Dots and Dashes,* were the source of much information for this book.

My heartfelt thanks to Barbara Burns, head of reference services, Crown Point, (Indiana) Community Library, and her colleagues Barbara Houk, Gail Olson, Suzanne Owen, and Catherine Salyers for reference help and for their unfailing interest in and encouragement of my writing efforts.

I was also fortunate to have near at hand Indiana's third largest library, the Lake County Public Library, where Director Carol Derner and her staff were always ready to help.

Prologue

For 15 years of my life, most of my waking hours were spent within hearing distance of a Morse telegraph instrument. Small wonder, then, that thoughts and recollections of the telegraph have filled my mind for all these years. In a recurring dream, I find myself in the little town where I was once a telegraph operator. Walking down the street, I come to the familiar-looking old office. The door is open, and there on the battered desk are the telegraph instruments, just as I remembered them from 60 years ago. Cautiously, I open the key on the Chicago wire. The sounder clicks—this line is still working! Grasping the key knob, I start to call "C," the call for Chicago. No answer. Then I try "G," for Galesburg. No answer there either. No one ever will answer now because it is a dream, a dream of people, places, and events that are gone forever. Some of the people still live, of course, but they too are all old-timers, living with thoughts of the past.

The great network of telegraph wires that once enfolded the nation like a cobweb has vanished just as surely as the spider's handiwork is erased by a sudden sweep of the broom. This book is about the telegraph, Morse's great invention that was the beginning of electrical technology. This is not a work of fiction. The truth is far more interesting than any product of the imagination. Where technical information is given, it describes actual methods and equipment used by the telegraph companies.

1. The Sign of Fire

O ye children of Benjamin, gather yourselves to flee out of the midst of Jerusalem, and blow the trumpet in Tekoa, and set up a sign of fire in Beth-haccerem: for evil appeareth out of the north, and great destruction (Jeremiah 6:1).

From the beginning of time, man has needed to communicate. This was particularly true during a period of constant warfare when it was vital to know what the enemy was doing. Other than sending a messenger, there seemed to be no way until someone thought of using signals of fire. This was limited to nighttime use, but it was better than nothing. At first the fire signals could convey only a very limited meaning; typically "no fire" meant "all OK," and "fire" meant "the bad guys are coming!" Crude as it was, the system could warn of approaching danger from miles away, faster than a messenger could travel. The Greeks made widespread use of fire signals and by building fires on strategically located mountaintops, could convey the message far beyond the range of direct vision. As the system got more sophisticated, more detailed messages could be sent by arranging one, two, three or more fires side by side, each number having a specific meaning.

In 1455, the Scottish Parliament passed an act establishing a bonfire or signal fire code, using the old word "bale." The Scots had one main preoccupation at the time, namely, "What are the English doing?" The signal code was therefore quite simple, consisting of three messages. One bale meant "The English are coming." Two bales meant "They are already here." Four bales was the signal of real emergency; it meant "They are here, and there are an awful lot of them!" When all England lived in dread of the Spanish Armada in Queen Elizabeth's time, watchmen were kept stationed all along the coast, ready to give the alarm. In *The Armada* Macaulay describes the night when the great fleet was finally sighted:

> From Eddystone to Berwick bounds, from Lynn to Milford Bay,
> That time of slumber was bright and busy as the day.
> For swift to east and swift to west the ghastly war-flame spread.
> High on St. Michael's Mount it shown; it shown on Beachy Head.
> Far on the deep the Spaniard saw, along each southern shire,
> Cape beyond cape, in endless range, those twinkling points of fire.

1

Fire signals were in use for some 20 centuries. Ruins of old signal towers can still be seen along the Spanish coast. In the United States, large numbers of earthen mounds are found in Butler County and elsewhere in Ohio. The prehistoric race that erected these structures did so for several reasons: military forts for defense against enemies, sites for religious ceremonies, and signal stations. Many of the mounds command extensive views of the country and of other mounds, so that fire signals could be relayed from one to another. Researchers who visited some of these sites over 100 years ago made notes as follows:*

> Within the enclosure are two stone mounds burned throughout. These burnt stones prove that powerful fires have there been maintained for long periods, and undoubtedly used as signals of alarm.
>
> These works are all protected by a perfect system of signal stations. Upon one of the highest hills in Madison Township stands the largest mound in the county. From it a fire on the Miamisburg mound could be readily seen. The watchman then lighting his fire could warn the watchmen on the other towers almost instantly.

Curiously, fire signals came into use again in 1942 when General MacArthur was being spirited away from Corregidor on a PT boat. Lieutenant Bulkely, commanding the PT squadron, had elected to stay close to the islands on his port bow to avoid choppy water farther from shore. This turned out to be a mistake because shortly huge bonfires sprang up on the shores of Cabra and the Apo Islands. Japanese coast watchers had spotted the boats and apparently not having radios, were using the time-honored fire signals to alert Japanese sentries on the larger islands of Luzon and Mindoro.

The plains Indians of North America made extensive use of smoke signals for daytime communication. Charles Russell's painting *Smoke Signal,* now in the Amon Carter Museum, Fort Worth, Texas, is probably accurate in depicting how the smoke signals were used. On a high vantage point, a small fire was built. Then green grass or other vegetation was added to produce a dense smoke. A blanket was used alternately to cover and release the smoke, making possible a crude form of telegraphy. For nineteenth-century travelers on the western plains, a smoke signal was ominous. It meant that someone was watching and waiting, for what purpose no one was never sure. From elevated points on clear days when the wind was calm so that the smoke went straight up, the signals could be seen for many miles across the western plains. During the afternoon of Sunday, June 25, 1876, Capt. Anson Mills, Third Cavalry, was on a scouting expedition from the camp of Gen. George Crook on Goose Creek, Wyoming Territory. Far to the northwest, the captain saw a column of smoke. It was not a signal that the captain saw. Without knowing it, he was seeing the smoke from the Battle of Little Big Horn.

*J. P. MacLean, The Mound Builders *(Cincinnati: Robert Clarke, 1887).*

As far back as 480 B.C. there are accounts of signals being flashed by the reflected rays of the sun. Brightly polished metal such as warriors' shields were the usual reflectors since glass mirrors were still unknown. Emperor Tiberius is said to have ruled Rome from the island of Capri for the last 10 years of his life, depending on sun-flashed signals from the mainland to keep track of things at home. Anyone who has been temporarily blinded by the brilliant flash from an automobile window on a sunny day can appreciate the inherent power of the sun's rays for signaling. Even though the ancients knew this, they were unable to make effective use of the principle because they lacked a dot-dash code to spell out words.

Visual signals given by flags, or lighted torches, originated in the mid-seventeenth century and were always useful for short-range communication. It is one of the old methods that has survived until modern times. During the American Civil War, a great deal of signaling with flags and torches was done from tall towers erected in the field. The Cobb's Hill tower near Petersburg, in use during 1864, was 125 feet high. For daytime signaling, a single large flag was used. There were three basic movements of the flag. Waving to the left indicated the numeral 1; to the right meant 2; and a dip to the front was 3. Where a letter was composed of several figures, the motions were made in rapid succession without any pause. Letters were separated by a very brief pause, and words or sentences were distinguished by one or more dip motions to the front.

The Meyer Code Used in Flag Signaling

A	11	K	1212	U	221
B	1221	L	112	V	2111
C	212	M	2112	W	2212
D	111	N	22	X	1211
E	21	O	12	Y	222
F	1112	P	2121	Z	1111
G	1122	Q	2122	&	2222
H	211	R	122	tion	2221
I	2	S	121	ing	1121
J	2211	T	1	ed	1222

The Meyer code was officially discontinued in 1912. Orders from the War Department specified the International Morse Code as the General Service Code of the army, to be used for all visual signaling, radio telegraphy, and cables using siphon recorders. The American Morse Code was specified for use on Army telegraph lines, short cables, and field lines.

The military two-flag semaphore system is still in use today, and when done by skilled signalmen is very fast over relatively short ranges. The Navy in particular has always favored this method of signaling between ships, especially when radio

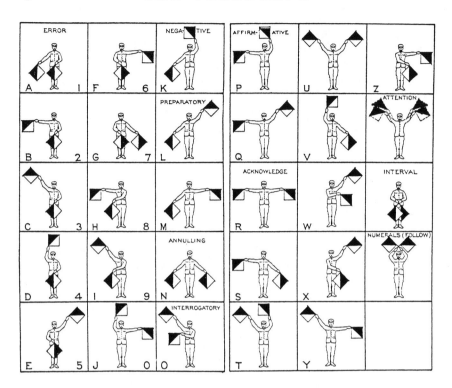

Two-flag semaphore code (*Signal Book United States Army 1912*) (courtesy Government Printing Office, Washington, D.C.).

silence must be maintained. Some operators become so skilled that they can dispense with the flags and communicate rapidly using hand motions alone over short ranges. Wigwag operators face each other and move the two flags to the stylized positions corresponding to the letters of the alphabet. During the American Civil War, there were some attempts to use lighted signals of various types for night signaling. Most night signaling of which there is a record was done with lighted torches and the Meyer code used for flag signaling.

A patent issued in 1862 to L. O. Colvin and G. H. Gardner of Philadelphia detailed a clever signal light to be used on the mastheads of ships. The device employed an oil lamp together with a shutter. The shutter, electromagnetically operated, was used for sending flashes of light in the Morse code. The inventors suggested that certain messages could be sent in cipher where it was necessary to avoid interception. The Smithsonian Institution has a patent model of this invention. There seems to be no record of its being put to practical use. Blinker lights later became very useful signaling tools, but they had to wait for the invention of the incandescent lamp, around 1880.

Chappé semaphore and code used (courtesy Morse Telegraph Club Quarterly — *Dots and Dashes*).

Before the electric telegraph, the first successful telegraph lines used the visual system of movable displays to convey messages. Originally used to report the arrival of ships as they approached port, the idea was later expanded to include chains of relay towers by which a message could be sent far beyond the range of direct observation. One of the best-known systems was that of Chappé in France. The Chappé brothers were three French schoolboys who were attending schools in the same general area. They were prohibited from visiting with each other in person and were inspired to develop a method of visual signaling that used movable arms on tall masts. The idea worked so well that the Chappés attempted to interest the French government in adopting it. However, this was during the French Revolution, and new ideas were automatically regarded with suspicion.

Eventually reason prevailed over hysteria, and the brothers were voted 6,000 francs for an experimental line. The project received a favorable report in a communication dated July 2, 1793. Reference was made to sending and receiving a "*telegramme*," believed to be the first use of the word in communications. One of the first lines ran from Paris via Montmartre to Lille. It was over this line that the first formal telegraph message was probably sent on August 15, 1794. It brought news of the capture of Quesnoy from the Austrians.

The Chappé brothers fell out of favor with the government when Louis Philippe ascended to power in 1830. The Citizen King did continue to expand the semaphore system, and by 1844, France was crisscrossed with 5,000 kilometers of line having 533 stations. Telescope making became a profitable business because every semaphore station needed at least one! Although extremely slow compared to the electric telegraph that was to come later, the Chappé system achieved some results that were little short of miraculous for that time. Messages were received in Paris from Lille in 2 minutes; from Calais in 4 minutes, 5 seconds; from Strasbourg in 5 minutes, 52 seconds; from Toulon in 13 minutes, 50 seconds; from Bayonne in 14 minutes; and from Brest in 6 minutes, 50 seconds. Under normal conditions a message could travel from Paris to Behobie in the far southwest corner of France in about 40 minutes.

Normally considered a daytime device, the Chappé system was adopted to night use by mounting torches or lanterns on the movable arms. Claude Chappé (1763–1805) served as chief engineer of the sempahore system. Like many other early inventors, he became involved in strife with others who claimed priority of the invention or were just jealous of his success. In 1805, while under extreme pressure building a new line from Paris to Lyons, Chappé became despondent and took his own life at age 42.

In England, development of visual telegraphs started in earnest when a British officer, campaigning in France, observed the enemy using Chappé's semaphore to direct troops in the field. Some of the early English systems used a display of large rectangular panels that could be displayed in different patterns instead of the arms of the semaphore method. In England, where signaling was at that time regarded as strictly a military activity, progress lagged in times of peace. After the peace of Amiens in 1801, many signal stations on the eastern and southern coasts of England were abandoned and the land given back to the former owners. The defeat of

Napoléon in 1814 and his banishment to Elba caused another abandonment of signal stations. With Napoleon's escape, active work in signaling again resumed.

The semaphore was now the preferred method, and a line was completed in 1815 linking London with Chatham via West Square, Southwark, Nunhead, and Red Hill. By 1836, Wheatstone was transmitting electrical signals from London to Birmingham, and the last of the semaphore stations was closed on December 31, 1847. In the early 1840s receipt of the "India Mail" was a matter of utmost urgency to the British. When the dispatches landed at the port of Marseilles, they were carried by fast horses to the port of Calais where a fast boat was waiting to rush them to England. A summary of the most important news was taken from the dispatch bag at Marseilles and sent to Calais by the French telegraph, thus arriving in England far ahead of overland transport.

The idea was clever but did not reckon with the resourcefulness of the French journalists. These worthies procured the services of some expert semaphore operators who could readily eavesdrop on the telegraph. In this way the French papers were regularly scooping their English counterparts on dispatches from the India Mail. The English were furious but were unable to do anything more than complain bitterly! It was probably not too difficult to recruit semaphore operators who were willing to work against their former employer. The French semaphore operators or *stationnaires*, were not exactly a happy group of workers. Deliberately chosen were individuals of low intellect who would presumably follow orders without asking questions. Pay was low, and even that might be withheld if the government was a little short of cash. Negligence could be punished by imprisonment, and each station was under the iron rule of a chief operator, who could fire a worker on the spot.

In America, development of visual signal systems was confined largely to schemes for advanced reporting of the arrival of ships from abroad. In those days, when a ship left port, it vanished into the great unknown stretches of the sea, and there was no knowledge of its whereabouts until it arrived at the distant port. Those that didn't arrive were presumed lost with all hands. Under these circumstances, observation stations in a position to spot vessels while they were still far offshore could provide a much-appreciated service to the public.

One of the first marine reporting telegraphs in America, established by Jonathan Grout of Belchertown, Massachusetts, ran from Martha's Vineyard to Boston using 14 intermediate relay stations. The Vineyard afforded a good vantage point for spotting vessels from the West Indies and South America as well as coastwise traffic. Grout charged pretty stiff fees, ranging from $10 for reporting a small coastal vessel to $40 for a large ship from a distant port. The high fees drove customers away, and by 1807, Grout was out of business and bankrupt. Legacies from this pioneer line are the seven locations between Martha's Vineyard and

Boston bearing the name Telegraph Hill and Telegraph Street in Dorchester, which leads to the old signal station.

Christopher Colles of New York established a semaphore line for reporting the arrival of vessels off Sandy Hook in 1812. Colles tried to interest the government in a semaphore line extending from Passamaquoddy to New Orleans, a distance of 2,600 miles. By his calculations, a message of the length of the Lord's Prayer could be sent over the line in 36 minutes, 13 seconds. He asked, "Will not this be rapid enough?" Colles never received any encouragement for this project, and even his Sandy Hook line was abandoned after a few years. Telegraph Hill in San Francisco is a reminder of the days when a signal station there announced the arrival of ships. Ship arrival was a very important event to the residents of that landlocked city.

Around 1817, James M. Elford of Charlestown, South Carolina, devised a marine signaling system using seven blue-and-white flags. Displayed in various combinations, the flags could indicate a large vocabulary of signals. John R. Parker, who was agent for Elford's flag system, also set up a semaphore telegraph on Long Island in 1824 to relay ship arrival information. All American ships had been assigned individual numbers, and when a captain was nearing port, he hoisted the flags indicating his number. These numbers were known in all the principal American and English ports and made it possible to identify and report approaching vessels.

The success of the marine telegraphs inspired continual agitation for the construction of cross-country lines, and in 1837 a memorial was presented to the 24th Congress praying for the construction of a visual telegraph line from New York to New Orleans. It was estimated that messages could be sent over the line from New Orleans to Washington in one hour. Relay stations no more than eight miles apart were required, and their cost would be $300 each. In the debate that followed this proposal, one of the leading objectors was none other than Samuel F. B. Morse, who stated correctly that his electric telegraph would soon make all visual systems obsolete. Fortunately, Congress took no action on the semaphore proposal. All visual telegraphs, no matter their nature, were subject to the vagaries of the weather. In London, where the problem was understandably severe, the Admiralty reported that its telegraph was out of service a total of 133 days during the fiscal year 1839–1840.

One of the most successful and widely used visual signaling systems, the heliograph, did not appear until 1865, long after most visual systems were considered obsolete. The factor that established the heliograph was the existence of the Morse alphabet of dots and dashes, widely used for land telegraph and submarine cable operations. The ancients understood the principles of reflected sunlight, but no one ever got around to devising a code for the letters of the alphabet. Signal codes of some type had existed long before Morse, but none of them ever reached a level of universal acceptance, and they were mostly forgotten by the time Morse published his code.

Early in the nineteenth century, Gauss, a German mathematician, had discovered the tremendous potential of the sun's rays reflected from a plane mirror. Through experiments he was able to demonstrate that even a small mirror one inch square could send flashes that could be seen over a distance of seven miles. The silvered glass mirror, invented in 1840 by Justus Liebeg, paved the way for the heliograph. A heliograph comprises a plane mirror and a means for keying the flash according to the Morse code. Simple as it was, the instrument did not emerge until the mid-nineteenth century.

Like the American army, the British did not have a separate Signal Corps organization until the 1860s. The first British signal school was established at Chatham in 1865. Shortly after, a young officer named Henry Christopher Mance (1840–1926) became interested in signaling with the sun. Mance, later to be knighted for his achievements in engineering, knew of the use of mirror instruments called heliotropes in the triangulation of India. The Indian survey, one of the great engineering projects of the nineteenth century, required accurate location of high mountain peaks to serve as control points for the ground survey. Bright fire pots were used at night and the heliotropes by day. It is not known whether any Morse code signaling was done by heliotrope, but it is certain that prearranged signals were exchanged.

By this time, the original American Morse code had been modified to form the International or Continental Morse code. The latter code had been adopted in 1851 for use on submarine cables. In 1865 it was designated as the official service code of the British army. The simple and effective instrument that Mance invented was to be an important part of military communications for the next 40 years. Limited to use in sunlight, the heliograph became the most efficient visual signaling device ever known. In preradio days, it was often the only means of communication that could span ranges of up to 100 miles with a lightweight portable instrument.

The Mance instrument employed tripod-mounted mirrors, with one mirror linked to a key mechanism. The key tilted the mirror enough to turn the flash on and off at the distant station in accordance with the dots and dashes of the Morse alphabet. Range was line-of-sight, with atmospheric conditions establishing the upper limit. The British army found the Mance heliograph ideally suited to field operations in India and Afghanistan. It was used to transmit daily reports and orders to and from the remote mountain posts and for tactical communications when troops were in the field. (One hundred ten years later, TV pictures were to show Afghan guerrilla units using British pattern heliographs in their conflict with the Russians.) The present Afghans have found the helio useful for the same reasons as their British enemies of old; namely, a simple uncomplicated mechanism that requires no batteries or complex maintenance.

In 1877, Chief Signal Officer Albert J. Meyer of the U.S. Army obtained some heliograph instruments from the British for experimental purposes. Meyer sent six instruments to Gen. Nelson A. Miles, who was assuming command of the Yellowstone Department in Montana. Miles became an enthusiastic user of the heliograph. When he was transferred to Arizona in 1886 to take command of the Apache Indian campaign, he saw it as the ideal place for heliograph operations. There were few roads and telegraph lines, and widely separated army commands were often at a disadvantage through lack of communication. Miles established a heliograph communications network throughout a large part of Arizona and New Mexico, taking advantage of strategically located mountain peaks for relay stations.

The annual report of the secretary of war for the year 1895 contains the chief signal officer's report on the Glassford expedition that established the world's heliograph distance record. It reads as follows:

> In developing the more important electrical communicating devices of the Signal Corps, other methods of signaling that are absolutely essential adjuncts have received due attention. Heliography is perhaps the most important of these methods to a rapidly moving army, operating over a country where the use of electrical instruments is inadvisable or temporarily impracticable.
>
> The former world's record for long range heliographing was surpassed 58 miles during the year through the zealous and intelligent exertions of Capt. W. A. Glassford, Signal Corps, and a detachment of signal sergeants by the interoperation of stations on Mount Ellen, Utah and Mount Uncompahgre, Colorado, 183 miles apart. This unprecedented feat of long distance intercommunication by visual signals was made on Sept. 17, 1894, with Signal Corps heliographs carrying mirrors only 8 inches square. It was accomplished only after much discomfort and some suffering, due to severe storms on the mountains and to the rarified air to which the parties were subjected for ten days. The persistence, skill, and ingenuity of Captain Glassford and of the signal sergeants engaged in this result are highly commendable.

Captain Glassford's report the the chief signal officer:

> On the morning of September 10, as prearranged, we were ready and began with the sunrise to direct our glasses and flash in the compass direction of Mount Ellen, for not even the Henry Mountains group, of which Mount Ellen is one, was visible. No answering flash was seen until about 1 o'clock in the afternoon, when we caught the first glimmer of the Mount Ellen flash, which appeared through the telescope of a deep reddish hue and to be about as bright as the planet Venus and with the same apparent disk as presented by that planet in our glasses. It was visible for only a short time, however, though long enough to settle definitely the position of that peak.
>
> On the morning of the 11th the flash from Mount Ellen was again seen for a short

time, and the Mount Uncompahgre flash was also recognized by the signalmen on the former. The 12th, 13th, and 14th were stormy, and the lower plateau intervening between the peaks seemed covered with a thick dust and haze which interposed a veil too thick to penetrate.

The 15th being more favorable, the flash from Mount Ellen could be distinctly seen, and at sunset the whole Henry group of mountains was outlined against the distant horizon. We could get their signals, but it seemed impossible for the party on Mount Ellen to read ours, hence interchange of messages was not yet successful. On the 16th the Ellen flash was dimly seen and feeling sure that they had received our message I began sending several messages, with directions that they be repeated back. One of these messages was sent time and again, so that it could, if only received in parts at a time, be put together and the complete message so made out.

On the morning of the 17th the horizon was clear, the Ellen flash distinct, and their messages read quite easily. The repeated message of the day before was sent by our party several times, and then our glasses were trained on the Ellen station. I knew that if they sent back the same message they had read our signals. About 10 o'clock we received the closing part of the message and read it without difficulty. When finished it was begun again and the whole message was received this time. Thus we knew that our flash had transmitted and the signalist's eye—183 miles distant—had caught the words sent by the speaking sunbeam.

Distances of 183 miles were never used in practical communication, 75 to 100 miles being about the maximum. The world's record did add to the prestige of the Signal Corps and demonstrated beyond all doubt the potential of the simple mirror signals. Persons who have traveled in the region of the mountains involved can truly admire what was accomplished. Some of the most rugged country in North America, with widely separated parties having no direct communication with each other, dependent solely on foot or horse-drawn transport, and the need to be self-sufficient for food—that was the nature of the challenge. Organizing such an expedition today would still present a few problems. In 1894 it was a miracle.

Remnants of some of the old heliograph stations are still found on the mountaintops today. At Fort Bowie, Arizona, ceremonial demonstrations of the heliograph are sometimes staged on Bowie Peak, an important relay point during the Indian campaign. The American army at first used the Mance pattern instruments from England. Later the United States had its own version that employed a leaf shutter to interrupt the light beam for keying instead of the mirror-tilting method used by Mance. The heliograph was used in the Spanish-American War in 1898. By the time of World War I, wireless and field telephones had pretty well taken over the army's communications, but heliograph instruments were kept on hand until the mid–1920s. Some were kept at Corregidor in the Philippines for backup communication with the mainland in case of radio failure.

The last great use of the heliograph was during the Boer War in South Africa,

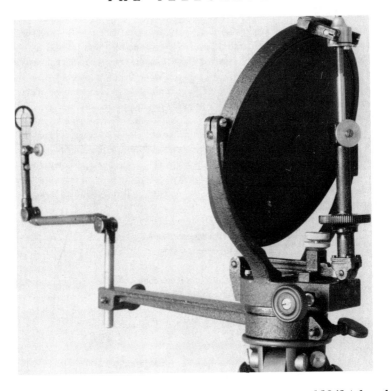

Mark 5 heliograph instrument as used in the Canadian army until 1941 (photo by Lewis Coe).

where both sides used it. The terrain and climate, as well as the nature of the campaign, made the heliograph the logical choice. For night communications, the British used some naval searchlights, brought inland on railroad cars, and equipped with leaf-type shutters for keying the beam of light into dots and dashes. In the early stages of the war, the British garrisons were besieged in Kimberly, Ladysmith, and Mafeking. With land telegraph lines cut off, the only contact with the outside was via light-beam communication, helio by day, searchlight at night.

In an effort to improve communications, five Marconi "mobile wireless units" were sent out from England. Unfortunately, with wireless still in its infancy, these units were of little value. In the siege of Ladysmith, telegraph lines were cut off on November 2, 1899, and from then until the relieving army arrived on February 28, 1900, the heliograph was the only connecting link with the outside world. Cloudy days were tedious for the inhabitants of Ladysmith because no news could be received. One person recorded such a day in his diary, writing, "Heavy weather had settled upon us and had blinded the little winking reflector on Monte Cristo Hill."

As the relieving army, commanded by Sir Redvers Buller, approached the city, his signal officer, Capt. John Cayzer, attempted to establish communication by helio. There were problems with Boer operators who intercepted the British flashes. When Cayzer finally reached a station claiming to be British, he devised a test. "Find Captain Brooks of the Gordons," he signaled. "Ask him the name of Captain Cayzer's country place in Scotland." Captain Brooks, when found, did not immediately grasp the purpose of the question and remarked, "Well, I always thought Cayzer was an ass, but I didn't think he'd forget the name of his own home!"

Canada was the last major army to keep the heliograph as an issue item. By the time the mirror instruments were retired in 1941, they were not used much for signaling. Still, the army hated to see them go. One officer said, "They made damn fine shaving mirrors!"

By 1900, the era of visual signals of any kind was drawing to a close. Rapid developments in the art of wireless, or radio, promised to solve the problem of communicating without wires. The two-flag semaphore, searchlights, and masthead blinker lights still survive today as a means of auxiliary short-range communication. The word "heliograph" now is likely to draw a questioning look. Latin students, of course, quickly translate it to "sun telegraph." Modern encyclopedias often do not have any entry for "heliograph." Nevertheless, the heliograph was an important signaling device for 40 years or more and has not been totally forgotten by modern engineers. When the first microwave systems were being designed, it was realized that light waves and microwaves would follow essentially the same line-of-sight paths. Old heliograph instruments were brought out of obscurity and tested under various conditions. The results enabled accurate predictions of the ranges that could be covered between microwave relay towers.

A final tribute to the usefulness of the heliograph comes in the signaling mirrors that are included in most survival kits. Although the mirrors may have a limited usefulness in many situations, they are so compact, lightweight, and inexpensive that it would be foolish not to include them. Today's military men have no need for beacon fires, flags, or semaphores. They can speak to each other with a variety of compact field radios or for longer ranges set up a portable earth station to access a satellite for worldwide communication.

2. Quick as Lightning!

Canst thou send lightnings, that they may go, and say unto
thee, Here we are? (Job 38:35)

Lightning was the supreme force to the ancients, and for many years it was the only manifestation of electricity in any form. The very early attempts at an electric telegraph were all based on the use of static electricity, the kind that makes hair stand on end and causes sheets of paper to stick together.

Some of these early telegraphs worked, but due to the temperamental nature of static electricity, they were never put to practical use. For one thing, static charges will rapidly escape from a wire. This made it necessary to use carefully insulated wires, sometimes running in glass tubes. As early as 1753, an experimenter had suggested a telegraph employing wires for each letter of the alphabet. A charge applied to a wire for a particular letter would cause a pith ball on the other end to move. In 1816, Sir Francis Ronalds of England demonstrated a more practical electrostatic telegraph that needed only one wire. He had eight miles of wire in his experimental line suspended on silk threads. At each end of the line were dials rotating in synchronism. When an impulse was transmitted, the desired letter was displayed on the distant dial. Ronalds was able to exhibit his invention to the British Admiralty, at that time using only the visual semaphore telegraph.

After a successful demonstration, Ronalds asked for a decision on the matter. The reply he received was probably typical of the times, and illustrates the difficulty that early telegraph inventors had in getting support:

> Mr. Barrow presents his compliments to Mr. Ronalds, and acquaints him with reference to his note of the 3rd inst., that telegraphs of any kind are now wholly unnecessary; and that no other than the one now in use will be adopted.

After a put-down like that, it would take a very determined inventor to carry on! None of the telegraphs using "static" electricity was ever put to practical use. Much later, in 1855, after the Morse telegraph was an everyday reality, an incident occurred that illustrated the power if not the practicality of static electricity. In the fall

14

of 1855, two young Scots named Andrew Carnegie and Robert Pitcairn were working as operators for the Pennsylvania Railroad at Outer Depot Pittsburgh, and Altoona, Pennsylvania. One evening there was a brilliant auroral display, and the Morse wires were seriously interfered with by atmospheric electricity. The two young men, 20 and 19, respectively, decided to test the atmospheric current on the line. With that object in view, they disconnected the main-line batteries of the circuit they were using and grounded the line at each end. Then, at intervals during the next hour, they were able to communicate with each other using only the electric power abstracted from the air by the telegraph line.

Although attempts to build an electrostatic telegraph persisted into the first quarter of the nineteenth century, practical telegraphy had to wait until inventors became aware of the pioneering work of Hans Christian Oersted, (1777–1851) and Alessandro Volta (1745–1827). Volta's work established the existence of a new kind of electricity, soon to be referred to as galvanic electricity. It could be generated by chemical action (batteries) and harnessed to do useful work in a variety of ways. Volta's "voltaic pile" was the first battery. Composed of dissimilar elements, it generated a steady current used in many of the early experiments. Oersted established the basic principles of electromagnetism, the basis for all successful telegraphs that were to come. Sir Charles Wheatstone (1802–1875) was probably the first to make practical application of Oersted's experiments with magnetized needles. The two men had a cordial meeting in London in 1823. In 1839, Wheatstone wrote to Oersted:

> I have applied your beautiful discovery for the purpose of transmitting instantaneously, both visually and audibly, to great distances. The first electrical telegraph was established by Mr. Cooke and myself on the London and Birmingham Railway in the year 1837, and we now have a line in action 14 miles in length on the Great Western Railway between London and Bristol.

Wheatstone's needle telegraph was the first widely used telegraph in England. The first version used five needles controlled by five line wires. The needles were moved by magnetic action to different points on a circular dial. The various combinations indicated the letters of the alphabet. In 1837, a five-needle telegraph was being worked between Fenchurch Street and the Blackwall railway station when three of the five dials broke down, probably due to line trouble. The telegraph clerks then made up a code of their own for working with two needles. The results were as good if not better than the five-dial arrangement. Later it was found that only one needle and one dial were needed, and this became the standard for the needle telegraph. Some of the needle machines continued in operation well after the adoption of the Morse system in England. This incident seems to illustrate again the fact that some of the developments in telegraphy were not the result of carefully thought-out research but the spontaneous creation of practical workers who simply went ahead and devised solutions without waiting for directions from above. The classic example, of course, was the development of "sound reading" in the United States, where operators just got tired of waiting for the tape to come out of the register and wrote the message down by listening to the sound instead. Wheatstone went on to become one of the most famous names in telegraphy, and some of his inventions are still in use today.

Wheatstone was among the first to understand and make use of the electrical laws established by Georg Simon Ohm. He made an effort standardize the unit of resistance later called the ohm. In his work with units of resistance. Wheatstone made use of a balanced "bridge" measuring circuit that had been invented in 1833 by Samuel Hunter Christie. This circuit came into prominence due to its use by Wheatstone and has been referred to as the Wheatstone bridge ever since. This was a source of great embarrassment to Sir Charles, who repeatedly tried to give the credit to Christie. Wheatstone at this time was already a brilliant scientist and did not need additional laurels based on another's man's work. During a lecture in 1843, Wheatstone attempted to set matters straight when he said: "Mr. Christie in his 'Experimental Determination of the Laws of Magneto-Electric Induction' printed in the *Philosophical Transactions of the Royal Society for 1833*, has described a differential arrangement of which the principle is the same as that on which the instruments described in this section have been devised. To Mr. Christie must, therefore, be attributed the first idea of this useful and accurate method of measuring resistances." The bridge principle was to become one of the most important circuits used in telegraphy and is still an important part of many modern electrical circuits.

Some of the nineteenth-century scientists who paved the way for the electric telegraph have been memorialized by giving their names to electrical units. Thus, Ampere, the unit of quantity; Henry, the unit of inductance; 'Oersted, strength of magnetic field; Ohm, unit of resistance'; and Volt, electromotive force. Wheatstone is not in this group, yet his contributions to telegraphy outshadow his considerable achievements in other fields, acoustics and light. For his needle telegraph, Wheatstone pioneered the use of polar keying, that is, the transmission of positive and negative voltage to indicate "mark" and "space." This was in contrast to the American Morse telegraph, which used only one polarity switched on and off to signal mark and space. Polar keying became an important factor in developing high-speed telegraphy, and the idea of using opposite polarities was essential in the design of the duplex and quadruplex telegraphs that came later. Keying by alternate polarity is still the underlying principle of today's high-speed digital-data transmission systems. Wheatstone was on good terms with his contemporaries in the field of science, the only exception being the disputes that developed with his early partner in the telegraph, William Fothergill Cooke. Joseph Henry visited Wheatstone during 1837, and evidence of the association between the two men exists in the form of two coils of copper strip, made by Henry, that were found in the surviving collection of Wheatstone's apparatus.

Using punched paper tape for transmission and automatic recorders, the Wheatstone high-speed telegraph system gave the British post office one of the world's best telegraph systems as early as 1881. It was soon adopted by Western Union in America, which hoped to bring over English technicians to assist in operating it. When the British adopted the "Marconi Beam System" to link the empire with shortwave radiotelegraphy in the 1920s, the post office system of high-speed operation was used. Other radiotelegraph services throughout the world also used the same method. Although worldwide communication is now handled almost exclusively by satellites, wherever radiotelegraph stations are still in operation, the Wheatstone system is in use. One of Wheatstone's lesser claims to fame was his invention in 1838 of the stereoscope, that favorite amusement device of Victorian parlors. Stereoscopes in good condition with accompanying picture cards are avidly sought after in the antique trade today.

As telegraph systems proliferated in the early part of the nineteenth century, better batteries to generate the required electrical power received much attention. One of the most promising of these was the Daniell cell, invented in 1833 by Professor John Frederic Daniell, an English chemist. The Daniell battery generated electricity by the same chemical reaction used in the later "gravity battery." Only the physical arrangement of the components was different.

The original telegraph batteries used by Morse were made up of Grove cells. The Grove battery was a powerful and dependable source of electricity. However, it was a rather complicated and expensive assembly, requiring both a zinc and a pure platinum electrode together with both nitric and sulphuric acid for the solution. The Grove was unique among primary cells in that it developed a voltage of 1.96 per cell in contrast to the 1–1.5-volt output of other cells. Ultimately the Daniell and the even simpler gravity cell became the standard. These latter cells gave an average of only 1 volt per cell, but this was not a great handicap as more cells easily made up whatever voltage was required. The Daniell and gravity cells had the further advantage of being perfectly suited to the closed-circuit Morse system. Other primary cells deteriorate rapidly on closed circuit. The Daniell and gravity cells have the opposite characteristic, giving longer life if left on a closed circuit.

A number of early telegraph inventors, including Morse, considered the so-called chemical telegraph. In this system, a chemically treated paper tape passes underneath an electrode. When a signal is received, the electrical action on the chemically treated paper produces a blue mark. One of the best known of these chemical systems was that of Alexander Bain, of Scotland, who received an American patent in 1848. Several Bain lines were in operation in competition with the Morse system. Morse sued Bain for infringement but was not sustained in court.

The courts held that Bain's device was sufficiently different from Morse's to warrant the granting of his patent. In his original patent Morse had a broad claim to the use of any form of electromagnetism in telegraphy. This claim was finally disallowed by the Supreme Court in a decision that pointed out that Morse's claim would have made any future developments in telegraphy impossible; all forms of telegraphy employed some use of electromagnetism. The Morse interests finally obtained control of the competing Bain lines and converted them to Morse operation.

The Bain system worked well enough but had one serious weakness. There was no problem as long as the Bain wire was isolated from other telegraph circuits. As lines increased in number, the Bain lines would pick up false signals from the other lines by induction, resulting in false and confusing marks on the recording tape.

In 1855, David Hughes of Kentucky invented a printing telegraph that showed a lot of promise. It employed a type wheel similar to that of modern printers. The Hughes printer was widely used in Europe but did not come into use in the United States, largely because of the entrenched position of the Morse interests. By 1855, the simple Morse key and sounder was answering the communication needs of the country so efficiently that all printing systems were at a disadvantage. Even the best of the printers represented a rather complicated mechanism of delicate adjustment. Printers required a good line wire in comparison to the Morse instruments, which could operate over some of the poorly constructed "beanpole and cornstalk" lines that characterized much of the early telegraph construction.

Alfred Vail had invented a well-designed printing telegraph in 1837. It employed the type-wheel type of mechanism similar to the later Hughes machine. Vail made no effort to promote his machine or obtain a patent for it, perhaps because he always scrupulously adhered to his commitment to the Morse patent or he honestly believed that printing telegraph machines were too far ahead of their time. The modest and self-effacing character of Vail was revealed when he wrote, in reference to telegraph printers, as follows:

> The instrument employed by Professor Morse has but a single movement, and that motion of a vibratory character; is light and susceptible of the most delicate structure, by which rapidity is insured; the paper is continuous in its movement, and requires no aid from the magnet to carry it. The only object that can be obtained by using the English letters, instead of telegraphic letters, is, the one is in common use, the other is not. The one is as easily read as the other, the advantage then is fanciful and is only to be indulged in at the expense of time, and complication of machinery, increasing the expense, and producing their inevitable accompaniments, liability of derangement, care of attendance, and loss of time.

Having thus talked himself out of it, Vail devoted no further attention to the printing telegraph. Likewise, all the other ideas for printers were set aside and did not reappear until after the turn of the century.

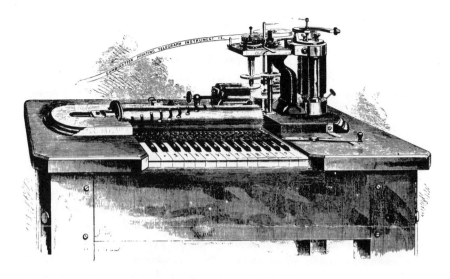

House Printing Telegraph.

In 1846, Royal E. House invented a telegraph instrument that printed the letters of the alphabet directly. The House instrument was far ahead of its time yet showed enough promise to encourage the formation of companies using it instead of the Morse system. The mechanism was improved and patented again in 1852, in part to avoid conflict with the Morse patent. The machine was rated at 1,800 to 2,600 words per hour. One press dispatch of 3,000 words was sent in an hour. In spite of its performance, the House machine suffered some serious problems that limited its practical application. It was a complicated and delicate mechanism, not easily repaired by the operators in the field. The House printer required a high-quality line wire to function properly and many early-nineteenth-century telegraph lines were of marginal quality. A serious drawback was the necessity of two operators to run the machine. One man, known as the grinder, was required to turn a crank operating the machinery. In 1846, there were no electric motors available to run a printer. The House printer soon lost out to the simple and uncomplicated Morse system, which required only one operator and would work over almost any kind of line wire. At least one House machine survived and was exhibited by Western Union at the 1933 Century of Progress in Chicago.

The House machine printed the received message on a narrow paper tape. The tape was folded up and placed in an envelope for delivery to the addressee. No attempt was made to paste it on a message blank as was done with the tape printers that came much later.

By the time of World War I, great progress had been made with the printing telegraph, and the machines handled most of the heavy traffic between major cities.

Using punched sending tape to actuate an automatic transmitter, speeds up to 200 words per minute could be obtained.

In 1868, Western Union brought the English telegraph authority Cromwell Fleetwood Varley to the United States to make a comprehensive survey of American telegraph operations. Varley was to find many problems that needed correcting. The American telegraph industry was the victim of too rapid expansion that left many details to chance. It was found that American lines were using a hodgepodge of instruments with different characteristics (ideally, all the instruments on a single wire should have identical resistance values). Out of Varley's work came a standard for line relays specifying windings of No. 32 silk-covered wire having 150 ohms resistance. Varley also introduced American technicians to standardized methods of making tests to locate faults on telegraph lines. The so-called Varley loop became a standard test in the industry. Varley's tests involved making systematic records of line resistances along a given route when the wires were in good condition. Using these recorded values in comparison with the measurements obtained under fault conditions enabled very accurate locations of faults. With wires in good condition and careful measurements, wire chiefs could often locate faults within one span between line poles.

Inventions of the past often seemed to emerge at precisely the point in history when they were timely and sensational. Others, appearing almost after the fact, have received relatively little notice from the public. Such was the case with the "machine for writing by electricity" that was invented well after the Morse telegraph and the telephone were in widespread use. All of the early telegraph inventors, including Morse, thought in terms of a visual reading device. Except for the accidental discovery of "sound reading" Morse instruments around 1850, visual reading might have been the only method, and an entire era of history involving the colorful Morse operators would have been bypassed.

It was not until 1886 that inventors became interested in the idea of transmitting handwriting by wire. The first machine, the "writing telegraph," actually saw some limited commercial use. The writing was received on a moving paper tape, and since there was no pen-lifting mechanism on the receiver, all of the individual letters were joined by a continuous line on the tape. Telegraphic writing soon attracted the attention of Elisha Gray, the man who lost the telephone patent to Bell by the merest technicality and a strong presumption of fraud. Gray developed a practical machine, which he patented and christened the "telautograph." Gray's machine had a pen-lifting mechanism, and the received message was written in conventional format on a wide sheet of paper.

A company called the Gray National Telautograph Co. was chartered in 1888 and purchased the patent rights for the machine from Elisha Gray. The telegraphic writing created a sensation at the 1893 World's Fair in Chicago. An improved machine in 1895 staged an impressive demonstration in transmitting handwriting

431 miles from Cleveland to Chicago. In 1900, Foster Ritchie, a former Gray assistant, perfected a new design using basically different principles that represented a great improvement over the original. This was the machine that was marketed for the next 30 years. At this time, telautographs were normally short-range instruments. They had technical limitations that prevented reliable performance at distances much over five miles.

Even with its limitations, the telautograph managed to find a sphere of useful applications and held its share of the market in competition with the rapidly expanding telegraph and telephone industry. It remained a device that was little known to the general public since the applications were mostly in large metropolitan areas. A typical application was in the old Dearborn Street railroad station in Chicago where a telautograph in the main concourse kept baggage and mail handlers informed of train movements. Perhaps the ultimate triumph of the telautograph came in the late 1890s when it was selected by the U.S. Army for fire-control communication in the coastal defense system.

First tested at Fort Wadsworth, New York, the system was eventually installed in the most important coastal forts of both Atlantic and Pacific coasts. The nineteenth-century equivalent of Star Wars, the coastal defense guns were the wonder of the age. Before the days of air power and submarines, the only defenses needed against enemy attack were the coastal artillery batteries placed to protect important seaports. As typified by the guns at Sandy Hook and Fort Hancock, New Jersey, that protected New York harbor, the installations utilized the highest technology then known and were shrouded in extreme secrecy. In an 1898 article, the *Scientific American* lamented that no one from the media had been permitted to inspect the Sandy Hook installations since 1895.

The guns were aimed on the basis of data received from observers stationed some distance away, and a reliable method was needed to transmit the data. Telephone or telegraph was not practical due to the deafening noise in the gun pits when the battery was firing. Special military models of the telautograph were designed to enhance ruggedness and reliability. The receiver units at the guns were enclosed in heavy brass, waterproof cases suspended on shockproof mounts. A plate-glass window enabled the message to be read without opening the case, and a small electric bulb illuminated the paper for night reading. None of the coastal guns was ever fired at an enemy, although there were active concerns when tension mounted with Spain in 1898.

Redesign of the telautograph instrument that took place between 1940 and 1960 incorporated the latest developments in electronics. The modern versions are not limited in range and will operate on any channels normally used for telecommunication, including microwave and satellite facilities. Large numbers of the telewriters, or telescribers, as they are now called, are still in use throughout the world. Hospitals, hotels, and factories find them ideal for quick, errorless interchange of

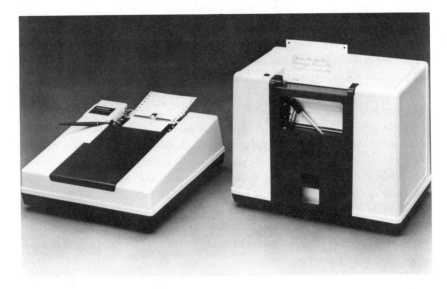

Styled as modern business machines, the current model telautographs still find many applications. For 98 years these machines have been unique in their ability to reproduce an exact replica of a written message at a distant point (photo courtesy Telautograph Corp.).

written information. The current machines are a far cry from the first models, yet they still do the same thing—transmitting a written message by wire. Officials of the Telautograph Corp. say that facsimile machines have now taken over most of the needs for communication that were first filled by the "writing telegraph" of 1888.

When the Morse telegraph began, all circuits between stations consisted of one or more actual metallic conductors, called in communications parlance a physical circuit. In contrast, today's circuits are almost entirely derived from some type of radio facility, either microwaves or orbiting satellites. Fiber-optic cables and modern undersea cables constitute a physical link between stations, but not in the sense that the old telegraph lines did. In a typical communications link today, about the only physical wiring involved is the connection from the customer's premises to the nearest telephone switching center.

Breathtaking as modern technology is, there was a certain fascination with the old circuits that united widely separated points with an actual thread of copper wire. Some very long circuits could be set up by the old methods. In 1884, the Indo-European Telegraph Co. in London staged a remarkable demonstration in setting up a line between London and Calcutta. The route was via Emden, Germany; Odessa, Russia; Tehran, Persia; Karachi, Agra; and Calcutta, India. Every foot of the way was traversed either by undersea cables or land telegraph lines. The British

post office once operated a regular circuit to Australia that consisted entirely of physical connections. The signals traveled from London to Canada via ocean cable, then across North America via Canadian land telegraph line. On the west coast of Canada, the signals were hooked on to an island-hopping undersea cable across the Pacific Ocean and thence to the Australian continent.

When we consider the perplexities encountered by those first line builders between Washington and Baltimore, it almost seems that history would have been better served if radio had been invented first, avoiding completely the problem of line construction. Also, if the planned underground cable had worked, it might have avoided a whole era of desecrating the landscape with overhead pole lines. Morse and his men worked at a time when even the simplest principles of electricity were little understood. Even the great scientist Faraday, who should have known better, once declared that a smaller conductor would be better for the transatlantic cable because it would not require as much electricity to fill it up! (Conductor efficiency increases in direct proportion as the cross-sectional area of the wire is increased.)

With learned opinion at this level, it is no wonder that Morse's crew had to agonize over every detail. Facts that a few years later were known to any journeyman telegraph lineman just did not exist in practical form. It is not surprising, then, that no one knew how to go about insulating the wires where they attached to the poles. Ezra Cornell, above all a practical man, also did his homework and was thus aware that glass was a good insulator of electricity. At his suggestion, the first insulators were glass plates with the wire sandwiched between.

Theoretically on track, the glass plates had problems. The glass had to be set in slots cut in the wood crossarms, a slow process. Also, the recessed mounting created a trap for moisture. Cornell's next idea was inspired by the glass knobs on the bureau drawers in his hotel room. Cornell's glass knobs were pretty close to the final form of the glass insulator, but they were too small, easily broken, and subject to high leakage in wet weather. Then followed a few years of the wildest experimentation, with every conceivable material, including wood, being tried for insulators. Telegraph promoter F. O. J. Smith topped all the others when he flatly declared that insulators were unneccessary. Smith built some lines with the wires just nailed to the supporting poles and trees. The uninsulated lines worked in dry weather, but when it rained, there was big trouble. In Smith's "folly" can be found one of the reasons why the Morse system was able to dominate the telegraph field in the early years. Morse instruments could easily be adjusted to work satisfactorily over lines of high current leakage. Years were to elapse before telegraph lines were of uniform high-quality construction, and the Morse system was simply better adapted to lines of uncertain performance.

Even after lines were built to uniform specifications and well insulated, heavy leakage could occur. When this happened, an operator might not know his station was being called – the instrument was silent. A prudent operator, not hearing any signals, would then "adjust" – moving the magnets farther from the relay armature – then signals once more came in loud and clear. With glass finally emerging as the preferred material, the last great advance in insulator design came with Cauvet's patent of 1865. This patent covered the glass insulator with internal threads molded in for mounting on an oak or locust mounting pin with matching threads. One of the problems with earlier unthreaded insulators, which were simply pushed on to the mounting pin, was that they were easily pulled off by any upward pull on the line wire. The threaded insulator and pin solved this problem nicely. After 1865, improvements in insulators were mostly centered on the invention of high-speed automatic glass-molding machines that could produce insulators in huge quantities at low unit cost.

The great boom in the telegraph industry during the last half of the nineteenth century created a huge demand for insulators. After 1876, the developing telephone industry added to the need. With some pole lines requiring as many as 2,000 insulators per mile, the extent of the demand can be imagined. A large industry sprang up to meet the need. One company alone, Whitall Tatum, listed a production of 67 million pieces during the period 1925–1938. Hemingray, one of the largest producers, was located at Muncie, Indiana, from 1890 to 1969 and turned out many millions of insulators in over 75 styles before shutting down. After World War II, when communication lines started going underground, the need for insulators rapidly diminished and none were manufactured in the United States after 1975.

It was inevitable that insulator collecting would become a popular hobby. Thousands are still available, ranging from the common ones to the ultra rare whose price may be in the four-digit range. Enthusiasts belong to the National Insulator Association. The association holds national conventions yearly and publishes a monthly magazine, *Crown Jewels of the Wire*. Collectors happily hike routes of old pole lines in remote areas, hoping to find a rare specimen. Most of these collectors feel quite strongly that someday these bits of glass will be the only tangible evidence of the great network of wires that once crisscrossed the nation.

The first telegraph line between Washington and Baltimore was strung with comparatively light-gauge copper wire, probably about No. 14 Awg. Here the choice was dictated by the necessity of salvaging wire from the ill-fated underground cable. The light copper wire was fairly adequate from an electrical standpoint but compared to the later techniques of line building was a frail thread indeed. Some of the other early lines used the same light-gauge copper wire, mainly because it was considered prudent to follow the previous example that had proved successful. For one thing, early builders couldn't open up a Graybar catalog and choose from dozens of wire sizes, all neatly tabulated according to size, weight, ohms per mile, and tensile strength. Wire manufacture in 1844 was an infant industry; orders had to be individually negotiated with the factory.

One must marvel that the early builders were able to get wire in the relatively large quantities they needed as most wire uses of the time involved only short lengths. Some idea of the general lack of knowledge prevailing in the early days is seen in the debate between insulated and bare wire for line purposes. The first builders labored under the misapprehension that the line wire had to be insulated. It came as good news that bare wire was just fine as long as it was insulated where it attached to the poles.

The high cost of copper wire finally tempted some brave soul to try iron wire as a substitute. Iron wire was not as efficient electrically as copper, but this deficiency could be allowed for by using higher line voltages. The lack of efficiency was more than compensated for by the lower cost and much greater tensile strength. In time, the standard telegraph line wire was high-grade No. 6 galvanized wire. If put up in cool weather, it could be pulled up tight by block and tackle. In warm weather a little slack had to be allowed for contraction during cold weather.

The lines were usually taut as fiddle strings. A slight breeze would start a musical hum on the wire, which could be heard by placing one's ear on the pole below. By the late 1920s, as telegraph technology became more and more advanced, the old iron wire was gradually replaced with the more efficient No. 9 copper wire. Open wire lines were now carrying telephone circuits, broadcast program feeders, and high-speed automatic telegraph circuits, all needing the uniform characteristics of the copper wire lines.

Iron wire lines always had a problem of unpredictable resistance changes, due to corrosion in the many splices on a long section of line. There was never a more efficient conductor of electricity than a carefully built open wire line using copper conductors. They were costly to maintain, however, and required lots of space in terms of the number of circuits carried. The demand for circuits steadily increased, and by the time of World War II, sheer physical limits of space ruled out the use of open wire lines.

3. Father of the Telegraph

What hath God wrought! (Numbers 23:23)

Modern travelers familiar with airport delays can fully sympathize with the passengers of the sailing packet *Sully*, scheduled to depart from Havre, France, for New York on October 1, 1832. With all her passengers aboard, the *Sully* did not leave; she just rocked gently at the dockside for five tedious days before adverse winds died down, permitting her to get out of the harbor. Passengers dared not leave the immediate vicinity of the ship since the wind might change at any moment. Everybody just sat tight and waited. "Missing the boat" in those days was not just an expression; it was a disaster because it might take weeks to secure a new passage. Finally, they awakened on the sixth day to the pitching of the ship and the smell of the open sea—under way at last! Among the passengers was an American artist, Samuel F. B. Morse.

Morse was returning to America after a three-year sojourn in France, Italy, and Switzerland. Recognized as a competent painter in America, at 38 he felt that he needed additional professional training on the Continent. The trip was financed largely by commissions from Morse's friends for paintings of European subjects. When not studying or working, Morse spent much time socializing with his friends the James Fenimore Coopers. It was during this time in Paris that Morse painted *Gallery of the Louvre*. Cooper was often found at the Louvre, watching the painting. Mr. and Mrs. Cooper and their daughter are portrayed in one corner of the huge canvas.

Settling down to shipboard routine, the *Sully*'s passengers occupied much time with philosophical discussions of various subjects. It was soon apparent that Morse's favorite topic was electricity, a new field of science only then starting to become a matter of public interest. Morse had no scientific training, but as a university graduate had been exposed to what was then known about electricity. The experiments of Benjamin Franklin and some phenomena relating to atmospheric electricity were about the extent of the public knowledge. While in France, Morse had been invited to inspect the Chappé semaphore telegraph and had been visibly impressed. Later, he told one of his friends, "The semaphore was better than the mail system," and then added, "But this will not be fast enough. The lightning would serve us better." According to the Coopers and other friends, Morse often discussed the possibility of the telegraph during the rest of his stay in Europe. In later years, Morse could recall only his trip to inspect the French semaphore.

One of the passengers, Dr. Charles T. Jackson (see Appendixes, p. 176), often joined Morse in the discussions and made the observation that electricity would pass instantly through any known length of wire. Morse then said, "If this be so, and the presence of electricity can be made visible in any desired part of the circuit, I see no reason why intelligence might not be instantaneously transmitted by electricity to any distance."

From this point on, Morse became obsessed with the idea of an "electric telegraph," and he and the rest of his fellow travelers were under the impression that this was the first concept of an electrical telegraph. They had not heard of Lesage's frictional electric telegraph of 1774, an early proposal by Ampere, or the telegraph proposed by Peter Barlow, an Englishman, in 1824. For the remainder of the voyage, Morse was busy sketching ideas for telegraph equipment and recording many notes in a series of notebooks. Little did he know it then, but the notebooks, drawings, and conversations with Dr. Jackson were to figure importantly in some of the bitter patent litigation to come in the years ahead.

Much thought was given to the method of sending the electrical pulses that would spell out words. A number code was devised in which combinations of digits would represent words from a selected list. For receiving, Morse sketched a pivoted lever actuated by an electromagnet that would record the pulses on a paper tape. The possibility of chemical recording using the action of an electrical spark on treated paper was discussed with Dr. Jackson, who had training in chemistry. This was the method later brought to practical application by Bain. Other than the discussion with Jackson, Morse appeared to concentrate on the magnetic telegraph, which was to prove more practical than the Bain system.

To send the pulses corresponding to the numerals of his letter code, Morse sketched a metal bar having teeth in groups for the digits. These teeth would act on a lever with contact points to open and close the electric circuit to the electromagnet. Later to be known as the portrule, the device later had the teeth cast in the actual dots and dashes after it had been decided to abandon the number code in favor of dots and dashes to represent directly the letters of the alphabet. At long last, after six weeks at sea, the voyage of the *Sully* was over, and the good ship reefed her sails in New York harbor on November 16, 1832. As Morse was bidding farewell to Capt. William Pell, his parting comment was "Well, Captain, should you hear of the telegraph one of these days, as the wonder of the world, remember the discovery was made on board the good ship *Sully*."

As he greeted his brothers Richard and Sydney on the Rector Street dock, he quickly turned to his vision of the telegraph, with wires strung around the world.

His sister-in-law Louisa was introduced to the joys of having an inventor in her house when she discovered drops of metal on her parlor carpet where Morse had cast type for his telegraph sending machine. After a few days of dreaming, Morse had to face the hard realities of existence in New York. He was virtually penniless, the European trip having consumed all of his resources. Also, he had to finish the *Gallery of the Louvre*, brought home in unfinished form.

For the time being, then, work on the telegraph invention came to a halt, even though as Morse was to recall years later, "I never lost faith in the practicability of the invention, nor abandoned the intention of testing it as soon as I could command the means."

When *Gallery of the Louvre* was completed, it was placed on exhibition in rooms above Carvill's bookstore on Broadway at Pine. The painting, a huge canvas 73⅞ by 108 inches, reproduced in miniature exact copies of 38 great masterpieces then hanging in the Louvre. It was hoped that the painting would become important as a means of introducing the American public to the great art treasures of Europe. The work received critical acclaim from art experts but suffered a lukewarm reception by the general public. It seems that Americans of that era were more preoccupied with making money and taming the wilderness than with fine art.

Following an earlier painting, *Congress Hall*, into obscurity, the Louvre painting was finally sold to George Clark of Cooperstown, New York, for $1,200. After passing through the hands of several owners, the painting ended up in the collection of Syracuse University. In 1982, the painting came to the attention of Daniel J. Terra, the well-known collector of American paintings. Terra was able to purchase the painting from the university for $3.2 million with the conditions that it be kept in the United States and placed on public exhibition. It has a permanent home today in the Terra Museum of American Art in Chicago and is occasionally exhibited in other locations.

An important artistic commission Morse had hoped to secure was to decorate one of the panels of the U.S. Capitol rotunda, which were still unfinished. Despite the fact that he was one of the reigning American artists and president of the National Academy of Design, he was not even invited to submit sketches. As late as 1847, the so-called Inman panel in the rotunda was still unfinished, and Morse cherished a final hope that he might be called on to do it. Deeply involved in the affairs of the telegraph by this time, Morse might still have gone back to art if he had been chosen. It was not to be. At 55, he felt that art had abandoned him, and thereafter his time and energy was devoted solely to the telegraph. Morse could little have dreamed that 100 years after he decided to quit painting, he would be honored with a one-man show at the New York Metropolitan Museum of Art, with some 60 of his paintings on exhibit!

By 1835, Morse had received an appointment as a professor of art at New York University. Morse gave regular lectures and spent his spare time working on a crude model of the telegraph instrument he had first sketched on the *Sully*. This was a time of great sacrifice and poverty for Morse. His university income was small. He spent every available penny on the materials needed for his invention and at times had barely enough to buy food. Nevertheless, a crude model began to take shape in the rooms Morse rented from the university. The receiving instrument was the famous "canvas stretcher." Pictures of it are often pictures of replicas; the original is in the Smithsonian. A working replica was exhibited by Western Union at the Chicago Century of Progress in 1933. This machine used a pendulum-type swinging lever on which was mounted the recording pencil and the pole piece of the electromagnet. Directly below the pendulum, a paper tape was pulled across the frame by an old clockworks. As the swinging pencil lever was actuated by the electromagnet, the pencil traced a wavy line on the paper tape that corresponded to the received signal pulses.

The sender employed the "portrule" device with cast-metal teeth which would send digits 1 to 5 when actuated. After due consideration, the digit system was abandoned in favor of "teeth" in the form of dots and dashes, Morse having suddenly realized that the digital system would require a truly enormous dictionary for translation of messages. Eventually, the portrule itself was abandoned in favor of a simple contact-making lever that Morse called a correspondent, later called simply the key. The first crudely constructed keys were prototypes of the telegraph hand keys still in use today.

Early in 1836, Morse had tried to make his machine work through a length of 40 feet of wire without success. Professor Joseph Henry, in a disparaging letter to a friend, wrote in reference to Morse, "He found himself so little acquainted with the subject of electricity that he could not make his simple machine operate through the distance of a few yards." At this time Professor Leonard D. Gale, a professor of chemistry at the university, became interested in Morse's work, and Morse was to benefit greatly from Gale's association with the telegraph. It was Gale who quickly grasped some of the essentials of Henry's research in magnetism. Morse had been using only one cell of battery, or cup as it was called then. Gale recommended a battery of 20 cells. Also, Gale found that Morse's magnet was weak due to too few turns of wire around the core.

With the magnet wound with over a 100 turns of wire and the 20-cell battery (39 volts), the original Morse apparatus now worked through ever-increasing lengths of wire strung around the rooms. Finally, 10 miles of wire, wound on reels, was secured, and the instruments worked perfectly. The telegraph was now ready for demonstrations, and a caveat for a patent was filed October 3, 1837. Gale received a share of the patent in return for his valuable contribution. Gale would have taken a much greater place in telegraph history except for the fact that he was a mild-mannered, self-effacing man who did not leave a large amount of written memorabilia for researchers to pore over.

Joseph Henry, (1797–1878) pioneer in the electromagnetic research that made the telegraph possible (photo courtesy Library of Congress).

Early in 1836, Gale and Morse had discussed the principle of the relay, one of the most important instruments of telegraphy. In that day, there was considerable misunderstanding among scientists of the carrying properties of an electrical current through a conducting wire. Some thought that electricity would decay or die out in a certain length of wire. Gale was guilty of the false assumption that the telegraph would not work even at a distance of only 20 miles. Morse had grasped the principle of the relay and told Gale, "If a lever can be moved at any distance, it can operate a contact point and send a strong signal to the next point, and so on around the globe if desired." Actually, in later years, Morse circuits up to 300 miles long were common without relays. The relay principle was vital for the automatic repeaters that made transcontinental telegraphy possible.

Alfred Vail (see Appendixes, p. 176), one of Morse's friends at the university, had attended some of his classes. Showing considerable promise as a mechanic, Vail had a change of mind after graduation and decided to study for the ministry. Discouraged by illness, at 29 he was at loose ends, looking for something to do. He happened to drop in at Morse's rooms and saw one of the demonstrations of the crude equipment working through 1,700 feet of wire. The telegraph seemed to fire his imagination, as it had Morse's. He approached Morse with an offer of money and mechanical assistance to construct more acceptable models of the telegraph, to facilitate patent applications in the United States and abroad. Vail had no money of his own, but his family was pursuaded to advance money and make the facilities of the Vail iron works at Speedwell, New Jersey, available for constructing the telegraph equipment. An agreement signed between Vail and Morse on September 23, 1837, assigned a one-quarter share of the telegraph patent to Vail.

Telegraph historians have always indulged in much conjecture about how much of the telegraph invention could be credited to Vail. There is no way to know, since Vail's agreement specified that anything he invented was to be turned over to Morse, whose name alone would appear on the patent papers. It was apparent that Vail's contribution was substantial. The whole assembly of apparatus was redesigned and built in professional style, and it is very likely that most of the new ideas were Vail's.

Back in Europe again in 1838–1839, Morse was in pursuit of English and French patents for the telegraph. On this trip he was accompanied by F. O. J. Smith (see Appendixes, pp. 175–176), who was now associated with the telegraph as a financial and political adviser. In England, Morse was able to see the rival telegraphs invented by Edward Davy and Cooke and Wheatstone. It was soon obvious that the English patent office was going to protect its own inventors. In a final meeting, Attorney General Sir John Campbell asked if an American patent had been issued. When Morse said yes, Campbell told him, "America is large; you ought to be satisfied with a patent there."

In France, Morse received a cordial welcome and was quickly granted a patent. The patent, however, turned out to be meaningless because it would not be valid unless a telegraph line was in operation within two years. Construction of a line was bogged down in French bureaucracy. There was also a prospect of building a line for the Russian government. That dream too was shattered when Czar Nicholas refused to sign a contract. The czar apparently had an ill-founded fear that the telegraph could be used in some subversive way against his government.

Before leaving France, Morse visited with Louis Daguerre, whose process of recording images on metal plates was the beginning of photography. Morse was later to establish his own daguerreotype studio in New York. Among his pupils was Mathew Brady, the man who gained fame for his efforts in photographing the American Civil War.

Morse's dream of a successful telegraph could never be realized until he was able to construct a working line over an appreciable distance. In 1843, the fate of that dream lay with the U.S. Congress where a bill was pending to appropriate $30,000 for the construction of a line between Washington and Baltimore (see Appendixes, p. 167). When Morse left the Senate chamber after agonizing hours of waiting on March 3, 1843, the lamps had already been lighted, and there were still 140 bills awaiting action before the close of the session. Resigned to another defeat, Morse went home for the night.

The next morning at breakfast he had a caller, Miss Annie Ellsworth, daughter of the U.S. commissioner of patents. "I've come to congratulate you," she said with a broad smile. Morse, genuinely puzzled, replied, "For what, pray tell?" Miss Ellsworth beamed. "On the passage of your bill!" Morse had been a college classmate of Commissioner Ellsworth, and due to his close friendship with the family, there had been rumors of a romance with Annie. According to legend, it was on this occasion that Morse told Annie, "You have been the first to bring me this happy news. Accordingly you shall have the honor of composing the first message to be transmitted over the new line." About the first message there is little doubt. Annie's choice was "What hath God wrought!" from the Holy Bible, Numbers 23:23, and it was transmitted on May 24, 1844. (It should be noted that the punctuation of the message has been widely misprinted over the years, using a question mark instead of an exclamation point.)

On May 14, 1932, the Postal Telegraph Company transmitted to all offices and stations of the company the following message:

NEW YORK, NY, MAY 14, 1932

THIS MESSAGE IS IN COMMEMORATION OF THE ONE HUNDREDTH ANNIVERSARY OF PROFESSOR SAMUEL F. B. MORSE'S INVENTION OF THE TELEGRAPH. WHAT HATH GOD WROUGHT.

(signed) SCOVILL

[As received at Galva, Henry County, Illinois, 11:17 A.M.]

It is not known why Postal selected May 14 to send this message. On May 14, Morse would still have been in Europe. The concept of the telegraph invention is generally accepted to have occurred between October 6 and November 16 during the voyage of the *Sully* from Havre to New York.

With the congressional appropriation in hand, it was at last time to start construction of the Washington-Baltimore line. Morse had become friendly with Samuel Colt, inventor of the revolver. Colt had done some work with underwater insulated cable using electrical current to set off explosive charges. It was decided to lay the Baltimore line with underground cable. It would have been a wise decision, but the manufacturing methods of the time were unable to produce a suitable cable. F. O. J. Smith had enlisted the serves of Ezra Cornell (see Appendixes, p. 175) to design a cable-laying plow and superintend the work. Cornell came up with a plow not too different from those used today by the telephone company. A narrow blade cut a deep slit in the earth, and the cable dropped in and was covered as the machine moved forward.

Some nine miles of cable had been laid before electrical tests revealed that the insulation was faulty. Morse, sick with anxiety, took the Baltimore & Ohio to Relay, Maryland, and walked back along the track to where the telegraph men were working. Calling Cornell aside, he said, "Can't you contrive some plausible excuse for stopping this work for a few days? I want to make some experiments before any more pipe is laid, and I don't want the papers to know that the work is purposely stopped." Cornell knew all about the bad insulation and replied, "Yes, I can manage that." The mules pulling the plow were started forward, and at the first chance Cornell caught the point of the plow on a large rock. Extensive repairs would be required before the machine could be used again.

Some experiments were made with pipe manufactured by a different method. It too proved defective. The telegraph partners were now at a low ebb of depression: $23,000 of the $30,000 appropriation had already been spent; Gale had resigned; and an adversarial relationship had developed between Smith and Morse. Only Cornell and Vail seemed to be focusing on the problem at hand. Reading of Wheatstone's work in England, they discovered that he too had experienced trouble with underground wires.

Cornell and Vail urged Morse to adopt the only feasible alternative, stringing the wire overhead on poles. Poles were ordered in February, and overhead line construction started. Now the line worked. At the end of each day, a working circuit was available back to the starting point.

Morse supposed that this was the first telegraph pole line ever built in America. This was not really the case, since in 1826–1827 one Dyar had erected a few miles of experimental telegraph line on Long Island. The underground cable had four conductors, which were thought necessary to provide two circuits. The overhead line was strung with two conductors. It had been learned that a telegraph line requires only one wire with ground return; the two wires of the overhead line were just as effective as the four in the original cable. With the overhead line came the problem of how to insulate the wires. Almost nothing was known on the subject at that time except that glass was one of the best insulators. Accordingly, the first wires were sandwiched between glass plates held in a notch cut in the pole cross-arm.

In 1818, Morse, 27, was married to Lucretia Pickering Walker, 19, of Concord, New Hampshire. They settled in Charlestown (now Charleston), South Carolina, home of Morse's uncle. They occupied rooms in a boardinghouse on Church Street, which turned out to be as much of a home as they were ever to have. In 1824, Morse was trying desperately to establish himself as a painter in New York. His *Congress Hall* had been an exhibition failure. While in Washington on a business trip, he received word that he had been chosen to paint a portrait of the marquis de Lafayette, then being given a hero's welcome in New York. The portrait, considered one of Morse's best, is still owned by the city of New York and hangs in City Hall. At last, there seemed to be a chance to establish the permanent home for Lucretia and their three children that was so desperately needed.

Full of enthusiasm for his painting of Lafayette and enjoying the social life in Washington, Morse wrote faithfully to Lucretia, letters full of love and optimism for their future together. Morse was about ready to leave Washington when he received a grim letter from his father. Lucretia, convalescing from an illness, had passed away suddenly at 26. In one moment, all of Morse's great dreams were shattered, and he was left to face the future as a widower with three motherless children.

Seeking solace in his work, Morse returned to New York and entered upon a period of comparative prosperity. He had many friends in the artistic community who helped to ease his loneliness. Among them was the novelist James Fenimore Cooper, who was to be his good companion on a later trip to Europe. In company with his fellow artists, Morse was instrumental in founding the National Academy of Design in 1826. It superseded the older American Academy of Arts which was said to be controlled by wealthy art patrons and was actually in a position to dictate the livelihood of New York artists. Morse was elected as the first president of the National Academy and continued to serve in that capacity for the next 16 years.

At 56, Morse was wealthy, a sophisticated man at home in any company, at home in the society of Europe at a time when most Americans had never traveled beyond their own state. He was, by any definition, a very eligible widower. Yet he had never remarried following the death of Lucretia. There had been rumors of some romantic attachments through the years, but none ever came close to marriage vows. Now, for the first time, Morse had a home that was his own, a haven for himself and his three children. Called Locust Grove, the estate sprawled over 100 acres near Poughkeepsie, within sight of the Hudson.

It was the beginning of the happiest period of Morse's life, and the best was yet to come. At a family wedding he became aware for the first time of his cousin

Sarah Griswold, who was a bridesmaid. Morse had known her as a child, but now she was a strikingly beautiful young woman of 26. Sarah had been born with the handicaps of poor hearing and defective speech, handicaps she had largely overcome by diligent effort and training. Morse was visibly affected by the kindness she showed to his little son Finley, who was a backward child and was being ignored by his cousins. A proposal soon followed and was accepted. There was some family disapproval because of the age difference. Sarah was even accused of marrying Morse because he was rich. She responded, "Oh, I wish he was poor, and I would then let him know whether I loved him." Sarah was asked what she would do if Morse suddenly lost all his property. "What would I do?" she answered. "Why, support him with my own hands."

Sarah became an expert lip reader and was at scarcely any disadvantage when communicating with others. Once, at a social gathering she murmured to her companion, "See those people over there? They are talking about me." Morse declared that he was hardly aware of Sarah's handicap. Despite the age difference, it turned out to be an idyllic marriage, full of love and devotion, and was blessed by four children.

In 1851, Morse built a new house at Locust Grove, a handsome Italianate structure designed by architect Alexander J. Davis. Overlooking the Hudson, the home was filled with the books and mementoes of a full life. There was even a working telegraph line that was connected with the wires running along the riverbank below the house. With 24 rooms, the place afforded ample room for Morse and his growing family.

After Morse's death, the estate passed into the hands of the Young family and was held by them until Miss Annette I. Young died in 1975. In her will, Miss Young bequeathed the house and 20 acres of land to the people of New York to be enjoyed as an historic site. Her bequest also included sufficient funds to maintain the property in perpetuity. The property, which is on U.S. Route 9 two miles south of Poughkeepsie, was designated a National Historic Site by the U.S. Department of the Interior in 1963. Members of the New York chapter of the Morse Telegraph Club were instrumental in assembling a collection of suitable memorabilia for display in the home.

Morse is one of few men honored by a statue erected during his life. Telegraphers throughout the United States and Canada donated money to pay for the statue, which was unveiled on June 10, 1871. It still stands in New York's Central Park near East 70th Street. A large crowd of spectators was present, including Theodore Roosevelt, Sr., escorting Miss Leila Morse. Later that evening, Morse was the guest of honor at a ceremony held in the Academy of Music on 14th Street. A telegraph instrument was set up and connected to a circuit that reached all of the major cities of North America. Morse was particularly pleased to see that Annie Ellsworth was present for the occasion. At the appointed hour, Miss Sadie E. Cornwell, an expert operator, stepped to the telegraph table and sent a prepared message: "Greetings and thanks to the telegraph fraternity throughout the world. Glory to God in the highest, on earth peace, good will to men." The young woman left the table, and Morse, taking her place at the key, slowly tapped out his signature, "S. F. B. Morse." As he finished, the guests rose as one and gave a mighty cheer.

For some years, Morse and Sarah had maintained a winter home at 5 West 22nd Street, New York. It was here, on April 2, 1872, that Morse passed away after an illness of about two weeks. All over the world, the telegraph quickly flashed the news that its father was dead.

Throughout history it seems that a certain individual steps forth to fill the need of the moment. Just as often, it seems that the chosen individual is not ideally qualified for his place in history. Morse lived to see himself honored as the father of the telegraph, yet in many ways his contribution was minimal. He was not a scientist or a mechanic, and not a very good businessman. Nevertheless, he gave the world a successful telegraph system when all the others, better qualified, were muddling around with impractical schemes. Morse had the one redeeming quality of hardheaded single-mindedness that led him to pursue his dream of the telegraph to the exclusion of all else, even though he had to rely on the skills of others.

An improvident man, he existed through much of his life on money borrowed from friends and relatives. Not until the telegraph became extremely profitable did Morse have any financial stability. He was not an easy man to work for, or with, and tended to be imperious, capricious, and unreasonable in his relations with others. The faithful Alfred Vail once complained, "Whenever there is work to be done, the Professor is taken ill." On another occasion, when a big telegraph demonstration was scheduled in Washington, Vail said with thinly veiled sarcasm, "I hope the Professor will be well enough to accept the honors with the rest of us!"

Morse's faithful associates in the development of the telegraph, Cornell, Gale, and Vail, all left his side after the telegraph became a reality. The chief complaint was that Morse kept all the glory for himself and seldom accorded any recognition to the others. Under pressure of the bitter patent litigation of the 1850s, Morse lost status in the eyes of many because of his bitter and entirely untruthful attack on Joseph Henry (see Appendixes, p. 173), the man who had done as much as anyone to make the telegraph possible. In spite of his obvious shortcomings, Morse will stand as the father of the telegraph. He risked everything and by sheer determination gave the world a communication system that lasted for over 100 years. No one else came forward to do the job when it was needed.

Some of the best-known paintings by Samuel F. B. Morse and where they are on public exhibition

Benjamin Silliman
Gallery of Fine Arts, Yale University

Congress Hall, the Old House of Representatives
Corcoran Gallery of Art, Washington, D.C.

Charles T. Jackson
Macbeth Gallery, New York

Eliphalet Pearson
Addison Gallery of American Art
Phillips Academy, Andover, Massachusetts

Gallery of the Louvre
Terra Museum of American Art, Chicago, Illinois

Lafayette (bust)
New York Public Library, New York

Lafayette (full length)
City Hall, New York

The Muse (portrait of Susan Walker Morse)
Metropolitan Museum of Art, New York

William Cullen Bryant
National Academy of Design, New York

Note: There are dozens of other Morse paintings, mostly in private collections.

4. Toward the Setting Sun

Amid the ringing of bells, which pealed out the national joy at the union of the world's great seas by the magic belt of fire which now united them. — James D. Reid

Out from Omaha they rode, 400 strong, a small army of men carrying Springfield rifles and navy revolvers. With them were 500 head of oxen and mules and over 100 wagons. Organized by Edward Creighton with military precision, the expedition was as self-sufficient as careful planning could make it. Their objective was a pinpoint on the map, 1,100 miles to the west—Salt Lake City. They not only had to get there; they had to build a telegraph line as they went.

By 1860, the rapidly expanding network of eastern telegraph lines had reached as far west as the Missouri River at Brownville, Nebraska, and then north to Omaha. In California the network extended north to Sacramento and then east to Carson City, Nevada. With the Civil War imminent, thoughts were concentrated on joining the nation with a transcontinental line. The romantic pony express furnished the only link and required at least 10 days to bridge the gap between East and West.

Hiram Sibley (see Appendixes, pp. 173–174) of Western Union was successful in obtaining final commitments to the transcontinental project from groups both eastern and western. In 1860, Edward Creighton, the intrepid line builder, had made a survey of the entire central route, following the trail of the pony express. All concerned agreed that it was the most practicable route for the telegraph to follow.

Creighton left Omaha in November 1860 on his solitary surveying trip and reached Salt Lake City in mid–December. Enduring personal hardships that would have turned back a lesser man, Creighton pushed on to California for a meeting with Jeptha Wade (see Appendixes, p. 172) of Western Union in March 1861. Creighton and Wade returned to New York by way of Panama and reached there on April 12. By May 23, Creighton was back in Omaha ready to begin construction. Meanwhile, Sibley had been successful in getting Congress to pass a bill granting

Western Union a $40,000 yearly subsidy for 10 years (see Appendixes, pp. 165, 166). The subsidy was granted under condition that the line would be in operation by July 31, 1862.

Western Union could not have chosen a better man than Creighton. He had previous line-building experience with the early O'Rielly lines and later had extensive road-building experience. Creighton's survey for the telegraph line had pointed out what was clearly the best route across the western plains; eight years later, the Union Pacific railroad followed practically the same route.

The eastbound construction gang, led by James Gamble and assistant I. M. Hubbard, left Sacramento on May 27, 1861, with 25 wagons, 228 oxen, 18 mules and horses, and 50 men. They were delayed in getting through the Sierra Nevada because of the many westbound wagon trains on the narrow mountain roads and did not reach Carson City, where the actual line construction was to start, until late in June. There were many problems for the line builders in bringing needed materials to the construction site. Poles were normally obtained from local timber sources, but wire and insulators for the western section had to be shipped from New York around Cape Horn to San Francisco, then hauled overland to Carson City and beyond.

Although the entire project was organized by Western Union interests headed by Hiram Sibley, the actual construction was done by the Overland Telegraph Co. for the section from Carson City to Salt Lake. The Pacific Telegraph Co. built from Omaha to Salt Lake. Sibley had gambled on the success of the project by extending the telegraph to Fort Kearney the previous year. The eastern crew started line building at Kearney and set the first pole on July 4, 1861. In addition to the main construction crews, there were men working eastward and westward from Salt Lake City. An Overland Telegraph gang under James Street worked to the west from Salt Lake City. I. M. Hubbard was in personal charge of the crew working eastward from Carson City. For the Pacific Telegraph Co., W. H. Stebbins was in charge of construction on the line extending 400 miles east of Salt Lake. Edward Creighton had overall supervision of the 700-mile stretch west of Omaha.

As soon as Russell, Majors, and Waddell realized that the overland telegraph would soon be a reality, they prepared to shut down the pony express after its brief 16-month existence. Telegraph officials, however, knew it would be a big advantage to have riders carrying messages over the steadily diminishing distance between the eastern and western sections of the line. After receiving substantial financial inducement, the pony express continued until the line was complete. Then the colorful horsemen passed into history.

Once the line builders got into their stride, construction proceeded in an efficient manner. Most of the delays were occasioned by failure to get adequate numbers of poles on time. On the treeless plains west of Omaha, it was sometimes necessary to haul poles as much as 240 miles to the head of the line. The surveyors went first, staking the route in long straight lines as much as possible. Then came the pole wagons, dropping off poles at the right intervals. Next came the hole-digging party, followed by the pole-raising crew. Last came the wire party, raising the wire to the pole-top insulators and tying it in place. The contract called for 25 poles per mile, or a spacing between poles of 211 feet. (Telegraph lines in later years, carrying many more wires, often had poles spaced 40 to the mile.)

Temporary telegraph offices were set up at the head of the line after each day's run, keeping the field parties in constant touch with their respective headquarters. There were no power posthole diggers in 1861, and sinking a 12-inch-diameter hole five feet deep is no inconsiderable task. Yet experienced diggers learned to do it with the minimum of physical effort, using the special long-handled spades made for the purpose. Power hole diggers were available by the time the first transcontinental telephone line was built in 1915, yet well into the twentieth century many line gangs still dug holes by the time-honored method.

The transcontinental line was relatively easy to build since there was only one iron wire and no crossarms on the poles. It was still a mind-boggling accomplishment, done when every phase of the operation depended on human muscle aided by horses, oxen, and mules. Daily progress varied from three to eight miles per day, according to the difficulty of the terrain, the maximum achieved in flat country where there were no obstacles and the soil permitted easy digging. One record-breaking stretch of 16 miles was completed to reach a campsite with water. This would have involved setting 400 poles—a good day's work by any measure!

After Creighton and his crew had completed a substantial section of line across the plains, they were confronted with a new problem—buffalo. The great shaggy creatures, accustomed to life on the treeless plains, had never experienced the ecstasy of rubbing against something. Then they discovered the telegraph poles, made to order for rubbing. They rubbed with such vigor that whole sections of line were pushed over. Frantic for a solution, Creighton had his men drive long spikes into the poles near the ground. The buffalo loved it. The spikes made the rubbing even more pleasurable. Some wages even suggested that the buffalo were forming in lines to await their turn at a favorite pole! There never was an effective solution to the buffalo problem, except to hope that the herd would eventually drift away from the line. The final solution, when it came, was not a happy one. Eight years later, after the overland railroad was completed, the buffalo herds were practically wiped out by professional hide hunters.

Initially there had been considerable apprehension about how the Indians would react to the encroachment of the telegraph on their tribal lands. James Gamble, superintendent of the western crew, took the precaution of sending his associate James Street to confer with influential chiefs of the western tribes. Shokup, chief of the Shoshone, expressed much interest in what he termed the "wire rope express." Shokup was invited to go to San Francisco and meet Horace W. Carpentier, president of the Overland Telegraph Co. The chief traveled as far west as Carson City, then changed his mind. He issued a statement as follows:

> Shokup, Big Chief of the Shoshones, says to Big Captain at San Francisco, that his Indians will not trouble the telegraph line. Shokup is a friend of the white man. His people will obey him. He will order them to be friendly with the white man and not injure the telegraph. He would like to see Big Captain, but must return to his tribe, and cannot go to San Francisco.

Shokup kept his word, and the Indians remained friendly to the telegraph men on the western section of the line.

Creighton and the eastern crew also attempted to establish friendly relations with the Indians. The magical powers of the wire were demonstrated by giving electric shocks and allowing the Indians to send messages to one another from different points on the line. Gradually, the Indians lost their fear of the wire and began to create a nuisance. Sometimes their antics produced their own deterrent. A party of braves had pulled down a section of wire and were making off with it when a lightning bolt struck the line. Fleeing in terror, those Indians never came near the line again.

Indian attacks became more vicious as time went on. In 1864, St. Mary's stage and telegraph station in Wyoming was attacked by a band of 150 Indians. There were only five men on duty at the station. The Indians set fire to the buildings. The five men took cover in a dry well, and in one of the classic fights of the Old West, held off the Indians for 30 hours. Finally managing to slip away under cover of darkness, the men headed for South Pass. Through it all, the telegraph operator managed to hang on to his instruments and a coil of fine wire. As soon as it was safe to stop, they connected with the telegraph line and summoned help from Fort Bridger.

Severe damage to the line was occurring as late as 1865. After that, the increased presence of the U.S. Army pretty well ended Indian attacks on the telegraph. In addition to the buffalo and Indians, the fragile 2,000-mile length of wire was subject to natural hazards. Lightning strikes, high winds, blizzards, and floods all combined to keep line-repair crews busy. The rather frequent outages caused some critics to charge that the line was deliberately put out of order at certain times to facilitate speculation in the gold market. Line maintenance became a lot easier after the Union Pacific Railroad was built in 1869. Repair crews could then get to most of the line quickly by train.

As the line approached Salt Lake City, Creighton was especially anxious to maintain good relations with Brigham Young, knowing that the Mormon leader was all-powerful in the area. One of Young's sons was given a contract to furnish poles. Having second thoughts about the matter, Young asked for a new contract at a higher price, and Creighton reluctantly agreed. Brigham Young, hearing of the transaction, sent for Creighton and told him that the original contract was to be honored. Brigham Young proved to be a good friend of the telegraph and insisted that his people live up to their contracts with the telegraph company.

Far below the original estimates of time required, Creighton's Pacific Telegraph crew reached Salt Lake City on October 18, and six days later, on October 24, 1861, Gamble and the Overland Telegraph line arrived. The line construction, originally estimated to take at least two years, had been completed in an incredible four months. The line was immediately very profitable. In the first week of operation, the telegraph company was charging $1 a word for messages, even though the contract called for a rate of $3 for a 10-word message. At that time, the word count included the place of origin, time, and date, leaving only seven words for the actual message.

Within a week after the line opened, the rates were adjusted to the following schedule:

San Francisco to St. Louis, first 10 words: $5; additional words 45¢

To Chicago, first 10 words: $5.60; additional words 50¢

To New York and Washington, first 10 words: $6; additional words 75¢

The eastern half of the line, from Omaha to Salt Lake, had been financed by selling $1 million in stock. The actual cost of building the line turned out to be only $147,000. The complete line from Nebraska to California was conservatively estimated to have cost no more than $500,000, making it a handsome investment for holders of Western Union stock.

The eastern terminus of the transcontinental line was originally planned to be St. Louis, via a line from St. Joseph across the state of Missouri. By October 1861, activities of southern sympathizers in Missouri were causing disruption of both overland mail and the telegraph. A dispatch to the *New York Times*, dated Salt Lake City, October 3, 1861, commented on the problem:

Since Saturday our mail matter from the States has arrived as usual, but for ten days or a fortnight previously it was in abeyance somewhere, supposedly in Missouri. It is to be hoped that the fortunes of war will deal tenderly with the overland mail and telegraph, so that communications and travel between the two oceans will not be altogether subject to the caprices of the Seceshers. In view of the existing troubles in the state of Missouri, the sentiment here grows more in favor of the permanent transmission of the overland mail via Davenport, Iowa City and Council Bluffs, or Omaha City, and some agitative public measure may yet be taken on the question. . . . About thirty wagons, laden with insulators and wire for the telegraph west of this city, arrived here last Saturday, and as most of the poles are already up, the prospect is good for speedy communication between this city and San Francisco at an early date.

Rapidly mounting concerns about the situation in Missouri caused the telegraph companies to revise their plans and make Chicago the eastern terminus of the line. Through the energetic efforts of J. D. Caton, president of the Illinois & Mississippi Telegraph Co. (see Appendixes, pp. 172–173), construction was immediately started on a line that would connect Omaha to Chicago via Des Moines and Cedar Rapids, Iowa.

E. D. L. Sweet, in charge of the construction, had many difficulties due to wartime shortages of men and materials. In spite of the problems, the line was completed in January 1862. Citizens of Des Moines were thrilled to be in contact at last with the outside world. Previously there had been no telegraph or railroad in the Iowa capital. The first regular telegraph news appeared in the *Des Moines Register* on January 14, 1862, and the jubilant editor exclaimed, "The lightning and telegraph company have at length made us even with the Mississippi cities." The vital transcontinental line was now safely beyond reach of Confederate interference.

The completion of the transcontinental telegraph was reported in an almost matter-of-fact manner by the New York press. The newspapers, which had gone all out for the celebration of the ill-fated Atlantic cable of 1858, apparently did not want to go out on a limb again. The celebration for the Atlantic cable had been so exuberant that, among other incidents, City Hall was set ablaze by carelessly handled fireworks. *The New York Times* commented on October 26, 1861, as follows:

> The work of carrying westward the transcontinental telegraphic line has progressed with so little blazonment, that it is with almost an electric thrill one reads the words of greeting yesterday flashed instanteously over the wires from California. The magnificent idea of joining the Atlantic with the Pacific by the magnetic wire is today a realized fact. New York, Queen of the Atlantic, and San Francisco, Queen of the Pacific, are now united by this noblest symbol of our modern civilization.
>
> It is not likely that New York will repeat over this news the wild effervescence it displayed four years ago on the occasion of the Cable Celebration, when Cyrus the Great rode in an open chariot up Broadway, buried amid flowers, and borne on the voices of half a million vociferous worshippers, and the municipal temple was made a bonfire of in its honor.
>
> But an equal marvel is now quietly done, without fuss or flummery—an accomplished fact—a conquest of creative civilization. Between New York and San Francisco there lie three thousand miles: so that, if we have not actually put a girdle round the earth, we at least have a continuous stretch of telegraphic wire round an eighth of the girth of the globe....

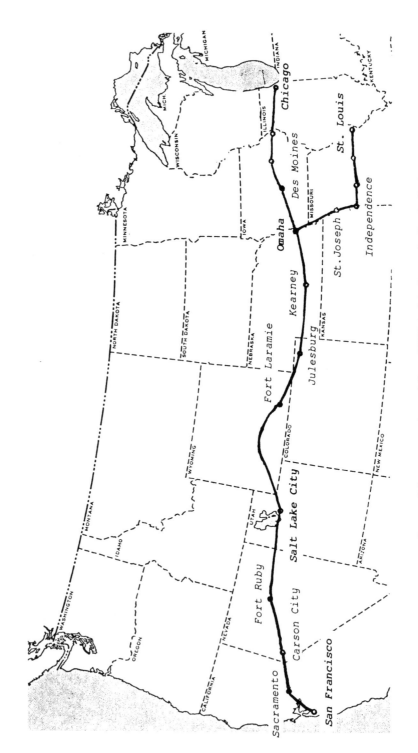

Route of the transcontinental line—1861 (original map by Lewis Coe).

It is easy for one to overlook the poetic element in this great achievement, so accustomed have we become to the telegraphic marvel. But what genuine grandeur is there in that wondrous line! From the Hudson it stretches across seven great and populous Free States to the Missouri River, a thousand miles—then across the Great Western Plains amid solitude and savages to the Rocky Mountains, as many leagues again—then leaping across the mighty chain of the Cordilleras—thence over hill and dale to the range of the Sierra Nevada, and from thence Westward still to the waters of the Pacific and the City of the Golden Gate—till the two extremes of the Continent are united by the magnetic wire, and the dwellers by the Hudson hail the settlers on the Sacramento.

The original transcontinental line followed wagon roads and the pony express trails. After completion of the Union Pacific in 1869, much of the telegraph line was relocated to run along the railroad. This greatly facilitated maintenance and protection of the line. Contemporary photographs taken in the vicinity of Promontory Point show poles with a short crossarm carrying two line wires, presumably one for the railroad and one for Western Union.

The 1941 movie *Western Union*, starring Randolph Scott and Robert Young, while mostly fictional, is nevertheless accurate in some details of the telegraph project. For example, when the sound of the telegraph instruments are heard on the sound track, they are spelling out authentic messages in Morse code. Published photos purporting to show construction of the transcontinental are often stills from the movie. The movie was based on Zane Grey's 1939 novel *Western Union*.

The first message sent over the eastern part of the transcontinental line was filed at Great Salt Lake City on October 18, 1861:

To—Hon. J. H. Wade, President of the Pacific Telegraph Cleveland, Ohio
Sir: Permit me to congratulate you on the completion of the Overland Telegraph Line west to this city, to commend the energy displayed by yourself and associates in the rapid and successful prosecution of a work so beneficial, and to express the wish that its use may ever tend to promote the true interests of the dwellers on both the Atlantic and Pacific slopes of our continent. Utah has not seceded, but is firm for the Constitution and laws of our once happy country, and is warmly interested in such successful enterprises as the one so far completed.
(signed) Brigham Young

First messages from California:

Oct. 24, 1861
To—Abraham Lincoln,
       President of the United States

In the temporary absence of the Governor of the State, I am requested to send you the first message which will be transmitted over the wires of the telegraph line which

Building an early telegraph line in the mountains of the West (photo courtesy Utah State Historical Society).

connects the Pacific with the Atlantic States. The people of California desire to congratulate you upon the completion of the great work. They believe that it will be the means of strengthening the attachment which binds both the East and West to the Union, and they desire in this, the first message across the continent—to express their loyalty to the Union and their determination to stand by its Government on this its day of trial. They regard that Government with affection, and will adhere to it under all fortunes.

Stephen J. Field
Chief Justice of California

San Francisco, Cal.
Oct. 24, 1861, 7:40 P.M.

To His Excellency, the President
Washington, D.C.

I announce to you that the telegraph to California has this day been completed. May it be a bond of perpetuity between the states of the Atlantic and those of the Pacific.

Horace W. Carpentier
President
Overland Telegraph Company

Edward Creighton (1820–1874) became a wealthy man through his holdings of Western Union stock and shrewd business ability. Even before his untimely death at 54, he had founded Creighton University and together with his brother John had been active in many civic projects that benefited the city of Omaha. Edward Creighton was actively involved in the building of the Union Pacific railroad, which followed essentially the same route he had surveyed in 1860. Creighton waged a bitter fight to have Omaha declared the eastern terminus of the Union Pacific. By 1868, it appeared that Omaha would get the terminal. Legal battles went all the way to the Supreme Court. After Creighton's death, the Court awarded the terminus to Council Bluffs, Iowa.

In the summer of 1884, 23 years after Creighton's wagon train headed west, a Postal Telegraph construction outfit headed west out of Omaha, following the Union Pacific. They were building a line from Omaha to Julesburg, part of a 933-mile Chicago-to-Julesburg circuit. Their work endured until 1947 when the line was dismantled as a result of the 1943 merger of Postal and Western Union. Traveling in luxury compared to Creighton's men, the Postal gang had three large custom-built camp wagons, each pulled by a four-horse team. A man-and-wife team presided over the dining wagon. The 24-man line crew had living quarters in the two bunk wagons.

A migratory life was common for telegraph construction men during the days when open-wire pole lines were in active use. As late as 1960, Western Union had some camp-car outfits, made from converted Pullman cars. Most Western Union lines paralleled railroads; the camp cars were a practical way to get the line crews close to the job.

On August 5, 1990, 129 years after Edward Creighton's wagon train reached Fort Laramie, Wyoming, with the westbound transcontinental telegraph line, a ceremony was held at Laramie naming the telegraph line as a national Electrical Engineering Milestone. The Institute of Electrical and Electronics Engineers

Postal Telegraph construction crew building west from Omaha in 1884 (photo courtesy J. Fred Smith).

Postal Telegraph construction crew building west from Omaha in 1884 (photo courtesy J. Fred Smith).

(IEEE) has sponsored the "Milestone" program as a means of honoring the great electrical inventions of the past. Through this program, the institute hopes to increase the understanding of electrical history among engineers and the public, and to encourage the preservation of the historical record of these achievements. The Milestones program is sponsored by the IEEE History Committee and coordinated by the Center for the History of Electrical Engineering, located at the institute's headquarters in the United Engineering Center in New York City.

It was appropriate for the ceremony to be held at Fort Laramie since this was the location of the original repeater station midway between Omaha and Salt Lake City. It was at first contemplated that repeaters would be provided to give direct transmission to Salt Lake where messages would be copied and manually retransmitted to the eastern or western part of the line. Later it was found that an automatic repeater could be used at Salt Lake, and thereafter the messages went directly from East and West.

5. The Military Telegraph

> *No orders ever had to be given to establish the telegraph.*
> —U. S. Grant

The date was April 9, 1865, and the historic conference between generals Grant and Lee had just been concluded at the McLean house. As Grant and his staff rode back toward their camp, the officers were in a jubilant mood. Grant, however, was quiet and preoccupied with his own thoughts. Then one of the staff said, "General, hadn't you better notify Washington of the surrender?"

The party stopped, and Grant, dismounting, asked for writing materials. Colonel Adam Badeau handed him a field order book. Sitting on a stone beside the road, the general wrote out one of the most important messages ever transmitted by the Morse telegraph:

HEADQUARTERS APPOMATTOX CH VA
APRIL 9, 1865 430P.M.

HON E M STANTON SECRETARY OF WAR
WASHINGTON

GENERAL LEE SURRENDERED THE ARMY OF NORTHERN VIRGINIA THIS AFTER-NOON ON TERMS PROPOSED BY MYSELF THE ACCOMPANYING ADDITIONAL CORRESPONDENCE WILL SHOW THE CONDITIONS FULLY

U S GRANT
LIEUT GENERAL

A rider galloped off, taking the message to the nearest telegraph office. Within hours, the entire country would know that the war was finally over. Flashing along the lines that paralleled the railroads, the message would soon reach even the smallest hamlet. The transcontinental line, completed in 1861, would carry the happy news to the Pacific coast.

The Civil War, often called the first modern war, was also the first to employ the Morse telegraph for communications on a large scale. Prior to the war, the U.S. Army did not have a signal corps as a separate organization. As a result, when the war started, the army had only a few people with any knowledge of the telegraph. To obtain the required numbers of operators and supervisors, a quasi-military unit known as the U.S. Military Telegraph Corps (USMTC) was formed. Thomas A. Scott and Andrew Carnegie came from the Pennsylvania Railroad to head the group. Western Union officials Anson Stager and Thomas T. Eckert were key men in the organization, which eventually included approximately 1,200 civilian operators. In 1862 Stager was commissioned colonel and placed in charge of all U.S. military telegraphs. Later, he held the rank of brevet brigadier general. Eckert was commissioned major and was in charge of Washington and the Department of the Potomac.

The members of the USMTC emerged as the unsung heroes of the war. Serving in the field alongside the soldiers, they were exposed to all the hazards of combat, yet they could not claim any of the benefits normally due a member of the armed forces. If captured, the civilian operators ran the risk of being shot as spies. Their services were applauded but after the war largely forgotten by the government they had so faithfully served. Unable to obtain any government benefits, some of the men in dire need were aided by Andrew Carnegie, their old boss, now their benefactor.

Both North and South employed telegraph scouts, highly skilled operators carrying pocket instruments and a roll of flexible wire in their saddlebags. The scouts often penetrated deep into enemy-held territory, tapping wires to obtain useful information. This was extremely dangerous duty. They could not remain long in one place without being detected and tracked down by enemy cavalry. When Confederate General Morgan staged his daring raid through southern Indiana in 1863, he was accompanied by Ellsworth, one of the most skillful operators in the South. The raiders tapped Union wires to learn the whereabouts of the troops pursuing them, as well as sending false messages to create alarm and confusion in the Ohio River counties.

The telegraph industry in later years developed a very strict code of ethics, some of it established by federal or local laws. Telegrams were considered private and confidential between the sender and addressee, and only a court order could gain access to message files. To interfere with delivery or make unauthorized changes in text of messages was a serious offense.

During the Civil War there was an incident that violated all the rules yet had a happy result. When Confederate General Hood invaded Tennessee in 1864, the opposing Union army was commanded by General George H. Thomas. Thomas, a methodical man, did not think his ragtag army was ready to fight and was working diligently to get it in shape before attacking Hood. In so doing, he incurred the ire of General Grant, who wanted immediate action. Finally, on December 15, over the

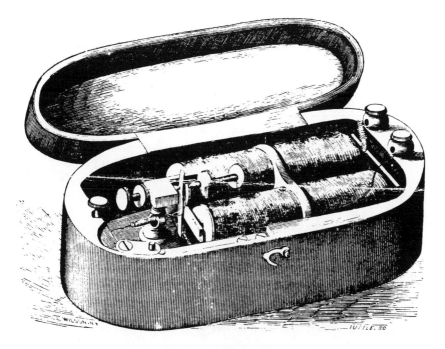

Pocket instrument as used by telegraph scouts. About six inches long.

objections of President Lincoln and Secretary of War Stanton, Grant filed a telegram relieving Thomas from command.

The message was given to Major Thomas Eckert, chief of the telegraph in Washington, for transmission. Some inner voice induced Eckert to hang on to the message for a while, knowing full well it was at the risk of a court-martial. Finally, as Eckert waited, two messages came through from Nashville, telling of Thomas's decisive victory over Hood. Feeling that he had made the right decision in violating orders, Eckert told Lincoln and Stanton what he had done and was assured that no action would be taken against him.

Jimmy Nichols was a 17-year-old telegrapher assigned to General Sumner during the 1862 Peninsular campaign in Virginia. On the march, Sumner asked Nichols if he could get in touch with McClellan. There was a telegraph line nearby, but Nichols had only three feet of wire with his portable instrument and did not want to cut the line down and disrupt other communicatons. Finally, the soldiers piled up a huge pyramid of cracker boxes under the wire so that Jimmy could reach it. Since it was dark, Nichols needed a lantern to work by and immediately became the target of enemy sharpshooters. Although the pile of boxes was repeatedly hit, Nichols was unhurt and carried out his assignment successfully.

Young Jesse Bunnell, the operator for Gen. Fitz-John Porter, having no horse to ride, was left behind in the retreat from Mechanicsville. Nearing Gaines's Mill, Bunnell saw that a battle was imminent. On his own initiative, Bunnell tapped a field wire and got in touch with McClellan's headquarters. McClellan was delighted to have a direct wire to the scene of battle. Bunnell was ordered to stay put, and a detachment of 15 mounted orderlies was assigned to him. Bunnell set up his instruments behind a large tree and for several hours kept McClellan's headquarters informed of all phases of the battle. Some of the orderlies were killed, and some of the messages that Bunnell handled were spotted with blood.

When General Rosecrans started to move south in the latter part of 1863, he set up headquarters at Crawfish Springs near the Georgia border with Tennessee. Assigned to him by official orders of the War Department was a civilian "investigator," Charles A. Dana, an editor of the New York Tribune. Rosecrans's comments on this were never recorded. In all probability they were not printable. Three military telegraphers were assigned to Rosecrans. One of them was Jesse Bunnell, later to become well known as the instrument manufacturer. On September 18, they established telegraphic communication with Washington via Chattanooga. Dana, whom the operators described as "talkative as a parrot," sent 11 telegrams to Secretary Stanton in one day.

On that same day, Rosecrans moved his headquarters northward to the log home of the widow Glenn, advising her to move to the next valley westward, as there would probably be a battle right in front of her place in a day or two. With much complaining, the widow finally moved, and not a moment too soon. Already there was skirmishing to the east, and the next morning, September 19, the great Battle of Chickamauga opened in full fury.

All day, Washington was kept informed of the progress of the battle. Disaster struck on the 20th when the Union line was breached and General Lytle was killed. Rosecrans hastily abandoned his headquarters in the Glenn cabin but left his telegraphers behind. The operators stayed at their post sending messages until the cabin was shot to pieces by shell fire. Then they followed the retreating army northward, setting up a temporary office on a stump. They were soon driven from that position and followed the last of the troops to the village of Rossville where General Thomas, the "Rock of Chickamauga," was at last slowing the Confederate advance. Jesse Bunnell was later with General Sherman on his drive to Atlanta. Bunnell was seriously wounded in the Atlanta campaign, his military career ended.

General Burnside, victim of the tragic defeat at Fredericksburg, was sent west to Cincinnati and in September 1863 sent on to Knoxville. Operator Charles Jacques went along with him. Along with Rosecrans's army, Burnside attacked General Longstreet, who had two divisions. After Gen. William P. Sanders was killed on the ramparts of Knoxville, Burnside assigned a position on the wall to Jacques and said, "Charlie, I want you to set up shop here and keep me informed of what goes on." A wire was strung to Burnside's headquarters where another operator was on duty.

On November 17, the fighting was furious. Assault followed desperate assault on the works, but they held firm.

On the 18th, Charlie's messages to the general ran like this: "They are attacking on the left . . . fighting hand to hand . . . troops so mixed we can't tell what is happening . . . Rebs fell back . . . they attack on the right . . . trying to outflank us, but make no progress . . . they attack the center . . . center holds firm." Twice the wire was shot in two, and the general's headquarters decided that the works had fallen, but this was not so. Jacques, creeping along the line, found the break and repaired it. After the battle, he got a raise in pay and promptly bought himself a new hat. Also, General Burnside brevetted him as a captain for bravery, another of those telegraph appointments that meant little except for a temporary raise in pay and a slight lift in spirit. No chance for a pension later on, or military honors when he died.

In May 1864, during Grant's Wilderness campaign, telegraphers were numerous and identified with the heaviest of the fighting. The operators were constantly on the move. Wires were regularly broken by shell fire. Making repairs was so dangerous that it was common practice to draw lots to see who would go out and fix the break. In the fierce fighting around Spotsylvania Courthouse, one of the operators, running for his life, lost his telegraph instrument. Thirty years later, a farmer plowing his field found the instrument. Oddly enough, the original owner heard of the discovery and showed up to claim it.

In May 1862, Maj. Gen. W. S. Rosecrans, probing into Tennessee, was anxious to learn something of the plans being made by his opponent, Gen. Braxton Bragg. It was decided to send two telegraph scouts deep into Confederate territory to tap the Rebel wires. Frank S. Van Valkenburg and Pat Mullarkey of the Military Telegraph Corps were detailed for the mission, which has been described by historian W. R. Plum. The two men were to tap a telegraph line on the Chattanooga Railroad near Knoxville. They were to find out whether Bragg was weakening his forces to send aid to Gen. Joseph E. Johnston at Vicksburg. They were also instructed to burn an important railroad bridge across the Tennessee River at Loudon.

Aided by Union sympathizers, the two finally made their way to a point on the Knoxville and Chattanooga Railroad between Le Noir and Loudon, about 15 miles from Knoxville. Here they proceeded to tap the telegraph line paralleling the railroad. First they took up the strain on the wire with a block and tackle. Then the wire was cut and the break insulated with a piece of leather. Before cutting the main line, they attached two fine wires, one on either side of the cut, and carefully arranged them down the back side of the pole, out of view from the railroad. The wire was placed back on its normal insulator, and only the closest scrutiny could reveal the tap.

A tap made in this way did not interfere with the normal working of the line;

An improvised telegraph office on a "cracker box" in the field (photo courtesy Library of Congress).

however, military operators were always suspicious of any unusual sound from the wire or a sending style that they were not familiar with. Most scouts used the Caton pocket instruments made in Ottawa, Illinois. The pocket sets had a sounder with all the adjustments of a full-size main-line sounder. The sending key was very small and not as easy to use as a full-size key; however, this was not a great handicap as the pocket sets were used mostly for receiving. The whole set was contained in a case about six inches long, very easy to carry and conceal.

From their hiding place on a bluff overlooking the railroad, the scouts listened to every message and even sent a few false ones to confuse the enemy. Finally they heard Knoxville say that their presence was suspected, and a man was ordered out to check the line. The scouts saw a train approaching, and on the rear platform was a lineman carefully watching the line as he went by. He saw nothing, but the next day he was ordered to patrol the line on foot. The men on the bluff saw him coming, stopping at each pole to look at it carefully. However, he did not climb the bluff, content to observe the poles from the railroad track. He reported again that the line was clear. The Union scouts had resolved to kill the lineman if he discovered them.

Some time later the scouts received truly alarming news. Their Union friends told them that cavalry had been ordered out to search the entire area. It was time to go, and for several days the Union scouts had to play hide and seek with the Confederate cavalry until they finally reached the Union lines on the Cumberland River. When they finally reached Nashville, they were barefoot and ill from hunger and exposure. In all the excitement they never had a chance to burn the bridge at Loudon. However, they had completed a mission of 33 days behind enemy lines and accomplished their primary purpose. Only after their return did they learn that spies in the North had informed the Confederate authorities of the whole plan. Under these circumstances, it was a miracle that Van Valkenburg and Mullarkey survived to tell their story.

In a day when armies moved on foot or horses, field telegraph lines could be strung fast enough to keep pace with the columns. Field commanders were able to keep in almost constant touch with Washington and one another. General Grant paid high tribute to the telegraph and gave a detailed description of field operations in his memoirs.

Personal Memoirs of U. S. Grant (vol. 2, p. 205):

> Nothing could be more complete than the organization and discipline of this body of brave and intelligent men. Insulated wires—insulated so that they would transmit messages in a storm, on the ground or under water—were wound upon reels, making about two hundred pounds weight of wire to each reel. Two men and one mule were detailed to each reel. The pack-saddle on which this was carried was provided

with a rack like a sawbuck placed crosswise of the saddle, and raised above it so that the reel, with its wire, would revolve freely. There was a wagon, supplied with a telegraph operator, battery and telegraph instruments for each division, each corps, each army, and one for my headquarters. There were wagons also loaded with light poles, about the size and length of a wall tent pole, supplied with an iron spike in one end, used to hold the wires up when laid, so that wagons and artillery would not run over them. The mules thus loaded were assigned to brigades, and always kept with the command they were assigned to. The operators were also assigned to particular headquarters, and never changed except by special orders.

The moment the troops were put in position to go into camp all the men connected with this branch of service would proceed to put up their wires. A mule loaded with a coil of wire would be led to the rear of the nearest flank of the brigade he belonged to, and would be led in a line parallel thereto, while one man would hold an end of the wire and uncoil it as the mule was led off.

When he had walked the length of the wire the whole of it would be on the ground. This would be done in rear of every brigade at the same time. The ends of all the wires would then be joined, making a continuous wire in the rear of the whole army. The men, attached to brigades or divisions, would all commence at once raising the wires with their telegraph poles. This was done by making a loop in the wire and putting it over the spike and raising the pole to a perpendicular position. At intervals the wire would be attached to trees, or some other permanent object, so that one pole was sufficient at a place. In the absence of such a support two poles would have to be used, at intervals, placed at an angle so as to hold the wire firm in its place. While this was being done the telegraph wagons would take their positions near where the headquarters they belonged to were to be established, and would connect with the wire. Thus, in a few minutes longer time than it took a mule to walk the length of its coil, telegraphic communication would be effected between all the headquarters of the army. No orders ever had to be given to establish the telegraph.

Perhaps the forerunner of modern news reporting was the telegraphic account of the battle between the Confederate ironclad *Merrimac* and the Union wooden frigate *Cumberland* in 1862. George Cowlam, a young military telegrapher was at his post near Newport News when the Confederate ironclad appeared in Hampton Roads bent on attacking Union ships. Although the shanty housing the telegraph office was repeatedly struck by stray shells, Cowlam stayed at his key. The terse messages he sent describe the action:

She [*Merrimac*] is heading this way.

The *Merrimac* is steering straight for the *Cumberland*—the *Cumberland* gives her a broadside—she keels over—seems to be sinking.

No, she comes on again—she has rammed the *Cumberland*.

God, the *Cumberland* is sinking, she has fired her last broadside and gone down.

Rolling telegraph office. U.S. Military Telegraph Corps battery wagon, Petersburg, Virginia, June 1864 (photo courtesy Library of Congress).

Other events of the war also foreshadowed the future of electrical communication. Professor T. S. C. Lowe, an enterprising balloonist, had made numerous ascents in captive balloons to observe the enemy. His ultimate achievement came at the battle of Fair Oaks, May 1862. A telegraph instrument was taken up in the balloon, connected to the military telegraph network by a trailing wire. The operator in the balloon observed enemy activity and transmitted the information directly to the military commanders.

With such intensive use of the telegraph, it seems odd that there was no telegraph in the White House during the Civil War. When President Lincoln wanted the very latest news from the battlefield, it was necessary for him to go across the street to the telegraph office in the old War Department building. He spent a great deal of time there reading the latest dispatches, finding the place restful compared to the constant hubbub of his office. Lincoln is said to have written the first draft of the Emancipation Proclamation while sitting in the telegraph office.

Whistling Cat, a stirring Civil War novel by Robert W. Chambers, tells the story of the Telegraph Corps with surprising accuracy. First published as a serial by

Liberty Magazine in 1931, it was later published as a hardbound book by D. Appleton in 1932. Now long out of print, the book is sometimes available from used-book dealers. Meticulously researched by Chambers, the story apparently draws heavily on the memoirs of Gen. Anson Stager, who was military commander of the Telegraph Corps from 1862 until the war's end.

One episode in the novel depicts the hero reading a Morse code message by touching the line wire to the heroine's tongue, which vibrated in accordance with the dots and dashes. "Instantly the electric pulsations gave to her tongue a vibratory movement like a telegraph armature. I could read the involuntary oscillations of her little pink tongue as easily as I could have read my own magnet." A similar incident was described by Stager.

The first army cipher used telegraphically in war was worked out by Stager, aided by D. Homer Bates, Albert B. Chandler, and Charles A. Tinker, the three young cipher operators in the War Department at Washington. It became the standard cipher of the army. Over a dozen new ciphers were devised during the war, whenever the one in use was captured by the enemy, or it was suspected that they had solved it. The Confederate ciphers were simpler than those of the Union. They were often solved and yielded useful information. Federal wiretappers were usually more successful than their southern counterparts because many Confederate messages were sent in plain English. In the Union service, almost all dispatches of any importance were encoded.

Operators assigned to commanding generals had exclusive custody of the highly secret cipher codebooks used in coding and decoding messages. They were sometimes placed in awkward positions due to the conflict between civil and military authority. General Grant once had to intervene on behalf of his cipher operator, who was being threatened with discharge from the service for refusing to turn over a cipher book to a subordinate officer on Grant's staff. Grant told the secretary of war that the operator had only obeyed orders and was not at fault.

Many of the Union army military operators were mere boys of 15. One 15-year-old, Willie Kettles, was working in the War Department telegraph office in Washington on the day that Richmond fell to the Union army. Willie was told to "turn down for Richmond"* and then had the distinction of copying General Weitzel's official message announcing the fall of Richmond, dated April 3, 1865, 8:00A.M. Secretary of war Stanton was so elated that he picked Willie up bodily and held him up to the window in view of the cheering crowds in the street.

On his visits to the War Department telegraph office, President Lincoln renewed his acquaintance with one of the cipher operators, Charles A. Tinker. In 1857, Tinker had been a telegraph operator at a hotel office in Pekin, Illinois, and had explained the workings of the telegraph to lawyer Lincoln, who was in town

---

To adjust the receiving instrument for the weaker signal coming from Richmond.

attending a court case. Lincoln called many of the operators by their first names and usually addressed the 15-year-olds as "sonny."

After the war, several members of the telegraph corps wrote books recording in detail many of the adventures and accomplishments of the members. One of the most comprehensive is William R. Plum's two-volume set, *The Military Telegraph During the Civil War in the United States* (Jansen McClurg, 1882). Other books: David Homer Bates's *Lincoln in the Telegraph Office* (Century, 1907), John Emmet O'Brien's *Telegraphing in Battle* (Reader Press, 1910), William Bender Wilson's *A Glimpse of the United States Military Telegraph Corps and of Abraham Lincoln* (Holmesburg, Pa., 1889).

Many of the old Civil War telegraphers advanced to executive positions in the telegraph industry in the postwar years. Jesse Bunnell founded the company bearing his name and became a leading manufacturer of telegraph apparatus. Carnegie, of course, became world famous for his philanthropic work. Albert B. Chandler was appointed a receiver in bankruptcy and directed the reorganization of the Postal Telegraph Company in 1886.

At war's end in 1865, the Union army had built an impressive total of 15,000 miles of military telegraph lines and handled over 6 million messages. During the Wilderness campaign alone, Dennis Doren, head of construction for the MTC, averaged 24 miles of line a day, some of it under fire or at night. During the same period, the Confederate army had erected only 1,000 miles of wire for military purposes. The Southern armies relied primarily on existing commercial lines for communications and did not have an extensive signal corps to provide field telegraph service.

Military telegraph operators in postwar years organized the Society of the United States Military Telegraph Corps. The group was active in lobbying in Congress for pension benefits for the operators who served. These efforts were never successful, and the only pensions ever received were those paid by Andrew Carnegie out of his private funds. By 1916, there were only 200 of the old operators left, and only 19 were able to attend the 35th and final reunion of the corps, held at the Hotel Astor, New York, September 1916.

The final gathering was addressed by Melville E. Stone, general manager of the Associated Press, who said in part:

> Today, the telephone has taken the place of the Morse operator in a very large measure, and today the telegraph companies are sending millions of messages without the Morse alphabet, by mechanical means. Let me say, however, that the Morse invention and the Morse operator and the Morse alphabet have been of incalculable benefit to mankind. You need have no regret for the work you have done. You have served your day and generation nobly. You have earned the gratitude of the world, and as to the future, all of these mechanical appliances and all of this progress which is inevitable, is builded on the foundation that you have laid.

Stone's remarks in 1916 were prophetic if slightly premature with respect to the Morse telegraph. Morse operators and the Morse system continued to play an important role in communications for at least another 30 years. It was true, however, that automatic equipment had largely replaced the Morse system on the busy wires connecting large metropolitan areas.

The Civil War Telegraph Corps was disbanded after the war, its role being taken over by the U.S. Signal Corps, which had been organized in 1861. The Morse telegraph continued to be an important part of military communications for another 50 years. In the great westward expansion of the United States after the Civil War, the army played a key role in building telegraph lines between the isolated military posts in the West.

One of the pioneer line builders for the army was Lt. A. W. Greely, later to become leader of the ill-fated Arctic expedition and finally brigadier general and chief signal officer. By 1876, Greely had strung 1,100 miles of telegraph line in Texas. He was forced to take an extended leave of absence due to poor health, returning to duty in 1878. General Meyer sent him to South Dakota. With only a sergeant, two men, and a four-mule wagon, Greely ran into a violent blizzard in the Badlands. "For 36 hours," he reported, "we lay buried in snow, suffering from high winds, no fire possible, and the temperatures down to zero. In a way the blizzard was a blessing, as no Indians would keep on the warpath in such weather." Reaching the Powder River, Greely ran into a captain with a full troop of cavalry, who promptly asked, "Where is the rest of your escort?" Told that there were only four in the party, the captain blurted out, "What damn fool sent you into an Indian country with only three men?"

After the invention of the telephone, the army started some limited experimentation with the new mode of communication. The military telegraph operator at Fort Sill, Oklahoma Territory, in 1879 was J. G. Hewett, who in addition to his other duties would copy Associated Press dispatches four times a day to keep the post up-to-date on the news. Hewett was sent two "Phelps Crown" telephones with instructions to try them out on the Fort Reno line by temporarily disconnecting the telegraph instruments at a time when the line wasn't busy. After the telegraph operators got the telephones working, they used to hold regular Sunday-afternoon telephone conversations between the two forts. Once, they invited Quanah Parker and some other Indians living on the Fort Sill reservation in for a demonstration. Listening on the line, the Indians were astounded to hear the bugler blowing taps at Fort Reno, 75 miles away.

The final challenge to the U.S. Signal Corps in telegraph line building came after the purchase of Alaska in 1867. The vast territory, having no internal communication or any telegraphic link with the States, needed the wires, and the Signal Corps was the only agency capable of providing them. The pioneer line builder of the Signal Corps, A. W. Greely, was by 1900 a brigadier general and chief signal officer. He at once embarked on a program to give Alaska a communications system and received a congressional appropriation of $450,550 in May 1900. The new system was to be called the Washington-Alaska Military Cable and Telegraph. The first progress came on October 29, 1900, when Capt. Charles Farnsworth, an extremely capable and resourceful officer, completed a telegraph line from Fort Egbert on the Yukon River to Dawson in the Yukon Territory of Canada. After his Alaskan experiences, Farnsworth served with General Pershing on the Mexican border in 1916 and later commanded the 139th Infantry Brigade in World War I. Farnsworth retired in 1925 as a major general but continued to lead an active life until his death in 1955 at 93.

The next vital link was to run from Fort Egbert to Fort Liscum near Valdez. Progress on this route came to a standstill after the departure of Captain Farnsworth. In the summer of 1901, Greeley sent a new officer to get things started on the important north-south route. The officer was only 21, and he had served in the Philippine Insurrection. He was Lt. William Mitchell, later to become the famous and controversial Billy Mitchell of air force fame. Mitchell brought youthful enthusiasm and a keen mind to the stalemated telegraph project, coming to the conclusion that proper transportation of supplies held the answer to the telegraph construction.

Hitherto only dog teams had been used for winter hauling, and the loads they carried were far too little for a heavy construction project. Mitchell decided to use horses and mules to haul in the necessary supplies during the winter, something that had never been done before. With the supplies in place, line construction could proceed during the summer months. There was a rather high mortality among the horses and mules used in winter, but it was a price that had to be paid for getting the job done. Young Mitchell quickly learned the facts of Arctic life in winter. Mercury thermometers and kerosene lamps froze in the intense cold. Special clothing was devised that permitted working in a temperature of 60 below.

Seeming never to lose interest or enthusiasm for the difficult assignment he had undertaken, Mitchell brushed aside one obstacle after another. Running out of funds, he telegraphed Greely for more and was astonished to receive $50,000. Rather than wait for an official warrant from the U.S. Treasury, he incurred obligations for the entire amount, explaining, "An officer who always follows the letter of the Book of Regulations instead of the spirit seldom gets anywhere." Unknown to Mitchell at the time, an error in telegraphic transmission had rendered the amount as $50,000 when it was supposed to be only $5,000, and General Greely had to get a special appropriation from Congress to cover the error. When Mitchell's men complained about working in the extreme cold, he simply banned thermometers from the construction sites. Line construction proceeded during the summer of 1902. The construction presented unique problems due to the permafrost soil, which would not support poles in summer. It was often necessary to use a tripod of wooden poles to keep the line pole upright. Overcoming all the problems, the telegraph line linked up with the Fort Egbert line at Tanacross Junction on August 24, 1902.

The following year saw completion of a line from Fort St. Michael on Norton Sound to connect with the Fort Egbert-Fort Liscom line. Mitchell himself made the final connection on June 27, 1903, and said, "America's last frontier has been roped and hog-tied." General Greely was generous in his praise of the men who built the telegraph lines in Alaska: "It is doubted whether in the peaceful annals of the Army, there have been met with nobler fortitude by the enlisted men equal conditions of hardship and privation. It is to be understood that the line of the Army has displayed in this work the same energy and endurance as the Signal Corps."

By 1908, the army began to experiment with wireless as a means of Alaskan communication. Eventually, wireless telegraphy was able to take over some of the old telegraph routes, which were very costly to maintain in working order. As wireless telegraphy advanced, it was found to be more reliable than the land telegraph lines. In 1904 the undersea cable from Valdez to Seattle was completed, the last link in the Alaskan system. Commercial messages always outnumbered military traffic and provided an income that paid for the upkeep of the land lines and cable. By 1922, the army had pulled out of Alaska, but the Signal Corps continued to operate the telegraph lines, now known as the Alaska Communications System. After World War II, communications in Alaska were greatly augmented by the so-called White Alice network, an advanced type of shortwave communication. Many remote villages that previously had only a single radiotelephone set for contact with the outside world could now enjoy regular telephone service.

Today, communications in Alaska are a far cry from the days when Billy Mitchell and his men struggled to erect an elemental Morse telegraph network. Modern telecommunications are provided to virtually every community of over 25 people in the entire state. A company called ALASCOM operates a complex network involving satellite earth stations, microwave links, and fiber-optic cables. A satellite called Aurora 1 in geosynchronous orbit over the Pacific serves the many earth stations throughout Alaska. The system is unique, the only one of its kind in the world. Plans for the future include connecting the Alaskan network to the latest technical marvel, the trans–Pacific fiber optic cable running between North America and Pacific Asia.

During World War I, when the first American Signal Corps units arrived in France, they were amazed to find the French still using outmoded methods dating back to the mid-nineteenth century. The Americans found some French operators still receiving by watching dots and dashes on a paper tape, something that hadn't been done in America since 1850. Maj. Frank H. Fay was placed in charge of upgrading the French telegraph service. His first problem was to improve the service between Chaumont and Paris, where the French wires were unable to handle the huge volume of wartime traffic. The French wires were still being operated in the "open circuit" mode, and there were no duplex terminal sets to increase the wire capacity. Fay went scrounging in Paris and found enough ill-assorted parts to build on the spot four duplex sets, two for Paris and two for Chaumont. The wires were changed to the American "closed circuit" system. The French continued to be amazed at the energy and efficiency of Americans. When they saw a line truck equipped with a special crane to string 8 or 10 wires at once, they just couldn't believe it.

The French telephone service was also found unequal to the wartime needs, and American ingenuity was again put to the test. On November 8, 1917, General Pershing cabled Washington asking for the formation of a Women's Telephone Operation Unit. The chief signal officer reported:

> The use of female telephone operators in France was decided upon for two reasons. The first of these was the unquestioned superiority of women as telephone switchboard operators, and the second was the desire to release for service in the more dangerous telephone centrals at the front the male operators on duty in the larger offices.

Although England had a sophisticated high-speed automatic telegraph system in operation by the time of World War I, not all of the facilities were that advanced. When American Signal Corps operators arrived there in 1917 with their bug keys and typewriters, they were astounded to find some English telegraphists still operating in a standing position, before waist-high key shelves, laboriously pounding out messages at about 10–15 words per minute. For the Americans, accustomed to sitting at a desk with the resonator at their ears, rattling away at 30–40 words per minute, it seemed like a throwback to the Morse telegraph of 1844.

6. How It Worked

The message is history! (Author)

Present technicians and engineers looking at the Morse telegraph consider it absurdly simple compared to today's complex technology. It was pretty simple, even by nineteenth-century standards, yet it evolved into a system that had no equal for almost 100 years.

To put Morse's invention in proper perspective, it is necessary to consider the state of life that existed in the America of 1832. There were only 24 states in the Union having a total population of around 13 million. A large part of the West was still uncharted wilderness. Railroads were still primitive in nature, and most travel was by horse-drawn stagecoach. Mail service was uncertain except along the post roads linking eastern seaboard cities. Oil lamps, candles, and a few gas lights were the only source of illumination. There was no practical application of electricity, and engineering as a profession did not exist. Contact with the rest of the world was limited to the sailing packets that typically took four to six weeks to cross the Atlantic. It was not surprising, then, that many citizens considered the electric telegraph as bordering on witchcraft.

Still not even dreaming that the human mind could decode telegraph signals directly, Morse used a cumbersome register, his original device for marking dots and dashes on a paper tape. This was the method used on the original Washington-Baltimore line and for several years thereafter on all lines. The recording feature was an important advantage claimed for the Morse invention. As time went on, operators listening to the clicking of the register mechanism hour after hour began to recognize the sound of individual letters and realized that they could read messages without looking at the tape. Over the years, different individuals came forward claiming to be the one who first used "sound reading." It is much more likely that it was something that was discovered by many operators at about the same time. Telegraph executive T. P. Shaffner, writing in 1859, declared: "Some years ago, as president of a telegraph line, I adopted a rule forbidding the receiving of messages by sound. Since then that rule has been reversed and the operator is required to receive by sound or he cannot get employment in first class stations." Many

operators developed the uncanny skill of being able to carry on a casual conversation with a visitor while sending or receiving a constant stream of messages.

One wire chief in the Boston office of the Postal Telegraph Co. once demonstrated the unusual stunt of copying a message in English and one in French simultaneously, writing with both hands. Other operators could lag far behind the sender and still put down a perfect copy. These were operators of extraordinary talent, yet even run-of-the-mill operators were regarded with awe by the uninitiated. It was this exceptional human skill that made the Morse system so successful. Morse lived to see sound operation become standard, but neither he nor other early telegraph inventors had any inkling that such a thing would be possible. All of them worked on some kind of recording device to display the received signals. People old enough to remember the telegraph seem always to remember the Prince Albert tobacco cans stuck in the resonator next to the sounder, even if they recall little else. This was not a universal practice by any means. Some operators did it just to change the "tune"of the sounder or possibly to distinguish between different instruments that were often operating at the same time.

Today the dot-dash Morse code seems like such a simple idea that it is hard to believe it took so long for somebody to think of it. It is certain that if a code had existed in practical form, a great deal of visual and electrical signaling could have taken place much earlier in history. Morse believed that he was the first to devise a code. Actually, some types of codes are believed to have existed as far back as the time of the Francis Bacon in 1605. Lomond of France supposedly had a code of some kind in 1787. Schilling, in 1832, had devised a code for use with the needle telegraph he had invented. Steinheil in Germany had devised a dot-dash alphabet for his telegraph in 1836, thus preceding Morse by at least two years. None of the early codes achieved any general acceptance or application in a practical way.

Morse's first attempt at a code came in 1832 when he used dots and dashes to represent numbers that could be translated into words. This system was found impractical due to the huge dictionary that would have been required to read messages. The first Morse alphabet using dots and dashes to represent letters and numbers directly was compiled in 1838. This version was revised in 1844 and became the "American Morse code" used thereafter on all land telegraph lines in North America (see p. 68). There has always been a question of who actually invented the code. Was it Morse, or Vail?

The best guess seems to be that the code was a joint effort. It would seem logical that Morse and Vail, working shoulder to shoulder on a common project, would have freely shared ideas on the subject. Morse always claimed the code for himself, with no effort to assign part of the credit to Vail. Vail, by the terms of his contract with Morse, was bound to assign anything he invented to Morse, and either for this reason or because of his modest nature, never made an effort to associate his name with the code.

TELEGRAPH CODES

American Morse Code	Continental or International Morse Code
A · —	A · —
B — · · ·	B — · · ·
C · · ·	C — · — ·
D — · ·	D — · ·
E ·	E ·
F · — ·	F · · — ·
G — — ·	G — — ·
H · · · ·	H · · · ·
I · ·	I · ·
J — · — ·	J · — — —
K — · —	K — · —
L ——	L · — · ·
M — —	M — —
N — ·	N — ·
O · ·	O — — —
P · · · · ·	P · — — ·
Q · · — ·	Q — — · —
R · · ·	R · — ·
S · · ·	S · · ·
T —	T —
U · · —	U · · —
V · · · —	V · · · —
W · — —	W · — —
X · — · ·	X — · · —
Y · · · ·	Y — · — —
Z · · · ·	Z — — · ·
& · · · ·	

Figures

	American		International
1	· — — ·	1	· — — — —
2	· · — · ·	2	· · — — —
3	· · · — ·	3	· · · — —
4	· · · · —	4	· · · · —
5	— — —	5	· · · · ·
6	· · · · · ·	6	— · · · ·
7	— — · ·	7	— — · · ·
8	— · · · ·	8	— — — · ·
9	— · · —	9	— — — — ·
0	————	0	— — — — —

Punctuation

American		International	
(.)	· · — — — · ·	(.)	· — · — · —
(,)	· — · —	(,)	— — · · — —
(?)	— · · — ·	(?)	· · — — · ·
(:)	— · — · ·	(:)	— — — · · ·
(;)	· · · · · ·	(;)	— · — · — ·
(-)	· · · · · — · ·	(-)	— · · · · —
(!)	— — — —	(!)	None at present
(')	· · — · · — · ·	(')	· — — — — ·
(/)	· · · —	(/)	— · · — ·
(	· · · · ·	(	— · — — ·
)	· · · · · · · ·	)	— · — — · —
(")	· · — · — · — ·	(")	· — · · — ·
(")	· · — · — · — ·		

Nevertheless, the legend has persisted that it was Vail and not Morse who invented the telegraphic alphabet. *Famous First Facts*, a respected library reference, states categorically that the first telegraphic communication system in which dots and dashes represented letters was invented by Alfred Vail of Morristown, New Jersey, in September 1837. However, no proof of this has ever been found. Even so, Vail's family would never admit otherwise, and in 1911 his grandson had Vail's tombstone in the Morristown churchyard inscribed as follows: "Inventor of the telegraph dot and dash alphabet." In developing the dot-dash code, it is said that the inventors consulted a printer's typecase to see which letter was used most often. This, of course, was the letter *e*, and it was assigned the symbol of one dot, the shortest in the Morse alphabet.

By the 1850s, undersea telegraph cables were being laid in Europe, first across the English Channel, then from England to Ireland. As this form of telegraphy started to increase, some shortcomings became apparent in the use of the American Morse code. Long underwater cables are characterized by a considerable time lag in transmission, which increases in direct proportion to the length of the cable. The American Morse, with its many dots and spaced dots, did not carry as well as on the land line telegraph circuits.

A code called the Austro-Germanic, which eliminated the spaced dots of American Morse, came into use on the cables. In 1851, an international conference at Berlin officially adopted the Austro-Germanic for use on cables, and it was called the International, or Continental, code. This became the standard code for cables, for land telegraph lines except in North America, and later on for "wireless," or radio, communication.

There were some minor changes in punctuation symbols in 1938; otherwise, the code used today for radio communication is the same as the 1851 version. In 1854, there was a proposal to adopt the International code for land wire telegraphy in the United States, apparently in the interest of having only one telegraph code for all uses. Such a storm of protest arose from operators and executives alike that the idea was hastily dropped. Apparently in the U.S. telegraph industry, no one wanted to start all over again.

Whatever shortcomings it might have had, the American Morse code lent itself beautifully to key and sounder telegraphy. Sent by a skilled operator using a "bug" key, the stream of dots and dashes rolled from the sounder with an almost musical cadence. As the sending speed increased, the receiving operator learned to copy many short words as characters rather than individual letters. Words like "the," "it," "on" were recognized instantly by the complete sound, not the sound of individual letters. Copying on a typewriter enabled the receiving operator to keep up with the fastest sending speeds. The old Morse operators were fantastic typists. They could keep up with the message, change message blanks, and mark number sheets without once interrupting a long string of messages. Surprisingly, a good many never used the touch-typing system. "Hunt-and-peck" is hardly the right term for the method they used, but they only used two fingers and were superfast on the keyboard. Telegraph typewriters had all capital letters, and messages were normally sent without punctuation marks because punctuation marks were counted and charged for as full words. Press messages, destined to become newspaper copy, were the exception, usually being sent with the reporter's punctuation included.

The American Morse code was a faster code to send than Continental. In Continental there are more dashes, with fewer dots and no spaced dots. Some studies have indicated that American Morse was at least 20 percent faster than Continental. This is true only in manual sending. With automatic senders, the speed can be brought up to any value desired. Today, American Morse is mostly a forgotten code. The sole exception may be in some railroad lines in Mexico, last refuge of the Morse telegraph, and among the members of the Morse Telegraph Club, who use it for traditional reasons.

Even the Continental is slowly going out of use. Once widely used in radiotelegraphy and on ocean cables, it is now more of an auxiliary to other means of communication. Oceangoing ships that were once required to carry a qualified radiotelegraph officer for safety reasons are now converting to automated systems for handling distress communications. When the great passenger liners were busy on the ocean, scores of coastal radiotelegraph stations were required just to handle the passenger messages filed on these floating cities. Amateur radio operators have long been required to have some proficiency in Continental code, which has always been the basic communication mode in an emergency. Even the amateurs may soon be relieved of any legal requirement to learn the code, yet many of them will continue to use it for traditional reasons.

In the 1860s, the Cincinnati office of Western Union was a large and very busy point for relaying telegraph traffic between East and West. George Kennan was an operator there in 1863. His descriptions of the office are preserved in documents on deposit at the Firelands Historical Society in Norwalk, Ohio. Kennan later became well known by virtue of his experiences with the trans–Siberian telegraph project. Kennan relates an incident that occurred when L. C. Weir, an operator with exceptional talent for copying behind the sender, decided to demonstrate his skill for Gen. Anson Stager, then head of the U.S. Military Telegraph.

Weir was working the eastern wire when Pittsburgh called saying they had 15 or 20 messages to send. Given a casual "go-ahead," Pittsburgh began to send at the rate of about 30 words a minute. Meanwhile, Weir made a show of searching his pockets for a pencil and failed to find one. General Stager, himself a good operator, looked on with interest and expected that Weir would stop Pittsburgh and say "Hold on a minute while I get a pencil," but this was not part of Weir's plan.

Rising lazily from his seat, he walked slowly across the big operating room where 12 or 15 other instruments were noisily banging away, went to the desk of Stevens, the chief operator, and asked for a pencil. Stevens got out his keys, unlocked his desk, and gave him one.

Weir went back to his table, looked at the pencil for a moment in a speculative way, then began to feel in his pockets for a knife to sharpen it with. Not finding one – or pretending not to find one – he again crossed the room and borrowed a knife from one of the local circuit men. Returning to his table, he sharpened the pencil deliberately, put a fine point on the lead, and then, taking a pad of soft paper in his lap, he put his feet up on the table and began to copy, making elaborate flourishes and curlicues as if he had worlds of time. Pittsburgh, meanwhile, had been sending steadily at the rate of 30 words a minute and was more than three messages ahead.

Weir finally stopped flourishing, settled down to business, wrote telegram after telegram with ever-increasing swiftness, and soon began to catch up. In 5 minutes he was only two messages behind. In 10 minutes he was within one telegram of the sender, and in a quarter hour he had recovered all the ground he had intentionally lost and was putting the words on paper as fast as they came from the instrument. General Stager watched the performance in silence, and when Weir had finally caught up, he said dryly, "That's all very fine, Mr. Weir; it's the most wonderful thing I have ever seen in the way of telegraphing, but I wouldn't do it again!"

The Morse sounder, the universal receiving instrument, consisted of an electromagnet that acted on a pole piece mounted on a pivoted sounding lever working between two stops. When the magnet was energized and released, the sounder gave a click. Slow and fast clicks corresponded to dots and dashes, which the operators could readily translate. For the basic circuit, the only additional equipment needed was a sending key for opening and closing the circuit. Only one line wire connecting stations was needed, the earth forming the return path for the line current. Morse had discovered this principle by accident in 1838, unaware of the 1837 discovery of the same thing by Steinheil in Germany.

Telegraph instruments were operated by direct-current electricity. Originally, batteries were used, and they were invariably of the so-called gravity type. Gravity batteries got their name from the two solutions of different specific gravity that were used. A blue copper sulphate solution in the bottom of the battery jar maintained a definite line of demarcation with the clear zinc sulphate solution at the top. Gravity cells had the characteristic of giving better life on a closed circuit delivering a small amount of power.

For this reason, Morse circuits were operated as series, closed circuit loops. The sending keys had shorting switches, which were always kept closed except when actually sending. The line was always under test with this arrangement. The

Modern version of the Morse recorder. Differs little in principle from the original recorders. Widely used to record numbers on messenger call circuits, fire alarm circuits, and even by the telephone company to monitor dialed telephone numbers (photo by Lewis Coe).

closed circuit mode was retained after motor generators replaced batteries around the turn of the century. In addition to the sounder, a mainline relay was used at many way stations. The relay had an electromagnet like a sounder and lightweight armature that was very sensitive. There were adjustments for the spring tension and the magnet pull, making it possible to adjust quickly for varying line conditions. The relay had a further advantage: The operator could shut off the noisy local sounder when not actually receiving a message. The muted clicking of the relay was enough to alert the operator when his station was being called. Sounders intended for mainline use without the intermediate relay were fitted with quickly variable adjustments.

Telegraph traffic was routed across the country in somewhat the same manner as the U.S. mail. Large centers, called relay offices, were the terminal points for dozens of branch lines covering a particular part of the country. A small office having a message for a station on its own way wire could call that station directly and send the message. Otherwise, the message was sent to the relay office, which then retransmitted it on another wire connecting with the desired destination.

Offices not having a large business were usually grouped together on one wire. All of the instruments on a way wire were connected in series, and each station heard all of the traffic going to the others. Each station had a one- or two-letter call

Top: Telegraph relay made by Bunnell and once used on the Nickel Plate railroad (photo by Lewis Coe). *Bottom:* Mainline sounder made by Bunnell and often used by Postal Telegraph (photo by Lewis Coe).

Top: The 17A (left) and 15B mainline sounders widely used by Western Union. Made by several manufacturers, including Bunnell and Western Electric (photo by Lewis Coe). *Bottom:* Pocket instrument, less than 6″ long. Made by J. H. Bunnell & Co. Instruments of the same pattern were made by other manufacturers. Has all the adjustments of a full size key and mainline sounder. Often used by linemen for test purposes (photo by Lewis Coe).

Resonator box on swinging arm placed sounder close to operator's ear. Cast iron swinging arm made by White Co., Worcester, Mass. (photo by Lewis Coe).

sign that identified it to the relay office. Messages going to distant parts of the country were placed on intercity wires to reach a relay office nearest to the destination.

Around 1900, when Morse operations were at a peak, the Western Union relay office in Chicago had operating positions for 880 operators on a shift. In such large offices it took operators of exceptional skill and iron nerves to hold down a job. For one thing, the noise in a large telegraph office was deafening. Dozens of sounders and typewriters going full blast, conveyor belts clattering, clerks shouting—all contributed to the general bedlam. Since some of the operators worked the same wire day after day, they became known to all of the operators on the line. Little pleasantries were exchanged when traffic permitted, and friendships developed, even though it was rare to meet in person.

Relay-office operators working the same wire on a regular basis soon learned to appraise the varying degrees of skill of the operators on the wire. It might range from a real high-speed hotshot on a large company's private wire to the slow, hesitant style of an elderly man or woman in a small-town office where only a few messages were handled per day. The way-station operators appreciated a good steady operator in the big city who didn't try to snow them under.

Long hours of sending with the simple Morse key caused many operators to

Top: Telegraph hand sending key made by J. H. Bunnel & Company, the original and basic sending instrument for Morse Code (photo by Lewis Coe). *Bottom:* Vibroplex "bug" key, made by the Vibroplex Company, New York (photo by Lewis Coe).

Opposite: Western Union relay office, Chicago 1901. Two rooms 46′×212′ provided space for 880 operators. Over two million messages per month were handled. Typewriters were in use, but there were no "bug" sending keys (photo courtesy Smithsonian Institution).

develop severe muscular pain in their sending arm. By 1900, as telegraph traffic became extremely heavy, inventors started working on automatic keys to make the operator's job a little easier. In 1904, Horace G. Martin patented his Vibroplex key, which is still being made and sold today for use in radio telegraphy. The Vibroplex employs a vibrating contact point to make the dots automatically. After Martin's patent expired, many similar keys were marketed, all known by the generic name "bugs."

By the late nineteenth century, telegraph technology started to get more complicated. As telegraph traffic increased, every possible method of increasing the line capacity was utilized. The duplex circuit was the first. It permitted sending and receiving at the same time over a single wire. Each station of a duplex had two operators, one sending and one receiving. Edison's invention of the quadruplex made it possible to send four messages over a single wire. Four operators worked at each end, two sending and two receiving. These devices gave an enormous increase in message-handling capacity without the expense of building additional lines. Thousands of small towns, however, were served by the single-line Morse instruments, essentially unchanged in principle since the 1850s. Telegraph lines up to at least 300 miles in length could usually be worked without anything more than the simple key, relay, and sounder equipment.

Longer lines sometimes required repeating instruments. The repeaters took the incoming signals and retransmitted them with new battery power to the distant station. Repeating instruments became very complex in application and were usually installed at larger offices where they could be kept in adjustment by specially trained personnel. The development of practical repeating instruments around 1860 made it possible to eventually work the transcontinental line straight through from New York to San Francisco. Originally, messages had been manually relayed east and west from Salt Lake City.

Direct current power to the lines was normally applied at the central relay office. On some long lines, power might be fed from both ends of the line. Way stations normally needed only a small source of power for their local sounder circuits, which could be supplied by a few cells of battery. Actual voltage on telegraph lines varied with the length of line, the type of instruments employed, and company practices.

The telegraph battery wagons of the Civil War carried 100 battery cells, giving a total line voltage of slightly over 100 volts. Telegraph motor-generator sets used in later years were typically rated at 150 volts, and this was an average line voltage when 150-ohm instruments were used. On some long lines, 300 miles or more, 150-volt generators were used at each end, making the effective line voltage 300. Such lines could give a pretty unpleasant shock when touched with the bare hand. Some companies used 30-ohm instruments with correspondingly lower line voltages.

Western Union, with its exclusive railroad contracts, usually followed railroad

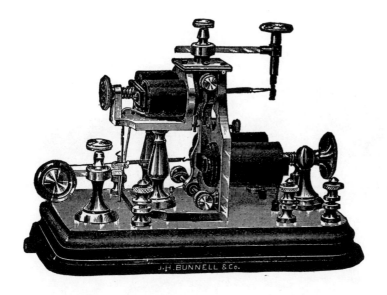

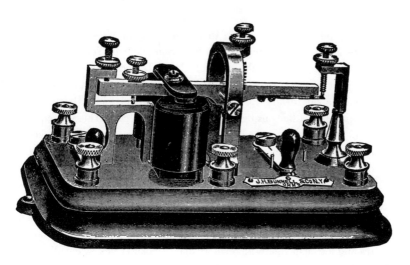

Components of the Milliken-Hicks, one of the first telegraph repeaters. Start-ing around 1860, the repeaters made long-distance transmission possible. Pre-viously, messages had to be manually copied and retransmitted at intermediate points if the circuit was much over 300 miles in length (J. H. Bunnell cata-log).

Lineman's test set circa 1910 – made by the Postal Telegraph Shop (photo by Lewis Coe).

right-of-ways with its lines. Western Union and railroad wires usually shared the same poles and were supervised by a Superintendent of Telegraphs, who was employed jointly by WU and the railroad. Postal Telegraph lines could be found on either public highways or railroads. On railroads, the Postal wires were typically on the opposite side of the track from the WU railroad wires. On the railroads, linemen could patrol lines using small hand or motor cars. This was convenient, but it could be dangerous as the light motor cars sometimes jumped the track. Also, the linemen had to get clearance from the train dispatcher before venturing out on the rails.

Linemen were the unsung heroes of the telegraph industry. Without them, any appreciable length of telegraph line would soon fall into disrepair and eventually quit working altogether. Long before the days of hard hats, cherry pickers, powered hole diggers, and massive boom trucks, the old-timers went out to do battle with the wires and the elements. With no more than a pickup truck, Klein pliers, "come-alongs," climbing spurs, and occasionally a helper, they had to rely mostly on their wits and a little luck to find and repair trouble. A capable wire chief could sometimes direct them to almost the exact location of a fault. At other times, they might spend hours in cut-and-try testing and line walking before the problem was located.

Model "A" line truck used by Postal Telegraph in the 1930s (photo by Lewis Coe).

Quite a few of the old-time linemen were capable Morse telegraphers and could cut in on a line and talk directly to the wire chief using the pocket instruments they carried. Line work in pleasant weather was still hard work. During winter blizzards, it was extremely demanding, even for a man of strong constitution. Linemen were "jewels in the rough," and in spite of their sometimes rough ways, many a young operator discovered that they were men of character, good and loyal friends. On mainline routes, the usual practice was to station a regular patrolman every 50 to 75 miles. These men were familiar figures along their routes. They had many local contacts whom they relied on for extra help when it was necessary. In case of widespread line damage, the telegraph company would dispatch a large line crew to make repairs.

Line work was considered so hazardous that the life insurance companies did not welcome applications from workers in that classification. Electrocution, either by contact with live wires or from lightning hits, was always a danger. However, injuries from falls and those resulting from derailment of rail motor cars were more common. This was before workers compensation and medical benefits were in force. The lineman was pretty much dependent on the charity of his employer if he got hurt on the job. When iron wire came into use for telegraph lines, it was at first not galvanized. To prevent rusting, the telegraph companies conceived the idea of coating the wire with tar. A more disagreeable job than covering mile after mile of wire with sticky, smelly tar can scarcely be imagined. Telegraph pioneer James D. Reid was once employed this way. He recalled that after a day on the line with mop and tar bucket, he was more or less unwelcome at the inns along the route.

Catastrophic damage to telegraph lines occurred when a tropical storm struck Galveston Island on August 16, 1915. Winds were 100 mph, and a tidal wave 7 to 10 feet high swept over the island. Some pole lines six miles inland were completely washed away. The Galveston telegraph office was inundated with eight feet of water. In a 15-mile stretch of line from Houston to Hempstead, 500 poles were down. From Houston to Spring, a distance of 27 miles, 400 poles were down. Emergency crews laid 20,000 feet of twisted pair wire and by the 19th had 20 wires working to Galveston.

One hundred seventy-five men were employed to carry in repair material by hand as all roads and railroads were washed out. Telegraph companies early recognized the inevitability of such disasters and were usually well prepared to cope with them. Western Union alone had emergency stocks of 1,000 miles of No. 9 copper wire, 500 miles of iron wire, and at least 150 miles of multiconductor insulated cable. In addition there were stocks of replacement poles at strategic locations around the country.

Communications and electric power services were all but wiped out in a large part of the Ohio River valley by the disastrous floods of 1937. Telegraph linemen

New York–Chicago main line of the Postal Telegraph Company, brought down by a sleet storm in January 1942. Scene is on the old Lincoln Highway near Merrillville, Indiana (photo by Lewis Coe).

were faced with the almost impossible task of restoring lines and bringing in portable generators to provide power for the larger telegraph offices. From messengers on up, the telegraph people responded in the tradition of public service. One group bringing an emergency generator to Louisville chartered a 30-foot boat to bring them and the generator across the Ohio River. Due to the rough water, the passengers were told to lie down on the bunks and not move around. One man said afterward, "When we reached the swift current, the boat jumped around like a cork, which made us, who could not see out, most uneasy."

Other emergency generators, arriving by train, could not be immediately unloaded because the army was in charge and gave first priority to food and medical supplies.

After some semblance of normal operation was made possible by the emergency power, linemen set out to find and repair downed lines. For the most part, they had to rely on small boats to reach the lines. In many locations the water was up to the level of the crossarms on the poles. R. A. Gantt, vice president of Postal Telegraph, paid high praise to his employees: "Our field forces quickly realized the danger and used their every resource to provide ways and means to keep traffic

Broadway at Maiden Lane, New York, in the 1880s showing the maze of overhead wires (courtesy Western Union).

moving. . . . With great personal sacrifice, they restored service and again upheld the highest traditions of the telegraph."

Although vulnerable to violent weather, open wire lines were relatively cheap and quick to build and served well during the great expansion of the telegraph system in the last half of the nineteenth century. As early as 1900, however, the need for more and more circuits started to create space problems for open wire lines in metropolitan areas. Poles carrying 25 crossarms with 250 wires were not uncommon. Such construction was complex and expensive, and easily put out of service by a variety of causes.

The next step toward increased circuit capacity came with both aerial and underground multiconductor cables. Then came cables with carrier current equipment, still further increasing circuit capacity. The cable systems were costly to build and maintain as they required rather closely spaced repeater stations to function.

In the 1930s, AT&T started its radio relay system and after World War II microwave networks proliferated throughout the country. With labor costs rapidly rising, only a few main-line railroads kept their trackside pole lines in service.

The majority dismantled the pole lines and switched to some form of radio communication. Few youngsters today will ever know the fascination of standing with an ear pressed to a telegraph pole, listening to the musical hum of the wires in the wind.

7. The Telegraph Companies

The sun never sets on the Mackay System.

By the end of the Civil War, Western Union was considered one of the largest and most successful private enterprises in America. In the early days of the telegraph, dozens of small independent companies struggled to obtain business. The hodgepodge of short lines running in random directions was not very efficient and often required many transfers between companies to deliver a message.

Using his New York and Mississippi Valley Printing Telegraph Co. as a nucleus, Hiram Sibley began buying stock and taking control of many of the small competing companies. Sibley's company had originally intended to use the newly invented House printer, but this was later abandoned in favor of the simpler Morse equipment. Sibley was joined in the venture by Ezra Cornell, Morse's early associate. As the lines extended slowly westward to the Missouri River, Cornell suggested that the new company be called Western Union. On April 4, 1856, Western Union was legallly organized, and Sibley was well on his way toward the goal of a single, efficient nationwide telegraph system.

Exclusive contracts were negotiated with most of the U.S. railroads, in many cases involving the joint building and maintenance of railroad and Western Union wires. In the smaller towns, the railroad station agent also acted as a Western Union representative, enabling the company to pick up and deliver messages in communities too small to warrant a regular commercial telegraph office. This gave Western Union a decided advantage in later years when Postal Telegraph started competing for traffic. Western Union could advertise direct telegraph service to many points that were far beyond reach of the Postal wires.

The success of the transcontinental line had inspired Western Union to think of an even larger project, a trans–Siberian telegraph line connecting North America with Europe. After the premature failure of Cyrus Field's Atlantic cable of 1858, many authorities believed that the only way to link America with Europe was by overland line across Alaska and Siberia. After the successful completion of the transcontinental line in October 1861, the *New York Times* commented editorially in its October 26, 1861, issue:

If there is ever to be electric communication with Europe, it will be by imitating the splendid example the United States has thus given in our transcontinental line. The bubble of the Atlantic submarine line has long ago burst, and it is now seen to be cheaper and more practicable to extend a wire over five-sixths of the globe on land, than one-sixth at the bottom of the sea.

Hiram Sibley went to St. Petersburg in 1864–1865 to begin negotiations with the Russian Government. The Russians offered to sell Alaska to Western Union. Sibley turned down this offer, but his recommendations to the U.S. government resulted in the 1867 purchase of Alaska by the United States. By 1866, line construction was well under way with some 850 miles completed into British Columbia.

The pundits of 1858 were proven wrong when the Atlantic cable was successfully completed and placed in service in 1866. The news brought an abrupt halt to the construction of the line through Alaska and Siberia. Construction crews were instructed to sell what they could of the line material, abandon the rest, and return home. One enterprising man sold a quantity of glass insulators to the gullible natives for use as "patent teacups." He apparently managed to get out of town before it was discovered that an insulator full of tea would tip over the instant it was set down! The completed line to Quesnel, British Columbia, was kept in operation as it furnished a needed link between Canada and the United States. The section north of Quesnel that had been completed was abandoned. Travelers in later years reported seeing native suspension bridges built with the salvaged telegraph wire.

For some time after Morse's demonstration of the telegraph in 1844, the public regarded it as little more than a clever stunt, or novelty, and seemed unwilling to use it for serious purposes. When one of the first lines in the United States, between Lancaster and Harrisburg, Pennsylvania, was completed in 1845, the first message, filed January 8, 1846, read, "Why don't you write, you rascals?" The sender probably didn't expect a reply. He just wanted to be able to tell his friends that he had sent a message over the new telegraph machine.

Eventually, of course, the telegraph was adopted with enthusiasm for all manner of business and personal messages. Morse's tragic experience at the time of his first wife's death in 1825 illustrates the lack of communication that existed before the coming of the telegraph. On a business trip to Washington, Morse kept writing letters to his beloved Lucrece in New Haven, completely unaware that she had died several days previously.

Business in the late nineteenth and early twentieth centuries made extensive and efficient use of the telegraph. Larger firms had their own telegraph operators with direct connection to the nearest telegraph relay office. Smaller companies could use the messenger service for pickup and delivery of messages. If there was

An old wood case telegraph call box. Turning the handle summoned a messenger (photo by Lewis Coe).

enough traffic, a call-box circuit was installed—a turn of the box handle summoned a messenger. Low night rates enabled messages to be sent out in quantity for special bulletins to dealers or salesmen. Morse operators handled such messages, known as "books," by sending the text only once. Then the addresses were sent, each with its own wire number.

At one time, the official government weather forecaster relied on telegraphed reports of local conditions by observers throughout the country. In the Midwest, where the weather report was vital to farmers during the growing season, a special report was sent by local observers early each morning. Sent at government rate, collect, the message gave the maximum and minimum temperatures for the past 24 hours, the measured precipitation, and the state of the weather at the time of dispatch.

With its transcontinental line, Atlantic cable, and exclusive railroad contracts,

Western Union had a virtual monopoly on telegraphic communication. This was accepted by public and Congress alike without stirring any "antitrust" sentiments, since after the early chaos in the industry it was pretty well accepted that a communications system was, by nature, most efficient as a monopoly.

Even the invention of the telephone, in 1876, had little immediate effect on telegraph traffic. Telephone service was for a long time quite limited. There was no transcontinental telephone until 1915. Shorter toll lines between cities were limited in carrying capacity. It was quite common for subscribers to have to "wait for a line." Voice quality on long-distance circuits was often poor. Furthermore, telephone service was relatively expensive, and many low-income families, especially in large cities, did not have phones.

The telegraph was the favored communications medium, and until around 1930 the term "telegraph" in the public mind meant the Morse telegraph, with operators reading the dots and dashes from a sounder and typing out the messages. Before typewriters came into general use around 1900, messages were handwritten, and telegraphers were noted for their beautiful script.

Jay Gould (1836–1892), the notorious New York financier, held the controlling interest in Western Union during the late 1800s. It was Gould's personal unpopularity wih certain men that brought the first serious competition into the telegraph field in 1881. James Gordon Bennett (1841–1918), publisher of the *New York Herald*, was a man of genius and completely outrageous personal behavior. It was Bennett who scored a great journalistic coup by sending Henry M. Stanley to Africa to find Dr. Livingston.

For all his talent as a newspaperman, Bennett was rapidly becoming persona non grata in New York society as a result of his wild escapades, which went far beyond the limits of good taste. The climax came at a gala New Year's Eve party in 1877, which was to have announced Bennett's engagement to Caroline May, a prominent society girl. Bennett, getting pretty well loaded as was his custom, completely shocked the guests by urinating into the drawing-room fireplace. The engagement was canceled instantly, and the girl and her parents went into seclusion. The next day, Fred May, the girl's brother, accosted Bennett as he was entering his office and publicly horsewhipped him.

Bennett responded by challenging May to a duel. It took place on January 7, 1877, on the old dueling grounds at Slaughter's Gap, Delaware. The Gap was favored by duelers; being near the state line, participants eould quickly flee into Maryland if the Delaware authorities attempted to interfere. Both men fired and missed, then shook hands and retired to a nearby tavern. This is believed to be one of the last formal duels fought in North America.

With hardly a friend left in New York, Bennett moved to Paris in 1877. To manage the *Herald*, he had to rely on a constant stream of messages sent over Jay Gould's Western Union cable. Running up extremely large bills for cable tolls,

Bennett appealed to Gould for a special discount on *Herald* messages. Gould refused to grant a discount on the grounds that he would have to extend the same rate to all the newspapers if he gave the *Herald* a discount. This was probably the start of the enmity between the two men, which was further enhanced when Gould discovered that Bennett was actively trying to start a rival cable company.

The feud really heated up when Bennett published a story in the *Herald* labeling Gould as "the skunk of Wall Street," complete with a cartoon showing Gould's face on a skunk's body. Gould fired back by publishing a vicious attack on Bennett, who showed his contempt by printing the story in the *Herald*, saying, "The proprietor of the *Herald* lost his reputation long before Mr. Gould was ever heard of."

In his efforts to establish a rival cable company, Bennett found a willing ally in John W. Mackay (1831–1902), who was also unhappy with the huge cable bills he was getting from Western Union. Mackay, a self-made man who amassed a huge fortune by investing in the Comstock silver mine in Nevada, was no stranger to the telegraph business. During his Virginia City days, he was a regular visitor to the telegraph office, at that time one of the busiest in the West. During the peak of the mining days, gold and silver speculators kept the wires busy with messages to San Francisco and New York. Still a bachelor, Mackay used to sit in the telegraph office by the hour and apparently had learned to read Morse code messages.

In 1867, Mackay married Marie Hungerford Bryant, a young and attractive widow who soon found the rather primitive society of Virginia City a little tedious when she had the Mackay millions at her command. She established a home in Paris, and her indulgent husband had no choice but to become a regular trans–Atlantic commuter. Like Bennett, he had to rely on the cable to run his business while abroad. Mrs. Mackay became one of the most popular hostesses in Paris, and her reception for President Grant in 1877 set a new high for entertaining in the grand manner. Never one to economize at the sacrifice of elegance, Mrs. Mackay had every stick of furniture in the house sent out and reupholstered in red, white, and blue silk for this affair. As a final touch, she wanted the French to decorate the Arc de Triomphe. When told that her request had been denied, she is said to have tossed her pretty head and announced loftily, "Very well, I'll buy their old arch and decorate it myself!"

It would be hard to imagine two men with more divergent backgrounds than John Mackay and James Gordon Bennett, Jr. Mackay was an Irish immigrant brought to the United States at the age of 9 in 1840. In 1851, he went to California and started work as a miner. A man of little or no formal education, his manners and speech reflected the influence of his years in the rough-and-ready atmosphere of a western mining camp. Nevertheless, he was a man of integrity and earned the respect of all who came in contact with him. He seemed to move easily in the highest circles of business and society, even though his early days had hardly prepared him for such a life.

Bennett, 10 years younger than Mackay, was a rich man's spoiled son. His father founded the *New York Herald*, the first penny newspaper in the city. However indulgent his father, he saw to it that the younger Bennett was thoroughly trained in the newspaper business. At 26, the son took over the paper after his father's death. Whatever his personal characteristics, Bennett had been steeped in the family business, and the *Herald* prospered under his management. After his wild days as a young man, Bennett achieved a measure of respectability in later years when he founded the Bennett international trophies in yachting, automobile, and aeronautical racing.

Seemingly unlikely partners, Mackay and Bennett formed the Commercial Cable Co. in September 1883. The first cable of the new company was landed in July 1884, and a second cable over the same route was completed in October. The Commercial cables ran from Waterville, Ireland, to Canso, Nova Scotia, then via Rockport, Maine, to Manhattan Beach just outside New York City. At Waterville, the cable was extended to Le Havre and Paris. A rate-cutting war with Western Union ensued before the rate was stabilized at 25¢ a word, a sharp reduction from the 75¢ previously charged by Western Union. The acknowledged loser in the cable-rate war, Jay Gould said ruefully, "There is no beating John Mackay. If he needs another million or two he goes to his silver mine and digs it up!"

Bennett and Mackay now had their cable but could not realize the full benefit from their investment because they still had to rely on Western Union for delivery of messages to inland points. To remedy this situation, in 1883, John W. Mackay invested $1 million to obtain a controlling interest in the newly formed Postal Telegraph Co.

Postal had been organized in 1881 to exploit the patents held by Elisha Gray for a harmonic telegraph. Postal started at a time when there had been frequent talk of a government telegraph service. This may have influenced the choice of a name, but Postal never had any connection with the U.S. Post Office. Gray's patent was for a system in which tones of different pitch could be sent over a single-wire circuit simultaneously. Gray's work on the harmonic telegraph was largely the basis for his bitter contesting of the Bell telephone patent. Postal also planned to use a new type of line conductor invented by Chester Snow. This wire employed a steel core with a copper outer covering, which gave it the tensile strength of steel with the good conductivity of copper. Such wire is still widely used today, known by the name Copperweld.

The harmonic telegraph was theoretically able to send 16 messages over a single circuit. In practice, only six channels proved workable. The harmonic system, although the forerunner of the carrier current equipment to come later, was shortly abandoned in favor of conventional Morse operation. For Postal, the great dividend of the harmonic telegraph was the building of high-grade lines with copper conductors paired and transposed to eliminate cross talk. This enabled Postal in later years to establish a limited long-distance telephone service between major cities.

Postal failed to generate adequate revenue and filed for bankruptcy in 1884. Albert B. Chandler, the old Civil War cipher operator, was appointed receiver. In 1886, the reorganized Postal, with Chandler as president, started to expand its lines and secured an exclusive contract with the Canadian Pacific Railroad, giving the company many exclusive destination points in Canada. With its Atlantic cables, the company now had service extending from Europe to most of the United States. Postal's first transcontinental line reached Los Angeles in 1894 by way of Denver, Albuquerque, Flagstaff, and Williams, Arizona.

After John W. Mackay's death in 1902, control of the company passed to his son Clarence H. Mackay (1874–1938), who became respected as a capable businessman in his own right. Under Clarence Mackay's direction, Postal made many improvements to its plant, hoping to attract a larger share of the telegraph market. In 1910, a new line was constructed from Omaha, via Salt Lake City, Reno, and Sacramento. This line was designed to resist the winter storms in the high Sierra. It used 45-foot poles and No. 4 copper wire and was often the only circuit working during violent storms. In 1924, Postal added a new southern route to the coast via Dallas, El Paso, southern New Mexico, and Arizona to avoid completely the weather interruptions that were common on the northern routes. This line used No. 7½ copper wire, paired and transposed for telephone service. Some of these Postal voice-grade lines played an important part in early network radio broadcasting. For some strange reason, the Bell system was at first not overly anxious to furnish circuits for radio networks.

Determined to span the Pacific, the Mackay interests formed the Commercial Pacific Cable Company and invested $12 million in a 6,912-mile cable extending from San Francisco to the Asian mainland via Honolulu, Midway, Guam, the Philippines, and Japan. The first 2,413-mile section from San Francisco to Honolulu was opened in January 1903. In 1928, after merger with IT&T, the company could boast of 73,004 miles of ocean cables and 386,093 miles of land telegraph lines, and say with pride, "The sun never sets on the Mackay System!"

By 1928, the Behn brothers and their International Telephone and Telegraph Corp. were expanding rapidly. Although Postal Telegraph was not noted as a very profitable company, it was seen in an attractive light by the Behns, who needed to enlarge their U.S. holdings to balance their extensive investments abroad. Clarence Mackay had received previous offers by business groups seeking to buy him out. None of the proposals had tempted him until he was approached by Colonel Behn and IT&T.

Sothenes Behn was a master negotiator who knew exactly how to entertain and cut deals with a man of Mackay's wealth and social standing. Besides his personal charm, Behn had some pretty impressive props to bolster his cause. At that time,

Clarence H. Mackay, pictured at about the time he took over the Mackay System after his father's death in 1902 (photo courtesy Special Collections, University of Nevada-Reno Library).

the newly erected IT&T headquarters building at 67 Broad Street was the showplace of lower Manhattan. Office windows on the upper levels commanded a breathtaking view of the Battery and lower New York harbor where majestic ocean liners shuttled back and forth to Europe. Behn's guests were entertained in the roof-top penthouse. The penthouse was reached by taking the public elevator to the 35th floor, then transferring to a small private elevator for the final trip to the top of the building. A skilled staff stood ready to serve luxurious meals in the dining room. The palatial oak-paneled boardroom provided an appropriate setting for negotiations that might involve millions.

The walls of the Cork Room were made of inch-thick Spanish cork, inlaid designs reflecting the company's involvement with the Spanish telecommunication system. With this kind of a backdrop, negotiations proceeded smoothly, and on May 18, 1928, the Mackay System, comprising Postal Telegraph, Commercial Cables, and a manufacturing subsidiary called Federal Telegraph, became part of IT&T.

For a time, it seemed that the new merger might be advantageous to both sides. It was not to be, however, and at times IT&T was forced to raid Postal's scanty resources to strengthen its own precarious position. There had been some talk of merging Western Union and Postal in the 1930s, but Congress refused to act on this proposal. The ultimate absurdity came in 1937 when the Justice Department charged Western Union and Postal, both fighting to stay alive, with conspiring to monopolize the telegraph industry. Reorganizing in 1939, Postal Telegraph limped along for a few years before bowing to the inevitable and merging with Western Union in 1943. This time there was no protest from the government, by now wise enough to recognize that a powerful monopoly would not emerge from the death struggles of two corporate giants.

Postal Telegraph and the Mackay System had some impressive credentials, but they were never able to match the Western Union competition. In 1927, Postal could claim only about 17 percent of the telegraph business. Western Union had the rest. Most of the old Postal lines were dismantled after the merger, although some of the high-grade copper wire circuits were kept in service as long as Western Union had any need for open wire cross-country lines. Postal's large stock of Morse equipment was junked since Western Union had long since switched to printer operation. A large part of Postal's automatic printing telegraph equipment was reconditioned and shipped to Russia as part of the World War II lend-lease program.

Shortly after the Postal negotiations, Colonel Behn was involved in another deal that had it turned out differently might have made IT&T a leader in world telecommunications. Behn needed an entrance to the profitable German market but had been blocked by Siemens, which had formed a partnership with L. M. Ericson, the Swedish telephone company controlled by Ivar Kreuger. The resourceful Behn was able to make a deal with Kreuger, paying $11 million for a block of Ericsson stock and giving Kreuger a seat on the IT&T board. Shortly after, Kreuger's fraudulent empire collapsed, and its owner committed suicide.

Using his Ericsson stock, Behn was able to work with Siemens in acquiring interests in telecommunications properties throughout Europe. At the same time, Behn picked up holdings in two other firms, Nippon Electric and Sumitomo Electric

Crossbar switchboard at the Postal Telegraph office, Galva, Henry County, Illinois, 1930. Office at Galva was opened in 1891 (photo by Lewis Coe).

Industries. Behn's intuitive business judgment told him to hang on to these properties.

Unfortunately, after Behn's retirement in 1959, the new CEO, Harold Geneen, promptly sold off the companies that Behn had so shrewdly acquired. Ericsson, Nippon Electric, and Sumitomo went on to become giants of the industry, with combined sales of $32 billion and enormous technological resources. It is widely believed that this marked the turning point in IT&T fortunes and ended the possibility of the company having any significant part of the world telecommunications business.

The Mackays, father and son, were always good newspaper copy. Clarence Mackay's second marriage was headline news in July 1931 when he took Anna Case of the Metropolitan Opera as his bride. The public was fascinated by the romance between Mackay, one of America's wealthiest men, and Miss Case, daughter of a blacksmith, who emerged from obscurity to become a star of the Metropolitan. Mackay, then 57, was 15 years older than Miss Case, who became the mistress of Harbor Hill, the palatial Long Island estate that had been the scene of many society events, including a dinner dance for the Prince of Wales in 1924.

Mackay had three children by his first marriage, and his daugher Ellin threw the family into an uproar when she married Irving Berlin in 1926. The thought of their daughter, a devout Irish catholic, marrying Berlin, a Jew, was almost too much. Mackay and Ellin were estranged for several years following her marriage but were reconciled by 1931, and Mr. and Mrs. Irving Berlin were among the guests at the Case-Mackay wedding. Aside from the religious difference, there was quite a social gulf between members of the theatrical profession and New York's high society. In spite of the misgivings, the Mackay-Berlin marriage endured until the death of Ellin in 1988. Irving Berlin died at age 101 in September 1989.

8. Under the Sea

They'll see lots of cables ere long,
For we'll twine, twine, twine,
And spin a new cable, and try it again,
And settle our bargains of cotton and grain,
With a line, line, line—
A line that will never go wrong.
—James Clerk Maxwell, 1857

In the history of nineteenth-century inventors and constructors there is probably no story more inspiring than that of Cyrus Field and the Atlantic cable. It is a story filled with heartbreak, crushing disappointments, and financial crisis, yet through it all the iron will of one man to succeed in a project that many thought impossible from the beginning.

By the 1850s, underwater cables were being laid in Europe, the most important the connections between England and the Continent. The cables were made practical by the discovery of *gutta-percha* as an insulating medium. This rubberlike substance from the juice of certain trees in Malaysia was first discovered by an English surgeon stationed in Singapore who brought it to England and obtained patents concerning its use. The success of the cross-channel and other coastwise cables inevitably turned thoughts to spanning the Atlantic. The vital need for such a cable was highlighted by an editorial comment in the *London Times*: "We nearly went to war with America because we had not a telegraph across the Atlantic."

The idea of a transatlantic cable came under immediate criticism from those who said flatly that it was impossible. One school said it was electrically impossible. These people, who had not yet become familiar with Ohm's law, held that the electrical signals would simply not pass through such a long conductor. They held to the outmoded theory that electricity gradually decays with distance and is eventually attenuated to zero. Morse saw the fallacy of this theory and freely predicted that the cable would work if the mechanical problems could be solved.

Those who said it would be mechanically impossible to lay such a long cable on the ocean floor had a more valid argument. After all, the manufacture of insulated wire of any description was in its infancy and surrounded by uncertainty. Robert Stephenson, engineer and famous bridge builder, cheerfully predicted that the cable could never be laid in deep water.

These were the kinds of objections that had to be overcome before investors could be interested in the project. In 1852–1853, Lt. Matthew D. Maury of the United States Navy had made extensive soundings of the Atlantic. Maury found that between Newfoundland and Ireland there was an undersea plateau that seemed to be suitable for laying a cable. The water was of fairly uniform depth, and samples from the bottom seemed to indicate that there were no strong currents to cause abrasion of a cable.

In 1854, Cyrus Field, his brother Matthew, and Maury met with F. N. Gisborne, who had been head of the unsuccessful attempt to operate a cable between Cape Ray and New Brunswick. After one of these meetings, Cyrus Field was looking at a globe and noticed how the land masses seemed to point out a cable route between Newfoundland and Ireland. He said to himself, "If a cable to Newfoundland, why not a cable all the way?" This was the beginning of Field's all-consuming ambition. He saw the Atlantic cable as the greatest achievement of the age, and he wanted to be its chief creator. Field, at age 34, had amassed a fortune in the paper manufacturing business and was looking for new worlds to conquer. His business ability enabled him to enlist the support of New York businessmen Peter Cooper, Marshall O. Roberts, Moses Taylor, and Chandler White.

On May 6, 1854, the New York, Newfoundland and London Electric Telegraph Co. was organized with a capital stock of $1.5 million. Peter Cooper was elected president. Samuel F. B. Morse was given a one-tenth interest to act as "advising electrician." Matthew Field was appointed chief engineer and started at once to build connecting land lines in Newfoundland. Cyrus Field went to England to place orders for cable and talk with those who had successfully laid some of the first European cables. The first attempt of the company to lay a cable from Cape Ray to Cape Breton Island ended in failure due to using vessels too small for the job. In 1856 this section was successfully laid, but by now the project had cost over a million dollars, and the resources of the original investors were exhausted. Field left again for England, the second of some 50 Atlantic crossings on cable business.

In 1856, Field organized the Atlantic Telegraph Company of Great Britain, with a capital of £350,000. Amid heated debate, a bill supporting the cable project passed the U.S. Congress and was signed by President Pierce on March 4, 1857. U.S. ships *Niagara* and *Susquehanna* were detailed, and the British furnished the *Agamemnon* and *Leopard*. The end of the cable was brought ashore at Valentia, Ireland, and on August 6, 1857, the vessels started westward with the cable.

Instruments on the ship were connected to the cable, and continuous communication with shore was maintained. After laying about 360 miles of cable, the vessels were hit by strong winds. This placed a heavy strain on the cable, and it soon parted. This ended the first attempt, but Field and his associates were undaunted and raised still more capital for another attempt the following year. This time it was proposed to have two vessels start from midocean and lay cable in both directions. Once again, there were several breaks in the first few miles, making it necessary for the ships to return to Valentia. Still optimistic, they tried again, leaving Valentia on July 17. Field was aboard the *Niagara*. This time luck was with them, and the *Niagara* entered Trinity Bay, Newfoundland, on August 4, 1858. The *Agamemnon* was simultaneously within sight of the Irish coast.

News of the successful cable laying triggered a series of wild celebrations in America. Field was hailed as the man of the hour. On September 2, a grand banquet was given by the Common Council of New York to honor Field and the officers of the two cable-laying ships.

Field concealed the deep anxiety he was feeling at the moment. All was not well with the cable. Clear reception from Valentia had been impossible during most of August, and now nothing had been received in the last 24 hours. When Field finally revealed that the cable was dead, it touched off a storm of ugly rumors. Charges were made that the whole thing was a humbug and that no signals were ever actually exchanged. Those who knew better kept their own counsel, but the cable was soon being referred to as the Great Atlantic Bubble.

Field, taxed by months of overwork and tension, was near nervous collapse when he heard the final word of failure. He broke down and cried like a child. Peter Cooper, in a moment of greatness, concealed his disappointment and said, "We will go on." Field recovered from his deep despair and again took up the burden of organizing for another try.

The failure of 1858 was almost certainly due to defective cable insulation. It was learned that while in the process of manufacture at the Glass-Elliot plant in England, large coils of cable had been left lying in the hot summer sun, melting the *gutta-percha* insulation. Some 35 miles of defective cable was discarded before the shipment left the factory. Obviously, much more was defective, and an unlucky gamble was taken in using it. Today, even the manufacturers of high-tech fiber-optic cable used by the telephone company take the precaution of labeling the reels "Do not leave in sunlight!" *Gutta-percha* was for years the only practical covering for underwater cables and was perfectly satisfactory if not damaged or exposed to high temperatures. The material made the ocean cables possible but also solved the problem of river crossings for the land line telegraph companies. Before suitable cables were available, river crossings were often made with wires suspended from high masts on the banks, and these were a constant source of trouble.

Returning to England in 1862, Field found it difficult to stir up much enthusiasm for the Atlantic cable project. The British government was still smarting from the failure of the Red Sea cable it had supported and was not about to run an even greater risk in the Atlantic. Business conditions were very unsettled in America with the Civil War threatening, and Field himself lost heavily when his paper company went bankrupt. There were notes of optimism, however. Julius Reuter estimated that his news agency would send £5,000 worth of messages over a cable in its first year of operation. Field, relentless in his pursuit of capital, once recalled that some of his friends would hastily dodge into the nearest doorway when they saw him coming down the street.

The first bit of encouraging news came when Field announced that the cable company had obtained a lease on the steamship *Great Eastern* for the next cable-laying attempt. The ship was 680 feet long, with a beam of 83 feet, displacing 27,000 tons. The largest vessel of her time, the ship had never been profitable in the passenger trade. The passenger business was just too limited to justify such a large vessel. She proved ideally suited to cable laying and was to be used in that service for many years to come. She was berthed at the Medway, and three tanks for cable were built belowdecks. The *Great Eastern* was the only ship then afloat that could carry all 2,300 miles of the Atlantic cable. The cable tanks weighed 2,000 tons, the cable itself 7,000 tons, and there was room for 8,500 tons of coal.

With all preparations complete, the cable ship departed from Valentia the latter part of July 1865. During the first 10 days, there were four signal failures in the cable. Each time, they had to reel in the cable, find the fault, and resplice. The faults were due to short pieces of wire that had somehow been thrust into the cable, breaking the insulated covering. On August 2, while repairing another fault, the cable slipped into the sea, and all efforts to retrieve it failed. The *Great Eastern* was then only 660 miles from Newfoundland. Even so, it was evident that nothing further could be done that year. It was another bitter disappointment for Field, but there was a ray of hope. The huge ship had turned out to be the ideal means for laying cable, and there was every reason to believe that another attempt would succeed.

A new company was organized, a new capital secured, and orders placed for new cable. It was manufactured at the rate of 20 miles per day. On June 20, 1866, the *Great Eastern* sailed from Sheerness with 2,375 miles of cable aboard. The ship left Valentia on July 12 headed for Newfoundland once more. This time there was no fanfare at the departure. Residents of Valentia were becoming accustomed to the departure of cable ships. The crew was constantly in touch with Valentia through the shipboard instruments, and everything proceeded smoothly. There were no breaks, no losses of the signal from shore.

At 7:00 A.M., July 27, 1866, Heart's Content was in sight. By 8:15 A.M., a happy Field was ashore, and by 5:00 P.M., the cable had been successfully landed and was working perfectly. On August 9, *Great Eastern*, with Field aboard, headed east again with the hope of finding the lost end of the 1865 cable. After several attempts, they finally found the cable end about 720 miles east of Newfoundland. With improved grappling equipment, they had the cable aboard at 2:15 A.M. on September 2.

It was a dramatic moment when the cable was tested and found to be working perfectly into Valentia. Field's first thought was to inquire if the just-laid cable was still working to Newfoundland and if the Gulf of St. Lawrence cable had been repaired. When Valentia signalled "both OK" Field once more succumbed to emotion. This time they were tears of relief and happiness. The long ordeal was over.

The recovered 1865 cable was spliced to the remaining cable in the *Great Eastern*'s hold, and the big ship headed back toward Newfoundland. The second cable was landed at Heart's Content on September 8 and worked perfectly. The recovery and successful operation of the 1865 cable seemed to capture the public imagination even more than the laying of the 1866 cable. Now was the time for cable critics and detractors to disappear quietly into limbo. However, one French scientist, Bobinet, who had freely predicted failure would not change his mind even when confronted with the evidence of successful operation!

Latimer Clark, a cable company engineer, went to Valentia to make a final test of the cables. He asked the Newfoundland operator to connect the two cables at that end to make an unbroken circuit of 3,700 miles across the Atlantic and back. Clark then improvised a tiny battery, using a borrowed silver thimble, an acid solution, and a piece of zinc. (Remember, this was 1866, and batteries couldn't be purchased at the nearest drug store!) The battery that Clark created would have been comparable to a modern wristwatch battery in electrical power, yet it was enough to send a current through the cable and deflect the sensitive galvanometer used as an indicator. With a fine flair for public relations, Clark had borrowed the thimble from Miss Emily Fitzgerald, whose father, the knight of Kerry, owned the land where the Irish cable terminal was located.

If Georg Simon Ohm had lived to see this dramatic proof of his laws for distribution of electric current, he would probably have smiled and said, "I told you so!" By 1900, there were 13 cables crossing the Atlantic, but they were seldom all working at once. The original 1865 cable failed permanently in 1873. The 1866 cable was in service until 1877. All cable companies kept repair ships constantly at sea ready to do maintenance work. Locating and grappling for cables became a well-developed matter of routine. During the America's Cup races of 1899, the cable ship *Mackay-Bennett* was moored over the New York cable, which it picked up and tapped to send news bulletins directly to London and Paris.

The cables became more reliable as better manufacturing methods were devised. Duplex terminal equipment came into use in 1871. Using duplex, messages could be sent simultaneously in both directions, greatly increasing the message capacity. Signaling speed on the early cables was limited to around 10 words per minute due to the large capacitance that stored electricity, causing a time lag in transmission. In 1924, Western Union pioneered the use of permalloy-loaded cable, which introduced a value of inductance having the opposite electrical sign from capacity. This canceled out the time lag and made much higher signaling speeds possible. The final developments by both Western Union and the telephone company included underwater repeating amplifiers sealed into the cable at regular intervals. This made both voice and high-speed telegraphy possible for the first time.

Before the days of the cable, European news dispatches were put ashore at Halifax and telegraphed from there to New York. There was much acrimonious squabbling among the telegraph companies and the Associated Press concerning the handling of this profitable traffic. This method of handling European news vanished overnight with the coming of the direct cable to Europe. The new cable immediately proved very profitable. In 1867, Field was able to pay off all of the creditors in full and add 7 percent interest. Cable stock that once sold for 30 guineas per £1,000 was now paying £160 interest per annum.

Field, who had started his business career as a $50-a-year apprentice in A. T. Stewart's New York department store, was now one of America's wealthiest men, so much so that his name was associated with the robber barons of the era—Sage, Gould, Drew, and Vanderbilt. It was wealth that brought the tragic end to his life. He made unwise investments in the stock of the Manhattan Elevated Railway Co., buying huge blocks of stock on very slim margin. The notorious Jay Gould moved in for the kill, forcing Field to sell Manhattan stock at a loss. He was almost penniless again. The final tragedies of Field's life were the death of his wife and the insanity of a son and daughter. A broken man, he died in his sleep on July 12, 1892. He was buried in the family plot at Stockbridge, Massachusetts. The inscription on his tombstone reads:

Cyrus West Field
To whose courage, energy and perseverance
The world owes the Atlantic telegraph.

In 1868, a new cable to the United States was proposed by English and French interests headed by Julius Reuter in England and Baron Emile d'Erlanger in Paris. The Anglo-American cable company vigorously opposed the new venture and sought exclusive landing rights in the United States from Congress. Congress granted the concession to the French cable, holding that Anglo-American was not entitled to an exclusive monopoly on cable business. The new cable was laid in 1869 by the faithful *Great Eastern*. It ran from Brest on the Breton coast to the island of St. Pierre just off the Newfoundland coast and then to Duxbury, Massachusetts, for a total distance of 3,333 miles. This was almost double the distance of the Ireland-to-Newfoundland route of the first Atlantic cables. The tanks on the *Great Eastern* had been increased in size to hold 2,584 miles of cable, enough for the run from Brest to St. Pierre. A smaller vessel carried the remaining cable from St. Pierre to Duxbury. This cable was absorbed by the Anglo-American company about four years after it was laid.

The original cables laid by Cyrus Field had all landed at Heart's Content, Newfoundland. Landing in Newfoundland had the advantages of the shortest undersea route, but there were disadvantages as well. European traffic, both sent and received, had to travel via land telegraph lines from the cable terminal in Newfoundland. This introduced some delay and possibility of errors, and the land lines were subject to interruption from weather or other causes. A group of English investors saw the advantages of a direct cable to the United States and formed a company they named the Direct United States Cable Co.

An English shipbuilding firm was engaged to build a cable-laying vessel. Called the *Faraday*, the ship was 300 feet long, with a 52-foot beam. Designed as a cable ship, the vessel had three tanks for cable. The *Faraday* was double-ended and could be conveniently steered from either end. This was an improvement over earlier cable ships, which had to stop and turn around if it was necessary to pick up cable. Owners of original cables opposed the new cable in every way they could. The new company is said to have had trouble in purchasing adequate quantities of *gutta-percha*, essential for cable manufacture. Overcoming all of the problems, the new company landed its cable at Rye, New Hampshire, in July 1874. The eastern terminal was Ballinskelligs Bay, Ireland. During the winter of 1874–1875, a permanent cable house was built in Rye. The company brought 16 experienced cable operators from England, Scotland, Ireland, and Wales.

The cable worked well from the start and was kept in operation 24 hours a day, seven days a week. The circuit was operated in duplex, enabling simultaneous transmission and reception. During the Russo-Japanese peace talks held at the Portsmouth Navy Yard in 1905, the cable was exceptionally busy sending messages to the governments of Russia and Japan. The biggest traffic day for the direct cable came on August 8, 1914, when 30,000 words were handled. The cable remained busy for the duration of World War I. It was considered important enough to be guarded by contingents of the U.S. Marines and the U.S. Naval Reserve for the duration of the war. After the war, traffic declined on this cable. The Rye cable house was permanently closed in 1921. The old cable building still stands on Old Ocean Boulevard, Rye, New Hampshire, and the state of New Hampshire has a historic marker on Route 1A to mark the location. It is said that remnants of the old cable can sometimes be seen at low tide. In the same location there are also visible stumps of trees, relics of the Ice Age "sunken forest." Other than the Commercial Cable Company's 1884 cable, the last major Atlantic cable to be laid in the nineteenth century was that of the French Telegraph-Cable Co., in 1897. Originating in Brest, France, the cable was landed at Orleans, Cape Cod, Massachusetts.

A cable office building had been erected in Orleans in 1890, and the first French cable had been extended from Duxbury, Massachusetts. For a number of years, cable messages from Orleans were forwarded by regular Western Union and Postal wires. Later, the cable company built its own private line into New York City. Finally, in 1932, a direct circuit between Cape Cod and New York was leased from AT&T. At this time, the cable signals were automatically repeated to New York, eliminating manual handling at Cape Cod. The French cables were cut by the Germans during World War II and were not reopened until 1952. The new high-speed transatlantic cables laid by AT&T spelled the end of the old-style cables, and in 1959 the French Cable Company leased the circuits it required from AT&T. The Cape Cod cable office was permanently closed in November 1959. The French cables were some 1,200 miles longer than the Anglo-American cables landing in Newfoundland, making their transmission speed correspondingly slower.

In 1971, a group of local citizens, mindful of historic values, purchased the cable property and established the French Cable Museum. The old station has been preserved in all its details and is open to the public during the summer months. The site is listed in the *National Register of Historic Places*.

Undersea cables were subject to a variety of hazards, some due to natural causes and some man-made. In time of war, enemy cables were considered fair game. The Allies quickly cut all the German cables leading to America during World War I. Ship's anchors occasionally snagged cables, but most of the cables were landed in remote spots where there was little ship traffic. Serious damage to the Atlantic cables occured in November 1929 when a severe earthquake rocked the ocean floor in an area just south of Newfoundland. Twelve of 21 Atlantic cables were broken at this time, and it was many months before they were repaired as the cable ships were handicapped by unusually severe weather in the area.

The last of the traditional telegraph cables across the North Atlantic was abandoned in 1966, a century after Field's first cable. It was now more economical for cable and radio companies to lease telegraph channels in the new telephone cables or in the space satellite radio facilities. The wide-band telephone cables that have been in service since 1956 are now being augmented by fiber-optic undersea cables. A new fiber-optic cable connecting North America with Asia will soon be tied in with the Alaskan communications network.

9. Learning the Trade

And thine ears shall hear a word behind thee...
(Isaiah 30:21).

The ability of the human brain to function as a decoder of telegraph signals will probably never be adequately explained. Dr. Donald Hebb, recognized as one of the foremost theoreticians on the brain, after a lifetime devoted to the subject, at age 79, admits that he is still searching for an explanation of the human memory. Probably not much different from the process by which a child learns his native language, there are still unique aspects to telegraphy that defy explanation.

Morse telegraphy on land lines passed out of general use over 40 years ago, and use of Morse on manually operated radiotelegraph circuits is rapidly declining. It is quite likely that this ability of the human mind that made us such capable telegraphers will never again be used in any practical way. It was the accidental discovery of "sound reading" that catapulted the Morse system into the widespread acceptance that made it the dominant mode of communication for 100 years.

It may not be too far-fetched to draw a parallel with modern computer technology and consider the brain as a PROM (programmable read only memory) reacting instantly to the symbol *dot-dash* and identifying it as the letter *A*, *dash-dot-dot-dot* as *B*, and so on. Computer programs have been written that will take Morse code input and display it on the screen as English. However, the human computer does something that the electronic version can never master. The electronic computer can accept only limited variations from a mathematically correct version of the dots and dashes to make a perfect copy. The human mind can accept dots and dashes sent at random speeds and spacing with all the individuality present among different sending operators. Unlike a computer memory that can be loaded in seconds, the human version requires a lot of time to program. The receptiveness, or talent for learning telegraphy varies widely among individuals. Some persons can master code in three months; others may take a year or more to become proficient. It is strictly a time-oriented process, and this is particularly frustrating to students who can absorb other types of learning in record time. Individual IQ seems to have little to do with it; the Ph.D. has to follow the same route as the grammar-school dropout.

Students of telegraphy have always thought of receiving as the most difficult part to learn. This is probably because receiving has to be done with the sender setting the pace. One missed word, and there is nothing to do but "break" and start over again. Every operator can probably remember the circumstances when with trembling fingers he copied his first real message on a working telegraph line. Sending, on the other hand, lets the operator set his own pace, and since he has the message before him, there are no strange and unfamiliar words coming from the wire.

Superlative receiving skill was always admired in the trade, but many pros feel that sending skill is a greater accomplishment. One has only to listen to amateur radio operators who can rarely send a complete sentence without making a mistake to appreciate the skill of the commercial telegrapher who used to send at high speed hour after hour without making a mistake. After a while, receiving becomes an automatic process for the professional, requiring little concentration and with little likelihood of a mistake unless the sender makes it. Sending requires concentration on the message, making sure it is sent exactly as written, keeping up good speed combined with clarity. Good senders developed a style that was fast but at the same time clear and easy to read.

The capacity of the memory to retain code characters becomes all the more remarkable when we consider that many operators were versed in the two telegraph codes and could switch from one to the other at will. Morse's original code of 1844 was used on land lines in North America. After 1851, the International or Continental code was used on ocean cables and for land wire telegraphy outside of North America. Continental also became the standard code for radiotelegraphy. In large metropolitan operating centers there was often a concentration of facilities consisting of Morse telegraph, ocean cables, and radio. In such places, there were many operators who could sit in on any mode of communication. Today, some of the old Morse operators have learned International code so they can participate in the hobby of amateur radio. Some of the Morse operators, including young persons who have learned American Morse for traditional reasons, have terminal equipment enabling the operation of Morse sounders directly from off-the-air radio signals. In this way, the authentic sound of the telegraph can be heard without the need for wire lines between stations.

The click of a Morse sounder is basically different from the sustained-tone signal of radiotelegraphy. Young radio operators, who have never heard the Morse telegraph in operation, tend to express wonder that anyone could make sense of the stream of clicks coming from the sounder. Actually, the sound pattern from the Morse instrument is just as distinctive as the radio signal. Operators with experience in both modes usually think of the Morse sounder as being easier to copy than a radio signal. The signal from the sounder on a normal wire is clear and distinct; there is no fading or interference as is often the case on a radio circuit.

Whenever the code is being discussed, it is common to hear someone say, "I learned the code once but have long since forgotten it." Every experienced operator knows that this is nonsense. One who has truly learned the code is not going to forget it, any more than he will forget his native language. Many of the old telegraphers who have not touched a key for 50 years or more often demonstrate their skill at public exhibitions of the telegraph. Of course, they are a little bit rusty and may forget some of the routines of the old operating days, but it all comes back in short order. The person who "learned the code once" probably only memorized the letters of the alphabet and never stayed with it long enough to have his mind programmed with Morse.

Probably the majority of Morse operators were self-taught. The learning process consisted of first memorizing the characters of the letters and numerals, then hours of practice sending. Receiving practice was a little harder to arrange unless one had a fellow student to do the sending. There were mechanical sending machines that used metal disks or punched tape; however, the disadvantage of these was that the student soon memorized all the tapes or disks.

During the Morse era, there were no cassette tape recorders. Telegraph instruments were available from mail order catalogs for years, and there were instruction books for the guidance of students. Before the days of amateur radio, building a "backyard" telegraph line was often a favorite project for electrical enthusiasts. Most of these lines were merely between houses in the same block. Others were on a more ambitious scale. The Bear Valley line in Wisconsin during the 1880s extended from farm to farm for a distance of 10 miles. The best receiving practice for the student was to listen to the wires at the local railroad station or telegraph office. This was usually easy to arrange; serious students were encouraged. More than one student got his first professional experience by giving a little unauthorized time off to the regular operator.

A common mistake among beginning telegraph students was to spend too much time with slow-speed receiving practice. After reaching the first plateau of learning, where the student could make solid copy receiving at 5 to 10 words a minute, it was tempting to continue practice at the low speed where the student felt comfortable. Practice at a higher speed, where the student was getting a whole word only now and then was more effective, even though it was discouraging at first. After a while the student was surprised to hear whole sentences coming through, and the learning process was almost complete.

Within the ranks of Morse operators there were fields of specialization. Operators on stockbroker wires became adept at handling numbers, fractions, and the cryptic letters used in board marking. Press telegraphers became masters of the large Phillips code vocabulary. Those who worked in such special categories tended to become imprinted with the routines used. Even though they were among the highest-skilled operators, they sometimes required a little familiarization before switching to commercial messages in plain English. The transition from general telegraphy to one of the specialized fields was even more difficult. Only an operator with unusual talent and suitable temperment could hope to cope with the frantic pace of some of the special fields of telegraphy.

There was a time when telegraphy was considered an attractive profession, particularly for the young person who was not bent on college. It was a job that still had a certain glamour to it, and the pay, while not high, was usually more than that for other small-town jobs. There were a large number of telegraph schools that flourished until the 1920s. The advantage of the schools was that they kept the student on a regular practice schedule, which is the only way the code can be programmed into the mind. Also, the schools could introduce the student to the accounting procedures that were an important part of most telegraph positions.

A famous American manufacturing company owes its beginning to a nineteenth-century school. George S. Parker was a teacher of telegraphy at the school in Janesville, Wisconsin. At that time, typewriters were not yet in use, and telegraphers used pens or pencils to copy the messages. Some of Parker's students were using the early versions of the fountain pen and found them unreliable, continually asking Parker to get their pens working again. Parker finally decided there must be a better way and proceeded to invent a pen of his own design. Somewhat reluctantly, he found himself in the pen-manufacturing business and founded the Parker Pen Company that is still headquartered in Janesville.

One of the largest and best known of the telegraph schools was Dodge's Telegraph, Railway Accounting and Radio Institute at Valparaiso, Indiana. Founded by telegrapher G. M. Dodge in 1891, the school had a high standing with railroad and commerical employers. A Dodge student was almost always assured of a job after graduation. A Dodge publication in 1917 stated: "The demand for railway agents and operators, radio operators and commercial telegraphers so far exceeds the supply that the prompt transaction of business by these companies is being greatly hampered." Instruction at Dodge was thorough, and the school even had working railroad lines cut in on its practice tables so that students could test their receiving skill by listening to actual telegraph traffic. Dodge's *The Telegraph Instructor* was the school textbook and was also widely used by home students of telegraphy. The Dodge school taught telegraphy and related accounting exclusively; other schools were often business colleges that had added a course in telegraphy to their curriculum. A few railroads had their own in-house schools teaching telegraphy and the accounting procedures used by that particular company. In general, it was probably easier for a student to qualify as a commercial operator. The railroad telegrapher often worked as a station agent with a variety of duties, including ticket selling and freight and express transactions.

In addition to the resident schools, there were a variety of home-study courses. Some of these were potentially helpful for the student who would follow them faithfully. There were, of course, no shortcuts, no way to beat the inexorable time factor required to program the code into the mind. The home courses usually included a disk or tape sending machine to give the student receiving practice. Today, students learning code to be amateur radio operators have even tried listening to code in their sleep, a practice of doubtful benefit.

Old-time Morse operators could not operate in their sleep, but it is true that an operator could recognize his own station call while soundly asleep and quickly awaken and answer. This unique ability was a godsend for the operator at a lonely railroad station on night duty. When routine tasks were finished, it was common practice for the operator to curl up on a desktop for a few winks. Even though there might be three or four Morse instruments chattering away, the operator knew he would awaken instantly when his call came through. Ted McElroy, a famous code speed champion and manufacturer of telegraph equipment, had a novel idea for code instruction. He sold a special telegrapher's typewriter that had the Morse dot-dash symbols printed on the keys in addition to the letters and numbers. The idea was for the student to learn Morse and touch-typing at the same time.

A practice suggestion for the student operator, found pasted in the box of an old code practice machine:

> The following words, with their repetitions, constitute one-half of all writing. Practice sending and receiving them until you can handle all of them without having to think how they are spelled. Have them sent to you until you can read them as words. This is your first step in learning to copy behind. Listen to one word being sent while copying another.

ONE HUNDRED WORDS WHICH CONSTITUTE HALF OF ALL WRITING:

it	what	their	who	ever	he	can	was
at	give	these	from	part	of	now	after
and	which	be	said	where	see	that	is
they	under	on	such	shall	more	have	any
time	could	had	most	go	very	with	but
must	an	seen	great	to	than	we	not
like	no	will	often	may	many	if	has
made	his	know	do	upon	those	all	are
as	were	into	so	them	today	you	one
my	some	wood	use	your	in	say	for
him	take	every	then	come	us	how	through
this	make	by	only	other	our	out	should
when	or	there	the	—	—	—	—

"CATCH" WORDS TO SEND AND RECEIVE:

doze	Erie	lazy	extra	Irish	jury	six	Jack
size	quick	zero	—	—	—	—	—

SOME OF THE SCHOOLS THAT TAUGHT MORSE TELEGRAPHY IN THE U.S. AND CANADA

Arkansas
Bohlinger College, Little Rock (1915)

California
Heald's Business College, Oakland (1906–1907)
Southern Pacific Telegraph School, Oakland
Southern Pacific Telegraph School, San Francisco (1918)
Wiggins (Frank) Trade School, Los Angeles

Colorado
Midwest Business College, Pueblo
Opportunity School, Denver
Union Pacific Telegraph School, Denver

Georgia
Southern School of Telegraphy, Newnan (1888)

Illinois
Chicago Radio & Telegraph Institute, Chicago (1920s)
Jones School of Telegraphy (W.U.), Chicago (1916)
LaSalle Extension Univ. (correspondence), Chicago
Morrow Telegraph School, Chicago (1940–1950)
Decatur School of Telegraphy (ICRR), Decatur (1940s)

Indiana
Dodge Institute, Valparaiso (1874–1940)
Western Union Telegraph School, Valparaiso
Valparaiso University, Valparaiso (1878)

Iowa
Iowa Institute of Telegraphy, Marshalltown
Miller's Business College, Keokuk (1880)

Kansas
Arkansas City Telegraph College, Arkansas City (1895)

Opposite: **Turn-of-the-century mail order catalogs featured the advantages of learning telegraphy.**

Emporia Business College, Emporia
Kansas Wesleyan College, Salina (1912)
Santa Fe Telegraph School, Topeka (1916)
SL-SF Railway Telegraph School, Fort Scott (World War II)
Western Telegraph Institute, Wichita (1886)
Wichita Telegraph College, Wichita (1913)
Wichita Commercial College, Wichita

Minnesota
Barry Telegraph School, St. Paul
Gale Institute, Minneapolis

Missouri
Chillicothe Business College, Chillicothe
Fultz Telegraph School, Kansas City
Midwest Telegraph School, Kansas City
Railway Communication School, Kansas City
Southwestern RR Telegraph School, St. Louis (1916)
St. Louis Telegraph School, St. Louis (1940s)

Nebraska
Boyles Business College, Omaha
Commercial Extension Business College, Omaha
National Railroad Schools, Omaha (1950s)
Union Pacific Telegraph School, Omaha

North Dakota
Northern Pacific Telegraph School, Jamestown

Ohio
Cincinnati Telegraph School, Cincinnati

Oklahoma
Flory Telegraph School, Oklahoma City
Phillips (Jess) Telegraph School, Wister

Ontario
Cassan School, Toronto

Oregon
Benke Walter Business College, Portland

Quebec
Elias Business College, Montreal
Thomas Institute, Quebec City

Texas
Brantley-Droughn Business College, Fort Worth
Southern Pacific Telegraph School, El Paso (1940s)
Tyler Telegraph School, Tyler

Washington
Northern Pacific Telegraph School, Tacoma (1950–1960)
Seattle Railroad School, Seattle
Spokane Telegraph School, Spokane

West Virginia
C&O School of Telegraphy, Huntington

Wisconsin
Northwest Telegraph School, Eau Claire (1916)
Reidelback School of Telegraphy, La Crosse
Valentine Telegraph School, Janesville (1902)

10. Life of a Telegraph Operator

Why don't you use your other foot? — Thomas Edison

Early in the morning of July 6, 1876, J. M. Carnahan, manager for the Northwestern Telegraph Co., at Bismarck, North Dakota, was awakened by a vigorous knocking at his door. Like most small-town telegraphers, Carnahan had been called out before in the wee small hours. This time there appeared to be an unusual sense of urgency in the message requesting him to come to the telegraph office as soon as possible.

When he saw the dispatches he was asked to send, Carnahan knew why. Normally routine army dispatches from Bismarck were sent to Fargo for retransmission to other points. Now Carnahan called Fargo and asked for a direct wire to St. Paul. The Fargo operator, sensing something out of the ordinary, queried, "What's up?" Carnahan's reply was a terse "All Custer's killed." Immediately patched through to St. Paul, he commenced a 22-hour stint at the key sending the official dispatches with the grim details of the Custer massacre.

The steamer *Far West* had arrived around midnight bringing the tragic news of the June 25 battle. It had taken 10 days at full steam down the Yellowstone and Missouri rivers to make the trip. Among the passengers on the *Far West* was Commanche, the horse ridden by Capt. Myles W. Keogh. Badly wounded, Comanche was the only living thing found on the battlefield. Responding to careful treatment, the animal recovered and lived to be 30. Given a place of honor in the Seventh Cavalry by official orders, Comanche was never ridden again. At each formal ceremony of the regiment he was saddled and bridled and paraded in formation. After his death at Fort Riley, Kansas, Comanche's body was preserved by taxidermy and can be seen at the Dyche Museum, University of Kansas, Lawrence.

At St. Paul, there were only two telegraphers available, Will Gridley and Ed Hughes. They too faced a long ordeal, handling thousands of words of military traffic relating to the disaster. The two men worked side by side, one receiving from Bismarck, the other relaying the messages on to Washington and other eastern points. Not until the official military traffic was cleared were the wires opened to press messages. Newspapers across the country clamored for details, and a large volume of press traffic clogged the wires for days afterward. Carnahan, working alone, set a record for telegraphy under pressure that has never been equaled. The thousands of words were sent with the simple hand key, which as every operator knows, is very tiring to operate over a long period.

Two courageous female telegraph operators who stayed at their posts in spite of deadly danger played central parts in the events of the Johnstown Flood in 1889. Miss Emma Ehrenfeld was a Pennsylvania railroad operator at South Fork, Pennsylvania. She came to work as usual at 7:00 A.M., May 31, 1889, little realizing that it would be the most eventful day of her life. Torrential rains and floods had created great fears that the South Fork dam on Lake Conemaugh was in danger of breaking.

As early as noon on the fateful day, a telegram had reached the railroad agent at Johnstown: SOUTH FORK DAM IS LIABLE TO BREAK NOTIFY THE PEOPLE OF JOHNSTOWN TO PREPARE FOR THE WORST. This message, sent by Ehrenfeld after an excited man came to the railroad tower and gave the warning, was disregarded by railroad personnel; there had been false alarms like this before. At 1:52 P.M. another message was sent by Ehrenfeld. Due to wire trouble, it had to be carried by messenger to a point on the railroad where the wire was working. It read: THE WATER IS RUNNING OVER THE BREAST OF LAKE DAM IN CENTER AND WEST SIDE AND IS BECOMING DANGEROUS.

In about 30 minutes, still another, more urgent message was sent from South Fork: THE DAM IS BECOMING DANGEROUS AND MAY POSSIBLY GO. This last message was received in Johnstown near 2:45 P.M. Hundreds of lives might have been saved had it been taken more seriously. In South Fork, railroad personnel had been warned to keep a sharp lookout up the valley; there was a good view from the telegraph tower. Suddenly alerted by the sight of people running, the people in the tower saw the water coming. Emma recalled later: "It just seemed like a mountain coming." Then, "without waiting to get my hat," as she put it, Emma and the two men in the tower ran for their lives. They made it to high ground and safety only minutes before the telegraph tower was swept away.

The Western Union operator in Johnstown was Mrs. Hettie M. Ogle, a Civil War widow who was a veteran of 28 years with the telegraph company. Mrs. Ogle also ran the local telephone switchboard. Since she always signed her reports "H. M. Ogle," many Western Union employees thought she was a man. Around 2:45 P.M. Mrs. Ogle received a telephone call from railroad operator Decker, who was concerned enough by now to pass on the final warning message from South Fork.

By this time, water was starting to rise in the Western Union office, sending Mrs. Ogle and her daughter to the second floor of the building. Near 3:00 P.M., Mrs. Ogle notified her Pittsburgh office of the situation and said it would be her last message since her wires would soon be grounded by the rising water. Emma

Ehrenfeld escaped with her life. Mrs. Ogle and her daughter Minnie stayed at their post too long. Their bodies were never recovered.

Morse telegraphers in a small town acquired a special identity. They might not always be known by name, but everyone knew it was the "man from Western Union" or "He works at the interlocking tower on the railroad." The telegrapher was privy to most everything that went on in the town. He had the details of business transactions, social matters, and tragedy before anyone else. In general, operators kept the trust and maintained an impersonal attitude toward the messages they handled. This was not always easy when they had to deliver a message of sorrow to someone they knew. Unfortunately, for many citizens who did not normally use the telegraph a great deal, a telegram was bad news: "Father died come at once."

During the 1930s, financial houses sometimes sent out large books of telegrams to random addresses trying to sell some investment. One operator got such a message for a woman who he knew was a widow living in very modest circumstances. Nothing to do but deliver it. As he approached the house, he heard someone cry, "My God, it's the telegraph operator!" The poor woman came to the door white-faced and trembling with apprehension. The operator quickly put her fears at rest: "It's not bad news, Mrs. Olson. They just want to sell you some stock!"

Operators in small one-man offices had a special responsibility in handling money transfers. For this reason, they were bonded by a surety company. When a money-transfer message was sent, the operator had temporary custody of the sum. Normally it was deposited in the company bank account as quickly as possible. Money transfers were paid by issuing a check. These telegraph checks were as good as cash, and the operator had a pad of blank forms.

Occasionally an operator might yield to temptation and try a fraudulent operation with money transfers. Due to the elaborate safeguards employed, these schemes were seldom successful. Operators involved in fraud would never be bonded again, making it unlikely that they could find further employment by the telegraph companies. Petty fraud could occur when an operator overcharged a customer for a telegram, reporting the correct tariff and pocketing the difference. Even this was risky. The companies had traveling auditors who would appear at the counter, file a dummy message, and check back later to see if the correct amount had been reported. Office monthly reports had to balance to the penny, and a close count was kept of messages sent and received.

Although the pay was low and the hours long, most small-town telegraphers felt they had a pretty good job. As long as an operator did his work and kept regular hours, he was seldom bothered by higher authority. The district superintendent might drop in occasionally; other than that, the operator was pretty much his own boss. There was plenty of time for reading, working on hobby projects, or visiting with friends.

Many women were employed as operators and managers. In fact, telegraphy was one of the first white-collar jobs where women could compete on a more or less equal basis with men. Few if any women ever made it to the top administrative jobs, but otherwise there was little distinction between sexes. Women seemed to have a special talent for telegraphy and were usually top-notch operators. One of the very first female telegraphers was Sarah G. Bagley. She was in charge of the Lowell, Massachusetts, office of the New York and Boston Magnetic Telegraph Association when the company opened its Boston line on February 21, 1846.

With many women working the wires, telegraphic romances were not uncommon. Sometimes these flourished; sometimes they came to an abrupt halt when the operators met for the first time. A couple who worked in the large Cincinnati office of Western Union in the 1920s were in the habit of going out together every night on their "SR" (telegraphic parlance for "short relief," now known as a coffee break). One night they were gone for over an hour, and the supervisor bawled them out upon their return. "Why, didn't you know? We just got married."

Harry Moorman, the Western Union veteran from Cincinnati, likes to tell the story of "Marie, the beautiful check girl":

> I was working the end position of a table right where the check girl stood, gathering messages which came off the conveyor belt, which she hung in front of the operators on the proper hook. She was just hired that morning. She was very beautiful. I got into a conversation with her, and helped her find the correct places to take the messages. I wasn't very attentive to what I was copying, and got two messages in a row destined Chillicothe, Missouri, which I made Chillicothe, Ohio. Two blue tags [errors] resulted and I was told to take the afternoon off without pay. I went to a race track in Hamilton, Ohio, and lost $25 to boot. One of my bad days!

Brigham Young was an enthusiastic supporter of the telegraph and rendered effective assistance when the transcontinental line was built through Salt Lake City. Young also was active in building telegraph lines throughout the Utah territory. One line ran from Salt Lake to St. George, thence through Pipe Spring and on to Kanab, the southernmost town on the Mormon Wagon Road. The telegraph operator at Pipe Spring was Luella Stewart, teenage daughter of a local rancher, who had taught herself the Morse code to be the operator. Later she married David King Udall, an English-born convert to Mormonism, and the couple settled at St. Johns. Luella Udall became the matriarch of the extensive Udall family in Arizona, the mother of Supreme Court justice Levi Udall, and grandmother of Congressman Morris K. Udall and his brother the former secretary of the interior Stewart Udall. Throughout her long life, Mrs. Udall recalled her days as the telegraph operator at the lonely Pipe Spring station.

Easily one of the most famous telegraph operators of all times was Thomas A. Edison. Although remembered by the public largely for his inventions of the incandescent light and the phonograph, Edison's career was founded on his early days with the telegraph. As a youth, Edison had saved the life of a small child who was in danger of being hit by an approaching train. The child's father, the railroad stationmaster, taught Edison the art of telegraphy to show his gratitude. While still a teenager, Edison worked at many different locations as an operator and in time became a first-class expert, especially gifted at receiving.

Once, when an exceptionally fast operator was trying to get him to "break," Edison just kept on putting down perfect copy until the messages were finished. Then, taunting the sending operator, he asked, "Why don't you use your other foot?" Edison could have ended his days earning a good livelihood as a telegraph operator, but his keen and active mind could not long endure routine activity, and he was often dismissed because of unauthorized tinkering with equipment. He had an unquenchable thirst for knowledge and once started on a project to read every book in the public library. He had actually read word for word through 15 feet of books on the shelves before deciding that selective reading of certain volumes was a better way to acquire knowledge.

At 21, the young telegrapher abandoned the key forever and thereafter devoted his time to consulting work for the telegraph companies, which soon recognized his talent for solving technical problems. One of America's most prolific inventors, Edison received 1,093 patents during his lifetime. The first successful device was the automatic stock ticker, for which he was paid $40,000. Eventually setting up his own factory to manufacture the ticker, Edison gathered the financial resources that made it possible to set up a laboratory and machine shop to work exclusively on development of new ideas.

In 1877, Western Union signed a five-year contract, agreeing to pay "laboratory expenses incurred in perfecting inventions applicable to land lines of telegraph or cables within the United States." Clearly, Western Union wanted the gifted Edison on its side, not inventing for some competing company. Edison had entered the telegraph field at precisely the time when new and advanced methods were badly needed. The rapid increase in business activity in the United States had resulted in a volume of telegraph traffic far beyond the capacity of the original single line, key, and sounder equipment. The invention of a practical duplex that doubled wire capacity in 1872 was soon followed by Edison's quadruplex of 1874. The "quad" gave each existing wire the capacity to carry four messages at one time.

As a youngster of 17, Edison had worked in the military telegraph office at Memphis, Tennessee. He never forgot his old comrades of Civil War days, many of them teenagers like himself when operators for the U.S. Military Telegraph Corps. In 1916, members of the Military Telegraph Association were entertained with lunch and a personally guided tour of the great Edison laboratories at West Orange, New Jersey. In 1920, old-time telegraphers asked Edison to make a recording of his telegraphic sending. Edison at first demurred, citing the fact that he had been primarily a receiver and had only nominal skill as a sender. However, he finally yielded to pursuasion to make the record for history. A special Morse wire was set up between Edison's library at West Orange and Western Union head-quarters at 195 Broadway, New York. On July 20, 1920, David Homer Bates, famous Civil War telegrapher, went to 195 Broadway and copied the historic message, which was simultaneously recorded on a wax master at the Edison Re-cording Studio:

To the telegraph fraternity —
Amid the activities of a busy life full of expectations hopes and fears my thoughts of early association with my comrades of the dots and dashes have ever been a de-light and pleasure to me I consider it a great privilege to record in Morse characters on an indestructible disc this tribute to my beginnings in electricity through the telegraph and with it a god speed to the fraternity throughout the world.

Edison.

Copies of this historic message have been made on magnetic tape and are highly treasured by Morse enthusiasts today.

New operators just entering the field often started with vacation or sick-relief assignments. Then, with a little experience, they were in a position to apply for permanent jobs that came along. For many years the telegraph companies opened seasonal offices at national parks, summer resorts, and army camps. These assignments were ideal for young unmarried persons as they usually offered oppor-tunities for an interesting social life after working hours.

An unusual telegraph job was that of board marker in stock and commodity exchanges. Before the days of electronic displays, the large quotation boards were marked by operators who got their information from Morse sounders positioned along the bottom of the blackboard. Telegraphers were found in a variety of unusual locations. One man spent many years working on the swinging bridge of the Milwaukee Road at Sabula, Iowa, on the Mississippi. The railroad had to have an operator on the bridge to keep the dispatcher informed when the bridge was opened for the passage of river boats. At one time, many operators worked for the oil pipeline companies. Telegraphic communication was essential to coordinate the ac-tivities of pumping stations along the line.

Business firms sending and receiving a large number of messages often had main-line Morse wires in their own offices. The operators were employed by the customer rather than the telegraph company. They enjoyed a privileged position on the wire as they sometimes generated more telegraph revenue than the public office in the same city.

In the large relay offices, a premium was placed on speed in message handling. A special class of operators were the so-called bonus men. To promote increased

speed in traffic handling, the telegraph companies offered a bonus to operators who could exceed the normal quota of messages sent and received. A first-class operator was usually capable of handling around 60 messages an hour. Some of the bonus operators could exceed this speed and still maintain acceptable accuracy.

Itinerant operators who drifted from job to job were called "boomers." During the years when Morse operators were often in short supply, the boomers could pick up and move on short notice, always pretty sure of finding work in the next location. Hiring was often done by just sitting a man down and letting him work a busy wire to test his telegraphic skill. No embarrassing background checks or questions such as "Why did you leave your last job?" Boomers were usually expert operators, but they often had alcohol-related or personality problems that kept them perpetually on the move.

An unusual telegraphic assignment fell to the late Stuart Davis, who traveled with President Franklin Roosevelt as his personal telegrapher. In those years, the Morse telegraph was still regarded as the most dependable communications tool. Davis had a small oak carrying case for his instruments. Anywhere wire lines were available Davis could set up his portable instrument and be in a position to access the worldwide communications network. FDR once told him, "I'm always glad to see you with that pretty little box."

Harry Moorman of Cincinnati, Ohio, treasures the memories of his 40 years of service with Western Union. When the late Lowell Thomas, radio newscaster and author, came to Cincinnati, Moorman was regularly detailed to act as his telegrapher, receiving the news dispatches essential to Thomas's radio broadcasts. The two men became personal friends, and Moorman received autographed copies of all the Thomas books.

Another association resulting in a continuing friendship was with the late sports-caster Red Barber. In 1934, permission was granted by most major league baseball teams permitting telegraphed accounts of the games to be sent to distant cities for broadcast on radio. Until the late 1930s, many major league owners had prohibited live broadcasts from the ballparks, fearing it would cut attendance. Barber was engaged by station WSAI in Cincinnati to do the play-by-play broadcasts, and Moorman was assigned as his telegrapher. The announcer looked over the tele-grapher's shoulder and read the bulletins as they came in, translating them into a reasonably coherent account of the game.

Former president Reagan, while a young radio announcer in Iowa, used to broadcast games in this way. The telegraphers had a special shorthand to facilitate the quick bulletins necessary to follow the action; SIC meant "strike one called";

Opposite: **Telegraph office, Dalton, Georgia, 1890. Operator's chair with glass telegraph insulators on legs. Once a common practice (photo courtesy Georgia Dept. of Archives and History).**

S2F, "strike two fanned"; PTF, "pitcher to first"; FB, "foul back"; NTG AX, "no runs, no hits, no errors, none left."

A favorite Moorman story concerns the day in 1931 when President Herbert Hoover was scheduled to touch a button in Washington that would set off a dynamite blast signaling the start of construction of the Hoover Dam in Arizona. Western Union had furnished a special telegraph circuit, routed through Cincinnati to Arizona, to trigger the explosion. Moorman, then working as a wire chief in the Cincinnati office, came to work that morning and since no one had advised him of the special wire, started his routine wire tests, which he did every morning. The blast went off as scheduled, but Moorman was never sure whether it was the president's signal from Washington or his wire testing that did the job.

Normally there were no occupational hazards associated with being a telegraph operator. However, when electricity is involved, the unexpected can happen. One operator returned from lunch to find his office filled with blue smoke. A heavy lightning bolt had struck the wires some distance away. Every main-line fuse in the office was blown out. The fuses had been blown apart with such force that the copper ends were embedded in the plaster ceiling. That operator counted himself lucky to be out of the room when it happened. In another instance, an operator pulled a plug from his switchboard and was startled when it drew an electrical arc two inches long. A frantic search did not locate the trouble locally. It was finally ascertained that a power line had fallen on the telegraph wires about 50 miles away. Operators habitually avoided touching the metal parts of equipment since just the normal line voltage could give an unpleasant shock. This was probably all that prevented a tragedy.

Pictures of old telegraph offices often show the operator's chair with glass line insulators stuck on the legs. This may have been done in the belief that it would protect the operator from electrical shock or merely to emphasize his position as "lightning slinger." A more practical reason might have been to make the chair slide easily over rough wooden floors. Operators were seldom injured by accidental contact with high voltage, but line crews were not always so lucky. In January 1944, a Western Union line crew was engaged in dismantling some of the old Postal Telegraph lines after the merger of the two companies. Foolishly disregarding safety procedures, they attempted to pull out a section of wire using another piece of wire, instead of rope to do the pulling. Three men on the ground were killed and one seriously injured when the wire unexpectedly swung into contact with a high-voltage power line.

11. Press and Other Services

Be it true or false, so it be news. — Ben Jonson

With the coming of the Morse telegraph, the nature of newspaper work changed. Instead of printing local news and week-old accounts of events elsewhere, newspapers could now publish news from distant places within hours of the event. A special bond seemed to exist between reporters and telegraphers. They often worked shoulder to shoulder at major news events, and the work of one complemented that of the other.

James Gordon Bennett, Sr., and his penny paper, the *Herald*, was quick to utilize the new telegraphic news service. Bennett was cordially disliked by his competitors, but they had to admit that he was regularly scooping them on important news stories. At the close of the Mexican War, it was decided to approach Bennett with a proposal for a cooperative news service using telegraphic dispatches to the members.

The meeting was attended by representatives of the *Journal of Commerce, Courier and Enquirer, Tribune,* and *Express,* and was held in the office of the *Sun,* New York's other penny paper. This meeting, in 1848, marked the beginning of the Associated Press, only four years after the first telegraph line was placed in service. During the first years of its existence, the AP sent and received its dispatches over regular commercial wires. In 1875, it started to set up its own network of leased wires connecting the member newspapers. Prior to 1852, messages were referred to as "telegraphic dispatches"; the term "telegram" had not yet been coined.

The beginning of the Associated Press as it exists today came in 1892 when the association was incorporated under the laws of Illinois. The first competitve newsgathering organization was the United Press, founded by E. W. Scripps in 1907. In 1909, a third group entered the field, the International News Service, founded by W. R. Hearst. The UP and INS merged in 1958 to form United Press International, UPI.

The Morse system was used exclusively until about 1917 when some of the main circuits were changed to mechanical printers. Morse hung on for at least 10 years

123

more in some areas. As long as it was available, Morse was preferred for many purposes such as running accounts of baseball games and other sporting events. A reporter could dictate an account of the action to a telegrapher, and the copy was usually on the way to the press room by the time the game was over. As late as October 1936, a large contingent of Morse operators was on hand to send stories covering the speech of President Roosevelt at Harrisburg, Pennsylvania. Even after the discontinuance of Morse by the Associated Press, most metropolitan newspapers had a few telegraphers on the staff and found them useful for special assignments.

The Associated Press was innocently involved in a classic newspaper headline goof, which probably ranks close to the *Chicago Tribune* headline of 1948 proclaiming Dewey winning by a landslide over Truman. On Memorial Day 1933, the editor of the Walsenburg, Colorado, *World Independent*, a small daily, had received his last AP news dispatch of the day. His deadline was getting close, and he wanted to get in the name of the winner of the Indianapolis 500. He wired the AP bureau in Denver to send the name of the winner as soon as possible. The AP wired back, "Will overhead 500 winner." Unfortunately, the editor was a new man, not familiar with the AP jargon, which really meant they would send a story on the winner as soon as the race was over. The poor editor, however, read the message literally, and went to press with the headline "WILL OVERHEAD 500 WINNER!" The accompanying lead story added a few imaginative details of how Overhead came from behind in the final 250 miles to win. (The real winner that year was Louis Meyer.)

An Associated Press telegrapher who remained in one place any length of time often endeared himself to the editor he served. His unique position as a representative of AP gave him the frequent opportunity to be a public relations man. Operators going to a new assignment were advised as follows: "Go over there and make yourself a member of the family. Turn out clean copy. Study the paper's style—its capitalization, abbreviation, and punctuation. Make yourself useful in every way possible, and always keep in mind that to the newspaper editors you are the AP. They rarely see any of us in the bureau, but they see you every day."

Associated Press telegraphy was a man's game because it was a hard grind six days a week, sometimes with a double shift on Saturdays. There were some exceptions, and the AP had at least nine women operators in 1920. A sizable city with one daily newspaper was likely to have one AP operator; if it had two papers, it had two operators, one on the day shift, the other on nights. These were the first men in town to hear news from the outside world. If a Sunday edition was involved, the night operator was off Saturday night, and the day operator, always off on Sundays, worked two shifts on Saturday—and was glad to get the extra money. Press telegraphers were so expert that they could converse with a visitor, go for a drink of water, without missing a word of incoming copy. Actual working time for the day

Typical operator's position in the bay window of a railroad station. Many operators liked to put a tobacco can in the resonator to give the instrument a distinctive sound. Shown is the restored C&EI depot at Rossville, Illinois (photo by Lewis Coe).

was 7 hours, 10 minutes. The wire was shut down 30 minutes for lunch. Twice a day the sending operator would say "Take ten," a most welcome command.

Reporters on assignment could stop at any country telegraph office and file a dispatch. If the story was more than a 100 words or so, the telegraph operator would call the traffic chief in the relay office and request a direct circuit to the destination. The press associations and major metropolitan newspapers had direct wires to the telegraph relay offices, and the circuits could be set up in minutes. The simplicity of the Morse equipment made it practical to run a temporary wire to the scene of the action. The operator could quickly connect his instrument and be ready to go in minutes; no external source of power or complicated terminal equipment was needed. The methods used in the Morse days seem hopelessly antiquated now, but they did produce impressive feats of news gathering.

In the days when political candidates often traveled by train, the accompanying correspondents depended on the telegraph to get their stories to the papers. The late A. J. Long, a veteran Western Union manager at Salem, Illinois, got word one day in 1948 that President Truman's train would be passing through Salem and would drop off press messages at the depot. An unusually large file was expected because General MacArthur had just announced that he would not run against Truman that year. Long was requested to be at the depot to pick up the envelope, which would be thrown off as the train passed through town without stopping. The envelope was retrieved on schedule, and Long worked late that night sending the stories to St. Louis and other cities. After getting a few hours' sleep, Long was back in his office at 7:30 A.M. While eating breakfast, he glanced at the morning St. Louis *Globe Democrat*, and there on page one was the story he had sent a few hours previously.

The New York *Herald* scored one of the great beats in journalistic history with its coverage of the Custer massacre in 1876. Col. Clement A. Lounsberry, editor of the *Bismarck Tribune*, was a *Herald* correspondent. One of his reporters, Mark Kellogg, had accompanied the Custer expedition and was killed in the battle. After the arrival of the steamer *Far West* in Bismarck bearing the news of the disaster, Lounsberry headed straight for the telegraph office. His reporters brought in every scrap of information they could get from the returning troops, and working 24 hours straight, Lounsberry filed a lengthy dispatch to the *Herald*. The final telegraph bill was $3,000. Lounsberry was paid $2,500 for his scoop, which enabled the *Herald* to beat other papers by four days.

Press telegraphers were among the elite of the Morse fraternity. Not only were they lightning fast with the Morse code, but they had to be masters of the Phillips code as well. Invented in the 1880s by Walter P. Phillips of the Associated Press, the Phillips code was a special vocabulary of about 3,000 symbols for English words and phrases. The normal working speed of a Morse operator was 30 to 40 words per minute. Phillips decided that too much time was spent spelling out common words and phrases used over and over in press dispatches. After typewriters came into use for copying, most operators could type at a much higher speed than any Morse man could send. Phillips reasoned that by using his symbols, press dispatches could be transmitted much faster, around twice the normal sending speed of an operator who was spelling out all the words in full.

Some of the single-letter symbols:

B	"be"	N	"not"	W	"with"
C	"see'	O	"of"	X	"in which"
D	"in the"	P	"per"	Y	"year"
F	"of the"	Q	"on the"	Z	"from which"
H	"has"	R	"are"	4	"where"
J	"by which"	T	"the"	5	"that the"
K	"out of the"	U	"you"	7	"that is"
M	"more"	V	"of which"		

A typical sentence "cut in Phillips" might read: "IXB5 POTUS WILL ENTERTAIN SCOTUS AT RVT HOME IN HYDE PARK." The receiving operator typed it out as follows: "It is believed that the President of the United States will entertain the Supreme Court at the Roosevelt home in Hyde Park."

Press telegraphers not only had to be skilled in Morse and Phillips codes; they had to use Phillips in the proper context in case the Phillips abbreviation coincided with the actual text. A classic example occurred after World War I when a telegrapher was copying a Washington dispatch pertaining to the mandated Pacific islands, which the Allies had acquired from Germany. The dispatch listed several islands, including Yap. The operator made what he considered a perfect copy of the message and handed it in. Presently the telegraph editor appeared waving the message and demanding an explanation. The mystery was soon solved. YAP is the Phillips code for "yesterday afternoon." Instead of typing "Island of Yap," the operator had absentmindedly typed "Island of Yesterday Afternoon."

The original Phillips code was revised by E. E. Bruckner in 1914 and by William G. Gerlach in 1945. The code remained in use as long as any Morse press wires were operating. The changes made by Gerlach in 1945 were an effort to improve the code for teletype use. Gerlach said many years later that the changes he made, although minor, were probably ill advised.

Morse telegraphers often had a special talent for either sending or receiving. Some operators worked almost exclusively as "receivers," especially those in newspaper offices where they spent the day copying the incoming news. Others, sometimes known as "outbounders," excelled at sending.

When the Morse system was finally phased out of the Associated Press, it was a nostalgic moment for those who had grown up with the old methods. The following, from the editorial page of the *Kewanee Star-Courier* (Ill.) in 1930, pretty well expressed the feelings of the old-time newspaper men:

> In the Newark bureau of the Associated Press Peyton D. Petty, supervisor of operating personnel of the traffic department, sat down for the last time at a Morse circuit "bug." Well he knew, as did the dozen old time telegraphers gathered about him, that his three dots, dash, dot, and a long dash would silence the last hand sending circuit on the Associated Press network.
>
> Save for the staccato clatter of automatic printer telegraph machines and a few Morse relays, there was no sound in the bureau office. Slowly Petty began sending. At four points in the state of New Jersey—last refuge of the Morse operators—operators picked up the swan song of the telegraphers:
>
> "We are about to witness the death of a very romantic profession," went the dots and dashes.
>
> "It seems hard to visualize that about twenty-five years have passed and we are still lovers of Morse telegraph. However, it must bow to the inevitable and so—we must give up to the march of progress."
>
> "In the circumstances it falls to me to give the final 'thirty' on an Associated Press Press Morse circuit, the last of them all." So—"30-30. GM"
>
> P.D.P.

The code "30" is the old-time telegrapher's signal for signing off. "GM" is Morse code for "Good Morning." So passed the last Morse circuit, and with it a romantic, colorful profession.

The newspaper telegrapher cramped over a hand-sending key and typing copy as it came from a Morse relay was a fixture in newspaper offices for 40 years or more. Printer telegraph machines made their appearance in the early 1920s, but Morse operators refused to be replaced by mechanized equipment. Even though part of the Associated Press circuit in Illinois was printerized ten years ago, it was not until 1927 that the "iron mike" superseded the Morse operator in the Star-Courier's news room. When telegraphers left the news office, it represented the breaking of a tradition. With the Morse operators went much of the human drama which daily was compressed in a Morse circuit resonator.

Now the last Morse circuit has been closed. Railroads, like press associations are also replacing Morse operators with teletypewriter equipment. The old-time telegraphers have been doomed by technology.

The Morse telegraph first reached Phoenix, Arizona, on October 12, 1873, and the circumstances were recalled in an 1893 article in the *Arizona Daily Gazette*:

The line at first was a sorry apology for one, sort of hung up on mesquite trees and cactus for poles, but when it finally reached Phoenix the inhabitants had a jubilee. The office was established in the adobe building on the corner of Jefferson and First streets, and to that point concentrated the entire population of about 300 persons. Morris Goldwater [uncle of former U.S. senator Barry Goldwater] then used the building as a store, and to him fell the office of telegraph operator. He knew a little about it, and was kept busy explaining to the wondering multitudes how the curious thing worked. He could not read the instrument by sound, so an old Morse receiving machine was sent in, with its reel of paper tape on which the dots and dashes were marked. It really seemed incredible to send a message to San Francisco and receive an answer within a day. On July 2, 1881, the telegraph operator brought the news that President James A. Garfield had been shot and wounded. The telegraph line across the Salt River at Tempe was attached to the railroad trestle. When the trestle washed out in 1890, the line broke and Phoenix and the *Gazette* were without telegraph service from the south for several days. Service was finally restored by flying a kite across the turbulent river. A string attached to the kite was used to pull a wire from one bank to the other.

In 1864, President Lincoln was one vote short in his effort to get the antislavery amendment passed. In the territory of Nevada a fierce debate was being waged over the advantages and disadvantages of statehood. Finally, on July 27, 1864, a constitutional convention voted in favor of statehood and drafted a constitution. The decision was seconded by the voters in September. To speed the process of admission to the Union, the entire text of the constitution was telegraphed to Washington. It was one of the longest telegrams sent over the Morse telegraph until that time and cost $3,416.77. Two shifts of Morse operators worked to get the message on the wire. With the constitution in hand, Lincoln immediately issued a proclamation declaring Nevada the 36th state. Nevada's representative in Congress cast his vote for antislavery, and the amendment was ratified. The controversy surrounding the decision on statehood under wartime conditions inspired Nevada's state motto, "Battle Born."

Of the special services, perhaps the one most familiar to the public was the money transfer service. By a process that mystified many people but was actually quite simple, the telegraph company could transfer sums of money to any place in the world reached by telegraph or cable. The customer handed the originating operator the amount of the transfer, plus a fixed fee and extra charges if a telegram of instruction was sent at the same time. The originating office then filed a "transfer message," which was sent to the distant city. In sending a transfer message, code words were included that had to match exactly with the key lists at the checkpoints. The receiving operator issued a telegraph company voucher for the amount desired. These vouchers were readily cashed by the recipient. At the sending end, the principal amount of the transfer was deposited in the company's local bank account.

Electronic transfer of funds is now commonplace, but in the early days of the telegraph, it was not always fully understood by the public. One woman came into a telegraph office to wire the sum of $11.76. On second thought, she changed the amount to an even $12, explaining, "I'm afraid the loose change might get lost traveling over the wire."

One Western Union veteran has a favorite story concerning an unusual money transfer he once handled. A man came into the office and announced that he wanted to wire some money to his girlfriend in California. He wanted to telegraph the sum of three cents, no more, no less. The accompanying message read: "If you can't afford a stamp to write to me here is the money." That bit of sarcasm cost the fellow several dollars. The money transfer service was one of the last services offered by Western Union, long after it had any message business. A special organization will continue the transfer service under the Western Union name.

Flowers by wire was once an important part of telegraph services. An agreement with the Florist's Telegraph Delivery Association (FTD) made it possible to send flowers by wire to any point where the FTD had a member. The customer paid for the flowers, plus fees similar to those charged in the money transfer service. The FTD had agreements with both telegraph companies, and it was usually up to the originating florist to decide which company to use.

Before the telegraph, there was no standard time system in the United States. Time could be determined in various localities by astronomic observation, and in the cities jewelers often displayed ships' chronometers in their windows to enable the public to set their watches. In rural areas, sunrise, high noon, and sunset were the usual timekeepers. In 1865, the U.S. Naval Observatory at Washington, D.C., started supplying time signals to Western Union. After Postal Telegraph entered the field, it too received the time signals. West of the Rockies, the time signals came from the Mare Island Navy Yard in California.

For many years, it was standard practice on all railroad and commercial telegraph lines to interrupt normal traffic at noon, eastern standard time, to transmit the time tick. Telegraph operators stood by to check their office clocks. Western Union later had a clock service, leasing electrically controlled clocks to their customers. Postal never had a clock service but did at one time sell electric clocks with the Postal logo on the dial. These were synchronous electric clocks dependent on the 60-cycle power-line frequency for accuracy. The present standard time zones were established by the U.S. government in 1883.

In addition to the time ticks, the telegraph provided a new tool for astronomers in establishing accurate longitudes of widely separated places, making instantaneous time comparisons that had not previously been possible. During the early part of the twentieth century, the international boundary between Canada and Alaska had not yet been precisely located. With valuable gold strikes being made in the area, disputes were inevitable, and it became imperative to locate the border to the satisfaction of both parties. One of the classic projects of civil engineering history, the boundary survey started in 1906 and required seven years to complete. The first step was to locate the 141-degree longitude line with precision. At a place called Boundary on the south bank of the Yukon River, time signals from Vancouver transmitted on the American-Canadian telegraph line established the exact longitude with much greater accuracy than the astronomical methods previously used. This was the starting point of the historic survey, which reached the Arctic Ocean on July 18, 1912. The line south of Boundary was completed the following year.

Telegraph companies had many special services. Before the invention of the telephone, the telegraph was the only means of electrical communication. Private wires, complete with operators, could be used by those able to afford the service. A noteworthy case was the private wire of Gordon Bennett, Sr. (1795–1872), connecting his home in Washington Heights with the downtown office of the *Herald Tribune* and the Bennett town house on Fifth Avenue at 38th Street, New York. Assignment to the Bennett private wire must have been an unusual experience. More conventional were the private wires supplied to brokerage firms and other large business organizations. Temporary circuits were also available for ceremonial occasions, enabling a dignitary to press a button to signal the start of some special event or like President Hoover, setting off a dynamite charge to start construction of the Hoover Dam in Arizona.

Live television coverage from the battlefield was only a dream during World War II, but the latest methods of radiotelegraphy were utilized to enable news correspondents in the most advanced areas to file dispatches for direct transmission to New York. The Mackay Radio and Telegraph Co. made elaborate plans to place a mobile unit in operation soon after the D-Day landing in France. A complete portable station was carefully packed and scheduled to be unloaded on the Normandy beach. Unfortunately in war the best-laid plans go awry, and the carefully packed radio equipment was hopelessly lost in the vast confusion of supplies being unloaded at the beachhead.

The Mackay crew was forced to improvise. They acquired some military radio equipment and an army truck to transport it. Then they were off across France, staying close to the correspondents who accompanied the advance units of the army. It was a dramatic moment for all when they erected their field antenna for the first time and established communication directly with the Mackay operating headquarters at 67 Broad Street, New York. News reporters, including novelist Ernest Hemingway, were delighted that they could file dispatches without leaving camp. The headlong dash across France was rough on the radio transmitting equipment. When the radiomen realized that they had no spare tube left for the transmitter, one man was detailed to hold the remaining tube in his arms while they were on the move.

The radiomen were in much the same status as the military telegraphers during the Civil War. They were civilians, and although they were operating in forward combat zones, they had none of the usual benefits accorded a member of the military. They did have official U.S. military uniforms, without rank insignia. This was only a slight concession to ensure that they would not be shot as spies if captured by the enemy. Also, they were accorded the courtesy of a "simulated rank" as commissioned officers of various grades.

Radiomen, army officers and news correspondents often socialized. At one such gathering, each man was asked to get up and introduce himself. Hemingway got up and said, "I am Ernie Hemorrhoid, the poor man's Pyle!" (Ernie Pyle was then one of the best-known war correspondents.)

Following closely behind Patton's Third Army advance units, the radiomen soon found themselves deep in German territory. When the final surrender came, the advance units were soon surrounded by German soldiers, all anxious to surrender their arms to the first American they met. Even the radiomen, with their American uniforms, were singled out by German GI's for whom the war was over. One Mackay technician brought home a fine souvenir in the form of a P-38 Walther pistol. A distinguished-looking German officer handed him the weapon without a word. The Germans knew that American GI's, hearing of German atrocities, were in a vindictive mood and might consider any German still bearing arms fair game.

For at least 40 years, Western Union provided a special Morse circuit for the Morse Telegraph Club. The circuit interconnected the 36 U.S. and 4 Canadian chapters of the club during the local meetings held each year on the last Saturday of April to commemorate Morse's birthday (April 27, 1791). Western Union traditionally furnished the circuit without charge as a gesture of respect to the old-time telegraphers. Due to the closing of Western Union, 1989 was the last year for the nationwide "party line" that was the highlight of the chapter meetings.

Despite loss of the Western Union wire, Morse club members still manage to communicate with key and sounder. Some of them are amateur radio operators and use their equipment in connection with a simple terminal device to operate a conventional Morse sounder. Others are using a new method, "dial-up Morse," to operate key and sounder over telephone circuits. Using a modem of the same type used by computer operators to go "on line" and talk to distant computers, the Morse operators can set up a circuit to anywhere reached by the public telephone system. Of course, someone has to pay the tolls involved, but most of the old-timers feel it is worth it. S. F. B. Morse would undoubtedly be pleased to know that his century-old system is quite at home traveling over microwaves, satellites, and fiber-optic cable.

12. The Telegraph and the Railroads

Railway termini are our gates to the glorious and the unknown. – Edward Morgan Forster

The telegraph was on hand to record a great moment in railroad history when the transcontinental line was completed in 1869. The following news dispatch to the *New York Times* tells the story of the final ceremony:

WASHINGTON, May 10, 1869 – The completion of the Pacific Railroad monopolized public attention here today to the exclusion of everything else. The feeling is one of hearty rejoicing at the completion of this great work. There were no public observances, but the arrangements made by the telegraph company to announce the completion of the road simultaneously with the driving of the last spike were perfect. At 2:20 this afternoon, Washington time, all the telegraph offices in the country were notified by the Omaha telegraph office to be ready to receive the signals corresponding to the blows of the hammer that drove the last spike in the last rail that united New York and San Francisco with a band of iron.

Accordingly, Mr. Tinker, manager of the Western Union Telegraph office in this city, placed a magnetic bell-sounder in the public office of that company, corner Fourteenth St., and the Avenue, connecting the same with the main lines, and notified the various offices that he was ready. New Orleans instantly responded, the answer being read from the bell-taps, New York did the same. At 2:27 o'clock offices over the country began to make inquiries of all sorts of Omaha, to which that office replied:

"To everybody, keep quiet. When the last spike is driven at Promontory they will say 'Done.' Don't break the circuit but watch for the signals of the blows of the hammer."

[Telegraph wires were connected to the metal head of the spike maul and to the spike. Each blow was recorded as a tick on the nationwide telegraph network.]

At 2:27 P.M. Promontory Point, 2400 miles west of Washington, said to the people congregated in the various telegraph offices:

"Almost ready. Hats off; prayer is being offered." A silence for the prayer ensued. At 2:40 the bell tapped again, and the office at the Point said:

133

"We have got done praying. The spike is about to be presented."

Chicago replied: "We understand; all are ready in the east. From Promontory Point: "All ready now; the spike will be driven. The signal will be three dots for the commencement of the blows." [Then came the signals corresponding to the actual blows of the hammer.] For a moment the instrument was silent, then Promontory sent the word "done," and the continent was at last spanned with a continuous rail line from east to west.

W. N. Shilling, a Western Union employee from Ogden, Utah, had the distinction of being the operator at Promontory Point on the historic day. His telegraph table was set up alongside the track, and wires ran from it to the telegraph line overhead.

In addition to the bell signal at the Western Union office in Washington, a magnetic ball had been installed on a pole at the Capitol, arranged to drop when the signal was received from Utah. In New York, cannon fired a 100-gun salute, and the chimes at Trinity Church were rung. San Francisco went all out with a big celebration. A 15-inch gun at Fort Point fired the first round of a 220-gun salute, and fire bells were sounded throughout the city.

Although the formal ceremony of the golden spike took place on May 10, 1869, the actual completion of the work took place a day earlier. Chief Engineer G. M. Dodge advised Oliver Ames, president of the Union Pacific, by telegram on May 9 that the road had been completed to Promontory Summit.

The Morse telegraph and the railroads coexisted for several years before anyone thought of combining them for more efficient operation. The telegraph wires usually ran parallel to the railroad tracks. When not busy with messages, operators would gossip about the weather and politics, and sometimes comment on how the trains were running that day.

The man who changed things was Charles Minot, superintendent of the Erie Railroad. On September 22, 1851, Minot was a passenger on a westbound Erie train that was halted at Turners (now Harriman), New York waiting for an eastbound train to arrive. Delays of an hour or more were common in the days before telegraphic train dispatching. On this memorable day, Minot happened to glance at the nearby telegraph wire and had an inspiration. He went into the station and telegraphed to Goshen, the next station to the west, inquiring if the eastbound train had arrived there. Assured that it had not, he then ordered the engineer of the westbound train to proceed to Goshen.

The engineer flatly refused, considering it suicidal to proceed until the eastbound passed them at Turners. Minot finally took the throttle himself and ran the train to Goshen without incident. The engineer and conductor, taking a very dim view of the whole idea, sought refuge in the very last car of the train, which they considered the safest place to ride. After reaching Goshen, Minot again verified the location of the eastbound and in this manner brought the train into Port Jervis on time.

This was the beginning of telegraphic train dispatching, which remained in use on the Erie until 1888 when the block signal system became the primary method of train control. The telegraph was the mainstay of train dispatching until 1882, when some telephone dispatching systems were placed in service. By the time of World War II, at least half of the existing track in the country had been switched to telephone dispatching. The Morse telegraph continued to be a very important part of railroad communications, even after the advent of the telephone. The railroads traditionally used the telegraph to move a large volume of routine business. Train "consists," car orders, reservations, and administrative messages kept the wires busy along the major roads.

Railroads had pretty well phased out the Morse system by the middle 1950s. Telephones, teletypes, and computerized accounting were the new order of operations. A few scattered Morse lines were left in operation as long as there were operators still available to use them. As the old Morse operators went into retirement, the Morse equipment was quietly removed and passed into history without much fanfare.

When telephones first came into use, there was often idle debate about the reason. Some people had the idea that the telephone was faster and more accurate. Actually, the methods were equally fast and accurate. Using the telephone, the sending operator can speak only as fast as the receiving operator can write out the message—exactly the same speed as the telegraph. Either method is accurate, as standard train-order procedure calls for the message to be repeated back word for word to the sender, who must acknowledge the correct repetition with his personal "sign." The real reason for adopting the telephone was simply that it is much easier to train a person to handle telephone messages than teach him telegraphy. A large part of a station agent's work consisted of duties not related to communications. Persons who were otherwise well qualified to handle railroad work were not always interested in becoming telegraphers. The use of the telephone simply gave the railroad a broader choice in filling positions.

A station agent had to master many routines, not the least of which was selling passenger tickets. A ticket to the next station was easy. When it came to the yard-long tickets needed for long trips with changes to connecting railroads, the seller had to have a good knowledge of railroad procedures. One young telegrapher, fresh out of the Dodge school at Valparaiso, Indiana, was assigned to a small station in southern Indiana as his first job. All was going well until a man came in and wanted to buy a ticket to California, complete with stopovers and transfers to three or four connecting lines. The young station agent had no idea how to write such a complex ticket. He still tells the story of how he got out of difficulty: "I just sold the man a ticket to Louisville and told him to buy his California ticket there!"

Back in the days when the West was still wild, telegraph operators were often involved in harrowing experiences. In tiny western settlements, the railroad depot was the focal point for all that went on, and the telegraph operator was usually right in the middle of the action.

An operator named Warden Meyers was never to forget Christmas Day 1895 as long as he lived. Meyers was on duty at the isolated station of Weskan, Kansas, a howling blizzard raging outside. Suddenly a stranger appeared out of nowhere and entered the station. With true western hospitality, Meyers gave the man food and shelter in the waiting room.

Finally, the fellow left, as though leaving the vicinity. Instead, he went out to the station stockyard and set a wooden fence on fire. When Meyers ran out to see what had happened, the man produced a gun and robbed the operator of the few dollars he had.

Meanwhile, a train was approaching the station. The bandit forced Meyers to stand in the middle of the tracks at gunpoint. The operator managed to leap out of the way at the last possible moment, and as he did so, the gunman fired, and missed.

The engineer of the train saw the incident and reported it to railroad authorities, who promptly sent aid to Meyers. The gunman had vanished as mysteriously as he had arrived. A few days later, the stranger showed up at the station in Monument, Kansas, and tried the same stunt, setting the stockyard on fire. Here he was not so lucky. He was hunted down and shot and killed by a hard-riding sheriff's posse.

In the little town of North Redwood, Minnesota, the railroad station agent–telegrapher got a shipment of watches destined for a local jeweler. The jeweler refused the shipment. The normal procedure would have been to return the shipment to the sender; instead, the agent contacted the shipper and made arrangements to buy the watches. Advertising the watches at reduced prices, the agent quickly sold them all. It was the beginning of a business selling watches that eventually moved to Minneapolis.

The young agent's name was R. W. Sears, and in 1887 he hired a young Hoosier watchmaker named Alvah C. Roebuck to help him. The year 1893 saw the beginning of the mail order giant Sears, Roebuck & Co. The company now handled a line of general merchandise in addition to jewelry. The company moved to Chicago in 1895, and Alvah Roebuck retired that year. Sears hired Julius Rosenwald, a Chicago clothier whose guiding hand helped move the company from less than $800,000 annual sales in 1895 to more than $11 million a year five years later. If it had not been for a refused shipment of watches, Sears might have ended his days as a $50-a-month railroad telegrapher instead of retiring in 1909 at age 45 with an estmated worth of $25 million.

The simplicity of the Morse telegraph made it widely useful on the railroad.

When a major derailment occurred, a temporary telegraph office could be quickly set up at the site, providing convenient communications between the work crews and headquarters. In a similar manner, telegraphers were often assigned to crews working on routine track or bridge maintenance so that train movements could be controlled.

Railroad telegraphers were required to be familiar with the "book of rules," which detailed the procedures to be followed in a wide variety of situations involving train movements. In the past, many railroads used the "double order system." "Form 31" orders, governing train movements, required stopping the train and obtaining signatures from the crew. "Form 19" orders, "assisting orders," did not require signatures and could be handed to a moving train using "message hoops," which had a wide loop for easy catching by the trainman's outstretched arm.

Train orders have undergone many changes in recent years. The advent of radio has made it possible for the dispatcher to talk directly to train crews. Whatever the method, some principles have not changed since the beginning. Orders are transmitted according to a standard form, and they must be repeated word for word to the dispatcher and acknowledged before they are complete.

Before the days of radio, considerable attention was directed to the possibility of communicating with moving trains. Trains in remote areas where there were few intermediate stations simply disappeared into the unknown until they arrived at the next reporting point. At one time, some trains carried a telegraph operator who could tap the trackside lines with a portable instrument in case of trouble. This custom died out as trains and tracks became more reliable, making it hard to justify the expense of carrying a telegrapher aboard. Another idea was to use the principle of induction, permitting telegraphy to and from a moving train by utilizing the inductive coupling between trackside wires and a pickup wire on the train. This was the system used by Preece in England, and others, to telegraph across bodies of water. One system is credited to Thomas Edison and W. Wiley Smith. In the 1890s, the Lehigh Valley Railroad had such a system in operation.

Inductive telegraph systems for trains never went much beyond the experimental stage. They still required that the train carry a qualified operator and were probably not too reliable. For one thing, the trackside wires were not always exactly parallel with the rails. It was not unusual for the telegraph line to take a shortcut that did not follow the rails. At such locations, the induction signal would be lost. Also, there was the problem of stray pickup of unwanted signals, common to all the inductive systems.

Practical Hints for Railway Telegraphers
(from an old manual)

Look up and down a track before stepping between the rails. Make a practice of doing this, even if you are sure that there is not a train or engine moving within

Symbolic of the end – abandoned telegraph line along the Erie railroad overgrown with vines (photo by Lewis Coe).

two miles of you. It is an excellent habit to acquire. Practice this, and almost unconsciously you will form the habit, invaluable to a railway telegrapher, of exercising great caution before placing himself in positions of danger.

Do not lose your temper, and take it out on some operator along the line. Do not comment on the company's way of doing business. The dispatcher hears all that goes over the wires, and he is in a position to retard your promotion or help you along toward promotion.

Do your telegraphing while on duty, study it while off duty. Always try to be accommodating, unassuming, and quiet. Help old people on and off trains. Do not get out of patience if a traveling man asks a small favor. They often travel all night, put up at poor hotels, and feel out of sorts, but a good word from them circulated among other traveling men, will reach the officials' ears more often than in any other way.

From an 1867 telegraph operator's manual of the Cleveland and Pittsburgh Railroad:

Operators are required to be in their offices whenever the interests of the company may demand it, but the ordinary hours of duty at day offices are from

7:30 A.M. to 8:00 P.M. Night offices must be kept open at all hours of the day and night, except as provided in the book of rules. At least one operator must be in each office at the time of the passage of every train during business hours, and for not less than ten minutes prior thereto. Operators must inform Agents and Watchmen as to their place of residence in order that they may be found, in cases of emergency. They must not leave their offices in charge of substitutes nor may they exchange places with other operators without the consent of the chief operator. Students must not be received without the consent of the Superintendent of Telegraph, and when such consent is obtained, students must not be allowed to practice on the main circuit without special permission. Operators will ordinarily be allowed one hour for each meal, but must restrict themselves to a shorter time whenever the interest of the company requires it. . . . Operators must always disconnect their instruments from the circuit when about to leave their offices. A very good excuse will be required for permitting instruments to be injured by atmospheric electricity.

13. Without Wires

. . .For a bird of the air shall carry the voice, and that which hath wings shall tell the matter (Ecclesiastes 10:20).

The electric telegraph was still in its infancy when thoughts were turned to the intriguing idea of telegraphing without line wires. The first experiments were probably made in the hope of solving the vexing problem of river crossings.

Several years were to pass before a satisfactory underwater cable was developed. A great benefit of the Atlantic cables was the perfection of methods for manufacturing *gutta-percha*–insulated underwater cable. Previously, the only known method was to suspend the wire on high masts on the river banks. On major rivers such as the Ohio, the spans were excessively long, and the wire had to be high enough to clear passing riverboats.

These river crossings remained the weak links in the telegraph system. When the wire broke, as it frequently did, the usual practice was to carry messages across the river in a rowboat until the wire could be repaired. As early as 1842, Morse had discovered that he could send a useful quantity of electric current across a canal 80 feet wide, using the water itself as a conductor. In 1844, Morse's associate L. D. Gale made a series of experiments on the use of water conductivity for crossing rivers.

Following Gale's experiments, Morse made a report to the secretary of the treasury:

> As the result of these experiments, it would seem that there may be situations in which the arrangements I have made for passing electricity across the rivers may be useful, although experience alone can determine whether lofty spars, on which the wires may be suspended, erected in the rivers, may not be deemed the most practical. The experiments made were but for a short distance; in which, however, the principle was fully proved to be correct. It has been applied under the direction of my able assistants, Messrs. Vail and Rogers, across the Susquehanna River, at Havre-de-Grace, with complete success; a distance of nearly a mile.

Nothing more was heard of this method of transmission. The pressures of rapid expansion of the telegraph system probably kept construction confined to tried and true methods. Also, someone may have discovered the obvious—that river crossings by water conductivity could carry only one circuit in the same vicinity. Otherwise, there would be hopeless cross-current interference between circuits.

For many years previous to Morse's experiments, the possibility of communication without wires was discussed by scientists. Even the ancient Greeks who witnessed Thales's experiment of transferring energy from electrified amber to neutral paper probably dreamed of bridging greater distances by the same mysterious influence. The first recorded scheme proposed for telegraphing without wires by electricity was that of Silva, a Spanish physicist, who read a paper "On the Application of Electricity to Telegraphy" before the Academy of Sciences on December 16, 1795, at Barcelona. In this prophetic memoir, Silva advocated that a given area of earth be positively electrified at Mellorca and that a similar area be charged to the opposite sign at Alicante; the sea connecting these two cities would then act as a conductor when the electric difference of potential was restored, and by a proper translating device the transfer of energy could be indicated. This was strictly a theoretical proposal, and there is no record that it was ever tried in practice.

In 1837–1838, Steinheil, a German, had discovered the conductivity of the earth, one of the most important discoveries in electricty. It made the single-wire Morse telegraph possible and is still used today in all manner of telecommunications circuits. Steinheil also thought that under certain conditions the earth alone might be used for communication, but again the idea never got beyond the experimental stage.

As far back as 1617, a Roman named Famianus Strada claimed to have signaled without wires by using two sympathetic compasses. This was getting close to the principle of telegraphy by magnetic induction that was to get much attention before the invention of the "wireless." Induction is the property that causes a wire carrying electrical current to transfer, or induce, a similar current in an adjacent conductor with no physical connection.

The possibility of using induction for telegraphy was investigated in 1884 by Henry Preece, later to become Marconi's sponsor in wireless. Preece, later to be knighted for his work in the British post office communications system, discovered while working on the London telephone system that currents in one circuit were causing corresponding variations in the adjacent wires of another circuit without physical connection. Preece saw the possibilities of this phenomenon and by 1892 had succeeded in sending messages across the Bristol Channel between Penarth and Flatholm Island.

In 1895, the induction system was used for communication in Scotland between Oban and the island of Mull when a break occurred in the submarine cable. Telegraphy by induction seemed to show some promise, and there were experiments involving communication with moving trains. However, none of the inductive systems survived beyond initial experiments. Range was limited, and even more serious, it was a single-channel system; only one inductive circuit could be used in a given area.

Induction is one of the most important principles in electrical engineering and figures in the operation of almost any electrical device. As a communication medium, induction has survived today only in the wireless sound systems installed in museums, churches, and other public buildings. In a museum, for example, visitors can rent a headset and hear audio descriptions as they view the exhibits. These installations consist of concealed loops of wire encircling the area to be covered. A powerful amplifier feeds the audio signal into the loop, and the sensitive headphones pick up the signal anywhere in the area. This is indeed communication without wires, yet it is not what we call wireless or radio.

Early workers in inductive telegraphy were not even aware of another form of electricity, called electromagnetic waves. The first intimation that there might be a true wireless method of communication came in 1873 when Scottish physicist James Clerk Maxwell (1831–1879) published his *Treatise on Electricity and Magnetism*. Maxwell pointed out for the first time the existence of electromagnetic waves that would propagate through space. The new waves had characteristics similar to light waves and traveled at the same velocity, 186,000 miles per second. Maxwell's discovery was brilliant, but it was largely a mathematical hypothesis and had not been proved by actual laboratory experiments. Not until 1886 did German physicist Heinrich Hertz (1857–1894) verify Maxwell's findings by laboratory experiments.

Hertz set up a small spark gap coupled to an antenna. A short distance away was an identical antenna and spark gap. When he produced a spark at the first gap, a similar spark appeared at the other gap. In one stroke he had invented wireless, even though he did not grasp its significance as a means of communication. Hertz, a pure scientist, was satisfied that he could prove Maxwell's theories.

There is a similarity between the early discoveries of the electric telegraph and the later discovery of wireless. Joseph Henry had demonstrated that he could ring bells at a distance, using batteries and magnetic attraction. In effect, he had invented the telegraph, but like Hertz he was interested only in the theoretical aspects of the experiment and made no effort to develop it into a practical system of communication.

Hertz died an untimely death at 37 and might have gone on to see the practical value of his discovery had he lived a normal lifespan. Even this seems doubtful. Before his death he had received a request for an opinion on the idea of using the Hertzian waves for communication and had given a noncommittal answer showing that he had given no thought to the matter. It remained for a young Italian boy reading Hertz's biography in 1894 to become obsessed with the goal of creating a practical wireless system using Hertzian waves.

Guglielmo Marconi, on holiday in the Italian Alps when he read the Hertz biography, was unable to begin experiments until the family returned to the Villa Grifone estate near Bologna in the fall. He had a clear vision of what might be accomplished with Hertzian waves but scarcely believed that he was the first one to think of the communication application. Years later he was to recall, "The idea obsessed me more and more, and in those mountains of Biellese I worked it out in imagination. I did not attempt any experiments until we returned to the Villa Grifone in the autumn, but then two large rooms at the top of the house were set aside for me by my mother. And there I began experiments in earnest." Throughout his early years of experimentation, Marconi was dogged by the fear that someone else had beaten him to the discovery of wireless. Marconi said, "My chief trouble was that the idea was so elementary, so simple in logic, that it seemed difficult for me to believe that no one else had thought of putting it into practice. Surely, I argued, there must be much more mature scientists than myself who had followed the same line of thought and arrived at an almost similar conclusion."

It has often been said that Marconi did not actually invent anything; he simply took existing knowledge and applied it to a practical method of wireless communication. The same thing was said of Morse and the telegraph. Marconi, of course, did his great work at a time when electrical knowledge was far advanced from the days of Morse. Basic electricity was pretty well understood; the telegraph and telephone were in existence; and the public was more enlightened about scientific matters than in Morse's day when the telegraph was often viewed as some kind of a trick. Public opnion in 1894 was a little more inclined to accept a miracle like wireless, but even then the whole idea was viewed with skepticism by many people.

By 1896, Marconi had perfected his apparatus to the point where he could apply for a patent and seek financial support. As a loyal citizen, his first move was to offer the invention to the Italian government. It was a bitter disappointment when the Ministry of Posts and Telegraphs, with characteristic governmental shortsightedness, turned him down without even an examination of his apparatus. Marconi took his ideas and equipment to England. On June 2, 1896, a provisional specification was filed at the Patent Office establishing the legal claim to priority of invention. Through influential friends of his mother, Marconi was able to get an interview with Sir William Preece, chief engineer of the British Post Office.

Preece, at 60, was one of the most talented telegraph engineers in Britain and had complete responsibility for the Post Office communications system. A curious mix of the most advanced technological knowledge and traditional Victorianism, Preece still drove to and from work in a handsome four-in-hand carriage. One might have expected such a man to be aloof, narrow-minded, and jealous of others working in his field. Marconi, only 22, must have been a little apprehensive about approaching the great man. Fortunately, Preece had that quality of greatness that is quick to recognize the accomplishments of others.

Preece listened carefully to Marconi's description of his apparatus and then, apparently having a prior engagement, assigned a young clerk in the office to take Marconi out for lunch. The talks continued that afternoon with some simple demonstrations of the equipment. Preece then arranged for several days of tests culminating in a rooftop demonstration for a group of senior officials and engineers. Marconi's equipment functioned flawlessly over the path between the General Post Office building in St. Martin's-le-Grand and another post office building in Queen Victoria Street about a mile away. When it was all over, Preece turned to Marconi and said, "Young man, you have done something truly exceptional. I congratulate you on it."

Progress was rapid after that. With the authority of the Post Office behind him, Marconi lacked for nothing to pursue his work in perfecting the wireless system, and communications were extended to greater and greater ranges. Preece realized that he had one of the great inventions of the century in his hands and meant to keep it for the British Empire. For a sea power like England, with far-flung colonial possessions, wireless had a potential value beyond calculation.

A company called Marconi's Wireless Telegraph Co. Ltd. was organized in 1897, and one of its first activities was a ship-reporting service for Lloyd's of London. Much favorable publicity was gained by the reporting of the Kingstown yacht races for the *Daily Express* of Dublin and a private link enabling Queen Victoria from her residence in the Isle of Wight to keep in touch with her son, Edward Prince of Wales, who was aboard the royal yacht moored in Cowes Bay recovering from a knee injury. Marconi came to America in 1899 to supervise reporting of the America's Cup races by wireless. He was already becoming famous, and when the *Aurania* docked in New York, he had to face dozens of reporters and a barrage of questions. He later recalled the occasion:

> I arrived in New York on 21 September and had to run the gauntlet as soon as I descended the gangway of numerous reporters and photographers who awaited me.
>
> The following day full and detailed reports of my arrival, my appearance etc., came out in dozens of newspapers together with more or less accurate accounts of what I had accomplished as regards wireless telegraphy until then. For some reason or other it seemed to come as a shock to the newspapers that I spoke English fluently, in fact "with quite a London accent" as one paper phrased it, and also that I appeared to be very young [he was 25] and did not in the slightest resemble the popular type associated with an inventor in those days in America, that is to say a rather wild haired and eccentricly customed person.

During this American visit, Marconi received a letter from a young man named Lee De Forest seeking employment. No action was taken on the application. Marconi could have had no way of knowing that he was losing the services of one of

America's future inventors, a man as gifted as Marconi himself. De Forest went on to invent the three-element audion, or vacuum tube, a device that marked a turning point in wireless, or radio, history. De Forest was also to start his own company and become one of the chief competitors of the Marconi company. As uses of wireless multiplied, a serious problem arose that had not been a factor in the early applications. The apparatus could not differentiate between two different signals reaching the receiver.

This was the principle of "tuning" a subject that was to be intensively investigated, and also the source of claims and counterclaims and endless squabbling among rival inventors. The Marconi company engaged in exhaustive research on the tuning problem, and by 1900 the famous "7777" patent was issued. It gave Marconi the exclusive right to use a tuning system that enabled nearby wireless stations to work sumultaneously.

Early activities of the Marconi company were not always in the public interest. Marconi-equipped ships would not communicate with ships or shore stations equipped by rival companies. This prevented wireless from being effective in emergency situations and required corrective legislation to end the practice. The Marconi equipment aboard the *Titanic* functioned flawlessly when she had to call for help after hitting an iceberg. The delay in receiving aid was not due to failure of the wireless equipment but to operators on nearby ships not being on duty in radio rooms. As a result of the *Titanic* tragedy, comprehensive changes were made in radio laws requiring a 24-hour watch on the marine distress frequency. This applied to ships carrying more than 50 persons. Smaller vessels usually had an "auto alarm" receiver that could detect distress calls when the operator was not on duty.

In the public mind, Marconi is probably best remembered for his historic achievement in transmitting the letter *S* across the Atlantic on December 12, 1901. Although widely acclaimed, Marconi was to experience a taste of the criticism that had been endured by Cyrus Field 43 years earlier when the Atlantic cable had been pronounced a hoax by the unknowing. There were those who said that Marconi could not have possibly bridged the Atlantic, that the *S* he claimed to hear might have been merely atmospheric noise in the headphone. Marconi was much pleased to have such distinguished electrical scientists as Thomas Edison and Elihu Thompson affirm their belief in his accomplishment.

The transmission of the letter *S* across the Atlantic merely proved that such a thing was theoretically possible, and it was not until 1907 that a fairly reliable commercial wireless service was operational. At the turn of the century, wireless was becoming an indispensible communication tool for ships at sea, and to some extent for point-to-point communication on land. The two limiting conditions were the transmitting equipment and the use of the low-frequency or long-wave portion of the radio spectrum. Prior to 1909, the high-voltage spark gap was the only known way to generate Hertzian waves. The spark gap was relatively inefficient and required extremely high power for long-distance transmission. The state of the art at the time held that only the longwave, low-frequency portion of the known radio spectrum was useful for communication.

In the years prior to World War I, improvements in transmitters were forthcoming in the Poulsen arc and the Alexanderson alternator. The arc transmitter was the result of research involving the ordinary carbon arc, then widely used as a source of illumination. It was discovered that besides giving a brilliant light the arc was also generating radio waves. For radio-transmitting purposes, the arc was operated in a closed chamber and subjected to a strong magnetic field. The arc design was adaptable to transmitters of all powers, ranging from one to five kilowatts for shipboard use up to giant units of several hundred kilowatts for shore stations.

The ultimate in high-power arc transmitters was reached in the two 1,000-kw stations built for the U.S. Navy at Bordeaux, France, during World War I. The Federal Telegraph Co., builder of the 1,000-kw units, was building a similar unit to be installed in China. In 1921, the Chinese contract was canceled, leaving Federal with the giant 65-ton magnet castings in storage. A few years later, Dr. Ernest O. Lawrence of the University of California started his historic work with cyclotrons, which like the arc transmitter required a strong magnetic field. The old arc castings made for China were donated by Federal, which also assisted with the winding of field coils. The result was one of the first successful cyclotrons used in atom-smashing experiments.

With Federal Telegraph controlling the patents to the highly successful arc system of transmission, competing companies developed the high-frequency alternator as a transmitter. Radio waves consist of alternating current, the same used in a home electrical system. The only difference is that instead of alternations of 60 per second, the radio alternations are much higher in frequency, 10,000 or more per second. Basically simple, an alternator transmitter consisted of a generator hooked to a radiating antenna. A practical transmitter, however, was an incredibly difficult problem in mechanical design and very expensive.

Dr. E. F. W. Alexanderson, of the General Electric Co., succeeded in designing a practical alternator, and the units he built gave satisfactory service for many years. The 200-kw transmitter at Kahuku, Hawaii, occupied a large transmitter house that was filled with the main machine and the required auxiliary equipment. The alternator was driven by a 500-HP motor and produced a radio wave of 17.6-kc. The antenna system consisted of 38 wires 5,000 feet long suspended on towers 300 feet high. The Kahuku station was part of the transpacific system operated by RCA in competition with Clarence Mackay's Commercial Pacific cable. The improved arc and alternator transmitters were much more reliable than the spark transmitters they replaced, but the limitations of the low-frequency channels remained a factor for several years.

High power and extremely large antenna systems were required to cover long distances. At Rocky Point on Long Island, New York, RCA had steel towers hundreds of feet high supporting their long-wave transmitting antennas. There was also a receiving antenna for reception from Europe at Riverhead, Long Island, that stretched out six miles over the scrub pine landscape. Some of these facilities were still in operation during World War II and offered a useful backup when signals on the normal shortwave channels were blocked out by magnetic disturbances.

Transmitting equipment continued to improve, and after World War I, vacuum-tube oscillators took over as the generators of radio-frequency energy. In the early 1920s, increasing attention was being directed to the shortwave or high-frequency portion of the radio spectrum. With amateur radio operators pointing the way, the Marconi company started intensive research in shortwave propagation. The result was the "beam system" linking the far-flung countries of the British Empire. Using modest power and highly directive antennas, it could communicate with any point on the globe. Marconi was to comment wryly that after recommending the expenditure of huge sums on long-wave stations, he had to reverse course and call for construction of the beam system.

In America, RCA and Mackay Radio started to establish international networks using stations patterned after the Marconi beam system. As early as 1902, Oliver Heaviside (1850–1925) had postulated the existence of a layer of ionized conducting gas encircling the earth that would act as a reflector of radio signals. The Heaviside layer, as it came to be called, was recognized as the reason for the phenomenal performance of shortwave radio. Waves were reflected off the layer and bounced back to earth hundreds or thousands of miles away. Long waves, on the other hand, tended to follow the curvature of the earth and were only occasionally subject to reflection.

All sorts of interesting facts came to light as research into radio continued. Engineers had learned how to design antenna systems with extremely sharp directional characteristics, like a searchlight beam. It had been assumed that radio waves arrived at a distant receiver via the great-circle course. Field investigations at receiving points proved that this was not necessarily true, and it was found that the incoming waves were considerably off the true great-circle bearing to the transmitting station. Extremely sharp beams at the transmitter turned out to be self-defeating and had to be modified to meet field conditions.

De Forest's invention of the audion, or vacuum tube, in 1906 not only paved the way for the improved transmitting equipment but resulted in highly efficient receiving equipment. When he invented the audion, De Forest did not seem to recognize the true potential of his discovery. In desperate need of cash, he sold license rights to the telephone company for a mere $50,000. For the telephone company, this represented one of the great bargains of all time because without the audion as a repeater amplifier, long-distance telephony would have been impossible.

By the early 1900s, wireless, or radio as it was now called, was the established medium for communication with ships at sea and to an extent competed with ocean cables for telegraph traffic. There was not much thought that radio could compete with the established land wire telegraph system. Outside of the United States, all communication was under strict government control, and competition with the land wire system would not have been permitted in any case. In America, where all the communications systems were privately owned, the government could not object to competitive efforts. In 1909, American engineers went to Denmark and obtained patent rights to the Poulsen arc transmitter. This was the beginning of the Federal Telegraph Co. The arc transmitters were much more efficient than the original spark-gap equipment and enabled reliable operation over greater ranges, even though the limitations of the long-wave mode still applied.

Possession of the arc patent gave Federal Telegraph a strong advantage over competitors who were still using spark-gap transmitters. The success of the arc system caused Federal to consider a system of domestic radiotelegraph stations that would compete with the telegraph system. By 1912, stations were in operation at Portland, Seattle, San Francisco, Los Angeles, Fort Worth, El Paso, Kansas City, Chicago, Phoenix, and San Diego. These stations were quite modern in design. Automatic keying apparatus enabled Morse code transmission at up to 80 wpm.

In 1907, Valdemar Poulsen of Copenhagen had invented, in addition to his famous arc transmitter, a surprisingly modern magnetic recorder, actually the forerunner of magnetic recording as we know it today. Poulsen's recorder would function with steel disks or steel wire and had high-fidelity reproduction of the recorded material. The steel wire version was almost the same as the wire recorders introduced to the American consumer market after World War II. The Poulsen "telegraphone" was adapted to the arc reception system. It permitted signals to be recorded at high speed, then slowed to a speed that could be copied by the operator. By the time of World War I, service to inland points had been discontinued due to unreliable daylight operation, particularly during periods of heavy summer static.

With relatively moderate distances and more uniform weather, the Pacific coast net proved much more reliable and continued in operation. The West Coast stations were given a complete overhaul after the war and remained in successful operation until World War II. Federal Telegraph communications services became a part of the Mackay Radio and Telegraph Co. in 1927, and the latter continued the domestic rate structure of "15 words for the price of 10" started by Federal in 1911.

The success of shortwave operations soon attracted the attention of promoters who saw the possibilities of relatively low-cost radio circuits competing with the land telegraph for the lucrative traffic between large cities. Government regulators discouraged many of the early proposals for domestic radio networks, knowing that

Switchboard at a Mackay Radio station circa 1933. Telegraph instruments were for communication with the main operating room. Candlestick telephone was used on the long distance lines of the Postal Telegraph Co. (photo by Lewis Coe).

the promoters were interested only in skimming off the more profitable intercity traffic. This was considered unfair to the established telegraph companies, who were providing service to the smallest hamlet. The first exception came in 1928 when the Universal Wireless Telegraph Co. was licensed to operate a domestic radiotelegraph network. Universal actually had a few stations operating in the Midwest before it went bankrupt due to inadequate financial backing.

It was not until 1933 that Mackay Radio and RCA Communications established successful domestic radio systems that competed with the domestic wire companies for traffic. Both companies used methods and equipment that followed closely the techniques used in the international service. Transmitting and receiving sites were located remotely from the city operating centers. A high degree of reliability was obtained, most failures being due to problems with the wire remote-control lines rather than the radio part of the circuit.

Messages were sent in International Morse code, using punched tape for sending and siphon recorders for receiving on paper tape that was decoded by the operators. In a sense, this was a reversion to the original Morse recording system, except that speeds of up to 200 wpm were possible. At top speed, the tape was usually split between two or more operators for decoding so that there was no delay in transcribing the messages. Customers of the radiotelegraph service were business firms having a large volume of intercity telegraph traffic. They were usually connected by direct wire to the radio operating centers and thus obtained a much faster delivery time between transcontinental points. Mackay Radio used the facilities of Postal Telegraph for local pickup and delivery of messages, and RCA had a similar arrangement with Western Union. Radiotelegraph service was available in New York, Chicago, New Orleans, Portland, Seattle, San Francisco, Los Angeles, and Washington, D.C. Other destination points were under consideration when World War II brought an end to domestic radio operations in 1942.

The domestic radio circuits were profitable from the start. They filled a need of the business community for ever faster communication. The circuits continued for some time after Pearl Harbor, but wartime censorship was being applied to all forms of communication, and the domestic circuits were shut down by government order in June 1942. The U.S. Signal Corps made some use of the facilities, but most of the stations were dismantled and the equipment utilized in some part of the war effort. The skilled personnel of the stations were for the most part transferred to the international services where there was a critical manpower shortage.

The domestic service never resumed after the war. The merger of Postal Telegraph and Western Union in 1943 had eliminated the possibility of competition in the domestic telegraph field, and newer methods of communication were starting to replace the traditional telegraph service. Ironically, radio, at first only a competitor of the land wire telegraph, is now almost the sole means of communication, by means of microwaves and space satellites.

14. Changes

To every thing there is a season, and a time to every purpose under the heaven (Ecclesiastes 3:1).

Heralding the gradual disappearance of the Morse telegraph was the appearance of tape printer machines in the early 1930s, which printed the message on a narrow paper tape. The tape preglued, was pasted on a telegraph blank for delivery to the addressee. The application of these machines in some smaller cities was at first limited due to the problem of synchronization. Sixty-cycle power-line frequencies were not yet precisely regulated, making it necessary to use tuning forks for adjusting printers to synchronous speed. At the Chicago Century of Progress exposition in 1933, both Western Union and Postal exhibited tape printers as the current state of the art.

The two telegraph companies, which even then were struggling to survive, encountered competition in the 1930s when AT&T and the Bell System introduced their teletype service. Frankly out to lure customers from the telegraph companies, the Bell System offered modern page printers installed in the customer's office, permitting direct communication with other teletype subscribers throughout the country. This proved an attractive proposition for larger companies, giving them the equivalent of a private telegraph line to points they needed to reach.

By the mid–1930s, AT&T had started operations with their microwave radio relay system. High-frequency radio beams were carried across country by relay towers spaced to give line-of-sight transmission. The limitation in circuit capacity imposed by the old open wire and cable toll lines was now removed. Microwave gave the Bell System hundreds of circuits over the main routes. The vastly improved telephone service made it easy for subscribers to pick up the phone and talk with someone directly rather than sending a telegram and waiting for a reply.

The Depression years took their toll of all businesses, and the telegraph companies were not excepted. The telegraph industry had grown and prospered on the premise of low-paid workers putting in long hours without overtime. Improved working conditions in other industries attracted young people who were no longer interested in telegraphy as a livelihood. By the end of World War II, it was becoming

151

Tape printers began to replace Morse operators in the 1930s. Tape was pasted onto a message blank for delivery to the addressee (photo courtesy Western Union).

obvious that the old system of delivering written telegrams by messenger was on the way out. Postal Telegraph was the first to go, selling out to Western Union in 1943. Western Union, meanwhile, tried every known technique to improve profitability.

The old wire lines, which were very costly to maintain, gave way to a modern microwave radio relay system. Aside from maintenance costs, many wire lines were abandoned because the railroads they paralleled went out of business. Western Union's "Telex" service was quite successful and countered the Bell System "TWX" competition. In 1970, Western Union acquired TWX from AT&T and amalgamated it with Telex. Aside from private teleprinter networks, Telex is the most generally available telegraph service today, with many listings in metropolitan phone books. By 1950, Western Union had 15 high-speed switching centers in operation. At these locations, incoming messages could be run through a "reperforator" to create a punched tape. The tape could then be routed by mechanical means to reach an outgoing wire for transmission to the desired destination. This was an attempt to improve the efficiency of the large relay offices where clerks on roller skates once carried messages from one wire to another. The "Westar" satellite system was placed in operation starting in 1974. Nine earth stations in the United

States gave Western Union enormous circuit capacity for every form of electronic communication, including television.

There was no way, however, to keep the hundreds of local Western Union offices open. A further complication was the closing of many railroads whose local employees had functioned as Western Union agents. A person wanting to send a telegram had to telephone it to Western Union, which in turn telephoned it to the addressee. People quickly realized that it was simpler and cheaper to call the addressee themselves. With rapidly mounting losses, Western Union had no choice but to call it quits in 1988–1989. Western Union Telegraph Co. was reorganized as Western Union Corp. to handle money transfers and related services that were still profitable. National Payments Network, a nationwide service offering electronic-based bill-payment services, was acquired in July 1989.

Starting in the 1930s, radio relay towers of AT&T Long Lines Div. gave the Bell System hundreds of circuits along major routes (photo by Lewis Coe).

In September 1988, Western Union sold its international private line service to Tele-Columbus AG, Baden, Switzerland, for $56 million. Early in 1989 the Westar satellite system was sold to GM Hughes Electronics Corp., a subsidiary of General Motors. Hughes Communications Industries was to operate the Westar satellites. In 1989–1990, AT&T acquired Western Union's business services group for $180 million. Included were Western Union's electronic mail, Telex, and packet-switched services.

From an early date Western Union management seemed to be aware of the company's role in history and took steps to preserve manuscripts and items of equipment. The Western Union Telegraph Museum was started in 1912 by H. W. Drake, an electrical engineer employed by the company. In the early 1930s, internal memorandums were sent out to Western Union divisional plant superintendents asking that old instruments be saved. Shortly thereafter, many old instruments

Clerks on roller skates once carried messages to the different wires in large relay offices (photo courtesy Western Union).

arrived from Western Union's many divisions around the country. In particular, many objects were sent from the engineering department laboratories. By 1936, over 500 objects had been collected. The museum was maintained by J. Schmid and 20 volunteers from the engineering division in their spare time.

In early 1969, Western Union officials decided to close the museum and use its space for offices. As an alternative to storage, Smithsonian curators suggested that certain material be transferred to the Smithsonian. Responding to the suggestion, J. E. Stebner, curator of the Western Union museum, donated many items to the Smithsonian, feeling that they would be permanently preserved and used in relating the story of communication.

In 1933, Western Union was represented by a comprehensive exhibit at the Century of Progress exposition in Chicago. Many instruments from the company's museum were included in the display. To detail the history of the telegraph fully, many original instruments were borrowed from the Smithsonian collection and replicated. These reproductions helped improve Western Union's collection. At the conclusion of the fair, the objects were returned to the renamed Western Union Engineering Museum.

In January 1971, Western Union officials proposed a transfer of the Western

Union museum to the National Museum of History and Technology (now the National Museum of American History) under an indefinite loan agreement, hoping to make the materials more readily available for exhibition purposes and use by historians. Later, in September 1971, the collection was received by the National Museum as a gift and was deposited in the Division of Electricity. The archival materials were transferred to the Archives Center in June 1986. The collection in the Archives Center consists mostly of manuscript materials from the Western Union museum. The material includes a series of fragmentary administrative records, a limited amount of correspondence, fairly useful reference materials on telegraphy, and a series of telegram examples from 1857 to 1948.

The collection is particularly strong in photographs. In addition to photos of Western Union facilities, pole yards, and employees, these are a wealth of images of telegraphic equipment and installations. The collection in the Archives Center is contained in 112 boxes occupying approximately 60 lineal feet of shelf space. The collection is classified in 11 series as follows:

1. General history of the telegraph, 1876–1963

2. History of the Western Union Telegraph Copany (WUTC), 1858–1956

3. WUTC administrative records, 1853–1956
   a. Annual reports of WUTC, 1869–1956
   b. Correspondence and forms, 1858–1956
   c. Postal merger inventory, 1943
   d. Pay (service) rolls, 1888–1948
   e. Ledgers and accounting, 1853–1903

4. Correspondence, 1848–1956

5. Notebooks, 1880–1942

6. Patents, 1840–1914
   a. Charles Buckingham patents
   b. Thomas Edison patents
   c. Elisha Gray patents
   d. Samuel F. B. Morse patents
   e. George Phelps patents
   f. Joseph Stearn patents
   g. John Skirrow patents
   h. Charles Wheatstone patents
   i. Miscellaneous patents
   j. Numbered patents
   k. Litigation

7. Scrapbooks, 1869–1956; news clippings, 1869–1956

8. Telegrams, 1857–1948

9. Western Union Telegraph Museum, 1869–1961
   a. Correspondence, 1860–1959
   b. Technical materials
   c. WUTC records
   d. Employee records
   e. Publications

10. Reference Materials, 1868–1964
    a. By Western Union, published, unpublished
    b. About Western Union, published, unpublished
    c. General telegraphy, published, unpublished

11. Photographs, 1858–1957
    a. Western Union buildings
    b. Pole yards and construction
    c. Western Union albums
    d. Equipment and offices
    e. Facsimiles
    f. People

The Western Union collection documents in photos, scrapbooks, notebooks, correspondence, records, and reference materials the evolution of the telegraph, the development of the Western Union Telegraph Company, and the beginning of the communications revolution. The collection is open to serious researchers, who should contact the Archives Center, National Museum of American History, for an appointment. The apparatus and equipment from the Western Union museum are now held in the Museum of American History's Division of Electricity and Modern Physics.

Until the mid–1950s, cast-off telegraph instruments were not considered to have any special value and were sometimes sold for scrap or carelessly dismantled by mindless tinkering. Only a few hobbyists showed any interest in them, and new ones were readily available from mail order catalogs. Finally, a few astute collectors realized that the era of the Morse telegraph was at end, making all telegraph artifacts eminently collectible.

Early collectors had a bonanza of material to choose from. When the Morse system was phased out of the large city offices, hundreds of items were available, not only those that had been in use but large stocks of spares. The city offices were usually disposed of by calling in a dealer who would bid on the whole lot, usually getting it all for scrap-metal value. These dealers for the most part were quite aware of the profit potential and held the items for retail sale to collectors. The prices realized were many times scrap value but still nominal when compared to current values. In rural areas, people who happened to be on the scene when the railroad station was torn down were often free to help themselves to anything they fancied. Many who acquired material in this way were not really collectors; they just had an intuitive sense that the things shouldn't be scrapped.

At the height of the Morse era, untold thousands of the basic keys, sounders, and relays were in use. The only communications artifact in greater numbers might have been the old hand-crank magneto-ringing telephones. Morse instruments were used by the two telegraph companies, the railroads, newspapers, stockbrokers, pipelines and the telephone company. For many years, the AT&T long lines department used Morse instruments for communication between test boards. In the days of open wire lines, voice circuits were too scarce to be tied up with company traffic. A Morse circuit could be derived from each telephone pair to serve as an order wire between stations. In the early days of network broadcasting, even the radio stations had Morse instruments so they could communicate with the AT&T men handling the program circuits.

The numbers of Morse instruments were such that for years they frequently turned up at flea markets, estate auctions, and surplus shops. By the 1970s, collector interest was starting to grow, and this was reflected in a gradual decrease in the number of instruments offered for sale and corresponding price increases. Nineteenth-century instruments were the first to disappear. Knowing collectors had gathered up most of them before the general appreciation of telegraph collectibles took place.

The exact age of instruments is difficult to determine. After 1900, many instruments were manufactured for years with little change in pattern. It is pretty safe to assume that instruments found today will be at least 50 years old since there was little reason to manufacture new instruments after 1940. Typically, the instruments can be even older, dating back to the early 1900s. Few instruments wore out in normal operation. Unless damaged by lightning or some accident, they were kept in service year after year.

A great many items showing up today have been damaged since being taken out of service. Careless handling and storage often result in bent or missing parts. Traditionally, the coils were covered with hard rubber tubing. These covers tended to get brittle with age and are often cracked or missing a section. The collector must look carefully at old instruments offered for sale; even a missing adjustment screw or binding post detracts from the value.

Since dealer stocks of used instruments have long been exhausted, the most likely sources for Morse equipment now are estate sales, garage sales, flea markets, and other collectors who dispose of duplicates. Fortunately for the beginning collector, Morse instruments still turn up often enough to enable starting a basic collection.

Top: "Box relay with key on base," a typical 19th century instrument, made by Western Electric and marked W.U. Tel. Co. (photo by Lewis Coe). *Bottom:* Western Electric sounder, about 1900, made from round brass tubing instead of the traditional brass castings (photo by Lewis Coe).

Collectors usually start with some of the basic instruments—the key, sounder, and relay.

The ordinary Morse hand key seems to be a favorite among collectors. Used by the thousands at one time, it is now one of the scarcer items, especially in nice condition. Sounders come in two basic types, mainline and local. Mainline sounders are fitted with extra adjustments and were used on the mainline without a relay. Local sounders are of simpler construction and were typically used in connection with a line relay. Mainline sounders are probably next to keys in collecting popularity. Nevertheless, relays are a nice collectible. The older ones have handsome brass parts mounted on a hardwood base with a cast-iron sub-base and have considerable cosmetic appeal. Instruments used in telegraph repeaters show up occasionally, but a complete repeater set consisting of at least four specialized relays rarely is found.

Telegraph manufacturers, numbering in the hundreds during the latter part of the nineteenth century, dwindled to less than a dozen companies that supplied the major users. The name most commonly found is J. H. Bunnell & Co. of New York. Founded by Jesse Bunnell, a famed Civil War telegrapher, the Bunnell Company became the dominant supplier and was known for the uniformly high quality of its products. Other manufacturers of high-quality instruments were the Western Electric Co., Foote Pierson Co., and the company shops of Western Union and Postal Telegraph. Signal Electric made many instruments, as did Manhattan Electrical Supply Company whose MESCO trademark is often seen.

The most collectible instruments are those made by the well-known companies for professional use by the railroads and commercial telegraph companies. Next in order of interest are the low-cost instruments typically sold by mail order houses and intended for student use on "backyard telegraph lines," especially specimens in like-new condition.

In 1904, the Vibroplex, or "bug," key was invented. It had a vibrating spring lever that made the dots automatically, saving the operator from much of the muscular fatigue that occurred with the ordinary hand key. The Vibroplex is still being made today for use in radiotelegraphy. Some of the older models are prized by collectors.

Perhaps one of the rarest collectibles is the glass-domed stock ticker formerly found in stockbrokers' offices. These are so highly prized now as decorators that most specimens are priced in the mid-four-figure range. Most instruments are probably of Western Union background. Due to the relatively smaller numbers, Postal Telegraph instruments have great appeal. The Postal Telegraph shop made many instruments, usually marked *Postal*, but some are unmarked. Postal, of course, used large numbers of instruments from the regular makers. Instruments are often marked with the name of a railroad or Western Union, which tends to add value.

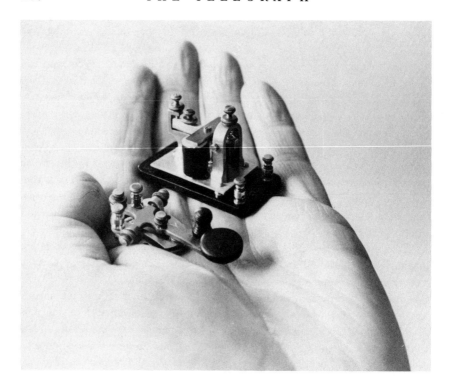

Any telegraph collector would like to get his hands on these miniature instruments once sold by J. H. Bunnell & Co. Now very rare, they were sometimes given as gifts to retiring operators (photo by Lewis Coe).

The odds are pretty much against it, but a lucky collector might even end up with a souvenir section of the original Atlantic cable. Tiffany's of New York bought a piece of surplus cable and cut it into short sections, neatly finished with a metal ferrule at each end. Some of them were sold with a certificate of authenticity signed by Cyrus Field himself. Just about everything connected with the Morse telegraph is now considered collectible. Metal office signs bring high prices at auctions. All sorts of paper items are in demand, including tariff books, messages blanks, advertising literature, and specimens of old telegrams. Some of the latter are quite interesting because they display beautiful Spencerian handwriting of the old-time telegraphers. Office furniture of all kinds, if marked with a telegraph company name, finds a ready market.

Coins and stamps associated with the telegraph are inexpensive and make a nice addition to a collection. The only coin generally available is the Canadian 1945 "Morse code nickel." This coin has dots and dashes spelling out the message "We win when we work willingly" around the rim of one side. Stamps include Thomas

Edison, 3 cents, 1947; S. F. B. Morse, 2 cents, 1940; Andrew Carnegie, 4 cents, 1960; Communications for Peace, 4 cents, 1960; and Centenary of the Telegraph, 3 cents, 1944.

Gone forever are the Morse operators with their "bug" keys and all-cap typewriters. Gone too are the trimly uniformed messengers, blue for Postal and olive drab for Western Union. The rough-and-tough linemen, with their Klein pliers and climbing irons, are all in the past now along with the cedar poles, the "black-jack" creosoted poles that were so miserable to climb, crossarms, insulators, and No. 6 iron and No. 9 copper wire. These things are all part of the past now, yet they kept the country going through 100 years of peace and war, and they deserve to be remembered. In their place are spotless rooms filled with pastel-colored electronic panels, giant dish antennas pointed skyward, and tall microwave towers.

When written messages are exchanged today, it is usually by means of fax machines operating over telephone circuits. Fax technology has improved to the point where machines are now affordable even to private individuals, and this may well be the "electronic mail" of the future.

Epilogue

It had been a pleasant summer day—warm but not oppressively so. In the little midwestern telegraph office where I worked, it was about time for the final ritual of the day: Comparing Numbers—Sent 2, Received 5. Not a very impressive total, but remember, this was a small office in the middle of the corn belt. Why was there a telegraph office there at all? Obviously not for profit. No, it was a strategic location for wire testing on the 100 miles of main line that ran along the Rock Island Railroad from Peoria, Illinois, to Rock Island.

Over the telegraph table, the big Seth Thomas clock ticked off the seconds until closing time. I'll always remember that clock. It had a golden oak case and a tick that was as crisp as the sound of breaking glass. Around the town square there was a stir of activity as preparations were made for Band Concert Night, the big summer social event of the week. The big clock ticked on, signaling the relentless passage of time and etching into my mind the memories of the glory days of the telegraph.

Appendixes

1860 Telegraph Act

AN ACT TO FACILITATE COMMUNICATION BETWEEN THE
ATLANTIC AND PACIFIC STATES BY ELECTRIC TELEGRAPH,
Passed by the Senate and House of Representatives
of the United States and Approved by the President,
June 16, 1860

Be it enacted by the Senate and House of Representatives of the United States of America in Congress assembled, That the Secretary of the Treasury, under the direction of the President of the United States, is hereby authorized and directed to advertise for sealed proposals, to be received for sixty days after the passage of this act, (and the fulfilment of which shall be guaranteed by responsible parties, as in the case of bids for mail contracts), for the use by the government of a line or lines of magnetic telegraph, to be constructed within two years from the thirty-first day of July, eighteen hundred and sixty, from some point or points on the west line of the State of Missouri, by any route or routes which the said contractors may select, (connecting at such point or points by telegraph with the cities of Washington, New Orleans, New York, Charleston, Philadelphia, Boston, and other cities in the Atlantic, Southern, and Western States, to the city of San Francisco, in the state of California, for a period of ten years, and shall award the contract to the lowest responsible bidder or bidders, provided such proffer does not require a larger amount per year from the United States than forty thousand dollars; and permission is hereby granted to the said parties to whom said contract may be awarded, or a majority of them, and their assigns, to use until the end of said term, such unoccupied public lands of the United States as may be necessary for the right of way and for the purpose of establishing stations for repairs along said line, not exceeding at any station one-quarter section of land, such stations not to exceed one in fifteen miles on an average of the whole distance, unless said lands shall be required by the government of the United States for railroad or other purposes, and provided that no right to preempt any of said lands under the laws of the United States shall inure to said company, their agents or servants, or to any other person

165

or persons whatsoever: *Provided*, That no such contract shall be made until the said line shall be in actual operation, and payments thereunder shall cease whenever the contractors fail to comply with their contract; that the government shall at all times be entitled to priority in the use of the line or lines, and shall have the privilege, when authorized by law, of connecting said line or lines, by telegraph with any military posts of the United States, and to use the same for government purposes: *And provided also*, That said line or lines, except such as may be constructed by the government to connect said line or lines with the military posts of the United States, shall be open to the use of all citizens of the United States during the term of said contract, on payment of the regular charges for transmission of dispatches: *And provided, also*, That such charges shall not exceed three dollars for a single dispatch of ten words, with the usual proportionate reductions upon dispatches of greater length, provided that nothing herein contained shall confer upon the said parties any exclusive right to construct a telegraph to the Pacific, or debar the government of the United States from granting from time to time, similar franchises and privileges to other parties.

Sec. 2. And be it further enacted, That the said contractors, or their assigns, shall have the right to construct and maintain, through any of the territories of the United States, a branch line, so as to connect their said line or lines with Oregon; and that they shall have the permanent right of way for said line or lines, under, or over, any unappropriated public lands and waters in the said territories, by any route or routes which the said contractors may select, with the free use during the said term of such lands as may be necessary for the purpose of establishing stations for repairs along said line or lines, not exceeding, at any station, one quarter section of land, such stations not to exceed one in fifteen miles on an average of the whole distance; but should any of said quarter-sections be deemed essential by the government, or any company acting under its authority, for railroad purposes, the said contractors shall relinquish the occupancy of so much as may be necessary for the railroad, receiving an equal amount of land for like use in its stead.

Sec. 3. And be it further enacted, That if, in any year during the continuance of said contract, the business done for the government, as hereinbefore mentioned, by such contractors or their assigns, shall, at the ordinary rate of charges for private messages, exceed the price contracted to be paid as aforesaid, the Secretary of the Treasury shall, upon said accounts being duly authenticated, certify the amount of such excess to Congress: *Provided*, That the use of the line be given, at any time, free of cost, to the Coast Survey, the Smithsonian Institution, and the National Observatory, for scientific purposes: *And provided further*, That messages received from any individual, company, or corporation, or from any telegraph lines connecting with this line at either of its termini, shall be impartially transmitted in the order of their reception, excepting that the dispatches of the government shall have priority: *And provided further*, That Congress shall at any time have the right to alter or amend this act.

Approved, June 16, 1860

Bill Passed by Congress Enabling Morse to Construct the First Telegraph Line, Between Washington and Baltimore

A Bill to Test the Practicality
of Establishing a System of Electro-   March 3, 1843
Magnetic Telegraphs by the United States.

Be it enacted by the Senate and House of Representatives of the United States in Congress assembled, That the sum of thirty thousand dollars be, and is hereby appropriated, out of any moneys in the treasury not otherwise appropriated, for testing the capacity and usefulness of the system of electro magnetic telegraphs invented by Samuel F. B. Morse, of New York, for the use of the Government of the United States, by constructing a line of said electro magnetic telegraphs, under the superintendence of Professor Samuel F. B. Morse, of such length and between such points as shall fully test its practicability and utility; and that the same shall be expended under the direction of the Postmaster General, upon the application of said Morse.

SEC. 2 *And be it further enacted*, That the Postmaster General be, and he is hereby, authorized to pay, out of the aforesaid thirty thousand dollars, to the said Samuel F. B. Morse, and the persons employed under him, such sums of money as he may deem to be a fair compensation for the services of the said Samuel F. B. Morse and the persons employed under him, in constructing and in superintending the construction of the said line of telegraphs authorized by this bill.

Morse Telegraph Club, Inc.

The Morse Telegraph Club is an international nonprofit organization devoted to maintaining the history and traditions of the telegraph. Its members include many old-time telegraph operators; however, the club welcomes membership from any interested person, and actual experience as a Morse telegrapher is not a requirement for membership. Members receive a quarterly publication, *Dots and Dashes*.

Full information concerning membership in the Morse Telegraph Club can be
obtained by writing to

> Mr. Robert A. Iwasyk
> Secretary/Treasurer
> Morse Telegraph Club, Inc.
> 12350 W. Offner Road
> Manhattan, IL 60442

or

> Mr. W. K. Dunbar
> President
> Morse Telegraph Club, Inc.
> 1101 Maplewood Dr.,
> Normal, IL 61761

Code Speed Records

After sound reading became standard, nineteenth-century Morse operators set
some fantastic speed records. Speeds around 55 words per minute were reached
in receiving contests. Long before the invention of the Vibroplex "bug" key,
operators reached speeds of around 50 words per minute sending with the ordinary
Morse hand key. These speeds were for short runs of five minutes or so in contest
exhibitions. On regular working Morse wires, speeds typically ranged from 30 to
40 words per minute.

Twentieth-century radio telegraphers, using the Continental Morse code, have
set some long-standing speed records. Ted R. McElroy, on July 2, 1939, in a contest at Asheville, North Carolina, received an incredible 75.2 words per minute.
Harry A. Turner, U. S. Signal Corps, at Camp Crowder, Missouri, November 9,
1942, transmitted 175 symbols per minute (35 wpm) using a hand key. Allowing
for the slower characteristics of the Continental code, Turner's record is believed
to be equal to the old 50-wpm speeds using American Morse code. Both of these
twentieth-century records were performed before witnesses and are currently listed
in the *Guinness Book of World Records*.

Chronology of the Telegraph

1832: Morse conceived the idea of the electric telegraph.

1838: First message sent using dots and dashes to represent letters of the alphabet
directly.

1844: American Morse code in final form. Washington-Baltimore line completed; message "What hath God wrought!" transmitted.

1848: Alfred Vail severs all connection with the telegraph. Associated Press formed.

1850: Sound reading replaces tape registers for receiving.

1851: Continental, or International, Morse code adopted. Telegraph first used in train dispatching.

1858: First Atlantic cable laid; fails after 24 days.

1860: Automatic repeaters enabled telegraph lines to operate over long distances.

1861: Transcontinental telegraph line completed.

1866: Successful completion of Atlantic cable.

1872: Stearns duplex permitted two messages to be sent simultaneously over a single wire.

1875: Edison quadruplex enabled four messages to be sent simultaneously over a single wire.

1880: Phillips code invented for press telegraphy.

1881: Postal Telegraph Company organized.

1904: Vibroplex automatic key patented.

1928: Postal Telegraph and Mackay System become part of IT&T.

1930: Closing of last Morse wire by Associated Press.

1943: Postal Telegraph merged into Western Union.

1989: Dissolution of Western Union Telegraph Co.

Glossary of Telegraph Terms

Black Jack	Telegraph pole coated with creosote.
Bonus operator	Skilled operator who can earn a bonus by handling more than the normal quota of messages.
Boomer	Itinerant operator who drifts from job to job.
Ground	A connection to the earth, either through stakes in the ground or underground water pipes.
Mainline sounder	Sounder with quickly variable adjustments for use directly in the mainline without a relay.
Paired and transposed	Two wires used together for telephone transmission. The two wires are reversed in position on the crossarm at intervals in a regular pattern to minimize interference from adjacent conductors.

Patch	A temporary connection, usually made with a flexible cord on a switchboard.
Relay	Sensitive receiving instrument connected in the main line to provide more positive operation of a sounder.
Relay office	Central telegraph office for receiving messages and retransmitting them to their destination.
Resonator	Thin wooden box holding a sounder. Directs the sound of the instrument to the operator's ear.
Sounder	The basic telegraph *receiving* instrument, producing a click when activated.
Way wire	"Party line" circuit connecting several smaller offices to the main relay office.
Way station	Intermediate office between main terminal points of a telegraph line.

Numbers Used as Abbreviations on Morse Telegraph Lines

1: Wait a minute.
2: Very important.
3: Give me the correct time.
4: Where shall I start?
5: Do you have anything for me?
6: I have business; are you ready?
8: Close your key; you are breaking.
9: Wire chief's call—wire tests.
13: Understand?
14: What is your weather?
18: What's the trouble?
19: Train order.
22: Busy on another wire.
25: Busy on another wire.
31: Train order.
55: Important
73: Best regards.
92: Deliver.

Secretary of War, General Orders, No. 1, Adjutant General's Office, January 20, 1879

In all instances in which United States telegraph lines are by order of the Secretary of War placed in charge of acting signal officers, who are thus made responsible for the construction, maintenance, and operation of the same, commanding officers and others will see that the especial duties of such officers are not interfered with, and will, upon application, render whatever proper assistance may be in their power. The lines form parts of one connected system of telegraph extending throughout the United States. They serve military, commercial, naval and other distant interests. The disabling of or interference with any part may cause complications not possible to be contemplated in the immediate vicinity. Official and military messages have precedence on all Government lines.

General Orders, No. 81, War Department, Washington, November 5, 1914

The officer in charge, Washington-Alaska Military Cable and Telegraph System, under the Chief Signal Officer of the Army, is charged with all that pertains to the technical handling and maintenance of the cable and telegraph lines and the receipt and disbursement of funds pertaining thereto, and will exercise supervision over the duties of the Signal Corps in connection with the construction, operation, and maintenance of all cables, telegraph lines, and radio installations of that system. The commanding general, Western Department, is charged with the discipline of all officers and enlisted men of the Army connected with the system, will render all practicable assistance in its maintenance and operation, and will cause such inspections to be made as will satisfy him that the discipline of the officers and men connected with the system is satisfactory and that their performance of duty is prompt and efficient.

Biographical Sketches: Men of the Telegraph

Oliver Heaviside (1850–1925)

Heaviside came from a family of talented artists and wood engravers, but he showed an early interest in complex mathematics. A diminutive man (5 foot

4 inches), he was by age 26 completely engrossed in mathematical investigations. He submitted many papers to scientific publications, and it was said that his work was so advanced that many of his peers had difficulty reading it. Heaviside worked to solve many of the problems in the rapidly advancing telegraph and telephone industry. His tools were pencils and paper; he did not even use a slide rule, working out equations by long-hand arithmetic.

He was the first to propose the principle of "loading," adding lumped values of inductance to improve transmission characteristcs of long telephone cables. A colleague, not understanding Heaviside's reasoning, complained that this would be like "putting bumps in the road to make the carriages run faster." In 1902, Heaviside had predicted the existence of a layer of ionized gas encircling the earth that would act as a reflector for radio waves. The "Heaviside layer" was to become one of the most important factors in shortwave radio propagation.

Heaviside complained that his contributions to telegraph and telephone science were never adequately recognized. This may have been partly his fault; his abrasive manner with others tended to repel those who might have sung his praises.

Jeptha H. Wade (1811–1890)

Wade became a telegraph operator after first working as a carpenter and daguerreotype artist. Advancing rapidly in the telegraph industry, he built the first telegraph line west of Buffalo, following the line of the Michigan Southern railroad. Later he built a series of lines in Ohio. A shrewd negotiator and businessman, Wade was the first president of the Pacific Telegraph Co. and was instrumental in perfecting arrangements for the first transcontinental line.

Wade was in California when Edward Creighton arrived there after his epochal survey trip across the western states. The two men returned to New York together via the isthmus of Panama. Shortly after, Creighton left for Omaha to begin construction of the transcontinental line. Like many early telegraph executives, Wade was proud of his early experiences as an operator and at his death was probably one of the oldest Morse operators in the country. His final years were spent in Cleveland, Ohio, where he was considered one of the wealthiest men in the city.

John Dean Caton (1812–1895)

A native of New York State, Caton moved to Illinois in 1833, locating in Chicago, then a town of 300 inhabitants. Having studied law, he obtained a license and opened an office as a lawyer. He eventually became chief justice of the Illinois Supreme Court, retiring from that position in 1864. His business interests led him into the new and rapidly developing telegraph industry. He was the chief shareholder and president of the Illinois and Mississippi Telegraph Co. At one time it was said that he controlled all the telegraph lines in the state of Illinois. The company was eventually sold to Western Union in 1867. The Caton Instrument Co. of Ottawa, Illinois, was known as the manufacturer of the compact pocket telegraph instruments used by telegraph scouts in the Civil War. The instrument company was later sold to the Western Electric Co. of Chicago. Judge Caton spent the last 30 years of his life in retirement traveling extensively. He was the author of several books, including *A Summer in Norway* (1875) and *The Antelope and Deer of America* (1877).

Joseph Henry (1797–1878)

A graduate of Albany (N.Y.) Academy, Henry worked as a schoolteacher, private tutor, and surveyor before being appointed a professor of mathematics at Albany Academy in 1826. Shortly after, he became interested in research involving electric currents and magnetism. His work became the foundation of the theory of electromagnetism as it is known today. He was honored by having the basic unit of inductance named the "henry." In 1832, he became a professor of natural philosophy at Princeton and continued his research, much of it anticipating modern developments in electrical science. Leaving Princeton in 1846, he became the first secretary and director of the Smithsonian Institution. Among his projects at the Smithsonian was the system for receiving weather reports by telegraph and using them as the basis for weather forecasts.

Morse's associate Leonard Gale had derived information from Henry's research that was vital to the electromagnetic telegraph. In the endless patent litigation that surrounded the telegraph, Henry felt that his work had been slighted. He once asserted publicly: "I am not aware that Mr. Morse ever made a single original discovery in electricity, magnetism, or electromagnetism, applicable to the invention of the telegraph." Unfortunately, what could have been a cordial relationship between Henry and Morse was an estrangement that continued until their deaths.

Hiram Sibley (1807–1888)

A self-educated and highly successful businessman, Sibley first became associated with the telegraph when he met Samuel F. B. Morse in Washington in 1844. In 1851, Sibley organized the New York and Mississippi Valley Printing Telegraph Company. In 1855–1856, as the lines expanded westward to the Missouri River, Sibley's associate Ezra Cornell christened the new company Western Union. With Sibley as president, Western Union started expanding and built the first transcontinental line in 1861. After the failure of the first Atlantic cable in 1858, Western Union embarked on a project to join America with the European continent via an overland telegraph line across Alaska and Siberia.

In 1864–1865, Sibley went to St. Petersburg to negotiate with the Russian government. Russia then owned Alaska and offered to sell the whole territory to Western Union. Sibley turned down the offer but made the facts known to the U.S. government, resulting in the 1867 purchase of Alaska by the United States. The trans–Siberian line was abandoned after the successful completion of an Atlantic cable in 1866. Associated with Cornell in the founding of Cornell University, Sibley established the Sibley College of Mechanical Engineering at Cornell. He also built Sibley Hall at the University of Rochester.

Ezra Cornell (1807–1874)

Cornell was a self-taught man with extraordinary ability in both business and mechanical design. He first became associated with Morse in 1842 when he designed a plow for automatically laying Morse's underground telegraph cable. When the underground cable proved impractical, it was Cornell who suggested stringing the wires on poles, setting the pattern of telegraph lines for years to come. After constructing the first Washington-Baltimore line in 1844, Cornell remained active in the telegraph industry, constructing many of the early lines between eastern cities. In 1855, he became associated with Hiram Sibley in organizing the national telegraph system, and it was called Western Union at his suggestion.

In his early days, Cornell was known as an indefatigable walker. With public transportation scarce or nonexistent, Cornell thought nothing of walking 35 or 40 miles to look after his business interests. A director of Western Union until his death, Cornell became a very wealthy man and devoted himself to philanthropy. He is remembered today as the founder and chief benefactor of Cornell University.

Amos Kendall (1789–1869)

Kendall's boyhood was spent on the family farm near Dunstable, Massachusetts. Graduating from Dartmouth College in 1811, Kendall entered the legal profession. He migrated to Kentucky, and remained there until 1829. Becoming involved in newspaper work, Kendall displayed talent as an editor and was inevitably led into the politics of the day. First a supporter of Henry Clay, he was later devoted to Andrew Jackson. Kendall's support was instrumental in helping Jackson carry Kentucky in the election of 1828. For the next 12 years, Kendall held various appointments in the Jackson administration. For eight years he was a member of the group of associates and advisers known as Jackson's "kitchen cabinet." Kendall's skill as a writer was employed extensively in the preparation of many of

Jackson's official papers. His final post in the Jackson administration was that of postmaster general.

Kendall's association with the telegraph began in 1845, when S. F. B. Morse employed him as business agent. His salary was based on a percentage of the profits. It was one of the more fortunate deals that Morse ever made in choosing his associates. Kendall was active in buying out smaller companies to form a larger, more efficient telegraph network. Kendall once said, "If it will pay 7 percent, we will build a line." Under Kendall's skillful management, the Morse system prospered, and by 1859 he and Morse had acquired comfortable fortunes. The final years of his life were devoted to religion and philanthropy. He was instrumental in founding Gallaudet College.

Dr. Charles T. Jackson (1805–1880)

Jackson, an 1829 graduate of Harvard Medical School, had a gifted mind and qualified as a professional in the fields of geology and chemistry. Best described as a brilliant but eccentric genius, Jackson had an unfortunate tendency to take credit for the achievements of others. His geological work in Maine, New Hampshire, and Rhode Island, although academically brilliant, was said to have little practical value. In 1846, he announced himself as the discoverer of surgical anesthesia, though his contributions in that field had been minor. Also in 1846, Jackson claimed to have discovered guncotton, which was announced by C. F. Schonbein in that year.

Jackson had devoted considerable study to electricity, and as a fellow passenger with Morse on the *Sully* in 1832, entered into long discussions about the possibility of an electric telegraph. Both men were under the delusion that they were the first to consider the idea. After Morse's demonstrations became well known and the telegraph appeared to be an invention of enormous potential, Jackson, true to form, claimed the honors of discovery for himself. In the later years of his life, due largely to his wild and irrational claims, Jackson was under such stress that his mind failed in 1873.

F. O. J. "Fog" Smith (1806–1877)

Smith's association with the telegraph began in 1838 when Morse signed him up as a business and political representative of the Morse telegraph patentees. It was a choice that Morse regretted for the rest of his life. In return for his services, Smith was assigned a one-quarter share of the telegraph patent, a share that he never failed to exploit. To accommodate Smith, the Vail brothers had to give up a quarter share and now had only a quarter share divided between them. Smith was actually of some service to Morse at a time when the company was struggling to get congressional approval for an experimental line. In those free and easy days, not much notice was taken of the fact that Smith, a member of Congress, was financially interested in a company that would greatly benefit if pending legislation was passed. In time, Smith became a very doubtful asset. He used his share of the patent rights to promote telegraph lines in competition with Morse and never failed to show up when there was some profit to be shared or to disappear when things were rough.

For all of his skulduggery, Smith was a learned man, a bibliophile who was said to have one of the largest libraries in his home state of Maine. Shoddy dealings seemed to follow Smith, even in death. The contractor who built his tomb cheated by partially filling the concrete forms with old newspapers. A few years later, when the shoddy concrete started to crumble, passersby could see old newspapers fluttering in the breeze on Smith's tomb.

Alfred Vail (1807–1859)

In 1825, Vail started work at his father's machine shop and displayed a strong talent for mechanical invention. He met Morse for the first time while attending New York University, having decided to study for the ministry. In 1837, he witnessed a demonstration of Morse's first crude model of the telegraph. Becoming fascinated with the telegraph, Vail could see many ways of improving the equipment. An agreement was made whereby Vail and the facilities of the Speedwell Iron Works, owned by Vail's father, would be made available for the development of the telegraph. Also, the Vails advanced certain sums of money since Morse was then penniless.

In September 1837, Vail and Morse signed a detailed contract in which Vail assigned his inventions to Morse. In return, he received a one-quarter interest in the U.S. rights and a half interest in any rights secured in France, England, Scotland, and Ireland. Only four years after the successful operation of the Washington-Baltimore line, Vail became disillusioned with the telegraph, feeling that his contribution to the invention had never been adequately recognized. On October 5, 1848, he wrote to his brother George: "The reason why I must give up remaining here is, that I am wearing myself out in the telegraph, for the interest of the patentees, without compensation, and the care and study is accumulating every day."

Henry O'Rielly (1806–1886)

A flamboyant builder of early telegraph lines, O'Rielly was a newspaper editor with no technical training of any kind. He was attracted to the telegraph merely because it was new and sensational and held a promise of big profits. In 1845, O'Rielly secured a contract with Amos Kendall and the Morse interests to extend telegraph lines to some rather vaguely defined points to the west. O'Rielly's lines were characterized by flimsy, hasty construction and were broken down most of the time. The contract with the Morse interests was soon voided, and O'Rielly embarked on a series of schemes of his own. The most ambitious of these was to extend lines south to New Orleans. This led to a head-to-head patent infringement battle with Morse. In litigation that eventually went all the way to the Supreme Court, O'Rielly lost and was declared to be openly infringing on the Morse patent.

Although O'Rielly is credited with building 8,000 miles of telegraph line, his main contribution seems to have been fostering dissension and legal battles in the telegraph industry. O'Rielly left the telegraph industry in 1853 and he worked at the New York Customhouse for 10 years before retiring.

Bibliography

Appleyard, Rollo. *Pioneers of Electrical Communication*. Books for Libraries, Freeport, NY, 1968.

Army Times. A History of the U.S. Signal Corps. Army Times Publishing Co., 1961.

Ault, Phil. *Wires West*. Dodd Mead, New York, 1974.

Carter, Samuel. *Cyrus Field—Man of Two Worlds*. G. P. Putnam's Sons, New York, 1968.

Cooper, Kent. *Kent Cooper and the Associated Press*. Random House, New York, 1959.

Davis, Burke. *To Appomattox: Nine April Days 1865*. Rinehart, New York, 1959.

Dodge, G. M. *The Telegraph Instructor*. 1921.

Harlow, Alvin F. *Old Wires and New Waves*. Appleton-Century, New York, 1936 (reprinted by Arno Press).

Hubert, Philip G., Jr. *Inventors—Men of Achievement*. Scribner, New York, 1893.

Jolly, W. P. *Marconi*. Stein and Day, New York, 1972.

Klein, Maury. *The Life and Legend of Jay Gould*. Johns Hopkins University Press, Baltimore, 1986.

Lewis, Oscar. *The Silver Kings*. Alfred A. Knopf, New York, 1947.

Mabee, F. Carleton. *Samuel F. B. Morse, The American Leonardo*. Octagon, New York, 1969 (reprint).

McCullough, David G. *The Johnstown Flood*. Simon & Schuster, New York, 1968.

Mitchell, Brig. Gen. Billy. *The Opening of Alaska*. Cook Inlet Historical Society, Anchorage, AK, 1982.

Nye, Col. W. S. *Carbine and Lance—Fort Sill*. University of Oklahoma Press, 1974.

O'Connor, Richard. *The Scandalous Mr. Bennett*. Doubleday, New York, 1962.

Porter, Gen. Horace. *Campaigning with Grant*. Bonanza, New York, 1961 (reprint).

Reid, James D. *The Telegraph in America, Its Founders, Promoters, and Noted Men*. New York, 1879 (has been reprinted).

Restak, Richard M., M.D. *The Brain*. Bantam, New York, 1984.

Sobel, Robert. *I.T.T.: The Management of Opportunity*. Truman Talley, 1982.

Thompson, R. L. *Wiring a Continent, History of the Telegraph Industry in the USA 1832–1866*. Princeton, 1947.

Vail, Alfred. *Eyewitness to Early American Telegraphy*. Arno, New York, 1974 (reprint).

Webb, Melody. *The Last Frontier*. University of New Mexico Press, 1985.

Index

DOMINANCE AND AFFECTION

DOMINANCE
&AFFECTION

THE MAKING OF PETS

YI-FU TUAN

YALE UNIVERSITY PRESS
NEW HAVEN AND LONDON

Designed by Sally Harris
and set in Goudy Old Style type.
Printed in the United States of America by
Vail-Ballou Press, Binghamton, New York.

Library of Congress Cataloging in Publication Data

Tuan, Yi-Fu, 1930-
Dominance and affection.

Includes bibliographical references and index.
1.   Dominance (Psychology)   2.   Love.   3.   Kindness.
4.   Interpersonal relations.   5.   Pets.   6.   Environmental psychology.   I.   Title.
BF632.5.T83   1984   152.4   84-3691
ISBN 0-300-03222-6

The paper in this book meets the guidelines
for permanence and durability of the Committee on
Production Guidelines for Book Longevity of the Council on Library Resources.

A portion of chapter four is reprinted, with permission,
from Yi-Fu Tuan, "Dance, Waters, Dance," *The Sciences*, September–October 1983.

10   9   8   7   6   5   4   3   2   1

That the most brutal of instincts should be the source of all civilization will not seem a paradox to anyone who understands what life is.
—George Santayana, *Dominations and Powers*

CONTENTS

ILLUSTRATIONS

PREFACE

This book is the most recent of a series of studies that I have undertaken in the last fifteen years to survey the broad themes of descriptive psychological geography. The first of these was called *Topophilia* (love of place), and it was followed by *Space and Place*, *Landscapes of Fear*, and *Segmented Worlds and Self*. In all of these works, my point of departure is a simple one, namely, that the quality of human experience in an environment (physical and human) is given by people's capacity—mediated through culture—to feel, think, and act.

How people feel, think, and act are the central questions for me, which explains why all my efforts in recent years have a strong psychological and philosophical bent. Thus, in the works cited, I have explored the nature of human attachment to place, the component of fear in attitudes to nature and landscape, and the development of subjective world views and self-consciousness in progressively segmented spaces. And now, in this current work, I wish to explore the psychology of *playful domination*—a special exercise of power that has the effect of making pets.

The word *environment* gives my efforts a geographical flavor and reflects my background in geography. *Environment* means "that which surrounds." It is a broad and loose concept that happens to suit my purpose. I use the term to include not only nature (climate, topography, plants and animals) and man-made spaces, but also other humans.

Finally, my approach is descriptive. Its aim is to point, collate, and clarify, to suggest possible ways of looking at the world anew, rather than to analyze, explain, and firmly conclude. The genre to which my writings belong is thus the essay. *Essay* means "the process of trying or testing," "an attempt," "a preliminary effort," and even "meditation" (Francis Bacon). An essayist is a writer of short compositions rather than exhaustive treatises; in the eighteenth century he is "one who makes trials or experiments." Scholarship may be viewed as proceeding in two stages, each of which calls for a special talent. First is the essay, wherein facts and ideas are imaginatively but also responsibly laid out and explored; then, if necessary, comes the further focusing on a particular problem and its detailed analysis. I believe that the social scientific understanding of human reality is flawed because too few scholars submit to the venture and discipline of the essay. Without this preliminary effort, research in compliance with a strict analytical methodology tends to become routine and sterile.

Perhaps the most pleasant part of writing a book is to acknowledge one's gratitude to those colleagues and students who have extended help and encouragement. I am happy to acknowledge here my indebtedness to Hans and Maj Aldskogius, Richard Berris, Thomas Clayton, Wayne Howell, Helga Leitner, Richard Leppert, Roger Miller, Berta Peretz, Philip Porter, Glenn Radde, Michael Steiner, and Sze-Fu Tuan. I also wish to express my gratitude to the University of Minnesota for providing me with a sabbatical leave and a generous Bush Award, and to the University of Wisconsin for the offer of a position, which was a boost to my morale as I work on a topic that, however intellectually exciting, is also in its nature rather distressful.

DOMINANCE AND AFFECTION

1 INTRODUCTION

Any attempt to account for human reality seems to call for an understanding of the nature of power. But if we use power as the key concept we build a picture of human reality that, for all its coherence and its ability to cover the facts, seems partial and distorted. Are people always trying, whether consciously or subconsciously, to dominate one another? Do they not also often cooperate? They do, although it can be argued that they cooperate only to dominate a third party—nature or human competitors. Is not love a social fact? It is. What role then does it play in human reality? To judge from the serious literature, fictional and scientific, love is *not* what "makes the world go around." In a pure state, it rarely appears even in serious fictional works except as a miracle or a momentary epiphany that has no lasting effect. In scientific literature, with the notable exception of the writings of Pitrim A. Sorokin,[1] *love* is indeed an inadmissible four-letter word. A treatise on social disorders may use such words as *passion*, *lust*, and *obsession*, but the states of mind they denote and the interpersonal relations they imply can readily be subsumed under the concept of power and dominance. Obviously, neither passion nor lust is love in the sense, for instance, that Saint Paul uses the word in 1 Corinthians. It may be that love as conceived by Saint Paul and by other great religious leaders is too rarified and too rare to make an impact sufficient to command the attention of the social scientist and the novelist of the social scene. There remains affection. It undeniably exists and is, moreover, common enough to matter in the day-to-day maintenance of the world. However, affection is not the opposite of dominance; rather it is dominance's anodyne—it is dominance with a human face. Dominance may be cruel and exploitative, with no hint of affection in it. What it produces is the victim. On the other hand, dominance may be combined with affection, and what it produces is the pet.

The effects of the exercise of power are everywhere and appear at different scales. In large and complex societies, perhaps the most striking effect is the transformation of nature. Forests are cleared and swamps drained to make way for human habitations. Trees are chopped down and rocks hewn to provide the raw materials of manufacture. Animals are harnessed to human service, consumed as food; their hide, fur, or feather are made into artifacts. This power to dominate nature was made possible by the invention of technical devices. One such device, before machines with moving wheels and levers were introduced, was the coordinated labor team—a machine made up of moving human parts. The existence of this human machine points to the fact that domination was exercised over people as well. People are killed or removed to make way for the habitations of the conquerors; people are enslaved to become a part of the functioning machinery of their master's household, commandeered to serve in a labor team or army and thus become a part of their master's armory of power.[2]

When objects stand in the way of the shakers and doers of the world, they are removed—unless they are perceived to have use and are so used. In either case, relationship to the object is impersonal. The lumberman bears no grudge against the forest, and the conqueror feels no hatred of a personal kind toward the conquered. Despite the horror of an act from the victim's viewpoint, the doer may not have been aware of his own cruelty because to him the victim has little or no interest and is barely a part of his visible landscape. A piece of timber that is made into a bench, an ox that is harnessed to a plow, a man that is turned into a tool—these are all acts of power directed toward practical ends. Power, however, can also be directed toward the ends of pleasure, adornment, and prestige. The objects that support *these* ends as distinct from those of a merely practical nature are regarded as valuable; they stand as visible elements in the landscape of the powerful; they are treated with favor, indulgently, as playthings and pets.

In many societies a distinction is drawn between a world of work and a world of play. Work presumes necessity, play freedom. We have to work to earn a living, whether as hunter-gatherer, shoe salesman, or public official. But beyond work there may be time, energy, and resource left over for play, which is something we do freely. Power and dominance pervade the world of work. People at work are people trying to master nature and life, and if they have sufficient power at their command they can significantly alter their part of the earth. The world of play, by contrast, has an air of innocence. Power is exercised in play, but playfully, with no lasting effect. Games may be vigorously pursued but they leave no enduring trace on the earth. In sophisticated societies, this distinction between work and play finds a parallel in the more specialized distinction between an economic realm and an aesthetic or cultural realm. The former suggests struggle—the need to control and dominate; the latter, by contrast, has an air of civilized calm, as remote from the burdens of necessity as from the passions of power.

There is no doubt that far more physical force is expended in the world of work than in the world of play, in the economic realm than in the aesthetic-cultural realm. However, if we think of power as a consciously felt possession and of the need to be master as a conscious need, then the distinction between work and play, economic activity and cultural activity is less clear. Consider a foreman at a construction site, with a couple of bulldozers at his command. Is he more a figure of power and dominance than an artist-gardener who, working with a few sharp tools and wires, "captures" wilderness and confines it to a glazed pot? Judging by the amount of earth moved, we would say that the foreman is, of course, a far greater figure of power. The foreman dominates nature, a judgment that we would not apply to the artist-gardener. And yet, from the standpoint of what an individual feels, it is not at all obvious that the foreman at the construction site feels more in control of his life and world than does the creator of miniature gardens of his. Indeed, we may argue that the artist-gardener is more a figure of power, more a person who wants to dominate his world. And the reason is that power, as a personal experience, must emanate from free will; and it is in the aesthetic-cultural realm rather than in the realm of practical affairs that the playful exercise of will is more likely to occur.

Compared with men of practical affairs, gardeners alter the earth only a little. But they alter it. Other aesthetic activities, such as writing poems and painting landscapes, do not have any obvious direct impact on nature and society, but the impulse to reduce—and thereby, order and control— is there. A poet looks at nature and captures its essence in a poem.

Something out there is taken into the human world, dressed in words and arranged in rhythmic order. Landscape painting is even more clearly a confident act of incorporation. Mountains and rivers—marvels of nature that far dwarf man—are caught by strokes of the brush on canvas or paper. Captive nature is then put in a frame, nailed to the wall of a house, there to be looked at and appreciated or to serve as a pleasing background (a touch of wildness) among the ordered events of social life. It cannot be mere coincidence that landscape painting emerged in Renaissance Europe, a time when Europeans took great pride in their cities and in their power over nature, and effloresced in China during the Sung dynasty (960–1279), a time known for its unprecedented expansion in commercial and economic life.

Power is subject to abuse. In the world of work this abuse is most strikingly manifest in the amount of damage done to nature and to people. Quantitative measures stand out: the thousands of acres of forest cut down to make way for roads, the thousands of humans enslaved to work in the silver or coal mines. In the world of play, the abuse of power is evident less in any quantitative measure of change as in the *character* of the change—in the ways that power has been used to distort plant, animal, and human nature for aesthetic ends, and in the ways that animals and humans—as pets and playthings—have been made to suffer indignities and humiliation rather than physical pain, curtailment of life, and death. And yet, there must have been pain in submitting to the excesses of training and disciplining; and as for the curtailment of life and death, we shall see in the following pages how great is the temptation for the powerful to reduce their pets (plants, animals, and humans) to simulacra of lifeless objects and mechanical toys—to the sort of frozen perfection that only the inanimate can attain.

On the uses and abuses of power in the economic and practical areas of life, a very extensive literature already exists. On such exercises of power in the aesthetic-cultural realm, little has been written; and we have noted that one reason is our tendency to dissociate power and domination from the world of pleasure, play, and art. This dissociation is easy to make because of the element of delight in aesthetic activities. How can we be said to abuse a plant when we take pleasure in it, even if part of the pleasure lies in twisting the stem into the shape of an antelope? Is it cruelty to breed a variety of goldfish with dysfunctional bulging eyes if such fish are well cared for and fetch a high price? Was it right for a lady of eighteenth-century England to keep a black boy as a pet? She thought so, for did she not dress the boy in finery and allow him special privileges? Of course, some of us are now inclined to disagree, arguing that the boy's dignity was compromised by his pet status and even by his mistress's acts of favor and indulgence. Affection mitigates domination, making it softer and more acceptable, but affection itself is possible only in relationships of inequality. It is the warm and superior feeling one has toward things that one can care for and patronize. The word *care* so exudes humaneness that we tend to forget its almost inevitable tainting by patronage and condescension in our imperfect world.

"Man's role in changing the face of the earth" is a popular theme in classrooms and scholarly treatises. It is concerned with power and domination; and *man* is the correct word because men, not women, have brought about nearly all the major changes for good and ill. Equally popular is the story of gardening, but literature on this subject appeals to quite a different class of readers. To them, gardening is an art form and has little to do with power play. In this book, I shall attempt to show that this is a mistaken view and that we fail to understand the nature of the pleasure garden unless we put power somewhere close to its center. The breeding and training of animal pets, the establishment of zoos, the story of the household servant and entertainer are other themes, each with its own specialized literature, each with its own clientele of readers, and all thought to be quite unrelated to the story of the garden. In this book, I shall show that this perception is incorrect. They are closely parallel themes, and none can be truly understood outside the context of the others. Moreover, all these themes can be put under the broad rubric of "man's role in changing the face of the earth." That which links them is power.

What has happened to the innocence of gardening, of keeping pets, and even of the feeling called affection? Are they all now to be tarred by the same brush of power? Are they all tainted by the urge to dominate? Yes, but power and domination are manifest in different ways: some are innocent, even benignant, others are savage, though perhaps most are both necessary and infrangible composites of good and evil. In order to appraise the operations of power in the aesthetic-cultural realm, we need to see them against the background of power in all its ferocity and pervasiveness in other realms as well. Against this broad background, we may conclude that the making and maintenance of pets is, after all, a relatively innocuous occupation. It often benefits the master, less often and more arguably the pet, and it is in any case inescapable.

2 POWER AND DOMINANCE

Power in itself is good. It is another word for vitality and effectiveness, states of being that all animals want. We admire power whether it is manifest in nature, in ourselves, or in our works. A thunderstorm is sublime and commands respect. The sight of water surging effortlessly out of a spring gives us pleasure, as does that of an athlete vaulting over a high beam with consummate grace. Happiness is to feel our sports car responding to our touch with alert and unstrained power on a winding mountain road. *Powerful* is a term of high commendation in the world of art. Thus we say of a symphony, a painting, or a poem that it emanates power, that it is strong. On the other hand, *feeble* and *weak* are the severest words of condemnation in the critical lexicon; any serious artist would much rather that his work be judged ugly than weak.

Yet *power* in Western society and particularly in our time has become a deeply suspect word. Mention it in social and political circles and we quickly envisage possibilities of abuse and corruption. Among artists the word arouses perhaps the least distrust. Despite the adage about poets being legislators to the world, they are more commonly viewed as figures of little power whose ability to change the world is limited to other people's passing moods and feelings. Like all makers, poets have to destroy in order to create, but what they destroy are merely pieces of paper, the loss of which is tolerable even if the completed poems should prove to be less than divine. In general, we take for granted that the finished artifact more than justifies the spoliation that precedes it. Every jug is superior to the clay from which it is made. The wonder of art derives

7

at least in part from the perceived disproportion between material that is used up and material that is created; between a marble block removed from the flank of a Tuscan hill and Michelangelo's *David*.

Humans have been reluctant to admit that the destructive act itself can give pleasure. It is not only that we *have* to break the egg to make an omelette; the breaking itself is pleasurable. Destruction is power—a dramatic way of being effectve. "To knock a thing down . . . is a deep delight to the blood," says George Santayana.[1] Parents will agree as they watch the first creative act of their infant, which is to knock down a pile of wood blocks. Infants are too ill-coordinated to put anything up, and it may be that they watch adults do so with envy; but they can always demonstrate their effectiveness by making a bowl of peas fly off the tray with a gleeful swipe of the arm.

Children, even when they are old enough to make things, retain a fondness for destruction. "Many children find knives irresistible," Colin Wilson notes. To them, "a surface of tight leather seems almost to ask to be cut with a razor edge." This destructive impulse is the same kind as that which leads youngsters to build "elaborate reservoirs of sand, fill them with water, and then poke a small hole in one of the walls for the pleasure of watching the water sweeping them away."[2] Adults are conditioned to repress the urge, and it is a rare individual who will confess it, as Wilhelm von Humboldt (1767–1835) has done: "The sight of a force which nothing can resist has always attracted me most powerfully—and I don't care if I myself or my best and dearest joys get drawn into its whirlpool. When I was a child—I remember it clearly—I saw a coach rolling through a crowded street, pedestrians scattering right and left, and the coach unconcerned, not diminishing its speed."[3]

"Who does not exult in fires, collapses, the ruin and death of friends?" John Updike asks.[4] Maybe many of us do, but it is an inadmissible feeling. War, however, sanctions violence. In a traditional war, not everyone is a victim. To those who destroy and to those who watch the destruction as bystanders, the theater of war can provide physical release and sensual-aesthetic delight. This conclusion is inescapable, says Glenn Gray, to "anyone who has watched men on the battlefield at work with artillery, or looked into the eyes of veteran killers fresh from slaughter, or studied the descriptions of bombardiers' feelings while smashing targets." As for sensual-aesthetic delight, "some scenes of battle, much like storms over the ocean or sunsets on the desert or the night sky seen through a telescope, are able to overawe the single individual and hold him in a spell."[5]

History is full of gory accounts of pride in destruction—the pride of power. An outstanding early example is Sennacherib's boast of the total annihilation of Babylon. (Sennacherib [705–681 B.C.] was the son of Sargon and king of Assyria.) "The city and its houses from its foundation to its top, I destroyed, I devastated, I burned with fire. The wall and the outer wall, temples and gods, temple towers of brick and earth, as many as they were, I razed and dumped them into the Arakhtu Canal. I flooded the city's site with water and made its destruction more complete than that by flood."[6] Destruction was a part of the process of creation—of the founding of a new city or civilization. This the Sumerians (but also the Assyrians and Romans) seem to have recognized. They felt the need to start with a clean field, with no vestige of defeated and vengeful spirits lingering over it. Moreover, the ancients—the Sumerians specifically—saw the establishment of civilization itself as involving not only order and lawful conduct but also evil (planned evil), falsehood, violence, and oppression. The Sumerian gods were essentially amoral, and the cities they had created partook of this amoral character at the core of their being.[7]

Life is power—a power that maintains itself and grows by incorporating others. Life is inconceivable without death and destruction. The mild M. Bergeret, a hero in Anatole France's novel Histoire contemporaine, says: "I would rather think that organic life is an illness peculiar to our unlovely planet. It would be intolerable to believe that throughout the infinite universe there was nothing but eating and being eaten."[8] Ernest Becker invites us to contemplate the living spectacle of all that we have organismically incorporated in the course of a lifetime. What would it be like? "The horizon of a gourmet, or even the average person, would be taken up with hundreds of chickens, flocks of lambs and sheep, a small herd of steers, sties full of pigs, and rivers of fish. The din alone would be deafening."[9]

Eating is a necessary and pleasurable activity that simultaneously takes pleasure in the object consumed. Eating, in other words, is an expression of love. Love is devouring. What we love we wish to incorporate, literally and figuratively. In a moment of exuberance, Chekhov exclaimed, "What a luxurious thing Nature is! I could just take her and eat her up . . . I feel I could eat everything: the steppe, the foreign countries, and a good novel." Robert Browning said that he had such a love for flowers and leaves that, every now and then in an impatience at not being able to possess them thoroughly, he wanted to "bite them to bits."[10] G. K. Chesterton confessed that in the Geological Museum certain rich crimson marbles, certain split stones of blue and green made him wish his teeth were stronger. W. N. P. Barbellion, reflecting on Chesterton's desire, concludes grimly: "There is no true love short of possession, and no true possession short of eating. Every lover is a beast of raven, every Romeo would be a cannibal if he dared."[11]

What is a magnificent civilization but one that has fed well on the resources of the earth? A distinguishing mark of civilization is extravagance—that voracious and seemingly insatiable appetite for the consumption and production of goods. Yet *extravagance* is not a word that comes most readily to mind when we contemplate society or civilization as a whole. That monumental pile of palaces and temples, theaters and parks, galleries and libraries, shops and emporiums, aqueducts and highways speaks of human achievement and is looked upon with pride. Why, in ancient Rome, did the bloody and expensive gladiatorial contests go on even when the Colosseum was half empty? What need was there for such entertainment? To go a step further, what need was there for the Colosseum itself? Few people dared to address these questions and pursue them to their logical ends because they would have cast doubt on the very grounds of civilization.

Extravagance in individual life-style does arouse, from time to time, comment and disapproval. Only a modicum of sensibility is required to frown upon the man who stuffs himself with food, grows obese, and lives as it were in his own ample cask of fat. A body cannot carry too many jewels without exciting ridicule. Tolerance for extravagance at the scale of a house is greater, perhaps because the house, though privately owned, is also a feature of the public landscape. Critical voices are, however, occasionally heard. Just look at the bathhouses of certain former slaves, wrote Seneca to a friend: "Look at their arrays of statues, their assemblies of columns that do not support a thing but are put up purely for ornament, just for the sake of spending money. Look at the cascades of water splashing noisily from one level to the next. We have actually come to such a pitch of choosiness that we object to walking on anything other than precious stones."[12]

Extravagance of the kind denounced by Seneca is a commonplace of all civilizations. In seventeenth-century England, the duke of Norfolk had ten seats, "including one in the very center of the city of Norwich, castles in four English counties and Norfolk House in London. One earl had nine seats, and one baron had eight. No family could possibly occupy so many houses at any one time."[13] Of course, these baronial mansions dominated the landscape and spoke eloquently of the power of their owners. How could the lords of the earth rule but by making their presence felt at all times? But this is not all. It seems to be in the nature of great power to go beyond practical politics and calculation. Power, if great, is free, extravagant, and whimsical. Why else would the fifth earl of Lonsdale give Lowther Castle 365 rooms? For that matter, why would one of the dukes of Bridgewater possess 365 pairs of shoes? Why is there a skating rink at Wentworth Woodhouse? Why did Lord Exeter need four large billiard rooms, and why were there twenty pianos at Woburn which nobody ever played?[14]

Human beings are themselves products of the earth that can be exploited and consumed in a variety of ways. When conquerors take over a country they have to decide what to do with the conquered. One extreme view sees the conquered simply as an unassimilable nuisance, like wild animals or tree stumps, to be wiped out. Another view, more sensible economically, sees the conquered as goods of varying value to be plundered. The wars of the ancient Romans reflected this latter view. "They made war," as Bertrand de Jouvenal puts it, "for its immediate gains of precious metals and slaves: the more treasure and the more ravaged victims that followed in the consul's train, the more applauded his triumph. The essential feature of the relationship between the capital and the provinces was the gathering of tribute. The Romans regarded the conquest of Macedonia as marking the date from which it had become possible to live entirely off the taxes paid by the conquered provinces."[15]

The nomads of central Asia, in an early phase of their conquest of their agricultural neighbors to the south, took the radical step of systematically slaughtering all the farmers and transforming their fields into pasture. A later solution, adopted under the nomads' leader Shih Lo in the fourth century A.D., called for the setting up of a military camp in the middle of China and then treating the whole country as a "hunting ground." Both strategies met with fierce resistance. The overrun Chinese could be neither eradicated nor plundered with ease. For the conquerors the one solution that had a chance of enduring success was to establish a government, based on the native model, empowered to collect taxes and draft labor in a systematic way. This solution treated the vanquished people as a resource to be widely used.[16]

Before the modern age, power meant primarily organized human power. Great cities and public projects were built with machines composed of human parts. Armies of people were sometimes employed. An inscription of the Han dynasty notes that the construction of a certain highway in A.D. 63 to 66 occupied 766,800 men. During the Sui dynasty, the Grand Canal (604–17) was built with the labor of one million men and women. Levies of this order severely disrupted farm life, causing widespread suffering even in a populous country. Deaths from sickness and accidents were commonplace. Clearly human lives counted for very little if they were those of peasants. From time to time, a cause of abuse was thought sufficiently flagrant to be recorded and thus enter history. Here is an example from the Northern Wei dynasty. The noblemen and high officials of the period considered it meritorious to build and endow Buddhist temples and houses. By A.D. 534, the city of Lo-yang had no fewer than 1,367 such establishments. One pious but ruthless official ordered the construction of 72 temples at great cost in human and animal lives. When a monk rebuked him, the official replied that posterity would see and be impressed by the buildings and would know nothing of the men and oxen that had perished.[17] From Europe, to take one case out of many, is this grim account of the wasting of workmen during the construction of Versailles. On October 12, 1678, the marquise de Sévigné wrote:

> The King wishes to go to Versailles on Saturday, but God, it seems, wills otherwise, because of the impossibility of getting the buildings in a fit state to receive him, and because of the great mortality afflicting the workmen, of whom every night wagons full of the dead are carried out as though from the Hôtel-Dieu. These melancholy processions are kept secret as far as possible, in order not to alarm other workmen.[18]

Contact with power often ends in death. What was once alive becomes inanimate matter. Thus trees turn into tables and chairs, animals into meat and leather. In war, humans become corpses. Short of death, trees turn into potted plants, animals into beasts of burden and pets. And humans? Confronted by power, they become "animals" and "things" or playthings. How is the human subject expected to behave in the presence of his lord? In the extreme case of despotism, he falls forward on all fours like an animal, strikes his head on the ground, and kisses the dust. In ancient Hawaii, political power was sufficiently terrifying to make the commoners crawl before their rulers. In Inca Peru, even the highest dignitary approached his sovereign like an animal, his back bent as though under a load of tribute. In pre-Conquest Mexico, prostration before royalty was a form of etiquette taught in the so-called colleges. Kowtow was practiced in China from the early years of the Chou dynasty, around 1000 B.C. The importance of prostration in the Near East can be amply documented, says Karl Wittfogel. "The records of Pharaonic Egypt describe the whole country as 'prone upon the belly' before a representative of the king. Faithful subordinates are shown crawling, and kissing (or sniffing) the monarch's scent."[19]

The monarch or despot sits. Sitting, Elias Canetti suggests, denotes the power and dignity of duration. We expect someone who sits to remain sitting. The downward pressure of his weight confirms his authority. The despot sits on a chair, "which derives from the throne, and the throne presupposes subject animals and human beings, whose function it is to carry the weight of the ruler. The four legs of the chair represented the legs of an animal."[20] In addition, guards stand stiffly by the ruler's throne. The stiffness suggests that guards are things—implements to be used. And before the ruler is the prostrate subject, a human person reduced to an animal in the presence of his lord.

These ancient expressions of power and servitude now seem to us grotesque. Yet their vestiges still linger in our world. "Boot licking," as a figure of speech, is still in use. Malcolm Muggeridge reminisces: "Whenever I think of the inexhaustibly interesting subject—the incidence and exercise of power—there is one incident which always comes back into mind. It was long ago, in the early thirties. I was having a drink in a café in Vienna. My companion was a free-lance journalist of sorts, and a propos of nothing and quite casually and ruminatively, he remarked, 'I sometimes wonder if I'm licking the right boots.' "[21] And Desmond Morris notes that in a modern Western metropolis, it is still possible for a man to sit on a throne and have his boots licked—that is, sit on a high chair and have his boots polished by a kneeling figure.[22]

Too often, the mass of humanity has been reduced to raw nature, and nature exists to be consumed by civilization for its glory. This glory, in a hierarchical society, is available only to the elect and consists in large part of luxury goods. What are luxury goods? Jean-Paul Sartre argues that luxury in its pure state exists only in aristocratic and agricultural societies. Luxury goods are essentially rare, *natural* objects. True, the products of nature have to be discovered, transported, and refined by people, and in the process they become artifacts. But Sartre contends that human labor itself, upon coming into contact with nature, is reduced instantaneously to a natural activity. "In the eyes of the rajahs, the pearlfisher did not differ much from the pig that noses out truffles; the labor of the lacemaker never made of lace a human product; on the contrary, lace made a laceworm of the lacemaker."

The aristocrat, says Sartre, "eats Nature, and the product he consumes should smell a little of entrails or urine." To a man of taste, the authentic luxury good should have, beneath its ostentatious appearance, "the carnal, clinging, humble, organic milky taste of the creature." A machine-made lace can never be a satisfactory substitute for the real article because it cannot replace the lacemaker's "long patience, the humble taste, the eyes that are ruined by the work."[23] Even today, when there is great respect for the kind of perfection that only high technology can achieve, the true luxury good must still carry a hint of human sweat and the organic. Manufacturers of Waterford crystal, for example, advertise their product as "Fire born of fire. Blown by mouth and cut wholly by hand. With heart." Perhaps more familiar is the boast of Rolls-Royce: "In the rear seats, you can snap on personal reading lights, listen to the sound of stereo, or simply lean back, close your eyes and let the warmth of deep Wilton carpets, the beauty of hand-rubbed walnut veneers and the scent of rich Connolly hides remind you that you are in a private world. It takes at least four months to build such a motor car, because it is built by hand and built to last." Volvo, the Swedish automobile manufacturer, also emphasizes human labor in its advertisements. "Each body panel is carefully fitted by hand; each seam is hand-burnished. . . . [And] the wood paneling is hand-polished to an elegant gloss." "Hand-burnished" and "hand-polished" suggest that it is the human oil and sweat, rather than wax or some chemical product, that give the panel its elegant sheen.

Sartre's pearlfisher dives into the sea and comes up with a pearl which is then taken away from him because it is not his to dispose of. His role is rather like that of the cormorant, trained by the Chinese since the twelfth century to dive into the river for fish; a ring around the bird's neck prevents it from swallowing its catch. Humans are not only hands and beasts of burden, they are also quaint animals that the people in power may find amusing to play with. For example, early in this century, pedestrians passing over Hungerford Bridge used to throw coins into the fetid mud banks of the Thames River and watch the children of the poor dive into the mud to retrieve them. The children were known as mud-larks. A more civilized form of this game is for passengers on luxury liners to throw money into the clear and shallow waters near tropical islands and watch the natives, nearly naked and lithe like seals or porpoises, plunge in for their paltry reward.

When people are treated like amusing performing animals, the line between condescension and sadistic taunt is thin. Healthy and young islanders who dive for coins may not feel humiliated; they may think of what they do as the day's work or even as fun. The passengers, on their part, may believe that they are simply combining charity with a bit of innocent pleasure. However, the structure of power that makes this game possible can lead to other games significantly less innocent. Consider the following story as told by eleven-year-old Theodore Roosevelt. During one of those grand tours of Europe that wealthy Americans were accustomed to undertake after the Civil War, the Roosevelt family came upon a group of Italian beggars. Young Teddy happily reported: "We tossed the cakes to them and fed them like chicken with small pieces of cake and like chickens they ate it. Mr. Stevens [a traveling companion] kept guard with a whip with which he pretended to whip a small boy. We made them open their mouth and tossed cake into it. We made the crowds give us three cheers for U.S.A. before we gave them cakes."[24]

Power is able to reduce humans to animate nature, and as such they can be exploited for some economic purpose or treated condescendingly as pets. From the viewpoint of power, however, animate nature remains imperfect. An animate being is imperfect because it moves and breathes, it has a biological rhythm to which it must defer, and it has a will of its own which can be made to cower but never can be totally defeated. For power to enjoy a supreme sense of control, humans must be reduced to something less than animate, to inanimate nature—to mechanical things. In varying degrees, civilizations have tried to provide their elites with this order of power in the realms of work, war, and pleasure.

How humans become machines in the realm of work is a dark tale that is often told. To do heavy work such as lifting stone blocks, people must

be organized into teams; their arms and legs must move in unison as
though they are the levers and beams of a machine. To do complex work,
especially if it is integrated with activities elsewhere, time must be rigidly
structured so as to overcome those impulses and rhythms of biological life
that do not synchronize with the needs of production. In Western Europe
during the fourteenth century manufacturers (taking their cue from
monasteries) began to use the bell to regulate the work schedules of their
workers. Protests and uprisings against the *Werkglocke* were frequent,
especially after bells pulled by hand were replaced by mechanical clocks
that attempted to break the day down into twenty-four equal and exact
parts. Jacques le Goff thinks "it might be possible to determine whether
the location of the crisis-ridden textile industry coincided more or less
with the region where mechanical clocks were to be found."[25] The
regulation of human activities by mechanical time, both that of the clock
and that of the manufacturing machine, became more and more a feature
of Western life and culminated in the factory line that ignored the
physiologic needs of its human "cogs." But human workers lack the
perfection of cogs; they have to go to the bathroom. The owners and
supervisors of a factory, by their attitude and behavior, can make the
workers feel that they are the weak and undependable parts of an otherwise beautifully running engine.[26]

In the military sphere, soldiers are instruments of war, part of a military
machine, cannon fodder. In this sphere, the reduction of the human to the
inanimate and mechanical is so extreme that the above characterizations
of the soldier should not be taken as mere figures of speech. Traditional
procedures in the training of soldiers resemble those used in the training
of performing animals, but the ideal of precision goes far beyond what
animals can achieve to that attainable only by machines. Marchers in a
parade must be perfectly in step; the drill line is ideally ruler-straight. An
incident reported by Piotr Kropotkin (1842-1921) perhaps best illustrates this ideal of inanimate perfection. In the reign of Nicholas I,
Kropotkin observed, an admired military man was a person "whose
soldiers were trained to perform almost superhuman tricks with their legs
and rifles; and who could show on parade a row of soldiers as perfectly
aligned and as motionless as a row of toy-soldiers. 'Very good,' the Grand
Duke Mikhael said once of a regiment, after having kept it for one hour
presenting arms,—'only, they *breathe!*' "[27]

In the sphere of pleasure, potentates have demonstrated their predilection for extravagance not only in their richly adorned palaces and gardens and in their numerous servants (some of whom were full-time entertainers), but also—more rarely and hence less well known—in a fondness for mechanical toys that simulate animate nature. Nothwithstanding all the goods and services offered by living organisms, from the standpoint of potentates animate nature still lacks the predictability and the undemanding presence of inanimate matter. In the presence of servants and slaves, and even of pet animals, potentates remain aware—however marginally—that they are not the sole possessors of consciousness and will. Hence the satisfaction to be found in mechanical toys and mechanical servants.

Consider the following two examples. (We shall refer to other cases later.) In the middle of the thirteenth century, a French artist-craftsman produced for the court of the Mongol Khan a large silver fountain in the form of a tree which delivered four kinds of drinks to guests through the mouths of lions and dragons placed among the leaves. At the top of the tree was a mechanical angel that could blow a trumpet. In this particular effort, however, the artist-craftsman's technical prowess failed to match his and his patron's aspiration. The arm of the angel could indeed move but only because it was manipulated by a hidden slave, and drinks flowed out of the fountains only because more slaves were hidden under the roof of the palace hall and from there poured liquors down long tubes. Why were the human servitors hidden? Why could they not have performed these simple tasks in the open? They could have, but from their master's point of view human servitors—by breathing, for example—lacked the timeless perfection of art objects.

The second example is from China and dates back to the early years of the seventh century. For the entertainment of the Sui emperor (Sui Yang-ti) and his guests, large toy boats were constructed that floated on water in winding canals. On some of the boats were men made of wood. When a boat paused before a guest, one figure would stretch out its arm with a full cup of wine. When the guest had drunk, the figure received the cup back and held it for another figure to fill. Immediately the boat moved on to its next stop. Apparently all these movements were performed by mechanical devices without the subterfuge of hidden human agents.[28]

3 GARDENS OF POWER
AND OF CAPRICE

"We are absolute masters of what the earth produces. We enjoy the mountains and the plains. The rivers are ours. We sow the seeds and plant the trees. We fertilize the earth. We stop, direct, and turn the rivers; in short, by our hands and various operations in this world we endeavor to make it as it were another nature."[1] This view of human dominance, so boldly stated by Cicero and so modern in tone, in fact rarely finds expression in premodern times, either in the classical Mediterranean world or in other high cultures. Much more common is the view that humans, for all the architectural and engineering feats that they have accomplished at nature's expense, have done little beyond submitting to the order of the cosmos, taken to mean, at one end of the scale, the movement of the stars, and at the other, the genius of place—the spirits that govern a particular locality. And nowhere is this belief more persistently upheld than for the pleasure garden. The pleasure garden is an emblem of innocence. It is a paradise in which men and women live in contentment, without work and strife. In Christian art and literature, it embodies a state before the Fall. The garden, in contrast to the city, is somehow not an artifact. Despite all evidences of human forethought and labor, it is viewed as though it were a gift of nature or of God.

Of course the garden—the pleasure garden—is an artifact. We may even argue that it is a purer manifestation of human will than are arable fields and villages because unlike the latter it does not answer to necessity. The pleasure garden, needless to say, is a plausible reality only to people who have satisfied their more pressing needs. The pleasure garden is a *jeu d'esprit*—a playful use of surplus power. This surplus power can be channeled into other activities such as sports and games, embroidery and painting, and abstract thought. But as an act of will, gardening is preeminent for two reasons. One is that the garden is a little material world in which people can dwell, and not simply a fleeting exertion, a project on paper, or an object for the contemplative mind. The other reason is that the garden, unlike a painting or a sculpture, has to be maintained thoughtfully and systematically; otherwise it will revert to nature. A garden, to remain perfect, requires constant vigilance. This is true of all gardens (except perhaps for the few that are purely sculptural) but surpassingly true of large formal gardens where the precise lines reflect the human desire to completely dominate both space and time. It is easy to envisage the rapid decay of Louis XIV's Marly estate when the annual sum of money garnered for its support fell from 100,000 *livres* in 1698 to less than 5,000 in 1712.

Gardens, with their air of innocent pleasure, aesthetic excellence, and religious import, have successfully hidden their roots in the exercises of power. What are these exercises? First are the acts of demolition. Before anything can be made, something must first be destroyed. We take for granted that in any artistic endeavor the finished product more than justifies the destruction that necessarily precedes it. With the making of a large garden, however, the things destroyed and removed may in their own terms have high human value—for example, farms and villages. Mencius (ca. 371–288 B.C.) was not pleased with the multiplication of gardens and parks in his time. He took them to be evidence of immorality among the rulers. "After the death of the Emperors Yao and Shun," he observed,

> the principles that mark sages fell into decay. Oppressive sovereigns, arising one after another, pulled down houses to make ponds and lakes so that the people knew not where they could rest in quiet, and threw fields out of cultivation to form gardens and parks so that the people could not get clothes and food. Afterward, corrupt speech and tyrannous deeds increased; gardens and parks, ponds and lakes, thickets and marshes, became more numerous; protected birds and beasts swarmed. By the time of Chou, the empire was in a state of great confusion.[2]

Landscaping, as a utopian venture, requires a clean slate. Whatever exists must first be removed. Feats of preparatory destruction, sometimes on a large scale, occur whenever and wherever landscape gardening has become a mania with the powerful and the rich, as, for example, in France and England during the seventeenth and eighteenth centuries. In England, the transformation of the rural economy has caused anguish among the displaced and it has inspired literary laments, notably that of Oliver Goldsmith in *The Deserted Village*. Destruction visited not only the landscapes of the humble. Old gardens, no longer in style, also suffered; they were gutted to make room for new ones. Lancelot Brown, a prolific designer of British gardens from the 1750s until his death in 1783 and famous for his creation of placid prospects, had a streak of ruthlessness in him. He and, to a lesser degree, his successor Humphrey Repton acted like vandals when they tore up old formal gardens (for example, the great parterres of Blenheim) and countless tree-lined avenues.[3]

With great power often goes capriciousness, which may itself be a symptom of boredom. Destruction, rather than being the necessary step preparatory to a sustained effort of construction, may be repeated in a restless and aimless quest for novelty. Thus at Marly, *bosquets*, or green chambers, were repeatedly taken down and put up to amuse the aging Louis XIV and his courtiers. Great stretches of thick woodland were transformed with lightning speed into broad lakes, where people were rowed about in gondolas, and were then changed back to forests so dense that daylight was banished as soon as the trees were planted. Louis, duc de Saint-Simon, observed: "I speak of what I saw myself in six weeks, during which time fountains were altered a hundred times, and waterfalls redesigned in countless different ways. Goldfish ponds, decorated with gilding and delightful paintings, were scarcely finished before they were unmade and rebuilt over and over again."[4]

Who built the great gardens? Whereas Michelangelo did indeed paint the Sistine Chapel, only an accepted convention of language allows us to say that André le Nôtre built Versailles. A great garden may be designed and supervised by a master artist but it is executed by a multitude of nameless artisans and laborers. Of Sui Yang-ti's imperial park near his capital, Lo-yang, it is reported that "the ground was broken over an area of two hundred *li* in circuit (about seventy-five miles) and the labor of a million workers, on the average, was required." The figure of one million is no doubt an exaggeration, but it does suggest that for the construction of an imperial park armies of workers had to be recruited. Once completed, such a park or garden may exude an air of formal calm or natural innocence, thus making it easy for people to forget its origin in forced labor, untold hardships, and death.

Consider two telling incidents, one from Japan and the other from India. By the fifteenth century, some of the gardens in Japan were already quite large. Surprising, by modern standards and values, was the spirit in which these projects were undertaken—its deadly seriousness, its extravagance in terms of effort and cost. Landscape gardeners and their aristocratic patrons, who themselves were well versed in landscaping art, placed the highest value on rocks of a certain kind. To procure them, no cost in human labor was spared. For example, Lord Akamatsu detailed 1,800 of his retainers to bring stones from Uzumasa to the shogun Yoshinori's garden several miles away. At another time, Lord Hosokawa engaged 3,000 men to move rocks into another estate that the shogun was constructing. Accidents were bound to occur in the course of these large operations, and even minor mishaps to the precious objects—rock or plant—could have dire consequences for the people involved. Thus, when the large branch of a plum tree presented by Lord Kuroda to the shogun was broken en route, the shogun was so angry that he ordered the imprisonment of three of the gardeners and the arrest of five young Kuroda knights considered responsible for the accident. Three of the knights fled into exile, two committed suicide.[5]

In Mughul India, the emperor Jahangir (1605-27) was as sentimental as he was cruel, a combination of traits not unusual in autocrats with a taste for beauty. He loved to hunt, and near his hunting lodge he built a drinking pool for animals, in memory of a pet deer. The emperor's human subjects did not always fare so well. In the twelfth year of his reign he wrote: "At this time the gardener represented that a servant of Muqarrab Khan had cut down some *champa* trees above the bench alongside the river. On hearing this I became angry, and went myself to enquire into the matter and to exact satisfaction. When it was established that this improper act had been committed by him, I ordered both his thumbs to be cut off as a warning to others."[6]

Gardens are a blending of nature and artifice; they are the product of horticulture and architecture. On the one hand, they consist of growing things, on the other, of walls, terraces, statues, and fountains. Histories of gardens often distinguish between two broad types—natural and formal (or artificial)—and hint that whereas natural landscaping expresses human adaptation to nature, formal landscaping reveals the human need to dominate. In fact, will and power lie behind both types, and it is hard to say which is more significative of the human wish to order and impose. A "natural" garden, because it contains clumps of trees and serpentine waters, may seem a more modest venture than does a formal garden with its stone terraces and lacery of fountains, but the naturalness of the former is a calculated illusion. Because this illusion is intended, we may argue that the natural garden is even more of an artifice—a product of artful cunning—than is the formal garden, in which no attempt is made to hide human design.

Whether a garden looks natural or not depends, in the final analysis, on the whim of the individual and of society. The taste of an individual is, of course, influenced by that of his society. However, an individual, if sufficiently self-assured and powerful, can run counter to society's taste. For example, although the prevailing style of gardening in Imperial Rome was formal and sculptural, that at Nero's Golden House was not. Suetonius described Nero's estate as having "an enormous pool, more like a sea than a pool, surrounded by buildings made to resemble cities, and a landscape garden consisting of plowed fields, vineyards, pastures and woodlands, in which every variety of domestic and wild animal roamed." Tacitus strongly disapproved of Nero's playground, not because it was adorned with "customary and commonplace luxuries like gold and jewels," but because of its "faked rusticity"—its "lakes, woods, and open spaces"—because of the "impudence with which Nero's architects and contractors sought to outbid nature."[7]

Toward the end of the seventeenth century and at the start of the eighteenth, landscape taste was turning away from the formality of earlier designs toward a style considered more romantic, natural, and what English critics called picturesque. Scholars have tried, without complete success, to account for this change of fashion. The lack of total success is not surprising if we frankly admit the component of whim in any exercise of power that is so free of necessity. Natural, picturesque, or formal? Whatever the decision, the power at the disposal of the landscapist must be equally large if the extent of the ground to be transformed is comparable. As a matter of fact, the more we know about the picturesque garden the more artifactitious and artificial it seems so that its real difference from the formal garden, in regard to the degree of "naturalness," is small and contracts to the amount of plant cover and to the dominance of curved as distinct from straight lines. Formal gardens boast many architectural and sculptural features: they are full of evidence of human handiwork. English gardens in the first quarter of the eighteenth century, although they moved deliberately away from Continental formalism, retained architectural profusion as an insignia of accomplishment. Chiswick, Claremont, Stowe, and Cirencester were all studded with temples, ruins, obelisks, classical seats, and Gothic bits and pieces. Fakery, no matter how blatant, was permissible if it produced the appropriate illusion. Batty Langley (1696–1751), in a book on rural landscaping, recommended the construction of ruins at the terminal points of avenues of trees, either ruins built of brick and plastered to imitate stone or painted on canvas and hung up. Where nature was the desired illusion, William Kent (1684–1748) went so far as to recommend the planting of dead trees "to give the greater air of truth to the scene."[8]

The most extraordinary example of a picturesque garden— extraordinary for its combination of naturalism and artificiality—was created, however, in France rather than in England, at Lunéville, in 1742. This curiosity, called *Le Rocher*, was an animated village constructed on the artificial rock bank of a canal. In its attempt to be both rustic and mechanically ingenious, both full of natural charm and self-conscious cleverness, it may be regarded as a prototype of the kinds of display offered at Fun Fairs and Disneyland. On *Le Rocher*'s constricted site were no fewer than eighty-two carved wooden figures arranged in a series of rural vignettes, among them a shepherd playing a tune on his bagpipe while his dog looked after the flock; a boy pushing a swing on which a girl was seated; a child stroking a dog that was eating a biscuit; men working at a forge, playing the violin, drinking and singing; women making butter and washing linen; a cock crowing; a hermit meditating in a grotto, etc. This was not a static and silent spectacle. The figures moved and made appropriate sounds. *Le Rocher* was not so much a garden designed for pleasure only as the model of an idealized society and world, although we should remember that all gardens, no matter how attenuated and frivolous their use, preserve somewhere in their founding the seeds of this ideal.[9]

Far from the pretentiousness and sophistry to which picturesque gardens were prone lay those "rain-washed wooded slopes and gentle stretches of greensward" created by Lancelot Brown (1716–83), which did look natural and expressed eloquently the English love of nature. Yet to Brown himself nature was but a raw goddess who always strove "for perfection, but who never achieved it without the Aristotelian dressing of man's divinely rational faculties." Brown aimed at ideal form. Behind all that surface placidity of grass and water, rolling hills and woodlots, was the desire to impose a pictorial perfection on landscape. To this end, he introduced buildings with classical and literary allusions, and he planted trees, marshaling them when necessary into straight lines, right angles, or wedge shapes exactly as though he were designing scenic wings for the theater.[10]

In trying to understand the origins of the eighteenth-century English garden, scholars have noted the penetration of the Chinese influence toward the end of the seventeenth century. Chinese gardens were well known for their disregard of the rectilinear, for their attempt to reproduce the subtle lines and spaces of nature. It was believed that the Chinese adapted to nature and did not try to impose on it the formal and geometric patterns of man; they did not try to force nature into, as it were, stiff court attire as French gardeners had done. Much of this belief was well grounded, except for the crucial point concerning adaptation. Whatever the Chinese themselves might have said in their philosophical and poetic moods, their gardens did not in fact exemplify the adaptive posture. Rather they were masterful creations, feats of engineering as well as of art, and full of the pride of power. This was true especially of imperial parks and gardens. The emperor Hui-tsung (1082–1135), for example, ordered the construction of a mountain 225 feet in height on the plain outside his capital, K'ai-feng.[11]

The manipulative and architectural character of landscaping was not restricted to works of imperial scale. Significantly, the Chinese speak of *building* a garden, not planting one, as is still done in English. A Western visitor whose prior knowledge of Chinese landscaping is confined to artistic and literary representations may well be surprised by the clutter of the Chinese garden. He is taken aback by the huge piles of rocks and perhaps even more by the extraordinary number of buildings. Plant life seems sparse. Except for rocks and pools of stagnant-looking water, everywhere his eyes are confronted by pavilions, temples, balustrades, and walls. Literary descriptions of a garden often give the impression that architectural features are separated from each other by wide expanses of space. This is the effect that writers wish to produce. In reality, however, not only small city gardens but even the larger ones in the countryside tend to be rather "busy" with artifice (fig. 1). Expansive vistas are unusual. It is as though the Chinese prefer the illusion of space to actual, unimpeded views.

That the garden is architecture rather than horticulture, and certainly not nature, is clearly manifest in the works of Western designers. One tradition treats the garden as an extension of the house. The garden displays human ingenuity and power expanding into and subduing nature, and not, as some modern interpreters would have it, nature making inroads into the human domain; nature does penetrate the house but only under strict house rules. In the ancient Roman world, not only did the rectilinear geometry of the house extend into nature's space, but the house's content of statuary, paintings, and benches also spilled into it. The ancients regarded the house and its grounds as a unit. Landscape architecture did not exist as a separate profession. In large estates, the same architects who designed the house also laid out its grounds.

The idea that house and grounds formed one architectural complex, the units adjoining each other or linked by a covered walk, persisted into later historical periods. For example, in the Middle Ages people were more likely to speak of "building" a garden than of planting one. (In this regard, they were like the Chinese.) Built features tended to dominate (fig. 2). Medieval gardens were "walled, fenced, hedged and palisaded much more closely than they are nowadays," Teresa McLean observed. "There was a good deal of stonework, carpentry, hedge-making, locksmithing and painting to be done in the making of them, and more of the same in the making of their mounds, fountains, benches, railings, paths and raised beds. Well-to-do gardens had to be built before they could be cultivated." The prominent garden walls were a source of pride and joy and a major status symbol. Disputes about them were frequently recorded.[12]

In the Renaissance period, such esteemed architects as Alberti, Vignola, Giuliano da Sangallo, Giulio Romano, and Bramante contributed to the art of landscape design as a natural extension of architecture into the surrounding space. Where nature proved to be difficult—where, for example, the terrain was uneven—a designer overcame it by architectural means. Thus, to construct the Belvedere gardens at the Vatican, the architect Bramante triumphed over the irregular site by the ingenious creation of three terrace levels and connecting stairways. His work was much admired and is now regarded as a landmark in the history of

Fig. 1. The Pai Shih pavilion in the Pan Mou garden, Peking. Originally designed in the sixteenth century, it was restored by Inspector-General Lin Ch'ing in the 1840s. Note the extremely artificial character of the garden—the potted plants and the stones standing on pedestals both within the pavilion and outside it.

Fig. 2. Garden depicted in a miniature of the fifteenth century. Note its architectural character: the wall, fences, raised beds, wheeled stands for climbing plants, and two potted plants.

landscaping. Architectural features such as pavilions, stairways, balustrades, and statues came to dominate Italian Renaissance gardens. Collectively they manifested an almost megalomaniac confidence in man's ability to control, transform, and improve. The skills needed to move earth, build retaining walls, terraces, pools, and avenues were also those needed in the military constructions of the period. Not surprisingly, Giuliano da Sangallo, Bramante, and other major architects of the Renaissance worked on both military fortifications and princely gardens.[13]

The prevalence of the architectural ideal entailed the subordination of plant life. In a formal garden, when the wind blew the branches on trees, shrubs or flowers did not sway, being too heavily trimmed for that. The variety of plants, apart from those exotics kept in museums of curiosities, was restricted. In a Renaissance garden, only those species that could be trained to meet an overall architectural design and its exactions were favored: for example, cypress, pine, ilex, laurel, box, juniper, and yew. Plants, regarded simply as architectural material, were forced into the solid geometric shapes of walls, mazes and labyrinths, rooms, temples, and theaters. We gain an insight into how far, in the sixteenth century, designers were willing to apply force in the service of aesthetic taste from Bernard Palissy's *Réceptes véritables* (1563). He wished to create a green temple in which living trees simulated classical columns and described the procedures in the chilling language of a surgeon.

> I will mark and incise the foot of the elm where I wish to make the base of the column; similarly at the place where I wish to make a capital, I will make incisions, marks or bruises, and then Nature finding herself injured in these parts will send help and abundance of sap and juice to strengthen and heal the said wounds. And from this it will come about that at these wounded parts a superfluity of wood will be engendered which will produce the form of a capital and base of a column, and thus as the columns shall grow and increase, the shape of the capital and base will widen too.

The unnaturalness of the procedure and of the desired outcome did occur to Palissy. In anticipation of criticism, he noted that his changes were not as extreme as those of a topiary gardener who might transform shrubs into the semblance of "a cock, a goose, and indeed several other kinds of animals." Moreover, Palissy believed that trees were a natural substance for construction, more natural indeed than stone; and the reason he gave was that stone columns, with their base and capital, merely imitated trees. He failed to see the irony of then making the trees imitate stone.[14]

Playfulness is a key feature of gardens. Not only do people play in the garden, but the garden itself is the product of a proud imagination able to construct a world full of magical and illusory effects. Landscape painting is one such effect: it magically captures a world and it creates an illusion of space. In China as well as in Europe, gardening and landscape painting are closely allied arts. A Chinese garden is a reduction of wild nature into a three-dimensional model attached to the domestic spaces of the house and circumscribed by a wall. A Chinese landscape painting is a more extreme reduction in two dimensions. A painted landscape scroll hanging on the wall of a study acts as a window that opens out to expansive space. Real windows exist in the garden partitions, through which one can see another segment of the landscape, and through a gate one can physically enter it. And yet a major function of such openings is to frame the garden beyond as though it were just a picture. Moreover, specialists on landscape design say that the whitewashed walls in a garden should be seen as the backdrop—a sort of paper scroll—in front of which rocks and plants are arranged as though they are elements of a painting. We see here paradox of a kind sometimes encountered in highly sophisticated cultures. Before the flat surface of a painting one is supposed to feel as if a three-dimensional world lies there into which one can enter. On the other hand, before the three-dimensional arrangements of a garden, one is supposed to imagine that a beautiful two-dimensional picture is being contemplated.[15]

An intimate bond between gardening and landscape painting also prevailed in the Western world. Both arts gave their practitioners a sense of control over nature and space. In the villas of Imperial Rome as well as in those of Renaissance Italy, landscapes of trees, birds, and orchards were sometimes painted on garden walls to create the illusion of a spacious countryside. By virtue of these murals, an owner sitting in his enclosed courtyard, rather than feeling hemmed in, was master of all that he surveyed, and what he surveyed included the painted scenes, which might well be of his landed possessions elsewhere.[16] During the seventeenth century, the stress on visual experience (prospects and views) reached a point such that the entire landscape garden seemed designed as stage scenes or tableaux to be looked at rather than as encompassing worlds into which one could unselfconsciously plunge and be immersed. In the seventeenth century and especially in the eighteenth, landscape gardeners were strongly influenced by landscape art, and some of them were themselves landscape artists. For example, André le Nôtre in his youth thought of becoming a painter. As a young man, he commissioned a picture from Nicolas Poussin. Later he bought more of Poussin's works as well as those of Claude Lorrain, despite the fact that Claude's landscapes are almost romantic in spirit.[17] Le Nôtre composed his gardens as a painter might compose a picture, except that his work was to be viewed from several angles, it being a composite of scenes; and these scenes were always framed by clipped hedges and, behind them, a wall of high trees. In England, already in 1650, Edward Norgate defined the landscape itself as "nothing but a picture of Fields, Cities, Rivers, Castles, Mountains, Trees or whatever delightfull view the Eye takes pleasure in."[18] The literature on gardens in the next hundred years was almost as much preoccupied with the arrangements of tints and colors, light and shade, and perspectives as the literature on landscape painting. William Kent, famed for his gardens, was also an architect, sculptor, and painter. He agreed with Alexander Pope (1688–1744) that "all gardening is painting," and he found another champion of this view in the architect John Vanbrugh (1644–1726), who, on being consulted about laying out the grounds of Blenheim Palace, exclaimed, "Send for a landscape painter."[19]

Playfulness in the garden takes a variety of forms. At its simplest, it is fun and games. A Chinese garden, for example, is not only the place for study, solitude, and contemplation, but also where children play with their toys (as many paintings show) and adults play chess or hold poetry contests enlivened by wine and food; less innocently, young nobles play at games of war in the imperial parks. Among European gardens, those that belong to the Tudor period were outstandingly lively. Multiple use was normal. Pictures of gardens show men and women engaged in a wide range of activities: playing cards, paddling, rolling on the ground, teasing monkeys, fishing in the ponds, splashing each other with water, making love, wandering about in the maze, and chasing each other. The Italian Renaissance garden was a place for meditation, philosophical discussions, and a center of botanic and medical research, but it was also a place for feasts, filled with joy, a place for the entertainment of friends, a place of intellectual as well as sexual freedom.[20]

One special kind of play, known both to China and to Europe, is rustic simplicity. In a garden elaborate with art, the high-born pretend to be simple farmers, thus imitating children who in their games pretend to be engaged in serious work. In China, a beautiful pavilion on an artificial island in a man-made lake may nevertheless carry a plaque that exhorts incongruously, "Farm with diligence." In the grounds of the Summer Palace near Peking there is still a row of farm buildings on Longevity Hill. The old empress dowager Tsu Hsi (1834–1908) used to enjoy watching her ladies struggling to feed the chickens on her farm. And, of course, in Europe we immediately think of Marie Antoinette leading the simple life on the dairy farm of Petit Trianon. The practice of establishing a rustic village in the midst of a grand estate also took root in other possessions of the Royal House of France, for instance, in the prince de Condé's park at Chantilly, at the duc d'Orléans' seat at Raincy, and on the property of Madame la Comtesse de Provence at Montreuil. At these farms and villages, the outward appearance of the little clusters of buildings spoke of simplicity and even poverty; inside them one would have found luxury and refinement. For example, at Chantilly, in Pierre de Nolhac's words,

> the barn with tottering walls, pierced with wretched skylights, became, once the threshold was crossed, a magnificent apartment with Corinthian architecture formed of columns in couples, painted red, fluted with silver and entwined with garlands of flowers; Cupids played in the clouds of the roofing, and the upholstery matched the curtains of rose taffetas, bordered with silver. Other hovels concealed a dining-hall, a library, a billiard room decorated with trophies of gardening tools. The imitation tavern with its well in the yard was really a kitchen provided with all the utensils necessary for serving a princely supper. The visitor, supposing that he was on a peasant's property, would have found, side by side with enchanted dwellings that seemed to have sprung out of a fairy tale, a real dairy, a stable full of cows, a mill that was really grinding corn, and a bakehouse where bread was baking.[21]

In the real world, events both natural and human are often beyond the control of individuals, no matter how powerful. In the world of pretense or theater, by contrast, conflicts may indeed arise but they can be resolved by the magic wand of art. Significantly, the history of the garden is entwined with that of the theater. In China, the garden has traditionally provided a setting for musical and theatrical performances. In late medieval Europe, revels, masques, and pageants were held in the garden. Italian Renaissance gardens—those of the Villa Mondregore and Borghese, for example—boasted permanent arenas and theaters for entertainment. By the end of the seventeenth century, France's gardens too might harbor permanent theaters. The *bosquets* of Versailles were green halls elaborately decorated with fountains, statues, and potted plants; they could seat as many as 3,000 spectators.

Not only did the garden contain the theater, but the design of the theater also influenced the design of the garden. In 1780, the architect Le Camus de Mesières urged landscape gardeners to use theatrical effects in their compositions. "Let us turn your eyes to our Theatres," he wrote in *Génie de l'architecture,* "where the simple imitation of nature determines our affections. Here in the enchanted Palace of Armida, all is magnificent and voluptuous."[22] In England, the close association between garden and theater is suggested by the fact that figures important in the literature and design of gardens such as Pope, Joseph Addison (1672–1719), and the third earl of Burlington (1694–1753) all had strong links with the stage. Vanbrugh, too, had been a playwright and was involved with the theater before he turned to architecture and landscape architecture.

Of course the garden is, in its own right, an artwork of power and imagination. The garden is power in a confident mood—witness the size and masterful layouts of some of its grander specimens; and it is power in a whimsical mood—witness the details of design. Each achievement in the technical sphere encourages the designer's imagination to fly higher. When the engineers were able to bring more water into the tanks of Mughul gardens, the single jet of former times multiplied into scores and even hundreds of fountains, as at the Shalamar gardens of Shah Jahan (1628–58) at Lahore. But even without the stimulus of major technical innovations, the mind is free to elaborate on details with abandon. Thus, the pool that is at the heart of the Persian concept of the garden evolved from a simple rectangular or circular tank into intricate lobate designs by the fifteenth century.[23]

In theory, the Chinese garden respects nature and the natural. But the more we attend to its details, the more artificial—indeed affected—it appears. Far from being an escape into the grand simplicities of nature, it is in some ways an old civilization's most contrived toy. Dissemblance is

Fig. 3. The great stones of Shih Tzu Lin (Lion Grove) in Su-chou. They are supposed to resemble sitting lions. The garden dates back to the fourteenth century. Photograph taken in 1918.

everywhere. Nothing is quite what it seems. Rocks represent wild and towering peaks, but also animals and monsters (fig. 3). In a novel written in the eighteenth century, a party of men viewing a newly built garden is confronted by "rugged rocks looking either like goblins or resembling savage beasts, lying crossways or in horizontal or in upright positions, on the surface of which grew moss and lichen with mottled hues or parasitic plants which screened off the light, while narrow paths wound around the rocks like the intestines of a sheep."[24] A rarer example of Chinese conceit is the rock stream. Rocks are arranged to suggest a stream bed that at any moment may be filled with tumbling water. This device, known to gardeners in the eighth century and perhaps even earlier, is meant to deceive the eye, for no water is likely to run through it.[25]

The architectural elements of a Chinese garden are richly capricious. Doors in the partitions may be simple rectangles, but almost as common are octagons and circles, and where circular they are known as moon gates. Doors, especially in the gardens of the late Ch'ing and early Republican periods, may also be shaped like a vase, gourd, flower petal, or leaf. Even more fanciful are the windows, which not only take the forms of flowers and fruits but also of such commonplace artifacts as fan, vase, carafe, urn, or teapot.[26] A figurative way of looking at things is strongly encouraged in the Chinese garden by its close link with poetry: the garden inspires poetry and is also the place where poems are frequently composed. Landscape features in the garden, rather than being allowed to speak for themselves, are often supplemented by evocative words, uttered in passing by literary viewers or permanently inscribed. Thus, rocks are "goblins and wild animals," as we have already noted, or they are one's "older brother"; pathways become "geese" and "meander like playing cats," pavilions over the water are "boats," and five pavilions set together become the "claws of the Imperial five-toed dragon."[27]

As a toy or plaything, the garden should be ingenious and full of surprises—and it is. Again and again in the gardening literature the designer is urged to avoid the obvious and seek the unusual and unexpected. Hiddenness and secrecy are desirable. A wall is to be "hidden by creepers," and buildings should be "partly concealed by trees." Sometimes the surprises can be extraordinarily elaborate, as the following case suggests.

Ni Ts'an, a Yuan dynasty painter, was once invited by his friend to see lotus flowers. Upon his arrival he saw nothing but an empty courtyard. His astonishment, however, was as great as his earlier disappointment when, returning to the same courtyard after the feast, he saw a pond full of lotus. The magic was a simple one. Hundreds of pots of lotus flowers were swiftly placed in the court-yard, which, being slightly sunk, became a pool when a water reser-voir discharged just enough water to submerge the pots.[28]

Another illustration of how far the ambitious garden-architect is wil-ling to go to create a magical world is given in the eighteenth-century novel mentioned earlier. Members of a party touring the garden enter a building and find, to their surprise, that its interior consists only of corridors, alcoves, and galleries, so that properly speaking it can hardly be said to have rooms. The partition walls have wood paneling, all exquisitely and fancifully carved, and they are pierced by numerous apertures of exuber-antly varied shapes. Shelving is concealed in the double thickness of the partition at the base of these apertures, making it possible to use them for storing books and displaying antique bronzes. False windows and doors in these ingenious partitions further heighten their magical effect. The garden building itself, already bewildering in its complex shifting spaces, is provided with additional devices that redouble its intricacy. The touring group's host, as he walks down a passageway, finds that another party similar to his own advances to meet him, only to realize that he is walking toward a large mirror. Circumventing the mirror, the group is confronted by "an even more bewildering choice of doorways on the other side."[29]

Surprises play an equally prominent role in the European pleasure garden. Builders and their patrons take pride in grandeur, but grandeur can be boring. Complementing the expansive open space and formal clarity is the principle of intricacy, bewilderment, and surprise: hence the mazes and labyrinths, the *bosquets* and the *giardini segreti*, the trick foun-tains and the excesses of topiary art. We may well wonder at the childish-ness of our forebears. Consider as one example among many the first garden apartment (*bosquet*) at Versailles—the Salle de Festin. An island ringed by canal water stood in the middle of a glade. Bridges to the island could be raised suddenly by a hidden mechanism, thus stranding the visitors. Practical jokes of this kind no doubt provoked much merriment among courtiers who in other respects were a sophisticated people.[30]

At Trianon, to give another illustration, the entire color scheme of the gardens was once changed during the short span of the Sun King's lunch.[31] (One's mind drifts inexorably to the harassed gardeners in *Alice in Wonderland*, who were obliged to paint the white roses red in short order.) Was the king's desire for the unexpected and the magical mere childishness, or did it reveal the mental state of a powerful monarch whose jaded appetite must be constantly stimulated by novelty? Perhaps the difference in personality between a spoiled child and a blasé aesthete is smaller than we think. The child, after all, is also easily bored and has delusions of power; his desires are fickle, he plays with things at hand— bending and twisting them, often destroying them in the end. Compared with the power of a child, that at the disposal of a nobleman and landowner is of course far from delusory. A potentate can command a large garden to be built for his pleasure. Such a work, however innocent and beautiful in appearance, may nonetheless also be an exercise in willfulness and force directed against nature. We shall explore how water has been compelled to perform and plants have been made to grow in whimsical disregard of their natural inclinations—how these elements of nature have become, for powerful people, sources of delight and flattering reminders of their ability to command and impose.

4 FOUNTAINS AND PLANTS

Water, although inorganic, is nevertheless widely regarded as in some sense "alive," even in modern times. Water, after all, moves. It *runs* over its bed and *jumps* over pebbles. The spring, we say, is the source of life—an ancient figure of speech that retains its appeal. Water can be trained to move fast or slow, in sharp bends or arrow straight, and even uphill. Water is harnessed by technology to irrigate fields and generate power. It can also be made into a plaything, forced to leap and dance for human pleasure.

Mencius asked, "Is it right to force water to leap up?" He was taking the position that human nature is inclined to act in certain ways and not others, using the movement of water as an analogy. "Water," he said, "will flow indifferently to east or west, but it will not flow indifferently up and down." Now, of course, he added, "by striking water you can make it leap up over your forehead and by damming and leading it you may force it up a hill, but do such movements accord with the nature of water?" Obviously not. "It is the force applied that causes water to behave thus."[1] Water is essential to an agricultural civilization that has established itself just beyond the margin of the steppes. The Chinese, since protohistoric times, have sought to control water. Their simplest and most ancient device takes advantage of gravity: water is drawn from a stream and led down ditches cut in a naturally inclined surface. However, since at least the Han dynasty the Chinese have also used the chain pump to force water upward so as to distribute it more effectively. Water has been made to perform against its nature, but this was done to satisfy primary economic needs. The question we now raise is, To what extent have the Chinese treated water as a plaything, taken delight in making it act against its nature out of a sense of power and of fun?

In creating the garden, the Chinese have not hesitated to change the course of streams, damming up their their natural flow and digging into the ground to provide more spacious beds. The pond or lake is an essential feature of the Chinese garden. Every technique of engineering and of art is used to make the body of water seem natural. Consider the West Lake of Hang-chou, perhaps the most famous of all the public parks in China. Its beauty has been celebrated by poets and artists for more than a thousand years. Even today, every tourist feels obliged to pay it the homage of a visit. The body of water is large enough to sustain the illusion of nature—indeed, of untamed nature. But the lake is in fact artificial. Created by a dike thrown across the sluggish streams of a delta, perhaps as early as the first century A.D., the lake survived only through dredging and periodic enlargement. Being shallow, it was always threatened by accumulating mud and aquatic plants. When Hang-chou was the capital of the Southern Sung dynasty (1127–1279) and use of the lake was intense, troops patrolled the lakeshores to prevent people from throwing rubbish or planting water chestnuts in it.[2]

Water, then, was manipulated—sometimes on a large scale—for pleasure. But did the Chinese, as Mencius put it, ever "strike water and so cause it to leap up"? In other words, were fountains and (in particular) upward-shooting jets a part of the Chinese repertoire of games played on nature? Until recently, it had been generally assumed that fountains were unknown in China before the Jesuit missionaries introduced them from 1750 onward—dramatically at Yuan Ming Yuan, the "Versailles of Peking." Joseph Needham argues, however, that evidence for the use of fountains may be found in almost every century after the Han. The earliest and clearest description of fountains and jets occurs in an account of a building called the Cool Hall (Liang Tien), built by the emperor Hsüan Tsung about A.D. 747. This hall, used for imperial audiences in times of intense heat, was cooled by water-powered fans, by ice applied to stone chairs, and (as the Chinese text put it) by "water forced to rise in the four corners of the hall, forming screens, which came down with a splash." Some three and a half centuries later, a man describing the glories of the Northern Sung capital, K'ai-feng, in the year 1148 mentioned a certain temple at which there were "two statues of the Buddhas Manjusri and Samantabhadra riding on white lions. From the five fingers of each of their outstretched hands, which quivered all the time, streams of water poured out in all directions." At a still later date, it was recorded of the last emperor of the Yuan dynasty (1260–1368), who liked mechanical toys, that among his possessions were dragon-fountains with balls kept dancing on the jets and dragons spouting perfumed mist.[3]

Despite such evidences, it is clear that the Chinese did not "cause water to leap up" at anything like the scale of the displays in Europe. How important were jets of water in other high cultures outside of the European tradition? Water, we know, lay at the heart of the Persian and Islamic gardens. Typically the Persian garden was divided into four parts by canals in the shape of a cross. At the center were a pavilion and a pool of welling water. This plan became firmly established by the Sassanian period (224–642). Its oldest element was the pool, which symbolized life that flowed effortlessly and joyfully. High regard, even worship, was directed at the welling water. Alien to the native Persian tradition were playful, high-shooting fountains, and yet once introduced they quickly caught the fancy of powerful rulers. Thus the great Safavid garden (seventeenth century) of the Hazar Jarib at Isfahan had as many as five hundred jets of water. The technology used to create such wonders, however, could be rather primitive. At the Ali Qapu Palace of Isfahan, a fountain played in a pool on the fourth floor. Power was furnished by oxen. A long chain of buckets plunged into a cistern buried beneath the ground and then raised the water to a tank on the sixth floor of the palace; from there water flowed into the pool below. As for attempts to make jets of water frolic in accordance with some predetermined pattern, these might call for balletic rather than mechanical ingenuity. Sometimes a fountain system worked only when nimble-fingered and swift-footed servants were in attendance. Donald Wilber reports: "We hear of such a system from an account of a visitor to the Bagh-i-Takhut, or Garden of the Throne, at Shiraz. His host was anxious to display patterns of spouting water and accomplished this effect by means of servants who dashed from nozzle to nozzle, holding wads of cloth over those openings not required at a given moment."[4]

In northern India, the Islamic gardens of the Mughul emperors boasted fountains in abundance as technology freed the imagination of the designers. A single jet here and there developed, by the middle of the seventeenth century, into hundreds of fountains all in one garden or into artificial rain such as that around the Lotus Pool at Udaipur. The Mughul emperors were fortunate in having in their service such outstanding engineers as Haidar Malik and 'Ali Mardan Khan, who were able to bring water from distant sources—by means of canals—into the garden-paradises of their patrons. Nevertheless, the jets of water in gardens of Islamic and Persian inspiration tended not to have the volume, force and thunder of European works at their height of development. The Oriental emphasis was on the simple spray or the single stream, multiplied, and on the delicacy of the water tracery that complemented the intricate carvings and ornaments of the architectural facades.[5]

In Europe, the history of the pleasure garden has its chief inspiration and roots in ancient Rome and, particularly, in the Rome of the Imperial Period. All Roman gardens have water as a major theme. Such, at least, is now our impression because all writers of the time who touched on the subject of the garden mentioned water with enthusiasm; and all archaeological excavations of villas reveal the presence of a complete system of pipes and ditches, even at places a private aqueduct to bring water in from afar should local sources or the supply from a large public aqueduct nearby prove inadequate. As for the small city garden, diggings such as those at Pompeii show, inevitably, the foundations of a pond and of fountains fed by lead pipes.[6] The importance of water is also made evident to us through the eloquent letters of Pliny the Younger. He possessed two beautiful villas, one near the sea at Laurentum and the other in the hills of Tuscany. Fond as Pliny was of his Laurentine estate he did reproach it for its lack of a running stream and of natural fountains. By contrast, the Tuscan villa was well fed by water from the hills, and Pliny responded to this gift of nature by having water everywhere, both inside and outside the house. Several rapturous descriptions appear in his letters to his friend, but one point of special interest to us is the comment on a fountain from which the water "shoots up into the air and is caught in the basin as it falls back."[7]

Pliny's villas were handsomely appointed, but far grander in conception and scale than anything Pliny could have envisaged was the emperor Hadrian's villa at Tivoli, some twenty miles from Rome, built between A.D. 125 and 136. Its dominant theme was water and marble. Reflecting on Tivoli's special aura, one modern observer, Eleanor Clark, has this to say: "Water was a prime element in architecture, here [in Tivoli] as in Rome, an element to be given shape, form, like other materials, subject to conceptions as varied—left flat and still or used in other simple ways on occasion, but probably more often elaborate in its faces and kinds of motion." Water provides an illusion of distance and is "the undefinable co-medium of light, serving purposes of luxury that later, when indoors was really indoors and glass was better, were taken over by wall-length mirrors and crystal chandeliers."[8]

In Roman estates, as at the Tivoli villa, water poured out of fountains, into baths, as cascades in nymphaeums, or stood still in elongated ponds. Water was everywhere. But one question remains. Did the Romans make the water jump? The answer is yes. We have, after all, a clear description of water shooting up in Pliny's Tuscan estate, although he did add that this display was intermittent, not continuous. The Tuscan topography, moreover, made it easy for natural hydraulic pressure to do its work. Hadrian's villa was less well sited for this purpose. Tivoli certainly had fountains, but how high did the water rise into the air? An answer to questions of this kind is made difficult by the fact that Roman writers used the word *salientes*, which could mean either ordinary fountains or jets of water. We are perhaps safe in assuming that, whatever the ambition of the time, elaborate sprays and high-volume jets of water were unlikely to be a prominent feature of the Roman garden. One reason is that the Romans lacked the technical knowledge to sustain the hydraulic pressure where this did not exist naturally by virtue of the topography. Despite the great advances made by the Romans in the art of distributing water and despite the architectural splendor of the aqueducts, their understanding of the principles of hydraulics was even less than that of certain Greeks whose works they knew and quoted. Available evidence suggests that the Romans guessed rather than rationally calculated the effects of head, slope, resistance, and other factors on the rate of flow.[9]

Near Hadrian's villa, at Tivoli, is the Villa d'Este, built for Cardinal Ippolito II d'Este from the year 1550 onward. The architect, Pirro Ligorio, sought inspiration from Hadrian's derelict villa. The hydraulic engineer was Orazio Olivieri, who successfully diverted and channeled a branch of the local river Anio so that an unlimited supply of water could descend the slope of the gardens. Although the Villa d'Este has been described as the most Roman of all gardens, it does differ from its classical predecessors in the sheer exuberance of its waterworks (fig. 4). For centuries the fountains of Villa d'Este have been one of the sights of Italy. Montaigne was there about 1581 and what struck him most was the volume of water. Besides volume, there was ingenuity. The *fontanieri* (fountain engineers) played with water in extraordinary ways. For exam-

Fig. 4. The massive fountains—the *fontana dell' organo idraulico*—devised by Orazio Olivieri for the Villa d'Este at Tivoli. (Drawing by Wayne Howell)

ple, at the Fountain of the Dragon the volume of the central jet could be varied so that, as Antonio del Re put it in 1611, "it made explosions like a small mortar, or many arquebuses discharged together; and at times it grew larger like a pavilion representing a downpour of rain." The *fontanieri*, says David Coffin, "treated water as a sculptor might clay, molding it into a variety of forms. Tall, thin jets vied with transparent veils or heavy cascades of water. In the center of the Oval Fountain jets of water formed the lily of the Este coat of arms, matching the lilies and eagles created of terra-cotta by the sculptors."[10] The best way to appreciate this hillslope wonder is to start at the bottom. Moving up, the visitor encounters first fish ponds overarched by gentle sprays of water; then, as the climb begins he sees glittering water staircases, then great fountains enclosed in garden rooms; then, after a steep climb, he sees finally one last silver jet spraying high into the sky as the great open terrace before the house is reached. This itinerary gives the impression that the higher one moves up the garden slope the higher the waters are made to jump: the contrast between the placid fish ponds at the bottom level and the high jet on the upper terrace, after a steep ascent on foot, can be singularly dramatic.[11]

This drama and this beauty were made possible by a most elaborate system of underground canals, culverts, water mains and pipes—the hidden machinery of a stage. Because an extensive infrastructure had been put in place and could be altered only with difficulty, the gardens of the Villa d'Este, four centuries after their construction, still resemble the earliest plans and engravings, and this despite the itch of a succession of owners to alter them in response to whim and changing fashion.[12]

Advances in hydraulic engineering made feasible the water fantasies of Renaissance and Baroque gardens—advances indicated by treatises that catered to the special needs of the ambitious gardener, such as Bernard Palissy's *Discours admirables* (1580), Olivier de Serres's *Théâtre d'agriculture* (1600), Salomon de Caus's *Les Raisons des forces mouventes* (1616), Israel de Silvestre's *Jardins et fontaines* (1661), and Jean François's *L'Art des fontaines* (1665). The mood of the times was that nature existed to be defied. "Forcer la nature" was a key phrase in the gardening literature. According to Montaigne, the grand duke Francesco de' Medici "chose an inconvenient, sterile and mountainous site—without springs" at which to build his villa (the villa at Pratolino) "so as to have the honor of sending for water five miles from there, and his sand and lime another five miles." In 1668, when the astute financier Jean Baptiste Colbert advised his royal master Louis XIV not to build his palace and gardens at the unpromising site of Versailles, the king haughtily replied: "C'est dans les choses difficiles que nous faisons paraître notre vertu" (It is in overcoming difficult matters that we make apparent our power).[13]

Water was a ceaseless obsession at Versailles—a locality that Saint-Simon once described as "that most dismal and thankless of spots, without vistas, woods, or water."[14] Without water? Eventually, Versailles became a fabulous City of Waters, although this was achieved at an enormous cost in money, labor, and human lives. In a first attempt to bring water to the gardens, the land nearby was tapped by underground drainage and all the moisture in the area was drawn into the reservoir through a system of pipes. This step proved inadequate. The next step was to build a tower and have water lifted up to it by means of a horse-operated piston pump. A Great Fête marked these accomplishments in the summer of 1668. Soon after, full-scale water displays were regular features of garden parties, consuming more water in a day than the public pumps delivered to the entire population of Paris of 600,000 people.[15]

As the garden continued to expand, so did demands for more and more water. The king turned to the rivers of France, unperturbed by the idea that fertile valleys might be dried up to feed his hydraulic toys (fig. 5). The first river to be tapped was the Seine, followed by the Bièvre and the Loire. Finally, with the approval of the great military engineer and architect Sébastien Vauban, it was decided to bring water from the river Eure, a tributary of the Seine to the west of Versailles. Work began in 1685. For three years, under the supervision of the minister of war, François Michel Louvois, thirty thousand soldiers labored day and night to bring water to the palace grounds through forty miles of canals and aqueducts. After eight million *livres* had been spent and thousands of soldiers had died of injury and malaria, the project was abandoned. Water remained scarce at Versailles, so much so that courtiers received only one small basinful each for their daily ablutions.[16] It reflects the spirit of the times that necessity had to yield to the exigency of play and display: there might not be enough water for the maintenance of bodily hygiene, but somehow enough water had to be found for the fountains, which finally reached the astonishing number of fourteen hundred at Versailles and Marly (Louis XIV's hermitage, some five miles from Versailles).[17]

Fountains were not only a key aesthetic element in the great gardens of the Renaissance and Baroque periods; they were also a toy, a sort of joke,

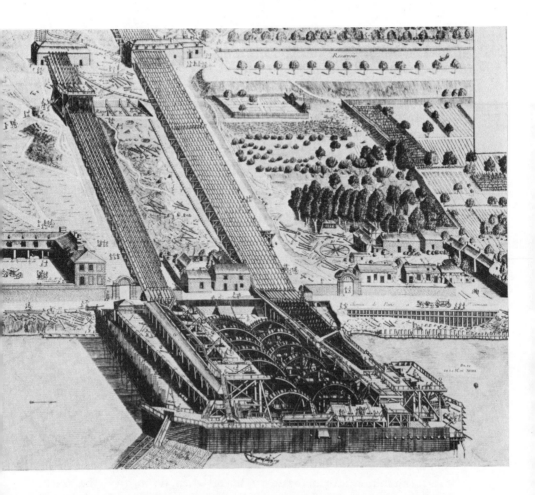

Fig. 5. The great Machine de Marly, completed in 1682, used an extraordinarily complex set of wheels to pump water from the Seine to an aqueduct (not shown here) that then supplied the fountains and lakes of Versailles. An anonymous engraving.

an expression of power in a frolicsome mood. The robust humor of fountains, which must seem childish to modern taste, was manifest not only in the jets of water shooting from the penises and nipples of human statues, but also in the widespread popularity of "water surprises." In England, one of the few improvements that Queen Elizabeth made at Hampton Court was "a splendid high and massy fountain" that spouted water at unexpected moments, drenching the spectators around it. In the gardens of the Alcázar at Seville fountains were designed to give a cold douche to unsuspecting visitors. At the château and parks of Hellbrunn, a few miles south of Salzburg (built by Archbishop Marcus Sitticus of Ems in 1614), practical jokes included shooting jets of water on the guests from artificial antlers hung on a wall and squirting them up from the seats of their chairs. In Italy, the Villa d'Este boasted several water tricks at the Fountain of Rome. Thus, the seats that were arranged along two sides of the piazza for people to sit while admiring the fountain contained secret holes through which water spurted to wet the buttocks of the weary beholders. Stairs that led to a little green patch below the cascade released a surprise jet of water which bathed whoever stepped on it "from the navel down." An iron gate in the middle of the bridge that led to the podium was contrived to eject two different streams of water at unsuspecting strollers (fig. 6).[18] Montaigne, while visiting Italy, was greatly impressed by the mechanical and hydraulic ingenuities of the Tuscan villa at Pratolino. At one place in the garden, he found an elaborate water trick: "On touching a spring, the whole grotto becomes full of water, and all the seats spout minute streams against you; and when, fleeing from the attack, you seek refuge on the stairs that lead to the castle, the motion of another hidden mechanism gives play to a thousand jets of water that inundate you with their showers till you reach the top."[19]

Apart from these surprises, which made the guests at least momentarily wet and uncomfortable, garden-builders were also immoderately fond of more innocent mechanical toys operated by water power. At the Pratolino villa, for example, hidden machinery made human figures move and, even more remarkable, made artificial animals jump into the water, drink, and swim about. At Hellbrunn, puppets swam around in a basin, spouting water the while; and birds piped among the stalactites. Perhaps the best known of these water-driven ingenuities is that at the Villa d'Este, praised by both Montaigne and (later) John Evelyn. On entering a part of the garden, Montaigne wrote, "you hear the notes of birds blended in harmony," artificial sounds produced by the impact of water falling on trapped air. "Touch a spring and you give motion to an artificial owl, which, on presenting itself on top of a rock, causes a sudden cessation of the previous harmony, the little birds being supposed to have become alarmed at his presence; then, on touching another spring, the owl retires, and the birds recommence, and you can continue this sport as long as you like."[20]

Forcing water to jump, spray, or weave into fanciful patterns waned in popularity with the growing acceptance of the picturesque and natural gardens from the end of the seventeenth century onward. As we have noted earlier, nature was still seen as a "raw goddess," and an artist-gardener was under obligation to perfect her form by eliminating her "false accidents." Lancelot Brown preferred placid or cascading waters to shooting fountains, but what he created was no less a total artifact, as William Cowper pointed out in the following lines:

He speaks. The lake in front becomes a lawn;
Woods vanish, hills subside, and vallies rise:
And streams, as if created for his use,
Pursue the track of his directing wand,
Now murm'ring soft, now roaring in cascades—
Ev'n as he bids![21]

Power makes it possible for the builder to act on a whim and do with nature whatever he pleases. Eventually, fatigue and boredom set in, or perhaps guilt; the builder then imposes a limit on what he does, persuading himself that not he but some external law derived from nature dictates such restraint. The excesses of artificiality are denounced, a "return to nature" is praised. Power is still exercised but with a proud and ostentatious restraint that confuses even further the meaning of *natural* in a work of art. We have seen how water was toyed with, particularly in the period from 1500 to 1700, when power was used with a childish lack of inhibition. Let us now turn to plants.

Playing and experimenting with plants take a variety of forms, some innocent and imaginative, others that must be described as extremely willful or perverse. One common form of play, practiced throughout the long history of gardening, is to uproot plants from their native habitats and transport them to a new and alien setting. To play and experiment at a regal scale, one must have the right kinds of material, and the more exotic

Fig. 6. The water trick over the bridge at the Fountain of Rome, Villa d'Este.
From Venturini's seventeenth-century engraving.

these are the more they are valued. Queen Hatshepsut of Egypt, who reigned from ca. 1486 to 1468 B.C., desired frankincense, a rare perfume that comes from the gum of the *Boswellia* tree. At that time the *Boswellia* could be found only in the land of Punt (Somalia) in East Africa. A mission was dispatched to bring specimens of the tree back to Egypt. This was done. The trees apparently flourished in their new home, under human supervision, each plant in its own pot of earth.

Since the time of Queen Hatshepsut, potentates everywhere— whosoever fancied gardens—spared no expense and effort to bring strange forms of life into their domain, thus enhancing its mystery and splendor. A time came when the entire world could be tapped for exotic specimens. By the early part of the seventeenth century, great Roman families were able to assemble flora from such distant places as India, the Cape of Good Hope, South and Central America, the Caribbean Islands, and North America. The multiformity of plants is suggested by Cardinal Barberini's collection. Among its more important specimens were Egyptian papyrus, the *Hibiscus mutabilis*, Judas trees, tamarind, sumac, yucca, begonias, passion flowers, exotic jasmines, large "Canadian" strawberries, tuberose, amaryllis belladonna, sprekelia or jacobean lilies, and the scarlet lobelia, or cardinal flower.[22]

Exotics from distant countries, in addition to providing prestige and an air of opulence, satisfied Renaissance man's yearning for the bizarre. This yearning could also be somewhat assuaged by unusual flora closer to home. In Tudor England, it would seem that certain flowers found favor merely because they were curious, such as the little trefoils called Snailes or Barbary Buttons that John Parkinson, in a book published in 1629, described as "pretty toyes for Gentlewomen." Flowers could be playthings, and some of them bore comical names such as Hose-in-Hose, the Foolish Cowslip, and Jack-an-Apes-on Horse-backe; the last name was used by country people for anything out of the ordinary.

Tudor gardens contained many useful plants, including fruit trees. Fruits matured into predictable shapes. The more playful horticulturists wondered, however, whether this had to be. Could not the shapes be altered into something more amusing? They could, provided the fruits were constrained by molds while still young. There seemed hardly any limit to what one could do. As Francis Bacon put it, "You may have cucumbers as long as a cane; or as round as a sphere; or formed like a cross. You may have also apples in the form of pears or lemons. You may have also fruit in more accurate figures, as we said of men, beasts, or birds, according as you make the moulds."[23]

The desire for power over nature, exhibited in the manufacture of curiosities, has led people to feign achievements and indulge in idle boasting, according to John Parkinson. Some writers wrote as though they had the means "of making flowers double as they list, and of giving them colour and sent [sic] as they please, and to flower likewise at what time they will." Some of these errors, Parkinson went on to say, "are ancient, and continued long by tradition, and others are of later invention: and therefore the more to be condemned, that men of wit and judgement in these dayes should expose themselves in their writings, to be rather laughed at, then believed for such idle calls."[24]

In Parkinson's time, people wanted to play with flowers and fruits as they wished but lacked the techniques to do so. This wish remains. Now, in the twentieth century, genetic science has made it possible for flower fanciers to be extravagantly imaginative and still hope for successful realization. A hybridist can now, writes Eleanor Perényi,

> take a simple flower and double or triple the petals, ruffle them, curl them. He can make an aster look like a chrysanthemum, a tulip like a peony, a marigold like a carnation, ad infinitum.... He can turn the colossus into a pigmy and vice versa. Above all, he can mess up the normal color range of a plant so that it no longer sends a familiar message to the eye. Burpee Seed Company for years ran a contest offering $10,000 to anyone who raised a white marigold. They never explained why a flower with gold in its name would be more desirable in white. They didn't have to, not to an audience trained to prefer any departure from the natural; chartreuse narcissus, mauve daylilies, pink forget-me-nots and those bi-colors inflicted wherever possible.[25]

Long before humans had the power to alter the color and scent of a plant or change it from a "colossus into a pigmy," they were able to alter the *shape* of a plant through the art of clipping. The viewing of plants as sculptural material to be freely transformed has deep roots in Western civilization; moreover, this attitude persists or is recurrent. In ancient Egypt, gardeners yielded to the temptation of clipping their trees into spherical and columnar forms. The ancient Romans were uninhibited in their playfulness. Hedge clipping had become an art, known eventually as

topiary art. Pliny the Younger heavily indulged. Describing his Tuscan villa, he noted how at one place
box trees were cut into numerous different shapes,
"even letters that spell out the name of the owner and
again of the artist." Such was the proprietorial and
artistic vanity of those times. Animal forms were executed in Pliny's villa and no doubt in the estates of
other Romans as well.[26]

Medieval gardeners played with plant materials by
creating arbors and clipped hedges. A fancy piece of
plant architecture was the labyrinth, known sometimes as the House of Daedalus. In England such a
labyrinth may have existed as early as the twelfth
century. Henry II is said to have hidden the Fair Rosa-
mond, his beloved, in a vegetal contrivance at Wood-
stock.[27] Whatever the status of mazes and labyrinths
prior to 1400, they were popular by Tudor times.
They appealed to the Tudor sense of fun and humor
and to their use of the garden for recreation and games.
A host enjoyed losing his guests in an intricate maze
and then rescuing them when they cried out for help.
From the evidence of pictorial art, we know that gardeners clipped certain individual trees and bushes into
fancy shapes. The crowns of trees set in the middle of
flower beds were sometimes cut to resemble triple
wreaths. On May Day, artificial fruits might be hung

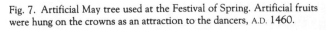

Fig. 7. Artificial May tree used at the Festival of Spring. Artificial fruits
were hung on the crowns as an attraction to the dancers, A.D. 1460.

on the wreaths (fig. 7). Some bushes might be cut into the shape of pheasants. Both the clipped tree with artificial fruits and the pheasant-shaped bush appear to have been inspired by ideas that the Crusaders brought home. Vegetal pheasants were a substitute for the real pheasants that strutted in an Oriental paradise; and the decorated, clipped trees could have been influenced by tales of bejeweled artificial trees in the palaces and gardens of the East.

Topiary art was known and practiced on a modest scale before 1400. In the course of the fifteenth century it began to acquire prominence in certain Italian gardens (fig. 8). One such garden belonged to Giovanni Rucellai, a rich Florentine merchant for whom Leone Battista Alberti served as architect and friend. Rucellai kept a diary during a time of forced leisure caused by the plague of 1459. In his diary the description of his garden is silent on the subject of sculpture, except for the terra-cotta vases. He lays stress, instead, on the clipped box. At one place in the garden the box is cut into the shapes of giants and centaurs, ships, galleys, temples, arrows, men, women, popes, cardinals, dragons, and all kinds of animals.[28]

Two literary works further bear witness to the popularity of plant architecture and sculpture during the second half of the fifteenth century. One work is the *Hypnerotomachia Poliphili* (Dream of Poliphilus), believed to have been written by Francesco Colonna, a monk of the Dominican Order in Venice, and first published there in 1499. Topiary effects tended to dominate Colonna's garden. Trees and bushes were made to look like pavilions and fountains and to simulate sculptures of animals. The second poetical work is *De Hortis Herperidum*, by Jovianus Pontanus, written about the year 1500. Jovianus may well have been thinking of Rucellai's villa when he made the following recommendations:

> When the tree, owing to the gardener's constant care and attention, begins to put out its branches and unfold its leaves, then choose the task for each, and make the formless mass into shapes of beauty. Let one climb to high tower or bulwark, another bend to spear or bow; let one make strong the trenches or the walls; one like trumpet must wake men to arms and summon hosts to battle. Thus, shall you by skill, time, native strength and careful nurture, convert the tree into many new forms, even as a thread of wool is woven into divers figures and colours in a carpet.[29]

Fig. 8. Topiary art: clipped box hedges as envisioned by the mid-fifteenth-century monk Colonna in his illustrated work *Hypnerotomachia Poliphili*.

The importance of topiary gardening varied in time and place. Among the Italians, early enthusiasm for at least the fancier forms began to wane toward the end of the sixteenth century. Increasing emphasis on the garden's overall design tended to curtail topiary ebullience. If fantasy required an outlet, it might take to stone rather than to vegetal sculpture: witness, the fantastic stone sculptures in Duke Vicino Orsini's garden at Bomarzo, near Viterbo, which included a winged dragon fighting a lioness (fig. 9), a colossal tortoise, bears, a Roman soldier seized in the trunk of an elephant, and giants.[30]

In France, topiary exuberance found expression in architectural rather than animal forms. The importance of green architecture in the ideal garden is clearly articulated in a work called *Traité du jardinage selon les raisons de la nature et de l'art* (1638) by Jacques Boyceau, an influential designer of his time and a forerunner of the style made famous by André le Nôtre. In this work, he favors rooms and pavilions made of trees, recommends that they be furnished with doors and windows and carefully maintained by constant binding and clipping. Even functional hedges, he says, can be transformed into an architectural feature in the landscape by being provided with fenestrations, arcades, and niches.[31] In England, Francis Bacon expressed a distaste for topiary fantasies, characterizing them as mere toys for children. On the other hand, his conception of a hedge was full of playfulness. "The garden," he wrote, "is best to be square, encompassed on all the four sides with a stately arched hedge.... Over the arches let there be an entire edge of some four feet high, framed also upon carpenters' work; and upon the upper hedge, over every arch, a little turret, with a belly enough to receive a cage of birds: and over every space between the arches some other little figure, with broad plates of round coloured glass gilt, for the sun to play upon."[32]

Despite strictures like those of Francis Bacon, topiary artworks continued to prosper in England throughout the seventeenth century, reaching indeed new heights of flamboyance toward the end of that period. Among the most flamboyant is that at Levens Hall, Westmorland, where a certain Beaumont began in about 1689 to create an outlandish green sculpture of umbrellas, mushrooms, and chessmen around the house (fig. 10). More significant as a measure of the taste of the times is how widespread these clipped hedges and trees were in the landscape. From the travel accounts of Celia Fiennes, written between 1685 and 1697, one

Fig. 9. A winged dragon fighting a lioness in the garden of Duke Vicino Orsini at Bomarzo, near Viterbo; mid sixteenth century. (Drawing by Wayne Howell)

gains the impression that at least in certain parts of England they jumped to the eye. Fiennes wrote: "Epsom is 15 miles from London, there are great curiositys in cut hedges and trees almost before all doores; they have trees in rows which they cut up smooth and about 3 or 4 yards up they lay frames of wood in manner of a penthouse, so plat the branches on it and cut it smooth; they leave the stem of the tree to run up and then cut it clear to the top which they cut in round heads. . . ."[33]

Topiary whimsy of the sort at Levens Hall inspired satire, of which the most cutting and best known is that of Alexander Pope, written in 1712. Pope concocted a bill of sales and among his wares were:

Adam and Eve in Yew; Adam a little shatter'd by the fall of the Tree of Knowledge in the Great Storm; Eve and the Serpent very flourishing.
The Tower of Babel, not yet finished.
St. George in Box; his Arm scarce long enough, but will be in a condition to stick the Dragon by next April.
A Quickset Hog, shot up into a Porcupine, by its being forgot a Week in rainy Weather.
A Lavender Pigg with Sage growing in his Belly.[34]

Pope's ridicule marked the beginning of a powerful shift in English taste, one that extolled prospects less obviously constrained by the forces of art and more evocative of nature. Both high-shooting fountains and topiary exuberance declined in importance during the eighteenth century. On the other hand, topiary caprice did not disappear. It continued to have practitioners throughout the eighteenth century, and indeed in the nineteenth century as well as in our time (fig. 11). It would seem that people do not easily forfeit their right to use their shears as they see fit. Hedge sculpture is fun and challenging and gives people a sense of power. A gardener employed to work on the estate of Lord Covehithe at Easton, Suffolk, in 1942, had this to say: "Topiary, there was a lot of that. It was a very responsible job. You had only to make one bad clip and the pheasant becomes a duck. The gardeners usually made up these creatures themselves. We are tempted to cut out something terrible sometimes. . . . But of course we never did. Even when we went on to mechanical hedge-trimmers we still kept topiary. There was a great pride in it, and in hedge-cutting of any sort."[35] Lord Covehithe's gardeners may have resisted the temptation to cut out "something terrible," but some Califor-

Fig. 10. The topiary garden at Levens Hall in Westmorland.

Fig. 11. An example of contemporary topiary caprice from the Green Animals Topiary Garden in Newport, Rhode Island.

nians were less inhibited. In 1981, certain residents in San Diego brought charges against their neighbors for having clipped their hedges into the shape of male sex organs. These topiary works, the plaintiffs claimed, were obscene and had ruined their view.[36]

Gardeners can play with plants in many ways. One time-honored way is to dwarf them, a procedure that is part of a larger effort to reduce wilderness to the size of a toy. Control over nature feels absolute when nature can be made to sit in the palm of one's hand. Although topiary art had come to mean plant sculpture by the Renaissance period, the word *topia* had other meanings in antiquity, one of which was "miniature gardens," such as those found in the peristyles of Roman houses. These miniature gardens were probably derived from landscapes in bas-relief on certain courtyard walls that date back to Hellenistic times. Bas-relief, freestanding miniature, and mural landscape art (which we have discussed earlier) were all attempts to bring nature, transformed and tamed, into the confines of the house. Some of the houses at Pompeii had mural paintings of gardens; others had, in addition, three-dimensional miniature landscapes. One such miniature showed a tiny water staircase and a pool adorned with Lilliputian herms, statues, and representations of water birds. On Pliny's Tuscan estate dwarf trees and gardens were laid out in imitation of country scenes. Whether he used rocks to simulate mountains is not clear. Rocks, an important feature in Roman garden design, were placed around grottoes to give them an air of wildness. Such landscaping around the grotto may be regarded as an attempt at miniaturization.

Although we find evidences of miniaturization in the Roman world, doubtless this process was and remains a specialty of the Orient. The miniature garden is a distinctive art form of China, Japan, and southeast Asia.[37] Nature's grandeur is scaled down so that it can be accommodated in a portable basin, to be placed on a stand in the garden or the house. What are the motivations behind the making of miniature landscapes? The most general answer is the desire for power, and this answer would be correct in both a magico-religious and an aesthetic-artistic context.

A typical miniature landscape in the Orient has three principal non-human components: rock, plants, and water. Rock stands for mountain, plants for trees or forest, and water for lake or sea. In China, which is a primary center of origin for miniaturization, rock may be the oldest as well as the most important of the three components. Without mountain,

Fig. 11. An example of contemporary topiary caprice from the Green Animals Topiary Garden in Newport, Rhode Island.

nians were less inhibited. In 1981, certain residents in San Diego brought charges against their neighbors for having clipped their hedges into the shape of male sex organs. These topiary works, the plaintiffs claimed, were obscene and had ruined their view.[36]

Gardeners can play with plants in many ways. One time-honored way is to dwarf them, a procedure that is part of a larger effort to reduce wilderness to the size of a toy. Control over nature feels absolute when nature can be made to sit in the palm of one's hand. Although topiary art had come to mean plant sculpture by the Renaissance period, the word *topia* had other meanings in antiquity, one of which was "miniature gardens," such as those found in the peristyles of Roman houses. These miniature gardens were probably derived from landscapes in bas-relief on certain courtyard walls that date back to Hellenistic times. Bas-relief, freestanding miniature, and mural landscape art (which we have discussed earlier) were all attempts to bring nature, transformed and tamed, into the confines of the house. Some of the houses at Pompeii had mural paintings of gardens; others had, in addition, three-dimensional miniature landscapes. One such miniature showed a tiny water staircase and a pool adorned with Lilliputian herms, statues, and representations of water birds. On Pliny's Tuscan estate dwarf trees and gardens were laid out in imitation of country scenes. Whether he used rocks to simulate mountains is not clear. Rocks, an important feature in Roman garden design, were placed around grottoes to give them an air of wildness. Such landscaping around the grotto may be regarded as an attempt at miniaturization.

Although we find evidences of miniaturization in the Roman world, doubtless this process was and remains a specialty of the Orient. The miniature garden is a distinctive art form of China, Japan, and southeast Asia.[37] Nature's grandeur is scaled down so that it can be accommodated in a portable basin, to be placed on a stand in the garden or the house. What are the motivations behind the making of miniature landscapes? The most general answer is the desire for power, and this answer would be correct in both a magico-religious and an aesthetic-artistic context.

A typical miniature landscape in the Orient has three principal non-human components: rock, plants, and water. Rock stands for mountain, plants for trees or forest, and water for lake or sea. In China, which is a primary center of origin for miniaturization, rock may be the oldest as well as the most important of the three components. Without mountain,

Fig. 11. An example of contemporary topiary caprice from the Green Animals Topiary Garden in Newport, Rhode Island.

nians were less inhibited. In 1981, certain residents in San Diego brought charges against their neighbors for having clipped their hedges into the shape of male sex organs. These topiary works, the plaintiffs claimed, were obscene and had ruined their view.[36]

Gardeners can play with plants in many ways. One time-honored way is to dwarf them, a procedure that is part of a larger effort to reduce wilderness to the size of a toy. Control over nature feels absolute when nature can be made to sit in the palm of one's hand. Although topiary art had come to mean plant sculpture by the Renaissance period, the word *topia* had other meanings in antiquity, one of which was "miniature gardens," such as those found in the peristyles of Roman houses. These miniature gardens were probably derived from landscapes in bas-relief on certain courtyard walls that date back to Hellenistic times. Bas-relief, freestanding miniature, and mural landscape art (which we have discussed earlier) were all attempts to bring nature, transformed and tamed, into the confines of the house. Some of the houses at Pompeii had mural paintings of gardens; others had, in addition, three-dimensional miniature landscapes. One such miniature showed a tiny water staircase and a pool adorned with Lilliputian herms, statues, and representations of water birds. On Pliny's Tuscan estate dwarf trees and gardens were laid out in imitation of country scenes. Whether he used rocks to simulate mountains is not clear. Rocks, an important feature in Roman garden design, were placed around grottoes to give them an air of wildness. Such landscaping around the grotto may be regarded as an attempt at miniaturization.

Although we find evidences of miniaturization in the Roman world, doubtless this process was and remains a specialty of the Orient. The miniature garden is a distinctive art form of China, Japan, and southeast Asia.[37] Nature's grandeur is scaled down so that it can be accommodated in a portable basin, to be placed on a stand in the garden or the house. What are the motivations behind the making of miniature landscapes? The most general answer is the desire for power, and this answer would be correct in both a magico-religious and an aesthetic-artistic context.

A typical miniature landscape in the Orient has three principal non-human components: rock, plants, and water. Rock stands for mountain, plants for trees or forest, and water for lake or sea. In China, which is a primary center of origin for miniaturization, rock may be the oldest as well as the most important of the three components. Without mountain,

there is no landscape: the same is less true of plants and water. One of the earliest mountain models is the "hill censer" (*po shan lu*).[38] Appearing some time during the Ch'in or early Han dynasty, it is a utensil of pottery or bronze fashioned into the shape of a cluster of peaked mountains. Holes in the *po shan lu* allow the incense burning inside to rise to the surface and waft over it like mist in the vicinity of towering peaks. To the Chinese, mountain and mist (rock and water) have been an age-old symbol of potency. This potency of nature the Chinese have sought to capture by various magico-religious devices, one of which is the hill censer. Another is the image of a sacred mountain hanging on the staff of a Taoist adept. By recreating a mountain on a much reduced scale the Taoist believes he can focus and contain its supernatural emanations and thus gain access to them. The further the size of a model is from that of the original, the more potent it is likely to be—an idea based on the analogy of the Taoist priest boiling down his medicinal stock to concentrate its essences.[39]

The miniature garden may contain only rock and sand. More typically, it contains also dwarf plants and water. The complete miniature has, in addition, tiny buildings and figurines: it is an entire world reduced in scale. When did this particular art form emerge? Literary evidence suggests that it existed in the T'ang dynasty, perhaps already in a high state of sophistication, and that it flourished during the Sung dynasty. Paintings of the Sung period show potted landscapes in people's houses, in their gardens (thus creating a model of nature within a model of nature), in outdoor areas where children play, and even in a silkworm nursery. Their presence in a silkworm nursery suggests that by this time the art form was no longer an elitist cultivation segregated from the work environment of ordinary people.[40]

The Western world tends to associate miniature gardens primarily with Japan, under the name of *bonsai*. Bonsai, however, is a Chinese term. Moreover, Japanese encyclopaedias assign a foreign origin to this art and note that it was introduced to the islands in the sixth or seventh century. Compared with Chinese practice, Japanese practice has retained a greater measure of aesthetic seriousness. Bonsai remains an elitist cultivation. One reason might be that in the course of the Tokugawa period (1603–1867), when peace was the norm, members of the warrior class found themselves increasingly burdened with leisure. A few gave up their high samurai status to go into the business world, but much free time remained. The more artistically inclined of these former warriors took up time-consuming hobbies, including the art of dwarfing trees. There appears to be a link here between the religio-asceticism of the military and the religio-aestheticism of bonsai.

Dwarfing trees, as done by Oriental masters, is one of the most refined ways of playing with nature. Clearly dwarf trees exist in the wild, in response to harsh climate and soil. Bonsai gardeners are people who have succeeded in imitating nature's own unrelenting severity. To rise to the top of their profession such artist-craftsmen, like preeminent generals and surgeons, must not merely tolerate but take pleasure in the exercise of force—in wielding the knife, scalpel, and shears. Stunting plant growth as such, we should note, is a standard practice of horticultural art, one that is by no means limited to Oriental gardens. In the Western world, we find it taken up in the making of low and thick hedges. Eleanor Perényi, in her book *Green Thoughts*, claims to discern a difference of attitude between European and American gardeners: Europeans are willing to turn potentially large trees into low dense screens with a regimen of pruning and training more sustained and savage than anything that American gardeners are willing to contemplate.[41]

It is, however, in the Orient rather than in Europe that the dwarfing and shaping of plants have reached their apogee. The history of these ancient practices has close ties with the desire to live to an old age and, if possible, forever. Taoism was an early source of inspiration. If the rock symbolized potency, the stunted and twisted plant stood for enduring life. In the same miniature garden, a gnarled dwarf tree might stand alongside a diminutive and bent human figure. Both are immortal. Moreover, both have achieved immortality through similar techniques. By slowing down the sap, a plant became stunted and took on the appearance of extreme old age; likewise, by slowing down the movement of breath around the body through respiratory exercises, the Taoist adept hoped to live to be a very old man, bent double with age, and able to enter the cavernous Other World as an immortal.[42]

Once the Chinese gardeners learned how to play freely with plant life, they sometimes succumbed to whimsicality. The religious significance of cavernous rocks and bent trees tended to be lost in games of power, and what the gardeners produced was more grotesque than either beautiful or portentous (fig. 12). In the twelfth century already, one could discern signs of excess in Emperor Hui-tsung's gardens, where the limbs of certain pine trees were knotted to look like canopies, cranes, and dragons (fig. 13). It says something of Chinese personality and culture that such extreme distortions have become an admired feature of the garden through the succeeding centuries, and that they remain an accepted practice in modern times.

Countries that have come under Chinese influence show a similar penchant for torturing (from the Latin word for twisting) plant life. In Vietnam, the limbs of garden trees, like those in China, might be warped into the semblance of animals.[43] In Japan, dwarfing and bending as in bonsai art have reached nimieties of refinement. Unlike ordinary garden trees which, though twisted, might still grow to several feet in height and would still have their roots in the common soil, the bonsai trees are only a few inches tall and their roots never touch the solid earth. To create a bonsai, the gardener must subject the plants to early and severe training. The plants themselves should be strong enough to withstand the rigors imposed on them. Pruning and wiring are basic techniques; others are tying, propping, and the application of jacks and weights. Open a modern bonsai gardener's kit and one will encounter an array of tools including a pair of side cutters for snipping wire; a thin screwdriver, with the upper edge bent at a 45 degree angle, to use as a cutting hook; a sharp penknife or scalpel; an assortment of copper wires, brushes, trowels, and tweezers. Any person who is aware of the contents of a tool kit and reflects upon what he finds there will question the view that the making of miniature gardens is a deeply humane art.[44]

Plant life has exigencies of its own that may conflict with human needs and desires. In dreams of the Other World, where perfection reigns, fruits and flowers often appear; they may well be an essential component of that perfection and yet attitudes toward them—and toward organic nature generally—are curiously ambivalent. In the Bible, Eden is a picture of organic innocence. By contrast, the City of God in Revelation is a thoroughly mineralized and bejeweled world in which neither tree nor water is to be found. In Zoroastrianism, the garden paradise is predictably filled with fruits and flowers, but it also has paths of burnished gold and pleasure pavilions of diamonds and pearls. Moreover, among those who qualify to enter this paradisiac world are the diggers of canals and builders of fountains and aqueducts—that is, people who have actively transformed nature and the earth.

Fig. 12. The ancient art of dwarfing and twisting trees is exemplified in this modern specimen in a Shanghai nursery. The trunk has been bent and wired until it has grown into a knot. (Drawing by Wayne Howell)

Fig. 13. A "deer-shaped" tree in a modern Hang-chou garden. The "dragon-shaped" tree in the gardens of Emperor Hui-tsung (1082–1135) may have resembled this plant. (Drawing by Wayne Howell)

Trees, fruits, and flowers are all highly desirable. But they do not last, or they blossom at inconvenient times. Oriental potentates have shown an inclination to substitute or supplement the natural growths of the earth with those made of materials that are less subject to decay. In the gardens of Emperor Sui (reign A.D. 604–18), outside of Lo-yang, when the leaves had fallen from the maples in autumn, the trees and bushes were decked with leaves and flowers made of glistening fabrics; and in addition to real lotuses, the lake was adorned with artificial lotus blossoms.[45] In Persia, under Islam, the love of trees, flowers, and fruits seems shadowed by the awareness that they do not last. Moreover, the impermanence of the organic hints at the limitation and impermanence of human power. Occupants of the Persian throne preferred the more enduring symbolism of the artificial tree. From an account by the poet Firdausi (ca. 940–1020), we learn that King Kay Khusraw possessed a tree which had a silver trunk and gold and ruby branches. In the Ghaznavid period of the eleventh and twelfth centuries, the court was decorated with trees of gold flanked by artificial narcissi in pots of silver. Similar trees appeared at the Mongol court in Iran during the thirteenth and fourteenth centuries. Materials other than noble metals and precious stones were also used. Craftsmen called the *nakhlband,* or "maker of artificial flowers," practiced an old though minor art in which paper, paste, wax, and paint were transformed into trees, flowers, fruits, and miniature gardens. People less wealthy than rulers and the nobility could afford these modest artworks, but they were not merely the ornaments of the less wealthy. During the Qajar period (1779–1925), vases containing paper flowers lined the avenue of approach to the ruler on his outdoor throne.[46]

Baghdad was the residence of the commander of the faithful, and thus a political and commercial center of the Arab world, for nearly five hundred years. Resplendent palaces and gardens were built on or near the banks of the Tigris during this period. Byzantine ambassadors, visiting Baghdad in the year 917, reported on some of the marvels. One of them was the new Kiosk (*gausak*), meaning a pleasure house surrounded by gardens. In the gardens were seven hundred dwarf palms, the trunks of which were entirely covered with pieces of teakwood held in place by gilded copper rings. Arabs venerated the palm, the tree of their true home. However, they seem to have found the stem ugly, and rich men spent money dressing it up in costly materials. The palm, dwarfed and dressed, went part way to becoming a precious artifact. Going all the way was the mineral tree, a feature common to Byzantine and Arab courts. A supreme example of it stood in Baghdad's House of the Tree, a palace compound that impressed the Byzantine ambassadors even more than did the Kiosk. The tree itself had eighteen boughs of gold and silver and innumerable branches covered with fruits made of precious stones. On the branches perched gold and silver birds, which whistled and sighed in harmony when a breeze passed through.[47]

The opulence of the Orient made a deep impression on the Crusaders. From the twelfth century onward, European gardens showed increasing signs of a taste for pleasure and the glitters of artifice, reflecting the influence of Byzantine and Arab courts. We have already noted that certain trees in medieval European gardens had their crowns clipped into the shape of triple umbrellas on which artificial fruits might hang. Some of the May trees, around which people danced, were made of metal. In literature, even before the Crusades, Oriental influence had penetrated the West by way of the Byzantine court. Thus Bishop Liutprand of Cremona, after seeing the imperial palace of Constantinople in 968, was inspired to give a detailed account of the throne and of the golden tree with its singing birds. By the thirteenth century, under the sway of recurrent tales from the Crusaders, the tree of noble metal and precious stones on which mechanical birds sang had become a standard emblem of paradisiac beauty and mystery (for example, the golden tree and singing birds of Wolfram von Eschenbach's *Titurel*) in the poetry of the West.[48]

Although trees, once planted, stay put, their branches and foliage grow and change as though possessed of a will of their own that must be constantly disciplined. There is pleasure in overcoming recalcitrance; and pleasure in the growing plant itself when it responds to human care. Plants can be disciplined and cared for like pets, but at times even vegetal pets are a nuisance. Leaves from the potted ferns that hang next to the bay windows—a fashion in decor that had taken over upper-middle-class homes by the last quarter of the nineteenth century—would drop upon and litter the windowseats and floor. As servants are more difficult to find and keep, the temptation grows stronger to keep plants that make no demands at all, which exist only as artifactitious imitations. In some private homes and even more in commercial establishments, to cut expense and bother, artificial greenery and flowers are substituted for real ones. The city may find that it can no longer quite afford the upkeep of live trees and may think of using, instead, plastic ones to provide the basic services of shade, pleasingly varied forms, and color.[49] But in the eyes of urbane designers, artificial plants are not mere substitutes *faute de mieux.* Aluminum trees are not intended to evoke pastoral nostalgia. What they do for a great city, especially to its entertainment district, is to enhance the ambience of glitter and glamor—to suggest a timeless world that denies the organic, with its inevitable hints of impermanence, growth and decay. Artificial trees are not a mere fad of the modern age. We have seen how venerable is the idea of the mineral tree and the mineral fruit. This desire for the inorganic, manifest in all high cultures, reflects a deep human ambivalence toward life.

5   ANIMALS: FROM POWERS TO PETS

In an offguard moment, C. S. Lewis assevered: "The tame animal is in the deepest sense the only natural animal. . . . Beasts are to be understood only in their relation to man and through man to God." Evelyn Underhill, Lewis's friend, wrote in protest: "You surely *can't* mean that, or think that the robin redbreast in a cage doesn't put heaven in a rage but is regarded as an excellent arrangement. Your own example of the good-man, good-wife, and good-dog in the good homestead is a bit smug and utilitarian, don't you think, over against the wild beauty of God's creative action in the jungle and deep sea? And if we ever get a sideway glimpse of the animal-in-itself, the animal—existing for God's glory and pleasure and lit by His light, we don't owe it to the Pekinese, the Persian cat or the canary, but to some wild free creature living in completeness of adjustment to Nature a life that is utterly independent of man."[1]

Underhill tried to restore for Lewis a sense of the power and grandeur of animals. This sense, weak in modern men and women, was at one time strong throughout the world. Wild and awesome nature assumed both vividness and specificity in the shapes of wild animals and monsters. The frontier history of the Western world is full of tales of encounters with beasts, natural and supernatural, that were a part of the imagery of wilderness and threatening chaos. First the desert and the steppe in the Near East and later the dark forests of Europe and North America were thought to be inhabited by ferocious animals, monsters, and demons. As late as 1707 the Puritan divine Cotton Mather could write about the "dragons" and "fiery flying serpents" that haunted New England's primeval forest. Even late in the nineteenth century, the imagination of lumbermen working in the remote forests of the Upper Midwest was able to produce a lore of fantastical beasts.[2] This fear of wilderness and tendency to populate it with strange animals was not, of course, confined to the West. It looms large in the frontier histories of other civilizations as well. For example, in China during the T'ang dynasty (618–907), when much of the tropical South was becoming known to settlers, poems that attempt to capture the flavor of the new country depict a fauna "turbulent with wild elephants, thunder-breeding dragons, monster sea turtles blowing up waves, and prodigious clams glowing in their subaqueous lairs." Even prose accounts tend to emphasize the awesome and the bizarre, such as reptiles and slimy invertebrates and "the hideous and demonic crawlers of the sodden soils."[3]

Initially, obscure beasts and monsters stood for the unknown and threatening forces of nature. Later, as the mind makes an effort to exert control, these inchoate forces were represented by more clearly envisioned animal deities and spirits, some of which were benign, many evil. Eventually, animal deities might be incorporated into the human world as part of an orderly worship. These steps, it is true, do not inevitably follow each other, but it is hard to conceive how the organized worship of an animal god can occur without an earlier stage, lost in prehistory, when the fear of unknown forces was diffuse and more likely to take the shape of protean monstrous presences.

The ancient Greek and Egyptian civilizations that we know best through historical and archaeological records have already attained the later stages of perception. To the Greeks, mountain torrents, exemplifying the rougher side of nature, were inhabited by water spirits. In art and literature as well as in folk belief, these turbulent spirits appeared as horse-shaped daemons—the centaurs and the seilensi. Nymphs, by contrast, were shaped like beautiful maidens and stood for nature's more gentle and beneficent aspects.[4] In Egypt, animals were incorporated as symbols of power into the heart of an articulated religious system in which, for instance, the falcon was another guise of the sun god Horus and the jackal was another guise of the god of the dead, Anubis. The animal itself might become an object of worship or be treated as though it were in itself sacred. This had happened to the cat. Originally, the cat was a symbol of the lioness, which was sacred to the goddess Basd. In time, however, the cat—all cats—assumed a sort of numinous power. When a cat died in the house, Herodotus reported, all the members of that household shaved their eyebrows. Dead cats were taken to the city of Bubastis where they were embalmed and later buried in sacred repositories. The investment of time and resources on the dead cats was immense. Excavators at the beginning of the twentieth century removed so many mummies that it was thought expedient to pulverize them and spread the product on the ground as fertilizer.[5]

The seemingly unlimited human capacity to see power and grandeur in the animal is illustrated by the lores of primitive cosmography and astronomy. In ancient Upper Egypt, the cow goddess of the sky (Hathor) was believed to have given birth to the sun. The sky was conceived as an immense cow whose legs are planted at the four corners of the earth and who is upheld by other gods. Modern astronomy retains the antiquated term *zodiac*, which means literally "the circle of animals." How could the ancient astronomers, as they gazed at the constellation of stars in the night sky, perceive any resemblance to animal forms? They surely could not— no more than we can do so today. They sought, rather, to honor the regions of the sky by naming them with the animals of their pantheon. These animals had such potency in the imagination of the ancients that they did not see any incompatibility of scale, absurd in its extremity, between the heavenly bodies on the one hand and animals on the other. Antiquity's conception of the stars as divine animals and as animal-shaped spirits found its way into the beliefs of the Middle Ages. For example, the animal-headed Evangelists or saints depicted on medieval manuscripts of the hermeneutic and mystical tradition appear to be derived from the animal-headed demons that represented the stars and governed the fate of men in early Jewish, Gnostic, and Christian mystic lore. Science in the late medieval period was also willing to see the stars not only as animate but as "super-animals." In the early twelfth century, Adelard of Bath, one of the first English men of science to travel to Spain and Sicily and thus expose himself to Mediterranean beliefs, was by no means surprised when his nephew asked him the starkly literal question, "If the stars are animals, what food do they eat?"[6]

When people want to express their sense of the force of nature, both in the external world and in themselves, they have found and still do find it natural to use animal images. On the cylinder seals of the first all-Mesopotamian empire (dating from ca. 2500–2400 B.C.), the imagery of beasts was able to project—for the first time—a feeling of monumental power and ferocity. Ever since, through the later phases of Mesopotamian and Assyrian art down to medieval heraldry, beasts have served to symbolize strength and aggression. In the heraldic art of the Middle Ages, animals embody power in a positive sense. Thus the lion symbolizes the virtue of strength and the eagle that of courage. Evil power is represented by monsters made up of parts of animals, such as the lion-headed eagle and the griffin—an eagle-headed lion.[7] Even in our time, when direct contact with wild animals is so rare, it is easy for us to associate strength and speed with some form of wild life. Power, even to the residents of a technopolis, is felt not as an abstract quantity measurable in dynes but as a bodily thrust and a passion. To project a feeling of power and speed, automobile manufacturers name their products Jaguar, Mustang, and Falcon, even though the clientele they wish to attract has no personal knowledge of these animals. Somehow jaguars and mustangs still project an image of power in a man-made world full of engines and machines that ought to convey energy in their own right, without borrowed feathers and claws from nature.

While in art and religion humans show an enduring tendency to see animals as the embodiment of power and as larger than life, in day-to-day existence they unhesitatingly dominate and exploit animals in myriads of ways. Even in art the aggrandizement of animals may be an indirect but highly effective means of exalting man. Rampant beasts are "captured" in art. As sculptural motifs on thrones and palace grounds or as emblems on heraldic shields they magnify and glorify their human owners. Envisage a Byzantine emperor of the ninth century, enthroned and about to receive a foreign ambassador in his great hall. Golden lions lay prostrate before him, griffins stood by his side, and rising behind him was a golden plane tree on whose branches exquisite birds displayed their gold-enameled plumage. Upon the ambassador's entrance, the birds raised their wings and sang, the griffins turned toward him, and the lions waved their tails and roared.[8] Thus mechanical wonders coated in noble metals and precious jewels substituted for real animals, but real animals—those with a reputation for ferocity and regal bearing—might also be kept in a potentate's court to underline the greater power and splendor of their master. In the court of Kublai Khan, Marco Polo was astonished by the perfect submissiveness of a flesh-and-blood lion. "You must know that a great lion is led into the Great Khan's presence; and as soon as it sees him it flings itself down prostrate before him with every appearance of deep

Fig. 14. Part of a second-century B.C. mosaic from Tunisia (now at the Museum of Antiquities, El-Djem), showing a Dionysian procession. The first known great animal procession was that of Ptolemy II (285–246 B.C.) on the feast of Dionysus.

humility and seems to acknowledge him as lord. There it stays without a chain, and is indeed a thing to marvel at."9

Potentates were ingenious at devising events that accented their power. One such event was the procession, at which animals often played a prominent role. Processions were a custom of ancient Greece, conducted ostensibly in honor of Artemis or Dionysus (fig. 14). Theocritus, in the third century B.C., mentioned a parade in which "many wild animals, among them a lioness" took part. A procession on the grandest scale occurred during the reign of Ptolemy II (285–46 B.C.) at Alexandria, then the cultural center of the Hellenistic world. The file of people and beasts took a whole day to pass through the city's stadium. Following an image of Dionysus came a long train of animals of all kinds. What could a well-placed spectator see? Elephants, four to each chariot, drawing twenty-four chariots. Eight pairs of ostriches in harness. Wild asses in harness. Six pairs of camels laden with spices. Two thousand and four hundred hounds of Indian, Hyrcanian, Molossian, and other breeds. After the hounds came one hundred and fifty men carrying trees to which were attached wild animals and birds of all sorts. These were followed by cages containing parrots, peacocks, guinea-fowl, pheasants, and "Ethiopian birds." Then came Ethiopian breeds of sheep, twenty-six white Indian oxen, eight Ethiopian oxen, a large white bear, fourteen leopards, four lynxes, sixteen cheetahs, a giraffe, and a rhinoceros. Somewhere in the procession were also twenty-four lions of great size.10

In the second century A.D., the geographer Pausanias saw at Patrae a "most magnificent" procession, which was a regular feature of the annual festival of Artemis. An unusual feature in the train was a priestess riding in a car drawn by stags—unusual because it requires high skill to put stags in harness. Great pride was taken in taming difficult wild animals and making them perform. Training animals to perform had developed into a high art in the Greco-Roman world during the first century A.D. Performing elephants were especially popular in the arenas of the Augustan age. Pliny the Elder noted that it was common to make them throw weapons into the air, fight duels, and go through some kind of "musical ride." In the reign of Tiberius (A.D. 14–37), they were taught to walk on a tightrope. At a gladiatorial show given by Germanicus, probably in A.D. 12, a dozen elephants danced and dined. It was particularly amusing to see these great, hulking beasts pick their way with anxious care to their places at the banquet among the seated guests. Pliny witnessed performing bulls fighting or rolling over at a word of command, letting themselves be caught and lifted by the horns, and even standing like charioteers in cars going at a gallop.[11] Seneca also alluded to the feats of tamers: one of them could put his hand into the lion's mouth, another dared to kiss a tiger, and a black dwarf could order an elephant to kneel or walk on a tightrope.[12] The emperor Heliogabalus (A.D. 218– 22) was reported to have driven lions, tigers, and stags in harness. A favorite practical joke of his was to turn his tame lions, leopards, and bears into the rooms of his sleeping and drunken guests at night. The mutilated beasts, toothless and clawless, were really just the emperor's roly-poly playthings. They could still do harm but were trusted not to.[13]

Tame and rare animals of great value were on their way to becoming inanimate art objects. The Byzantine emperor's golden lion and the Mongol Khan's flesh-and-blood lion were both treasured possessions; and even though one beast was alive, its freedom to act was so minimal that it too might be regarded as a prestigious artifact. Seneca observed that some of the tame lions in Rome had their manes gilded, a procedure that could be taken as a step in the conversion of an animal into an art object. Even the fish might be played with thus. Roman nobles of the late Republican period built elaborate ponds at their coastal villas and stocked them with snakelike murenas. It was said of Crassus that one of his murenas was adorned with earrings and a jeweled necklace. Pliny reported that Antonia, the grandmother of Caligula, also had earrings put on her pet murena.[14] An extraordinary example of this inclination is recorded for Mexico in the later part of the nineteenth century. Elegant women there took to the fancy of pinning hardy beetles (genus *Zopherus*) on themselves as crawling forms of adornment. To keep the adornments alive they must be put from time to time in damp, decayed timber. With such minimal care, the beetles could give satisfaction for months. As recently as 1962, Heini Hediger, then director of the Zurich Zoo, received some beetles from a lady returning from Mexico. On each, the upper side was studded with small flashing stones; a small screw ring had been inserted into the hard wing-covers and a glittering gold chain was attached to the ring.[15]

Potentates demonstrate their power by appearing to sustain a cosmos. One element of that cosmos is the menagerie. The keeping of menageries is a discriminative trait of high civilization, combining as it does the desire for order with the desire to accommodate the heterogeneous and the exotic. It has a long history. In the tomb of a grand vizier of Egypt's Old Kingdom (ca. 2500 B.C.) at Sakkara, archaeologists have found pictures of several kinds of antelope, some wearing collars, which means that they had either been bred in captivity or were caught and tamed when very young. Besides the addax (a large antelope with long spiral horns), the ibex (a wild goat), two different species of gazelles, and the oryx (an Arabian antelope with straight, sharp horns), archaeologists also discovered representations of monkeys and carnivores such as the hyena. Queen Hatshepsut sent collecting expeditions as far away as Somaliland. They brought back not only the tree that produced frankincense and other exotic plants, but also a large array of animals for her palace zoo, among them monkeys, greyhounds, leopards (or cheetahs), hundreds of very tall cattle, many species of birds, and a giraffe. King Solomon (reign ca. 974–37 B.C.) was the great farmer-zoologist of the Old Testament. The Bible records that, besides keeping great herds of beef cattle, sheep, and horses, he traded zoo animals with King Hiram of Tyre. "Once in three years came the navy of Tharshish, bringing gold, silver, and ivory, apes and peacocks" (1 Kings 10).[16] In China, the founder of the Ch'in dynasty (221–07 B.C.) gathered the vanquished lords and their families to his capital and destroyed the houses they had left behind. Beyond the city limits, he walled off a vast hunting preserve in which he domiciled the rare beasts and birds that were tributes from the vassal states. The hunting preserve that had been turned into a park became, like the capital itself, a microcosm of the sprawling empire.

> Unicorns from Chiu Chen,
> Horses from Ferghana.
> Rhinoceros from Huang Chih
> Birds from T'iao Chih.[17]

In the European Middle Ages, kings and nobles kept rare fauna on the premises of their palaces and castles, and townsmen might have maintained bear pits or a lion house. The reasons people kept wild animals were varied, ambiguous, and hard to disentangle. Vulgar curiosity, pride of dominion, prestige, and scientific interest were among the more important motivations. Despite the early bond established between hermit monks and wild animals as part of the paradisiac ideal, monasteries did not see any need to maintain a zoo, for symbolic reasons, in their midst. Indeed, the order founded by Saint Francis ruled in 1260 "that no animal be kept, for any brother or any convent, whether by the Order or by any person in the Order's name, except cats and certain birds for the removal of unclean things." A possible exception was the great abbey of Saint Gall, established in the ninth century in Switzerland. It is believed to have maintained a menagerie of rare animals, including badgers, marmots, bears, herons, and pheasants, presented to the monks as gifts.[18]

Secular potentates kept rare beasts mainly for reasons of pride and prestige. Nonetheless, a disinterested desire to know more about the bountiful manifestations of nature played a part. In this respect, Holy Roman emperor Frederick II of Sicily set an example for the great princes of the late Middle Ages and of the Renaissance. In Frederick's court, chivalry and learning were inseparably linked. The king believed that not only hunting and the martial arts but learning was a mark of nobility. To him, falconry was also a way of knowing bird life: it was a sport that simultaneously provided opportunities to study nature. Frederick was himself the author of a learned treatise called On the Art of Hunting with Birds, which he began in 1244 but left unfinished. Of course, wild captive animals also catered to his pride as king. On Frederick's many progresses and campaigns he surrounded himself with Saracen bodyguards followed by a train of scribes and astrologers, huntsmen and falconers. In addition, wild animals accompanied him—symbols of chivalry assembled in the flesh, as it were, to do homage to the king. "In November 1231, he arrived in Ravenna with a train of elephants, dromedaries, camels, panthers, gerfalcons, lions, leopards, white falcons and bearded owls," and in 1245, "the monks of Santo Zeno at Verona, in extending hospitality to the Emperor, had to entertain with him an elephant, five leopards, and twenty-four camels."[19]

Perhaps the greatest zoo of premodern times was that of the Aztecs in pre-Conquest Mexico. Accounts left by Hernando Cortez and Díaz del Castillo tell us that Lord Montezuma possessed a magnificent pleasure garden in which, among other wonders, rare aquatic birds lived in ten pools of water. The birds received food appropriate to their species. Worm eaters were fed worms, the corn eaters corn, fish eaters fish. Some three hundred keepers were employed exclusively to watch over these birds. The animals even had their own physicians. In one particularly large and beautiful house, Cortez noted, were kept many species of birds of prey. On the first floor of the same building were housed lions, tigers, wolves, foxes, and cats of every species. Both the birds of prey and the mammalian carnivores were fed poultry and, according to Díaz, also the flesh of human sacrificial victims. In another house lived human dwarves, hunchbacks, and other sorts of deformed men and women, each in a separate room. Like the other animals, the human exhibits also had their guardians.[20]

The inclusion of humans among the animals of Montezuma's menagerie is a reminder of the fact that to people of power humans too can be treated and "valued" as curiosities and pets. History swells with examples, which I will take up in later chapters. Here I should like to focus on the idea of public exhibition, as in circuses and zoos. Humans are put on display alongside of other animals, thus strongly implying that such humans are more like monkeys and bears than they are like "normal" people. But the same juxtaposition leads spectators to view the captive animals in a special way. Animals are like humans, only more openly carnal and sexual, more openly and therefore more disarmingly absurd. These aspects of animals are a major source of attraction for visitors to the modern zoo, as humans incarcerated in asylums were to their visitors in an earlier era.

Why put animals and humans on display? The correct and obvious answer is that they provide entertainment. Circuses of Roman antiquity were places of violence and bloodshed, and although they did indeed exhibit wild animals and human captives from foreign lands it was not so much the exotic appearance of these live imports as their enforced violence and killing that drew the crowds. The modern circus, which dates back to the closing years of the eighteenth century, was by comparison a very mild affair. Animals and people entertained by their acrobatic skills, or as in freak shows outside the big tent by simply being themselves, or by behaving as the paying customers expected them to behave, that is, according to stereotype. A major figure in the modern history of the circus is the American showman P. T. Barnum. His attitude toward his animal and human charges was tellingly indiscriminate. Just before his fall season in 1843, Barnum's orangutan fell sick. He cursed the beast for her expense and trouble. "D—n the luck," he wrote to his manager, "I have puffed her high and dry—got a large transparency and a flag ten by sixteen feet painted for her." Barnum had set great hopes on a goat, "but he *shits* so I can do nothing with him. . . ." Barnum also had high aspirations for the American Indians whom he advertised as brutal savages just brought back from killing white men in the Far West, but unfortunately for the showman, his human exhibits turned out to be "lazy devils" who pre-ferred to lie about the museum rather than act ferocious.[21]

The word *museum* is used advisedly. Barnum displayed his wares in places called museums. That word suggests to our mind an institution of learning and of dignity. And this was indeed how enlightened Europeans and Americans of the late eighteenth century conceived the museum: for them, the proper display of nature had a high educational value. By the middle of the nineteenth century, however, thanks to the spirit of show-manship that succeeded in drawing crowds of sensation-seeking (mostly lower-class) spectators, museums—with the exception of a few national institutions—had lost their serious purpose and had become primarily places for entertainment—places, as one American educator put it in 1852, "for some stuffed birds and animals, for the exhibition of mons-ters, and for vulgar dramatic performances."[22]

In the twentieth century, museums have regained their original high calling. The exhibits in a modern natural history museum are not intended to be mere objects of amusement. They are still supposed to give pleasure but pleasure of a thoughtful kind. Museums have moved away from the unimaginative display of stuffed birds and plaster Indians on pedestals or in glass cases. Instead, they offer well-designed dioramas showing the habitats of animals and humans in three dimensions. As visitors walk down the hall, they might see through one window penguins sunning themselves on the ice fields of Antarctica and through another an Eskimo family performing household chores outside an igloo in the Arctic wastes; or they might encounter across one glass pane hyenas rampaging through an African bush and across another Bantu herdsmen corralling their cattle. In a museum of natural history, neither the models of animals nor those of humans attempt to reproduce gestures and behaviors that merely amuse. What the visitors see are the normal activities of life. Nevertheless, both animals and humans are putting on a show: the context of illu-minated diorama, glass window, and darkened hall makes this theatrical element clear. And notice this fact. In a modern natural history museum, both humans and animals are on display, as peculiar animals and people were on display in circuses and in the Barnum-type of museum. An important distinction, of course, is that the exhibits of a modern museum are all models of live beings and not the live beings themselves.

In a modern zoo, live animals are exhibited. Conspicuously absent behind the bars of a cage is the species *Homo sapiens*. David Garnett, in his novel *A Man in the Zoo* (1924), imagines a man who offers himself to be shown as a member of the human species among the monkeys of the zoo. Garnett's idea is not so fanciful as perhaps he himself believed: exhibiting humans along with other animals, as we have noted, is an old and enduring game. Modern zoos emerged, however, out of the enlightened views of scientists at the end of the eighteenth century and during the early part of the nineteenth century. These people were seriously concerned with the scientific understanding of nature and with education. The idea of exhibiting humans would have deeply offended their sensibility. It is true that nineteenth-century society was still highly stratified; some people were deemed superior and others were thought to belong to the lower classes, and that term was used indiscriminately of the laboring poor and of the higher animals. Nevertheless, conspicuous rudeness or condescension to another human person was no longer acceptable. Toward captive animals, however, society was and is far more permissive.[23]

Although the purposes of a modern zoo are straightforward and commendable, human experiences of the zoo are likely to be ambiguous and mixed. The zoo, besides providing an opportunity for visitors to appreciate the variety and splendor of nature, allows them to feel superior to the caged beasts and to acknowledge aspects of behavior, such as eating and copulation, that they find disturbing and faintly disgusting when practiced by themselves.

One of the pleasures of visiting a zoo is feeding the animals (fig. 15). The act is generous and the pleasure is innocent, although both derive from a base of superiority and of power. Making another being eat out of our hand—*that* yields a special thrill all the greater if the animal is first made to beg and if it is large enough to crush us in another setting less structured in our favor. Visitors also derive merriment simply out of watching carnivores eat. *Our* eating is wrapt in ritual. The more civilized we are or think we are, the more uncomfortable we feel toward acts of devouring—especially of flesh—that support our own lives and that, in a more general and larger sense, lie at the foundation of the most refined culture. At the zoo we can confront this fact, not in ourselves, but in animals toward which we feel superior. The public, as zoo officials know, grows excited over the sight of lions devouring large chunks of bloody meat. So popular with the public is this simple act of survival that managers at the zoo may feel obliged to feed the lions once a day even though in the wild they eat a hearty meal at most once a week.

Fig. 15. Feeding animals in the London zoo. Cartoon by Richard Doyle in *Punch*, November 19, 1849.

Monkeys are a major source of attraction. The director of a famous circus grew indignant when not a half dozen visitors looked at a rhinoceros that had cost him twelve thousand dollars, while throngs crowded in front of a group of monkeys worth only forty-five.[24] Why do monkeys, even though they are not really rare, enjoy such popularity? One reason, no doubt, is that they resemble humans. Visitors can stare and laugh at them openly. Some visitors are especially attracted by the easy sexual behavior of the monkeys. Voyeurism is forbidden except when applied to subhumans. Monkeys, however, resemble humans so much that officials in some zoological gardens want them excluded on principle. Hediger observes that "in one of the largest zoos in the world a spacious open-air enclosure for baboons had to be pulled down because its inmates had behaved 'indecently.'"[25]

Animals of erect posture, according to Hediger, have a special appeal for zoo visitors. Could it be because an upright stance makes an animal seem more human? Most large animals have horizontal postures. A conspicuous exception is the bear, which may partly explain why it is a favorite with the public. Dogs are never so appealing as when they sit up and beg. A fish that has won worldwide approval, even among those who live inland and have never seen it, is the sea horse (*Hippocamus*). It is the only vertical fish. Ornaments made in the shape of sea horses are worn by women. Parrots and owls are vertical birds. The parrot is "almost human" with its upright posture and capacity for imitating human speech. The owl was a symbol of wisdom in ancient Greece and subsequently in other European culture areas, but it fails to command approval everywhere, no doubt in part because of its nocturnal life.[26]

The earliest modern zoos, those of Paris and London, were scientific enterprises. Public interest led to their opening to subscribers from outside the membership of scientific societies and to the establishment of public zoos in a number of European cities by 1860: besides Paris and London, these included Dublin, Bristol, Berlin, Frankfurt, Antwerp, and Rotterdam. Distinguished scientists such as Charles Darwin and Francis Galton were frequent visitors of animals at the London zoo. Artists, too, as students of nature found it rewarding to call on a Sunday outing. The great mass of callers, however, came for amusement rather than for any deeper appreciation of nature. Until well into the twentieth century, the crowds tended to be rowdy and cruel. Keepers had to be constantly on guard. A former keeper of the Moscow zoo wrote: "All day long a huge, annoying and rowdy crowd paraded before the cages. This crowd, which would have been panic-stricken by the sight of a single one of these beasts uncaged, delighted in seeing them so disarmed, humiliated and debased. The mob avenged its own cowardice with boorish calls and shakes of the animals' chains, while the keepers' protests were countered by the incontestable reply, 'I paid for it.'"[27]

This behavior toward caged animals bears a close resemblance to how, in an earlier time, people acted toward caged mental patients. In the early modern period (1600 to 1750), Europeans viewed the lunatic as the lowliest human creature, someone reduced almost to a state of pure animality though still possessing a soul that could be saved. Such was the low status of the mentally deranged that where the criminal and the madman were confined together, pity went to the criminal for the company he had to keep. Yet not only the rabble but the most refined members of society flocked into London's Bethlehem Hospital for the insane (popularly known as Bedlam) for entertainment. Just as people in the early part of the twentieth century might cruelly tease animals caged in the zoo, so in this earlier era visitors to Bedlam deliberately tried to enrage the inmates chained to their cells or intoxicate them with gin so as to obtain a wilder performance. Before its doors were finally closed to the public in 1770, Bethlehem Hospital came to admit 96,000 visitors annually. Receipts from the gates supported the institution.[28]

In colonial America, treatment of the insane resembled that of Europe. The first general hospital—the Pennsylvania Hospital—opened its doors to patients in 1756. The mentally ill were confined to the cellar. They were often chained to iron rings fixed on the floor or wall of their cells. The keeper carried a whip and used it freely. Lunatics were regarded as dangerous but also entertaining wild animals. Local people treated their out-of-town guests by bringing them to observe and tease the inmates. A cruel fantasy of the time was that the insane, like wild beasts, were insensitive to weather and therefore could be kept in their cells naked. The enlightened Dr. Benjamin Rush (1745-1813) fought against this sadistic practice, but he was hardly free of the notion that mad people were like animals. He believed, for example, that the insane could be "tamed" by the total deprivation of food, citing in support of his idea the fact that in India wild elephants were subdued by denying them victuals until they became thin shadows of their former selves. He also suggested that the methods used in breaking wild horses be applied to violent patients.[29]

We have already noted that monasteries, despite their aspiration to being a paradise on earth, excluded animals other than useful livestock from their midst. On the other hand, in the Western world, holy men from Androcles to Saint Francis have had the reputation of being able to charm wild beasts. In idealized pictures of the Garden of Eden, all creatures (including wild animals) lived in harmony under the benign overlordship of man. These pictures, as people have always known, could not be translated into reality unless the animals were harmless, tame, or under strict control. The resistance of wild animals to human control and the fact that the lion did not willingly lie down with the lamb aroused strong feelings of ambivalence in Europeans of the early Christian era and through the Middle Ages. It was sometimes argued, by the Eastern Church for instance, that animals were the incurably depraved instruments of Satan. Significantly, no animal appears in Dante's description of the Garden of Eden, and Dante himself was assailed by a panther, a lion, and a she-wolf when he emerged from the gloomy forest where the *Divine Comedy* begins. In G. B. Andreini's *L'Adamo, sacra representatione* (1617), several illustrations of Eden depict it as a *formal* garden in which wild animals obviously have no place. They are indeed shown, but at the entrance of the garden gate, with Adam naming them. In John Parkinson's *Paradise in sole* (1629), the frontispiece is a picture of the Garden of Eden. No animals are depicted in it, however. In their place is that curious creature known as the Scythian lamb, part plant and part animal, that people in the seventeenth century still thought to exist in the wilds of Asia.[30]

One animal can be admitted to paradise without hesitation and that is the bird. In medieval thought, birds resemble man in that they have two legs; they fly and hence resemble angels. These characteristics were interpreted to mean that birds did not participate in the original revolt against God. They were fit denizens of both the heavenly and the terrestrial pàradise. In the Oberrheinischer Meister's "little paradise garden" (ca. 1410), the Virgin sits reading and the Child is shown playing with his Mother. There are two trees and many flowering plants but no animals other than songbirds. The Eden of Guillaume Salluste du Bartas

(1544–90) contains a thousand sorts of birds. Milton's Paradise is full of avian choirs.[31] John Evelyn (1620–1706) wanted to build an aviary in his botanic garden large enough to hold five hundred small birds, including linnets and yellow hammers, finches, larks, thrushes, blackbirds, and robins. Since antiquity, sound has been an integral component of gardening art. The perfect environment, whether Elysium or Eden, should offer not only visual but also aural delights among which is the harmonious blend of bubbling water and warbling songbirds. By the Renaissance period, birds have come to be so closely associated with the garden that the earliest books on horticultural art, such as *La Maison rustique* (1572), discussed critically the relative musical merits of avian species. Birds, however, could not be allowed to fly free if their purpose was to provide concerts for human entertainment. An old custom called for the placing of caged birds in a secluded part of the garden and then covering up the cages with foliage so that visitors could hear them and enjoy the illusion of wandering in a natural forest.[32]

The botanic garden, sometimes spoken of as "the whole world in a chamber," emerged in the enlightened centers of Europe during the late sixteenth and early seventeenth centuries. Its proud boast was that it contained specimens from "the remote Quarters of the World." A characteristic design of the botanic garden shows it as divided into four parts to suggest both the idea of the quadripartite paradise of Persian origin and the idea of the four continents.[33] A problem with these botanic gardens, as their builders realized, is that they were only botanic. Where were the animals? Without animals, such gardens could neither claim to be a representation of the original Eden nor suggest man's dominion over the whole of animate nature. Architect-designers did try to include animals but these had to be kept in separate cells. Dead and stuffed animals were introduced into the grounds of some botanic gardens. These were all tacit admissions of the defeat of an aspiration which Europeans could not altogether give up, even in the seventeenth century—an aspiration rooted in the myth of Adam's power over beasts.

The dream that ferocious animals, on the approach of man, would kneel in docility and thus be a fit companion in a perfect world may be among the most vainglorious of human aspirations. It is not confined to Western culture. Evidences of it appear in other high cultures as well. Wherever man evisages a perfect world, elements of this dream occur and recur. Attempts to translate the dream into reality encounter the problem of how animals can be brought into the garden and made to seem a natural and integral part of it. Some of these attempts we have already noted. They will be recapitulated briefly here in order to underline the human need to associate with animals and to do so on the principles of dominion and control, in Eden as in practical life.

Wild and exotic animals have been considered an important component of the great hunting parks and gardens of imperial China. With sufficient space and number of caretakers, the animals could be kept in fenced-in compounds or allowed to run more or less free. The emperor in such a park could feel himself in tune with and in command of the whole of nature. The great hunting park-garden was, however, the exception even for an emperor. Most gardens were of a very modest size, especially those within the walls of a city. How could the animal presence be introduced into these small-scale, idealized worlds? There have been a number of solutions. Thus, even in the smallest garden, animals could be given a token presence as birds in cages and as fishes in small rock pools. Animals of stone and bronze substituted for live ones. Lions guarding the entrances to garden gates and halls were especially popular. These beasts managed to look simultaneously fierce and tame. They reared their backs and bared their teeth but, on the other hand, they showed neatly arranged swirling locks and doglike features.[34] In imperial gardens, sculptures of the deer and reptiles such as the dragon and the tortoise were often placed in front of the halls. The animal presence was also felt in the distorted limbs of trees and in deeply weathered limestone (figs. 3, 13). Both plants and rocks were shaped and arranged to suggest not only wild animals but even monsters. It is a curious fact that the Chinese garden, which supposedly represents an ideal world of harmonious beauty, should so often contain images of ferocity and strife. Bizarrely shaped boulders protruded from a ridge in the emperor Hui-tsung's fabulous garden outside of K'ai-feng. A monk observed that they resembled "tusks, horns, mouths, noses, heads, tails and claws," and that "they seemed to be angry and protesting against each other." Near the boulders was a display of contorted pine trees, "their branches twisted round and knotted to form all kinds of shapes, like canopies, cranes, dragons." Animals and animal passions were admissible into the garden only as art objects made of plants and rocks.[35]

In the European garden, animals made their presence felt in a variety of ways. A whole zoo might be carved out of yew and box hedges. One could see animal images in water shooting out of the mouth of a dolphin or out of the claws of a crayfish, models of animals (perhaps even mechanical birds) in the neighborhood of a grotto, stuffed animals in galleries that bordered a botanic garden, and beasts sculpted in stone, such as the fantastic display in the sixteenth-century villa of Duke Vicino Orsini. So many animal sculptures might be packed into a garden that it could seem the model of a zoo. The gardens of Henry VIII are a case in point. Henry took special delight in his "beestes," which were carved figures of animals painted and gilt, stuck on the tops of posts and placed everywhere about the grounds. In one small garden alone there were "11 harts, 13 lions, 16 greyhounds, 10 hinds, 17 dragons, 9 bulls, 13 antelopes, 15 griffins, 19 leberdes, 11 yallys [horned, mythical beasts], 9 rams and the lion on top of the mount."[36]

The Edenic ideal calls for the presence of both plants and animals, which unfortunately do not mix. The usual solution is to isolate the animals or use models. In the second half of the eighteenth century, a radically new solution was introduced by Lancelot Brown, who rid the garden of flower beds, trimmed hedges, and formal avenues of trees in favor of broad expanses of undulating turf. On this turf, cattle and deer could graze picturesquely right up to the front of the house. For the first time, animals (albeit very tame ones) were brought to the center of the garden stage.

6 ANIMAL PETS:
CRUELTY AND AFFECTION

Animal pets in the affluent nations of the Western world receive, as we all know, lavish care. In the United States, more than half of the households have a dog or a cat, or both, and some six billion dollars are spent on them every year.[1] Moreover, numerous reports, stories, and anecdotes attest to the personal devotion of owners to their charges. On the other hand, pets exist for human pleasure and convenience. Fond as owners are of their animals, they do not hesitate to get rid of them when they prove inconvenient. In the United States, for instance, there is the revealing statistic that approximately 15 percent of the total estimated dog population is destroyed yearly in dog compounds and animal shelters. Another revealing fact is that the majority of Americans keep their dogs for only two years or less. In other words, for these Americans dogs are kept so long as they are playful, endearing, and asexual pups. When they grow to a size that makes their presence in the house problematical and, above all, when they begin to respond to the imperatives of their sexual nature, the temptation to destroy them increases.[2]

One partial solution is neutering. No matter how fond owners are of their pets, the knife is allowed to be used on them with little or no regret because that is the only way they can remain manageable and "clean" playthings within the house. A sample population in Minnesota's Twin Cities area say that female pets ought to be spayed because their blood is "messy," "annoying to see," "dirty," and will stain carpets and furniture. Castrated male pets, they say, have the advantage of being more docile and less smelly. Apart from a number of practical conveniences to people of middle-class background, neutering makes it possible for them to forget the insistent sexuality of all animals. The cruelty of castration is suggested by the tools used. A modern company offering "all your animal health care needs" lists a variety of instruments that, together with accompanying diagrams, must shock all but the most hardened reader. How is one to choose? Should one use a relatively simple castrating knife ("a double-bladed scalpel and hoe in pocket guard") or a Double Crush Whites Emasculator? a Baby Burdizzo only nine inches long or a Stainless Steel Emasculatome? Farmers have to confront these instruments; pet owners in the cities, a much more genteel breed, are able to look the other way.[3]

Cruelty to animals is deeply embedded in human nature. Our relation to pets, with all its surface play of love and devotion, is incorrectly perceived unless this harsh fact is recognized. Cruelty in the sense of indifference to the pain and needs of another being is a product of necessity. Unlike some primates, humans are omnivores, with animal flesh an important constituent of their diet. Moreover, for half a million years protohumans and humans have been not merely scavengers but active and increasingly skilled hunters. To become skilled hunters, humans must have taken a certain pleasure in their task of running down prey and killing it. Work essential to livelihood was also a sort of game. Devising various methods of killing became a challenge that could be exciting and fun. The hunter's body and mind, and with them a disposition toward activity and unconcern for suffering, are thus an inescapable part of our heritage.

Indifference to the pain of animals has been frequently observed among hunter-gatherers. Consider, for instance, the Gikwe Bushmen of the Kalahari Desert, a people known for their gentleness toward each other and toward outsiders. But this gentleness cannot apply, for obvious reasons, to the animals they have to kill for food. A certain callousness toward animal suffering is evident even when hunger is not a pressing question. Elizabeth Thomas, in her book *The Harmless People*, describes an event which, because it is quite ordinary, reveals a hunting people's deep, unreflexive attitude toward animal life. A man named Gai was about to roast a tortoise which belonged to his infant son Nhwakwe. Gai placed a burning stick against the tortoise's belly. The tortoise kicked, jerked its head, and urinated in profusion. The heat had the effect of parting the two hard plates on the shell of the belly, and Gai thrust his hand inside. While the tortoise struggled, Gai slit the belly with his knife and pulled out the intestines. "The tortoise by now had retreated part way into its shell, trying to hide there, gazing out from between its front knees. Gai reached the heart, which was still beating, and flipped it onto the ground, where it jerked violently." Meanwhile, the baby Nhwakwe came to sit by his father. "A tortoise is such a slow tough creature that its body can function although its heart is gone. Nhwakwe put his wrists to his forehead to imitate in a most charming manner the way in which the tortoise was trying to hide. Nhwakwe looked just like the tortoise."[4]

The Bushman God was equally indifferent to animal life. There is the story of Pishiboro (one of the names of God) and his elephant wife, who was killed by Pishiboro's brother while pretending to delouse her. "The younger brother then built a fire, cut off the breast of the elephant wife, and roasted it. When it was cooked he sat up on the body of the elephant wife to eat it." Pishiboro, espying his brother, wondered: "Ah, can it be that my younger brother has killed my wife and is sitting on her body?" He ran forward and found his worst suspicions confirmed. "Pishiboro was wildly angry, but his younger brother handed him some of the roasted breast, which presently Pishiboro ate. The younger brother looked down at Pishiboro and said in a voice filled with scorn: 'Oh, you fool. You lazy man. You were married to meat and you thought it was a wife.' Pishiboro saw that this was true, so he sharpened his knife and helped his younger brother with the skinning."[5]

Eskimos are widely admired for their courage and superb skill in hunting. Not all their hunting devices require contact with the animal and physical courage, however. A few are as ingenious as they are cruel. One such device works as follows. A sharpened piece of springy whalebone is tied into a U-shape, covered with fat, and left out to freeze. Then the thongs are cut and the frozen baits strewn around. Hungry foxes and wolves swallow the baits. In their stomachs, the fat thaws and the whalebone springs open, piercing the animal's interior organs and killing it.[6] The traditional Eskimo economy makes the people absolutely dependent on the animals around them for food and as raw materials, plants being quite insignificant in these roles. The result would seem to be a sense of guilt and of fear, which is recognized in speech and legend. A legend has it that when Eskimos die of violence—as in accident, suicide, or homicide— they go straight to the Happy Hunting Ground. But if they are killed by an animal they may have to do a year of penance in the underworld of the Sea Spirit. Such death seems deserved and therefore does not call for immediate compensation.[7] More directly, guilt and fear are eloquently expressed by the Iglulik Eskimo Aua in the following speech: "The greatest peril of life lies in the fact that human food consists entirely of souls. All the creatures that we have to kill and eat, all those that we have to strike down and destroy to make clothes for ourselves, have souls, like we have, souls that do not perish with the body, and which must therefore be propitiated lest they should avenge themselves on us for taking away their bodies."[8]

Hunters may respect but they do not love the game they hunt. By contrast, pastoralists spend much time taking care of their livestock and are known to show strong affection toward it. Consider the Nuer of the Upper Sudan as an example. Although the Nuer grow some millet and maize, they are preeminently pastoralists dependent on the cattle for their livelihood. Cattle, to the Nuer, are not just a resource to be used. Far from it. They love their cattle. Moreover, this love appears to be without condescension. Cattle stand in quasi-equality with people. Personal names suggest such a relationship. Men may be called by names that refer to the form and color of their favorite oxen; women take names from oxen and from the cows they milk. Personal care of and pride in cattle among the Nuer is conveyed, touchingly, by Evans-Pritchard in the following paragraph.

> When [a young man's] ox comes home in the evening he pets it, rubs ashes on its back, removes ticks from its belly and scrotum, and picks adherent dung from its anus. He tethers it in front of his windscreen so that he can see it if he wakes, for no sight so fills a Nuer with contentment and pride as his oxen. The more he can display the happier he is, and to make them more attractive he decorates their horns with long tassels, which he can admire as they toss their heads and shake them on their return to camp, and their necks with bells, which tinkle in the pastures.[9]

Nevertheless, cattle are food and resource to the Nuer. They provide milk, meat, and blood. Their skins are a primary raw material for making the meager goods that the Nuer possess. Obtaining milk and blood from cattle presents no moral dilemma. Blood is not a staple article of diet; moreover, the Nuer believe that bloodletting practiced from time to time is good for the cow or the ox. But killing the beloved cattle for meat does present a problem, which the Nuer evade by pretending to eat only the

flesh of animals that have already been slaughtered for ceremonial and
sacrificial purposes. An excuse for a ceremony or a sacrificial rite is,
however, never hard to find. After such an occasion, the scramble for
carcass is uninhibited. Any animal that dies a natural death is eaten. Even
when a youth's favorite ox dies he must be persuaded "to partake of its
flesh, and it is said that were he to refuse his spear might avenge the insult
by cutting his foot or hand on some future occasion." The Nuer recognize
the dilemma of having to kill that which they love. "Nuer are very fond of
meat, and declare that on the death of a cow, 'The eyes and the heart are
sad, but the teeth and the stomach are glad.' 'A man's stomach prays to
God, independently of his mind, for such gifts.'"[10]

Pastoralists do not exist for the sake of their livestock. It is the other
way around, although this exploitative relationship is fudged by the care
that cattle herders *must* give to their charges, a care that in specific
instances can lead to genuine affection. "The Lord is my shepherd." The
deep irony of addressing Christ or a bishop as shepherd seems to escape
most people. To this day, the pastoral metaphor for the just ruler, with
roots in Plato as well as in the Old and the New Testament, is used in all
innocence. George Santayana, in his book *Dominations and Powers* (1951),
observes:

> If the shepherd were, as he must have been in the beginning, the
> owner of the sheep, his care for the flock would be naturally prompt-
> ed and limited strictly to his proprietory interests. He would not
> love sheep at all, but only wool and mutton. . . . Sheep are safe from
> wolves, but often deformed and helpless in their sodden pastures. It
> is a fate comparable to that of eunuchs or ladies of the seraglio, or
> lapdogs or other favourites of tyranny. If some fabulist ventured to
> put a description of their keeper into the sheep's mouth, it would
> surely not depict him as a ministering angel, but as a driver, a gaoler, a
> shearer, and a butcher.[11]

Hunting large animals and herding livestock are predominantly male
occupations. What, we may wonder, is the relationship between women
and animals in preliterate societies? Where hunting contributes significantly to livelihood, the men provide meat by chasing down and killing
large game at some distance from camp while the women scavenge or trap
small animals close to camp. Women do hunt and kill, but their preys—
small rodents and reptiles, grasshoppers and caterpillars, and such like—

have no prestige. For them, there is no glamor or pleasure in killing. Women share the task of dismembering the animals brought home by male hunters, and of course they do the cooking or help do it. Women's hands, like men's, are covered in blood, but for them the activity is a necessity, not a game and not surrounded by any mystique.

Although women kill and dismember animals, they may also grow fond of some. On islands of Southeast Asia and the Pacific Ocean, where the inhabitants hunt and fish as well as carry on some form of agriculture, pups and piglets are fed and nurtured by the women and become their playthings and pets. In 1825, J. Macrae wrote:

> I noticed a young woman walking along the street, and at the same time suckling several puppies that were wrapped up in a piece of tapa cloth hanging round her shoulder and breasts. This custom of suckling dogs and pigs is common to the natives of the Sandwich [Hawaiian] Islands. These animals are held by them in great estimation, little inferior to their own offspring, and my journeys to the woods in search of plants often afforded me an opportunity of being an eyewitness to this habit.[12]

Similar observations have been made by European explorers and scholars on other islands. As recently as 1950, a photographer was able to take a striking snapshot of a Papuan mother nursing with one breast a child of about two to three years old and with the other breast a piglet (fig.16).[13] Yet the tenderly nurtured animals are destined for consumption. Dog meat, in particular, is regarded by Pacific Islanders as a great delicacy. "Hawaiians," wrote a visitor in 1868, "have always been epicures in the article of dog meat. The kind they raise for their feasts is small and easily fattened. They are fed only on vegetables, especially kalo, to make their flesh more tender and delicately flavored." Dogs suckled by women "are called 'ilio poli' and are most esteemed." There is a suggestion here of dogs reared deliberately for the quality of their flesh. Pets they may be but are nonetheless eaten without much regret when desired as food. On the other hand, it has also been reported that the esteem and affection for a breast-fed pet may go so deep that killing it for food becomes impossible. A pup might be selected as the companion and protector of a child. If the child should die, the dog is killed and buried with its young master as a playmate in the other world.[14]

Fig. 16. Papuan (New Guinea) mother nursing her child and a piglet. Photograph taken by Douglas Baglin in 1950.

The old English word *game* means both amusement and hunted wild animals. Killing, even when it is a necessity, is also a sport. The anthropologist S. L. Washburn speaks of our "carnivorous psychology," which was fully developed by the Middle Pleistocene period, several hundred thousands of years ago. "It is easy," he says, "to teach people to kill, and it is hard to develop customs which avoid killing. . . . The extent to which the biological bases for killing have been incorporated into human psychology may be measured by the ease with which boys can be interested in hunting, fishing, fighting, and games of war. It is not that these behaviors are inevitable, but they are easily learned, satisfying, and have been socially rewarded in most cultures.[15] Among so-called civilized peoples, hunting is the traditional sport of kings and of the nobility. It has glamor. It is a martial art, the most highly organized and splendid of sports. In theory, the hunted animal should be a worthy antagonist in speed and cunning, or ferocity. It must have a chance to escape or fight back. Otherwise the killing would simply be the work of a butcher, not of a sportsman. The playful character of hunting and fishing, of course, is seen entirely from the human viewpoint. To the hunted animal, obviously, the chase is not a game but a matter of life and death in which the opportunities to escape are, more often than not, cruel illusions.

Hunting is a blood sport. Notwithstanding its modern-age aesthetic of red coats and of brass bugles flashing in the morning sun, it retains its flavor of violence in mud, sweat, blood, and death cries. Seemingly far more genteel is another quintessential activity of high culture, namely, breeding animals so that they turn into playthings and aesthetic objects. This activity presupposes an order of material abundance such that animals need no longer be seen as potential food, or even as sacrificial victims in rituals that have the promotion of fertility as their aim. It speaks of leisure and skill, and the desire on the part of those thus endowed to manipulate the reproductive processes of animals so that they turn into creatures of a shape and habit that please their owners.

As illustrations, consider two well-documented animals, the goldfish and the dog, the one bred purely as an animal pet and the other for a variety of reasons. Since the nineteenth century, the goldfish has become one of the most popular pets in the world, and nowhere more so than in its earliest homes—China and Japan. No Chinese home is complete without a *chin-yü*, which might be housed in a muddy pond or, at the other extreme, in a carved ivory and gilded aquarium. Every large marketplace in Japan has a *kingyo* stall at which connoisseurs of all ages discourse expertly on the relative merits of each specimen. In the Western world, almost every pet shop sells goldfish. Goldfish in small, glass bowls were at one time popular prizes at funfairs. Now, at American county and agricultural fairs they may be given away in plastic bags. London back-door hawkers used to exchange goldfish for old clothes. Although these practices have been on the wane since the 1930s, the use of the goldfish for interior decorations remains in favor. For a room furnished in the Oriental style, an aquarium stocked with black-colored Moors is consi-dered an elegant touch. For a modern room, the aquarium may be chromium plated and stocked with an American breed known as the Comet, developed in the 1880s. In the 1930s, society hostesses fashiona-bly substituted a bowl of goldfish for a bowl of flowers on their dining room table.[16]

The wild goldfish (*Carassius auratus*, or *chi yü*) is native to Chinese freshwaters. It is a greenish or grayish fish, not much esteemed as orna-ment but sold in markets as food. Red scales appear as a variant, and this striking color has been noted by the Chinese perhaps as early as the fourth century A.D. Even in its natural state the goldfish displays a broad range of variations, a fact that the Chinese took advantage of when they decided to interbreed the abnormal specimens to produce varieties that appealed to their aesthetic sense and even to their appetite for the monstrous. Domes-tication is known to have begun early in the Sung dynasty (960–1279). By the year 1200, we have firm evidence of the existence of a fancy breed, described as having a snow-white body with black spots, beautiful mark-ings, and a varnishlike luster. By the seventeenth century, the Chinese were breeding goldfish of many different colors in large quantities. In a work written in 1635, the two authors noted in detail the following colors and color combinations: deep red, lustrous white, white with ink spots, red with yellow spots, white with vermilion on the brow, vermilion with white on the spine, vermilion on the spine with seven white spots, white spine with eight red lines, and other banded varieties.

The shape of the body and of the fins and such anatomical details as the shape, size, and position of the eyes have undergone major changes during the sixteenth century and later. In the sixteenth century, goldfish with three, five, and even seven tails began to appear. Fish with compact and stunted bodies, known as the Egg Fish, emerged in the same period, as did the Telescope Fish, a variety with large, protuberant eyes (fig. 17). Ideally,

Fig. 17. The Telescope goldfish has been unable to adapt to its grotesquely protuberant eyes and is likely to injure them by swimming against hard objects.

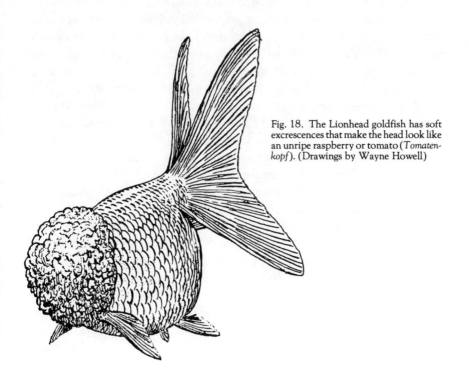

Fig. 18. The Lionhead goldfish has soft excrescences that make the head look like an unripe raspberry or tomato (*Tomatenkopf*). (Drawings by Wayne Howell)

the eyes of the Telescope Fish should be well-rounded, of equal size, and equally protuberant. However, it sometimes happens that only one eye bulges out in the desired manner, or that both bulge out but not equally. The Telescope Fish appears unable to adapt itself to the enlarged eyeballs. As an adult it is likely to injure them by swimming against hard objects and thus become blind.[17] Moreover, in a pond the protuberant balls may be sucked out by another fish. Minnows are notorious offenders in this regard. Among the more monstrous of the goldfish breeds is a latecomer, developed in Japan in the nineteenth century, widely known as the Lion-head, but also called the Hooded Goldfish, or the Buffalo-head in the United States and the Tomato-head in Germany (fig. 18). This breed is distinguished by wartlike excrescences that first emerge on the top of the head and then gradually spread downward over the cheeks and gill-covers, leaving only a small area under the mouth comparatively free. The excrescences are soft to the touch, and usually red, pink, or white in color. In the best specimens every excrescence is about the same size, and the fish has been aptly described as having an unripe raspberry for a head.

The goldfish is a pet. It has to be fed and cared for. As early as the tenth century, the monk Kao Tsan-ning wrote: "If goldfish eat the refuse of olives or soapy water then they die; if they have poplar bark they do not breed lice."[18] These lines provide evidence of the most careful observation and experimentation. It may be that monks who lived in large Buddhist estates with fine gardens have played an important role in breeding fancy goldfish. Emperors, we know, have enjoyed them as pets. Billardon de Sauvigny, in a tract on the goldfish first published in 1780, observes that the emperors make much of the fish and consider feeding them with their own hands among their daily amusements, but that nonetheless "it is the apartments of the women, where they are so much feted and lauded, petted and loved, that have made their fortune and spread them throughout the empire."[19]

For many centuries the Chinese people, high and low in society, have been able to enjoy the goldfish as pet. To the leisured class, however, it can also be treated as an art object. The fish in its aquarium, set upon a stool, is in its own world—one that does not impinge on ordinary human living space. In this respect, the goldfish differs from hard-to-confine pets, such as the dog, and is more like a potted plant or an inanimate work of art. The goldfish is also like an art object because new varieties can be produced so quickly through skillful human intervention. It occasionally happens that a fish fancier is so impatient that he bypasses the process of selective breeding altogether and seeks to impose change directly by dubious devices such as etching Chinese characters on the fish's body with acid or painting flower and other patterns on it.[20] Of course, it is fakery to offer such decorated pieces as the products of nature. Note, however, that this criticism cannot be directed at artifice itself, for the process of mating to produce the right breeds is at least as manipulative. Here, for example, is a semitechnical account of how to hand-spawn goldfish.

A mature male and female goldfish are placed for from twelve to twenty-four hours in a medium-sized aquarium, with some aquatic plants. As soon as the female has shed a few eggs, the male is removed and the female taken in hand and allowed to wriggle. Squeezing her is not necessary. The wriggling results in the ejection of a large number of eggs, fully as many as are ejected in the normal way. As soon as all the eggs are shed, the female fish is placed aside, the water given a gentle stir, to distribute the eggs over the plants, and the male taken in the hand. By gently squeezing him in the anal region the sperms are ejected and carried by the same wave to fertilize the eggs. This method almost guarantees all the eggs being fertilized.[21]

Remember that the procedure, described above in such a dry manner, has no other aim than to produce something appealing and decorative. It is an exercise in fantasy, another attempt to bend nature not so much to human needs as moods. Certainly the names given to the different breeds of goldfish are fanciful. Among those used by Chinese fanciers toward the end of the seventeenth century were: Seven Stars (a reference to the constellation Ursa Major), Eight Diagrams (a reference to divination), Lotus Terrace, Embroidered Coverlet, Eight Melon Seeds, Crane Pearl, Silver Saddle, and Red Dust.[22]

Goldfish is a special case of domestication, one that enjoys the advantage of being exceptionally well documented in literature and art for a period of one thousand years. The story of the goldfish is, of course, a mere detail in the broad sweep of the history of animal domestication, to which we will now turn. Domestication means domination: the two words have the same root sense of mastery over another being—of bringing it into one's house or domain. With a small animal like the goldfish, domination is not a problem. People can always control and play with it. Training is not in question. Although there are stories of how fish have been trained to respond to the call of a single master or mistress, the ability to perform on cue is not essential to its standing as a pet. Because fishes are confined to ponds and aquariums they cannot be a nuisance. The one real challenge, then, lies in altering their shape rather than their behavior. With large land animals, domination must be established if they are to be used or enjoyed. Certain large mammals can be tamed without domestication (where *domestication* means altering the genetic constitution of a species through selective breeding). Elephants, the largest land mammal, are an example. Although not domesticated, they are easily tameable. They have been trained to do everything from hauling timber to standing on their hind legs, wearing a petticoat, for the amusement of circus spectators.[23] Apart from the inherent difficulties of breeding elephants, which have a long gestation period followed by a long period of immaturity, there was no compelling need for humans to alter and control them by such means. With most other large animals, there was such need. Humans have found it necessary to tinker with their biological makeup because, unless this was done, such animals could not be tamed easily and, moreover, remain tame through their adult lives.

What were the directions of change? How have humans established their dominance over beasts that in a wild state were too large and fierce to be manageable? One direction of change was toward diminished size. A large animal was reduced to a smaller one—to a pet, the literal meaning of which is "small." Animal domestication began in prehistoric times, more than 10,000 years ago. One criterion by which archaeologists are able to tell whether the skeletons found at a prehistoric settlement belong to a domesticated species is size. How was the reduction effected? Could it have been deliberate? Even when attempts at control and taming were deliberate, the reduced size might have come about by more or less accidental means. At least this is the view of F. E. Zeuner, who thinks that farmers in early Neolithic times lacked the knowledge to bring about a diminishment in the size of large bovines in a calculated manner. Rather, he believes that something like the following sequence of events happened. Contact with humans first occurred when wild bovines, as was their wont, began to rob the fields. The farmers, already experienced with such domesticated species as the dog, the sheep, and the goat, took tentative steps to induct the bovines into the human fold. One step in that direction was to capture the young individuals and keep them as pets around camp. Some of these appealing captives were surely treated with kindness, but they could not as a whole have received consistent attention and care. Neolithic farmers, who made only modest demands on themselves for housing and food, were unlikely to provide the best possible living conditions for their captives. Animals thus kept deteriorated in health. Compared with their wild ancestors, their progenies became smaller and weaker and hence also more docile. Throughout the Neolithic period, the size of cattle decreased until, during the Iron Age, specimens were bred that would be considered dwarfs by modern standards. The height of their withers was little more than a meter.[24]

Manageability or control was the real aim. The smaller size helped. Another device, more direct and perhaps practiced as early as Neolithic times, was castration, which made the male animals more docile. Cutting off the testes of some specimens and not others meant that humans could and did interfere directly with the breeding process. In time, they gained mastery over even the large bovine. Once an animal became fully domesticated and docile, humans could deliberately seek ways to alter it so that it was even more useful and pleasing to them. They might try to make their cattle larger so as to yield more meat or be better draft animals, without however making them at the same time more fierce; and they might try to lengthen and alter the shape of the horns for religious reasons. With the horse, in a later stage of domestication history, humans have tried to make the animal both larger and smaller. Thus we have now at one extreme Shire horses and at the other extreme Shetland ponies. Certain aesthetic criteria probably also applied. In wild horses as well as in asses and zebras the mane is short and stands erect rather than falling gracefully to one side as in all breeds of the domestic horse. Moreover, the domestic horse boasts a longer and more elegant tail.

All young animals are docile toward the adults of the species. It suits human purpose, therefore, to breed animals such that they retain juvenile anatomical and behavioral traits through their entire life span. Other than size, the retention of foetal and juvenile traits is used by archaeologists as a criterion for evaluating whether a particular skeleton belongs to a wild or a domesticated animal. Among juvenile traits are a shortening of the jaw and of the facial region. Dogs commonly display these characteristics, but so do other animals—sometimes to an exaggerated degree—as in certain breeds of pig (Middle White, for example) and in cattle such as the South

American variety known as Niatu.[25] With the dog, reduction in the size of the muzzle results in smaller teeth. Not even the Great Dane and the Saint Bernard have teeth as large as those of their wild progenitor, the wolf, even though their body may be larger. Other juvenile traits in the domesticated dog are the short hair, curly tail, skin folds like the dewlap, and the hanging ears of many breeds. Hanging ears give the dog a conspicuously submissive look: think of the spaniel. Police dogs should have erect and pointed ears to avoid even the appearance of submission. Although docility is a desirable feature in a pet, it can become excessive. Fawning can be cloying and friendliness toward humans indiscriminate. Such behavioral traits, Konrad Lorenz believes, is a result of exaggerated infantilism. Dogs of this kind "are always over-playful, and long after their first year of life, when normal dogs have sobered down, they persist in chewing their master's shoes or shaking the curtains to death; above all, they retain a slave-like submission which in other dogs is supplanted after a few months by a healthy self-confidence."[26]

The impact of domestication on the dog merits a closer look for several reasons. One is that the dog is almost certainly the first animal to have been domesticated. In its long association with humans the dog has become diversified to an extraordinary degree, perhaps more so than any other animal species. Moreover, in the Western world at least, the dog is the pet par excellence. It exhibits uniquely a set of relationships we wish to explore: dominance and affection, love and abuse, cruelty and kindness. The dog calls forth, on the one hand, the best that a human person is capable of—self-sacrificing devotion to a weaker and dependent being, and, on the other hand, the temptation to exercise power in a willful and arbitrary, even perverse, manner. Both traits can exist in the same person.

An outstanding fact about the dog, to the naked eye, is its variability. The range in size is so large that it is hard to believe that its members all belong to the same species; and indeed the largest dog cannot breed with the smallest one for obvious physical reasons. A Chihuahua may weigh 4 pounds and a full-grown Saint Bernard 160 pounds, or forty times as much.

Legs vary from the squat extremities of dachshunds to the long, graceful limbs of greyhounds and salukis. At opposite extremes we see the undershot jaws and foreshortened heads of bulldogs and pugs, and the long, narrow heads of the borzois. Tails vary from a tight curl to a sickle shape. Manifold variations in the color, length, and texture of hair exist and there is even a permanently bald breed, the Mexican hairless, contrasting with the poodle with its continuously growing hair.[27]

The wild relatives of the dog—the wolf, the coyote, and the jackal—also show wide ranges in size, but their ranges do not match that of the dog. Moreover, none of them exhibit the anatomical contrasts and differences in hair color and length that appear in the domesticated canines. There is not, for example, the equivalent of the dachshund and the borzois among wolves. Skeletons of dogs from Neolithic settlements reveal as yet little differentiation: they all resemble those of the modern Eskimo dog. By 3000 B.C., however, distinct breeds were known in Mesopotamia: one was the heavy mastiff (a guard dog) and the other was the much more slender greyhound or saluki. From the art of ancient Egypt, we gather that several distinct varieties existed; and from the length of time covered by the representations and the consistency of type, we surmise that their distinctiveness was maintained with care.[28]

In Near Eastern antiquity, already, the dog was treated as an animal whose breeding line could be controlled and modified for human purposes. What were these purposes? What motivated humans to make changes in the breeding line? Foremost among the motivations, from antiquity to the modern period, was *use*—the use of the dog in hunting and as a guardian of the home. Dogs that helped the hunter were an instrument of survival. On the other hand, in agricultural civilizations hunting was relegated more and more to a subsidiary role in survival while taking on, increasingly, the status and function of a sport, not only among the elite but even—in time—among peasants. Thus, as early as the fourteenth century, farm laborers and servants in England might keep greyhounds and use them in hunting for sport, although no doubt they welcomed the game captured and killed as additions to their pantry.[29]

Once hunting became a specialized sport, the dog served as an instrument for attaining specific ends, defined by the nature of the sport but serving the larger general purpose of pleasure. Dogs that were at first only instruments of pleasure could later be the direct source of satisfaction whether as a status symbol or as a toy, or both. Nearly all the smaller dogs, which we now think of primarily as pets—playthings for the lap and boudoir—were once bred for hunting. Terriers, for example, derive their

name from the French *terre* and were bred to creep into the ground and
drive out small animals like foxes and badgers. They were known to
English hunters at least as early as the sixteenth century. Spaniels originated in Spain and were used both for hawking and for hunting birds
with nets. Richard Blome, writing in 1686, noted how the spaniel could
be trained to "couch and lie close to the ground," then trained to lie still
while a bird net was dragged across him, and then taught to associate lying
down with the scent of a partridge. Toy breeds existed in the sixteenth
century, and these later came to be known as King Charles spaniels. It is
hard to see what purpose they served other than as pets. Loyalty was early
recognized as one of their most distinctive traits. Thus Blome, in a book
devoted to the recreational employment of dogs, nonetheless took space
to write: "Spaniels by Nature are very loving, surpassing all other Creatures, for in Heat and Cold, Wet and Dry, Day and Night, they will not
forsake their Master. There are many Prodigious Relations, made in
several Grave and Credible Authors, of the strange Affections which
Dogs have had, as well to their Dead and living Masters; but it is not my
business to take notice of them here."[30]

The poodle is another example. It seems a frivolous and pampered
creature that has no conceivable use other than as a plaything and a social
symbol. Yet it was bred originally as a hunter. The word *poodle* comes
from the German *pudeln* (to splash in water). It was and is used extensively
by the French as a gun dog, and especially for duck hunts. A clipped
poodle looks ridiculous. What is called the lion clip (hair shorn from the
back and hind parts so that the dog looks like a heavy-maned miniature
lion) is more than three hundred years old; and far from being a mere
playful fantasy the clipping was done to make it easier for the dog to
progress through water. As for the ribbon tied to the hair on the head and
on the tail, this too was done originally for a practical end, namely, so that
the animal could be seen easily as it moved among the reeds. However, by
the reign of Louis XVI (1774–92) the poodle had already become a
fashionable pet in France. Poodle barbers practiced a lucrative trade along
the banks of the Seine. They ingeniously shaved various patterns on these
long-suffering animals, including true lovers' knots and monograms.
Thus a topiary art was applied to the hair of an animal.[31]

One breed of dog that seems to have lost all connection to practical use,
if it ever had any, is the Pekinese. It is hard to imagine how this hairy and
cuddly dog, which could be as small as four and one-half pounds, might

have the wolf as a distant ancestor. Yet in anatomy and physiology, in internal and external parasites, the wolf and the Pekinese are remarkably alike. Unique in the Pekinese is its exceptional retention of such babyish traits as a very short facial region of the skull, large brain case, big eyes, short legs, curly tail, and soft fur. Juvenility makes it easy to train the Pekinese into a pet and performer. On the other hand, the animal is reputed to be highly intelligent and independent. This combination of virtues, together with the appeal of its babyish features, accounts for the popularity of the Pekinese among European toy dog fanciers ever since it was introduced from China in the nineteenth century.

The story of the Pekinese in China is unclear. Writers on the subject differ widely as to when the breed appeared.[32] Miniature dogs were known in China by the first century A.D. They could be fitted under the table, which during the Han dynasty had very short legs. Small dogs were in vogue at court during the T'ang dynasty (618–907). Some of these were probably the Maltese type brought into China from Fu Lin or Byzantium. The prestige of these small hairy dogs, whether they were Maltese or proto-Pekinese, received a boost when they came to be associated with the legend of Buddha's lion. Lamaist Buddhism focused on the lion as a symbol of passion which Buddha was able to subdue; the subdued passion, in the shape of a diminutive lion, trotted by Buddha's heels like a pet. Kublai Khan (1215?–94), as emperor of China, favored Lamaist Buddhism. Lions were a part of his menagerie, and a tame lion or two even roamed his court. About this time the expression "lion dog" came into use. Dog of a certain type served as an emblem of the lion, acquiring its prestige as a mighty beast but also the prestige of that beast's association with Buddha. Were the Pekinese, then, a popular pet during the Yuan dynasty? We do not know. We do know that they flourished during the Manchu (Ch'ing) dynasty (1644–1911). Art works dating from the early K'ang-hsi (1662–1722) to the late Tao Kuang period (1821–50) clearly depict the Pekinese as well as other breeds of dogs. All Manchu rulers appear to have been partial to the Pekinese. They also favored the idea of the Pekinese as lion dog because of the implied comparison between themselves and Buddha.

To Chinese fanciers, the ideal Pekinese should have round cheeks "like dumplings." Their eyes should be large and somewhat protuberant, like those of a goldfish. The front legs were to be short, not straight and sticklike; they were to be shorter than the hind legs, with the intention of producing a rolling gait, the movement of a "plentifully finned gold-fish."[33] Thus the Pekinese was compared not only with the lion but also with the goldfish, that other favored pet among the Chinese. The compar-ison with goldfish implies the desirability of traits opposite to those of a lion: the Pekinese should be diminutive in size—an animal that one could handle as one would a small toy. Manchu breeders sought to produce specimens of tiny size such that they could be tucked into the sleeves of women's coats. During Tao Kuang emperor's reign, unscrupulous men tried to stunt the growth of the Pekinese through the use of drugs and various manipulative devices. Dowager Empress Tsu-hsi (1834–1908), who took her sobriquet of "Old Buddha" seriously, discouraged these practices while promoting the achievement of the same end through inbreeding. She was not very successful. Knavish fanciers continued to alter the size and shape of the Pekinese by devious means. One method lay in curtailing the exercise a dog should have over the period from the third month to maturity, with the aim of reducing its appetite and food consumption and hence rate of growth. A pup might be put in a close-fitting wire cage and kept there until it had reached maturity. Another method lay in holding a pup in the hand for days at a time, inducing by gentle pressure of the fingers a slight exaggeration of width between the shoulders. To achieve the desired result of a small snub nose, some owners broke the cartilage of the nose with their thumbnail or with a chopstick when the pup was from three to seven days old. Others massaged the nose daily in the hope of restraining its growth.[34]

Imperial patrons and respectable society frowned on all these practices for their cruelty but also because they were illegitimate shortcuts. The approved method was the slow one of selective breeding. In the case of the Pekinese, this procedure had been applied under the patronage of Man-chu emperors and the supervision of chief eunuchs over a period of several hundred years. The result was an appealing, healthy, and intell-igent animal that was capable of performing all sorts of tricks and of living to the ripe old age of twenty-five years.

Dogs, then, can be bred to some arbitrarily constructed standard without doing damage to their health and liveliness. On the other hand, examples can readily be cited of purebred dogs that do suffer from genetic and physiologic deterioration. The basic problem can be stated simply. It is rarely possible to breed a dog to arbitrary criteria of beauty and appeal and still have it retain functional vigor and intelligence. As Konrad Lorenz has pointed out, "Circus dogs which can perform complicated tricks demanding great intelligence are very rarely equipped with a pedigree; this is not because the 'poor' artists are unable to pay the price of a well bred dog—for fabulous fees are paid for talented circus dogs—but because it is mental rather than physical qualities that make good performing animals." As one example of rapid degeneration, among many that can be cited, Lorenz mentions the Chow. In the early 1920s, Chows were still natural dogs whose pointed muzzles, obliquely set Mongolian eyes, and pointed, erect ears called to mind their wolf-blooded ancestors. Modern breeding of the Chow, however, has "led to an exaggeration of those points which gives him the appearance of a plump bear: the muzzle is wide and short . . . the eyes have lost their slant in the compression of the whole face, and the ears have almost disappeared in the overgrown thickness of the coat. Mentally too, these temperamental creatures, which still bore a trace of the wild beast of prey, have become stodgy teddy bears."[35]

An animal may lose much of its natural vigor and still be serviceable as a pet. It is even desirable that a pet not be endowed with too much vigor and initiative. The pet, if it is to find acceptance in a well-run household, must learn to be immobile—to be as unobtrusive as a piece of furniture. The single most important trick taught a dog is instant obedience to the order "sit" or "lie down." A well-trained dog will lie down for hours at a stretch, upon command, even in a strange place, while its master goes off on business. The ability to stay put is a necessity in a hunting dog and it is clearly a great convenience to humans in a busy, modern household, where time is tightly organized. However, to some people, a dog's submission to command is desirable in itself. Power over another being is demonstrably firm and perversely delicious when it is exercised for no particular purpose and when submission to it goes against the victim's own strong desires and nature. Dog shows cater to the usual human vanity and competitiveness, but they also provide the occasion and the excuse to demonstrate openly and to public applause the power to dominate and humble another being. Here is an account of a dog obedience show which the author offers in all innocence but which may well serve as a prime example of refined cruelty.

Perhaps the hardest test required that the dog should be brought into the ring hungry and, when given a plate of his favourite food, sit by it until he was told to eat; the time was four minutes and the owner had to go out of sight, leaving the dog alone with his tempting plate.

Hundreds of people were watching when, on one occasion, Beeswing [a tiny Pekinese] came into the ring. He was ravenous and the four minutes must have seemed interminable; he endured for two and then, without moving from his post, slowly got up and, in Miss Cynthia's words, "sat on his bottom and begged." The crowd roared but he did not move a muscle. He had not broken the rules but instead of sitting on four legs sat on two; after another two minutes the judge called her; Beeswing saw his mistress come into the ring but knew he still must not move as she walked up and stood beside him. She had to wait for the word from the judge. It came, she released Beeswing who literally jumped on the food and gobbled it.[36]

In modern society, the owner of a dog may have someone else do the disciplining and training. He enjoys the product—a docile and friendly pet. The harsh story behind the making of a pet is forgotten. And the story must be harsh because the basis of all successful training is the display of an unchallengeable power. The dog must not be in doubt as to who is the master and as to the consequences of disobedience. Another repressed side of the story, so far as a genteel buyer-owner is concerned, are the processes of mating and breeding. These processes are either subsumed under "pedigree," when the past is in question, or steps to be taken under the supervision of specialists, when the progeny or future is in question. Breeding animals to achieve and maintain certain traits calls for an indifference to individual lives that is suggestive of nature's own vast wastefulness. "As soon as the bitch hath littered," explains a seventeenth-century English handbook, "it is requisite to choose them you intend to preserve, and throw away the rest;" and the kennel book of a Yorkshire dog-breeder (1691–1720) contains such laconic entries as, "three of this litter given to Br. Thornhill, the rest hanged, because not liked."[37] A modern breeder is well aware of the perils of inbreeding, which must nonetheless be carried through to fix a pattern. "Nature uses it extremely," one twentieth-century specialist on the subject says, "but nature is harsh and, if it leads to deterioration, nature has no mercy." The breeder must also show no mercy. He must be scientific and cruel in his play. He "must watch the effect of inbreeding as if through a microscope, and at the very first sign of deleterious effects, not only down must come the guillotine, but the litter that showed them must be destroyed: a step too far has been taken, a step back is necessary."[38]

Mating with the aim to produce progeny of a certain kind is, of course, a highly calculative and manipulative process. We have seen how the goldfish might be handled to produce the desired effect. A much larger literature, which reads at times like a laboratory manual and at times like pornography, exists for canines. That compelling desire to intervene decisively in the life of another finds a certain satisfaction in dog breeding. Life's urges and processes are, however, often imprecise; the breeder encounters difficulties that must be overcome. One is the time to mate, which varies with different breeds, within the same breed, and "even between individual bitches bred from the same parents. Dogs, also, vary in their attitude towards in-season bitches. Many will not touch a bitch until the red discharge has ceased. Some will mate a bitch at any time, if the bitch herself will permit it." Often she will not permit it. She has someone else in mind other than the well-groomed mate chosen by the breeder. Waiting for her to relent is useless. Force has to be applied. An expert advises: "Get a good firm grip on her ears. Someone else should then put a hand underneath her to steady her for the dog. With the other hand, a little helpful push at the right moment behind the dog might make all the difference. Steady him whilst he is tying the bitch; then when you are quite sure that the tying has taken place, gently turn him round, back to back with the bitch."[39] To ease the process of mating, it may even be necessary to put vaseline on the vagina and take the dog's member "into the palm of one's hand and exert a slight warming pressure." At un–scrupulous kennels, where breeding is a profitable business, bitches that do not show willingness are helped, and if they resist the help, they are forced, that is, muzzled and put into a sling to prevent them from resisting.[40]

The procedures just sketched are the impolite backstage activities. In front, for all to see, are the owners and their pets. How do people relate to the animals they keep in their house? How have attitudes changed in the course of time? Was affection—that personal involvement with the welfare of an individual animal—a common element of the bond? To these large questions I can provide here only suggestive answers. The key question for us, namely, the importance of affection in the bond, is also the most elusive for historical periods. That dogs have been highly valued pets since ancient times is beyond dispute. For example, remains of small

dogs have been discovered in the tombs of Egyptian pharaohs, dating
back to 2000 B.C. One specimen had ivory bracelets on its legs, and others
had collars of twisted leather. The teeth of many of these dogs were in bad
condition, which indicates that they suffered from pyorrhea—a consequence of being fed soft food.[41] In China, dogs were treasured and
pampered by many emperors, notably by Ling Ti (168-90), whose
favorites were given official titles; they ate the choicest rice and meat and
slept on costly carpets.

On both sides of the Eurasian continent, historical records abundantly
attest to the importance of the dog in high society. Difficult to ascertain
now is the precise character of the relationship between master or mistress
and pet. Without doubt, fine breeds served as a symbol of social worth.
They were protected and treated with as much care as other precious
possessions. However, unlike other possessions, the animal offered entertainment; it could be picked up and played with or used in some way (as a
rug or hand warmer, for instance); and it could be put aside anytime, even
kicked aside, when one's mood changed. Hints have come down to us that
in the past, as in the present, pets served a wide variety of purposes, that
they could be a source of pride and yet treated with cruel arbitrariness,
that even when human affection toward them was genuine and strong it
was more likely to be directed to a type or breed than to particular
individuals. Roman ladies were fond of little dogs. Pliny the Elder observed, however, that they also served a practical purpose. "As touching
the pretty little dogs that our dainty dames make so much of, called
Meltaei in Latin, if they be ever and anon kept close unto the stomach,
they ease the pain thereof."[42] Alcibiades possessed a large and beautiful
dog, noted in particular for its long, feathered tail. It was an animal he
could be proud of and which he surely valued, and yet, according to
Plutarch, he caused the tail to be cut off so that the Athenians might focus
on this eccentricity of behavior rather than on something worse.[43] The
behavior *was* eccentric and intended to shock. Still, we may wonder
whether an attitude of indifference, interspersed with bursts of effusive
attention, was not rather common for his time—and, indeed, of what
historical period would this attitude toward animals be untrue?

From the Renaissance period onward, portraits of notables often show
a dog or two, sometimes prominently placed in the center foreground,
along with other precious possessions—rich fabrics, furnishings, and
glimpses of landscape and landed property—all drawn with attention to

detail so as to suggest their material substance and tangibility. The dogs in such a world were certainly valued, but did they, individually, capture the affection of their master or mistress? Were they, for example, given personal names? In general, probably not. Thus G. S. Thomson, who studied the household of the fifth earl of Bedford at Woburn Abbey as it existed in the second half of the seventeenth century, has this to say:

> Many a dog appeared with his master or mistress in the portraits on the walls of the gallery at Woburn. Chiefly, these were spaniels, but one painting at least of the Earl himself, not at Woburn but at Chatsworth, shows a beautiful coursing greyhound standing by his master's side. But to be put into a picture was the only tribute paid to the dogs. No dog in the accounts, whether a spaniel or a coursing hound, is ever mentioned by name, or assumes the individuality of Tomson, the hawk. The entries are always on purely general lines— so many dogs to be fed and looked after.[44]

Fox hunting became a popular sport among aristocrats and the squirearchy in seventeenth-century England and continued to be so for the next two hundred years. The social flavor of the sport had not a little to do with the hunters' sartorial discrimination and with the presence of fine horses and dogs, which in the eighteenth century might well live in quarters more substantial than those of common laborers or of the servants who took care of them. And yet horses and hounds could also be treated harshly— whipped or kicked—when their masters and mistresses saw fit to do so, in a foul mood or in the heat of a chase. After a day in the field, wrote a riding-master in 1655, it "would pity the heart of him who loveth a horse to see them so bemired, blooded, spurred, lamentably spent, tired out." When worn out they were quickly discarded.[45]

Wherever animals were kept and brought up around the home compound, genuine affection toward them would develop, if only temporarily and sporadically, if only by the women who nurtured them and by young children who hugged and played with them. In Europe, society as a whole seemed to show a warmer feeling toward domestic animals from the seventeenth century onward. Dutch genre paintings of the period support this view. Whether the paintings are of landscapes or of house interiors, the dog is a common and conspicuous figure. Furthermore, just as the people and the interiors shown lack pretension—they are of the bourgeoisie and of low life—so the dogs depicted are not the prized possessions, the emblems of rank and wealth, but well-fed household animals and the mangier specimens of the countryside and the streets. Dogs in a bourgeois household were members of the family, participants in its daily round of activities as well as in its more festive occasions, and valued as such rather than for their pedigree.[46] There was sentiment, but of an unselfconscious and practical kind. More effusive sentiment—the hothouse product of a softer city life—emerged later, in the early decades of the nineteenth century. It was then that maudlin dog books began to reach many readers. Joseph Taylor's *The General Character of the Dog,* first published in 1804, enjoyed enough success to warrant two sequels, *Canine Gratitude* in 1806 and *Four-Footed Friends* in 1828. Schoolchildren were besieged by storybooks preaching kindness to animals.[47] In the same period appeared the immensely popular animal pictures of Edwin Landseer. Unlike the dogs drawn by such past masters as Paolo Veronese, Titian, and Velásquez, which showed the animals as they were engaged in their own thoughts and business, Landseer's dogs were drenched in human feelings and morality.

This highly sentimentalized view of animals was uniquely developed in western Europe and, later, in North America. What were the contributary causes? One general cause was simply the growing distance between people and nature. Wild animals and even farm animals were becoming less and less the common experience of men and women in an increasingly urbanized and industrialized society. It was easy to entertain warm feelings toward animals that seemed to have no other function than as playthings. Moreover, humans needed an outlet for their gestures of affection and this was becoming more difficult to find in modern society as it began to segment and isolate people into their private spheres, to discourage casual physical contact, and to frown upon the enormously satisfying stances of patronage, such as laying one's hand on another's shoulder.

To appreciate the *depth* of the bond between individual humans and their animals, we do well to read the numerous personal stories that have been recorded at different times and places. From antiquity, for example, are the well-known accounts of the devotion of Alexander the Great to his horse Bucephalus. He once risked war with an aggressive mountain tribe, the Mardians, when they abducted his horse. Alexander hand-reared his favorite dog, Peritas. At least one town in central Asia was named after the dog; in addition, a monument was built to its honor. With the world at their feet, potentates still seemed to need the blind devotion of animals, and to the animals they in turn might show the utmost concern and affection. Thus Louis XIV, to whom men and women constantly deferred, yet required the company of his setter bitches and always had seven or eight in his rooms. He fed them with his own hands so that they could learn to know him. Thomas Carlyle in his biography of Frederick the Great tells several stories of the king's tender feelings for his dogs. He is reported to have been found "sitting on the ground with a big platter of fried meat, from which he was feeding his dogs. He had a little rod, with which he kept order among them, and shoved the best bits to his favourites." In 1774, "wrapped in solitude, the King shut himself up in Sans Souci with his dogs, and afterwards he asked to be buried under the terrace of this little summer palace at Potsdam among his dogs." As he lay on his deathbed in 1786, he noticed that his greyhound bitch, which lay on a stool by his bed, was shivering. "Throw a quilt over it," he said, and they were probably his last words on earth.[48]

A tender romance of our time is that between the lonely writer T. H. White and his dog, a red setter named Brownie. The romance started coolly on White's part. He recalled how at first he thought of his pet as simply "the dog," rather as one thinks of "the chair" or "the umbrella." "Setters," he said, "are beautiful to look at. I had a beautiful motor car and sometimes I wore a beautiful top hat. I felt that 'the dog' would suit me nearly as nicely as the hat did." This casual appreciation deepened later into love. Brownie's near fatal sickness and White's nursing the setter back to health triggered the change. When, after eleven years of companionship, the dog did die, White wrote to David Garnett: "I stayed with the grave for a week, so that I could go out twice a day and say, 'Good girl: sleepy girl: go to sleep, Brownie.' It was a saying she understood. . . . Then I went to Dublin, against my will, and kept myself as drunk as possible for nine days, and came back feeling more alive than dead." More alive than dead. White, obviously, had to keep on living. Even before burial, when Brownie's body was still by his side, he wondered whether he should buy another dog or not. He pondered in a practical manner: "I *might* live another 30 years, which would be two dog's lifetimes . . . and of course they hamper one very much when one loves them so desperately."[49]

Konrad Lorenz, in his book *Man Meets Dog*, makes two points that may serve as defining the limits of human affection. One is the lingering tendency to treat even a valued pet as a convenience. Lorenz puts it thus: "If I ask a man who has just been boasting of the prowess and other wonderful properties of one of his dogs, I always ask him whether he has still got the animal. The answer is all too often . . . 'No, I had to get rid of him—I moved to another town—or into a smaller house.'" In this regard, it is significant that the mean age of household pets in California is only 4.4 years, with more than half being under 3 years. Household dogs are well looked after and yet they rarely grow old in the human family: they are disposed of long before they reach a ripe old age. The second point that Lorenz raises touches on the individuality of an animal. The death of a faithful dog may cause as much grief as the death of a beloved person. But Lorenz says, there is one essential detail that makes the former event easier to bear:

> The place which the human friend filled in your life remains for ever empty; that of your dog can be filled with a substitute. Dogs are indeed individuals, personalities in the truest sense of the word and I should be the last to deny this fact, but they are much more like each other than are human beings. . . . In those deep instinctive feelings which are responsible for their special relationship with man, dogs resemble each other closely, and if on the death of one's dog one immediately adopts a puppy of the same breed, one will generally find that he refills those spaces in one's heart and one's life which the departure of an old friend has left desolate.[50]

When we think of the power that one person exerts over another, the image that first comes to mind is unlikely to be that of mother and child. For when we think of mother and child we have an image of affection and tenderness—traits that we tend to dissociate from relationships of power. Another barrier to coupling power with motherhood is this. The word *person* suggests an adult. An infant or even a small child is still not thought of as a person in the fullest sense of that word. So, although a mother does have enormous power over her child, it is not quite perceived as power over another fully human individual. The child, in other words, is a pet and is properly treated as such.

Whatever views a mother may have toward her infant, in the actual practice of mothering she has to treat it as an incontinent young animal and even as a thing. She picks the infant up and puts it down with confidence and authority. She lifts its legs with one hand and with the other wipes its bottom. To change its diapers, she flips the child over with the nonchalance of a cook tossing a pancake. At a later stage, the child is toilet trained as the pup that is brought to live in the house must be toilet trained. The orders given and the manner in which they are given during such training are practically the same in both cases. The small child is a piece of wild nature that must be subdued and then played with—transformed into cute, cuddly beings or miniature adults as the mother or the surrogate mother sees fit. Its hair is curled, straightened, or tied with ribbons. Its clothes are put on and taken off—it must seem to the small child—at arbitrary times. The clothes themselves appear to have no bearing to the desires and needs of boy or girl. A child is dressed up largely for the convenience and pleasure of the adult. Once a child is mobile its movements have to be controlled. Inside the home, it is placed in a pen—caged in for its own safety and for the mother's convenience. Outside the home, the toddler may be put on a leash like a puppy. A child has not only to be trained but educated, and there too the mother plays a dominant role at a critical stage of growth. Women have perhaps always recognized this power. In the feminist consciousness of modern times it is openly avowed. "O how solemn, how great the responsibilities of a Mother," wrote Mary Hurlbut, a mother of four in New London, Connecticut, in 1831. Susan Huntington confidently if not arrogantly recorded in 1813 that the mother's task "is to mould the infants character into whatever shape she pleases."[1]

Attitude toward the child varies, of course, with culture and at different times within the Western tradition. Universally, the mother feels for her child. That is certain. But what is the precise nature of this feeling? To what extent is it consciously cultivated and articulated? The answers to these questions are less clear. One common perception of the small child, shared perhaps by adults in all cultures, is that it is a warm and soft animal pleasant to hold and hug. Jules Henry, reporting on the Kaingáng—a tribe of hunters and gatherers in the highland forests of Brazil—notes that the children there are greatly appreciated by the adults. The source of the attraction is a generic trait—the warmth and softness of their little bodies. Compared with this trait, the unique personalities of the children count for naught. Toddlers are at the beck and call of every adult. They sleep all over the place. They waddle up to older people and there, like pups, absorb the delicious stroking they can always count on receiving.[2] In a modern society, children do not waddle about naked in public spaces and they are not at the disposal of every adult. Yet we know how pleasant it is to hold a young child, to cuddle it to our breast. Do we hold a child as a loving, protective gesture, or do we *hold on to* a child—in moments of unease and self-doubt—as to a security blanket? There is evidence that in premodern times a European mother might take her infant to bed and hug it to herself with fatal consequence to the infant. One common reason given for infant death was "overlaying," or suffocation in bed. It may be that the infant was deliberately killed, but it could also be that it was used as a security blanket and hugged to death. In the Middle Ages, awareness of this possibility lay behind the warning periodically issued to parents that they must not coddle their children "like the ivy that certainly kills the tree encircled by it, or the ape that hugs her whelps to death with mere fondness."[3]

Infants are immobile and can therefore be picked up and put down by adults at any time. This immobility of infants was doubly ensured, in earlier ages, by the common practice of swaddling. Why infants were swaddled has several possible explanations. One is to straighten the child's limbs and to discourage it from assuming the animal-like foetal posture that is natural to it at that age. Another is to prevent the child, believed to be violent and animal-like, from doing harm to itself such as scratching out its own eyes. A third is convenience to adults. A swaddled infant is like an object that can be deposited anywhere. It can even be hung up on the wall or placed behind a furnace, out of one's way. A swaddled infant can also be treated as a toy and tossed about as one would a ball. This treatment of the child is almost too bizarre to be credible, and yet historical records indicate that it could occur, and not only as an isolated incident. It would appear, for example, that a brother of Henri IV of France, while being passed for amusement from one window to another, was dropped and killed. The little Comte de Marle suffered the same fate. "One of the gentlemen-in-waiting and the nurse who was taking care of him amused themselves by tossing him back and forth across the sill of an open window. Sometimes they would pretend not to catch him. . . . The little Comte de Marle fell and hit a stone step below." In the eighteenth and nineteenth centuries, doctors complained of parents who broke the bones of their children in what they described as "customary" tossing.[4]

Young children have been treated as sexual playthings. True of Western culture in the past and possibly in the present, the practice may also have occurred in other cultures. In Western society, sexual customs have changed so much that what we may now view with horror as sexual perversion and abuse was at an earlier time taken rather lightheartedly as a game or as acts legitimized by society. Using children for sexual purposes was a fairly widespread practice in classical antiquity. "Boys were not merely to be bought for money: they could even be hired by contract for a longer or a shorter time. . . . In Greece, at least in Athens and other harbour towns, there were brothels or houses of accommodation, in which boys and youths were to be had alone or with girls for money." Even where sex with freeborn boys was proscribed by law, men kept slave boys for pleasure. Children could be sold into concubinage, and one

Musonius Rufus wondered whether a boy sold by his father into a life of shame had the right to resist. In gymnasiums, teachers were exposed to the temptation of naked boys under their charge. Plutarch said that freeborn young Roman boys, when they played in the nude, might wear a gold ball around their neck as a warning to men that they were not to be molested. People who went too far in their sexual games with the young were, of course, censured. The emperor Tiberius went too far. Suetonius condemned him because he trained "little boys, whom he called his 'minnows', to chase him while he went swimming and get between his legs to lick and nibble him, and he let babies not yet weaned from their mother's breast suck at him." On the other hand, adults feeling the "immature little tool" of boys, which Petronius loved to describe, might perhaps come under the category of innocent fun.[5]

In Europe, as late as the seventeenth century, adults in all layers of society were extraordinarily uninhibited in using ribald language and engaging in overt sexual behavior before children. Indeed, children were often the target of sexual teasing. Their combination of innocence and partial understanding was a source of amusement to adults. The remarkable liberties that adults took with children have been recorded in art, literature, and other documents. One such document is the diary in which Henri IV's physician, Jean Héroard, noted the details of young Louis XIII's life. A modern reader would be shocked by what he finds there. Young Louis was treated as a sort of clever puppy at the disposal of every fun-seeking adult from his nanny upward in status to his royal parents. When Louis XIII was not yet one year old, his nanny made him laugh uncontrollably by waggling his penis with her fingers. The child soon learned to copy this trick. Calling a page, "he shouted 'Hey, there!' and pulling up his robe, showed him his cock." In high spirits, Héroard noted, he would ask the people around him to kiss his penis and nipples. The marquise de Verneuil wanted to put her hands under his coat and play with his nipples, but Louis objected because he was told that she might want to cut them off. Even the queen, his mother, joined in the games. She touched his organ and said, "Son, I am holding your spout." But most surprising of all was the day when both he and his sister were undressed and placed naked in bed with the king, and there they kissed and twittered to the king's great amusement.[6]

Before the twelfth century, parents no doubt had the most tender feelings toward their young, but these did not reach a level of reflexive consciousness to find expression in art and literature. In the Middle Ages, children, once they could stand on their own feet, were viewed as little adults; by the time they attained seven or eight years of age, they were made to work and could be exploited economically as though grown. Already in the thirteenth century, however, signs of a loving interest in childhood as a particular stage in life began to appear. The special needs of children and their unique ways of behavior were noticed more and more in later times. During the seventeenth century this interest was manifest in portraits, which became numerous and rather commonplace in noble households. For the first time, the secular family portraits began to be grouped around the child. A boy or a girl was the focus of pride and value as in other portraits a dog or a monkey might play such a role—or both child and animal would appear as necessary components of a loving household. In many paintings of this period, too, the child occupied a position of honor. Boys and girls were depicted, fondly, as taking music lessons, reading, drawing, playing. Some adults, however, allowed their fondness to take wayward paths. They took pleasure not only in the child's good behavior but also in its antics; indeed they encouraged its capers for their own amusement. They were also inclined to coddle the child and indulge it as they would a pet dog. Madame de Sévigné showed this tendency in her attitude toward her eighteen-month-old granddaughter. In a letter of 1670, the little girl is described as doing "a hundred and one little things—she talks, fondles people, hits them, crosses herself, asks forgiveness, curtsies, kisses your hand, shrugs her shoulders, dances, coaxes, chucks you under the chin: in short, she is altogether lovely. I amuse myself with her for hours at a time."

Not everyone was pleased with such foolish fondness. Montaigne, for one, could not accept the idea of loving children "for our amusement, like monkeys," or taking pleasure in their "frolickings, games and infantile nonsense." This critical attitude found wider acceptance in the next century. The moralist Claude Fleury, in a treatise on educational methods (1686), railed against the silly habit of praising and kissing children who have said something wrong but cute, or deliberately tricking them into making incorrect inferences for the laughter they provoked. "It is," Fleury wrote in words similar to Montaigne's, "as if the poor children had been made only to amuse adults, like little dogs or little monkeys." This view was repeated in M. d'Argonne's book on education. "Too many parents," he thought, "value their children only in so far as they derive pleasure and entertainment from them."[7]

Both male and female children can, of course, be treated as pets. However, in male-dominated, complex societies young male children are pets in a special sense, and what this is will need to be briefly explored. We hear the expression "mother's boy," "mother's pet." or "mother's little man." There is also the expression "teacher's pet," and in an American elementary school the teacher is likely to be a woman.[8] On the one side is the powerful and authoritative woman and on the other is the dependent little boy. In a male-dominated society, children are brought up in a household where the male head is seldom present except as a distant and awesome figure. The details of life are under the control of women. They are the figures of immediate authority with the vast power to give or withhold nurture. Adult males, those that the children see in the house most of the time, tend to have little power and low social status, being servants, slaves, or tutors. The mother is the commanding figure to small children. Her relationship with her daughter tends to be warm and unambivalent. The daughter is herself when young; the little girl's stages of growth replicate her own. For the little girl, growth is also unproblematic. She has her mother as a constant model. A child's playful activities become in time a woman's serious work: there is no sharp break between them.

In this type of society, the relationship between mother and son is more complex and tense. The son is of the opposite sex, a fact that the mother cannot ignore even when the son is an infant. Each time she bathes him she is aware of this difference. Each time she teases him, the sexual element—however innocent—is unlikely to be entirely absent. We should not be taken aback, or misinterpret, an engraving of the year 1511 depicting the holy family. The engraving shows Saint Anne pushing the child's thighs open as if she wanted to get at its privy parts and tickle them.[9] The picture illustrates the sexual frankness or innocence of the time. But if in a more prudish age the mother deliberately avoids touching those areas of her son, the consciousness of sex is still there—indeed, in a heightened form. The male child is loved because it is a child but also because it is male. Society places a higher value on the boy, a value that the mother shares in part because her own value in society rises by virtue of having produced a son. The son extends her power; he is her security and her gallant champion; he is her "little man." She wants her young son to behave like a little man and to strut a bit. She is amused by shows of precocious virility and can tease him cruelly if he reveals girlish traits such as wanting to play with dolls. On the other hand, he is chastised for his boisterousness, for his showing-off and aggression. The mother builds up the son's male ego and then cuts it down, ridiculing it contradictorily for both its crude power and its inadequacy.

Why this undercurrent of resentment? Why this temptation to play tauntingly with her son—a temptation that is unlikely to emerge in her relationship with her daughter? One answer lies in the nature of a male-dominated society. Women, however outwardly acquiescent, resent their subservient status. A wife resents a husband who spends the best hours of the day in the company of other men and treats her as merely the supervisor of his comforts, the mother of his children, or even more simply with an indifference born of familiarity and fatigue. A woman's anger cannot be directed at her husband and at man's estate in general. It can turn, however, on the son. In Greek myths, as Philip Slater has pointed out, the use of the son as a scapegoat for the father is ferociously and baldly expressed. "Medea kills her son in jealous rage against Jason (Euripides, Medea), while Procne, for identical motives, kills her son and serves him up to his father as a stew (Apollodorus)."[10] This is the strong stuff of passions. For the father's lesser sins, the son may also have to pay.

In earlier times and in other cultures, women have stood for awesome power that can be seen as either generative or destructive. Woman is the Great Mother, the source of all life and a nurturing goddess. She is also the Terrible Mother and takes the form of monsters in such places as Etruria, Rome, Egypt, India, Bali, and Mexico. The Great Mother is the ever fertile earth, the Terrible Mother is the ever hungry earth that devours her own children and fattens on their corpses.[11] In many societies, women as bearers of children and nurturers of plant life occupy a focal position in the structure of authority. "Whether the male chief is big or small," say the women of a West African solidarity group, "what matters is that he was given birth by a woman." Such women can protest a chief's action by treating him like a child.[12] They rely on ridicule and shame to get their way. No man can completely forget his former total dependence on a woman. In patriarchal societies, the men can never quite free themselves from the subliminal fear that they may yet slip back unawares into a childlike state and become once more women's appendages and play-things. As women's irresistible wiles seem endlessly varied, so are the forms of male subservience. Rousseau pretended to be concerned that the men of his time were so bound up with pleasing women, so careless of their own need for mental stimulation and physical exercise, and so incapable of defending themselves against the vacillating moods of nature that they were turning into a breed of lapdogs. In a poem called "On Woman," he describes her as that seductive and deadly being that "makes man into a slave, makes fun of him when he complains, overpowers him when he fears her, punishes him, and raises storms that torment the human race."[13]

Woman, both as nature and as culture, threatens man. As nature, she is a mysterious and violent force that needs to be propitiated or controlled. She is also fertility, nature's overwhelming abundance, and the threat to man there is the temptation of ease—of renouncing strife and culture for an indolent life on nature's ample lap.[14] As culture and artifice, woman represents a force that threatens to domesticate the male, emasculating him and curbing his freedom and wildness. To overcome his fears, man seeks the postures of domination and condescension. Insofar as woman is a force of nature, she must be tamed and harnessed to man's needs and desires. However, nature is not only powerful it is also unconscious, crude, irrational, and amoral. These are the defects of innocence—the innocence of nature and of the child. Woman in this other guise of nature is like a child. She can be condescended to and treated as a child. Woman, like nature and the child, is dumb—that is, without articulate speech. She is taught to be silent in the presence of her men. Speech does not become her, for it is either the prattling of a child or it is blunt and therefore ill-suited to the needs of public discourse.[15] Significantly, in Japan, flower arrangement is an art perfected by man, which is then taught to woman so that she can, without speech, express her sentiments to her lord.

On the other hand, the human male has also recognized woman as culture and the mistress of culture, including articulate and refined speech. Man's response to this perception is to treat culture as frivolity—the essentially useless trinkets and baubles of life—and to regard speech itself as evidence of ineffectiveness; woman speaks because she lacks the strength to act, that is, move material objects in the world. It would appear that man feels inferior, which feeling he tries to overcome by assigning to woman such subsidiary and subservient roles as vehicle for the continuation of his line, child, maidservant, fragile ornament, source of sexual pleasure and health, and plaything. All over the world, it is true, the general tendency has been far more to exploit women economically, to use them as laborers at uncongenial tasks, than to regard them as objects of prestige, playthings, and pets. But it is with the latter that we are concerned here.

When we think of women as playthings and pets, one image is certain to emerge and that is what goes on within the women's quarters, the seraglios and harems of patriarchal societies. Popular notion has it that these are paradises for the powerful and lascivious men who own them, that their denizens—the women—have no rights and serve no purpose other than as objects of prestige and of sexual indulgence. Reality is, of course, far more complex. Rules of etiquette and duty bind the masters almost as much as they do the women, and in some ways they can be as onerous. Yet in the end we must conclude that the women segregated in their compounds, almost totally out of touch with the outside world, exist for the use and pleasure of men.

Consider traditional China, where for more than two millennia men of the middle class and above have practiced polygamy. As early as the middle Chou period (ca. 700 to 500 B.C.), the king was believed to need the services and company of one queen, three consorts, nine wives of the second rank, twenty-seven wives of the third rank, and eighty-one concubines. (The numbers, after one, are multiples of three—three being a magical number of potency.) Why did the king need so many women? In cosmologic and medical terms the answer is that the king, because of the high level of his vital force (tê), required a large number of female partners to sustain it through sexual intercourse. Success in producing a strong and intelligent male heir for the throne was assured if union with the queen was preceded by a strengthening of the king's vital force through frequent copulation with women of the lower ranks.[16] Such belief was not confined to the ruler; it percolated down the heirarchy and was passed down the ages. By the Han period, custom allowed a middle-class householder to have three or four women, a man of the upper middle class six to twelve women, and a nobleman, a great general, or prince thirty or more wives and concubines. Justifying sexual indulgence as a health measure and as answering the social need to produce a vigorous male heir was understandably popular with the men. However, moralists periodically raised objections, increasingly so during the Sung dynasty. Thus Wan Mou (1151–1213), wrote:

The princes and noblemen of today keep large numbers of consorts and concubines, they use them as a kind of medicine---- But this will not prove advantageous to them; on the contrary, it will soon ruin their health. Even a superior man who understood [the Confucianist] Reason like [the famous T'ang scholar] Han Yü could not avoid succumbing to those teachings. So difficult it is to control one's carnal desires. Thus countless members of the gentry harm their body and lose their life through "those with the powdered faces and painted eyebrows," but they still persist in these practices and will not see reason.[17]

Where did the women come from and how were they obtained? No sure answer can be given for the more distant historical periods, not even for the large contingents assembled for the imperial palaces. However, reasonable surmises can be made. Van Gulik believes that during the heyday of empire (T'ang dynasty) the palace women "consisted of girls offered as tribute, both by the provinces and foreign and vassal countries; of daughters of prominent families keen on obtaining the Imperial favour; and of women recruited by palace agents. The palace agents used to scour the entire Empire for beautiful and accomplished women, and apparently took them wherever they found them, not despising even commercial or government brothels."[18] Thus, like rare birds or plants, women were picked and sent as gifts and tributes to the palace, where they were sorted out as to quality: the best went into the harem, the talented were trained to become performers, and the least desirable found employment as servants. During the sixteenth century, the procedure for obtaining palace women was somewhat different. Selection took place among the general population around Peking. "Young girls," wrote the modern scholar Ray Huang, "were nominated by the precinct and village elders according to quotas assigned to the communities, and subsequently went through many rounds of screening" before they entered the palace gate. Sometimes as many as three hundred were admitted as a group into the imperial household. Once inside the palace compound, the women would not see the outside world again and indeed would not see other males again except the emperor and the eunuchs.[19]

The Chinese emperor, in theory the absolute ruler of men, in fact led a life that was tightly circumscribed by tradition and customs which the civil officials (zealous Confucians) supervised. One area of the emperor's life that the civil officials could not touch was the women's quarters. The women were the emperor's property. Among them and within the inner courts he was free to behave as he wished. He could and sometimes did bathe naked with his ladies in the palace ponds. Dallying thus, the emperor was vulnerable to murderous attack. To forestall this possibility, all doors giving access to the inner apartments were kept barred and guarded. Security measures also necessitated another practice, attested for the Ming and Ch'ing periods but probably dating back to much earlier times. It was this. To guard against the possible but unlikely event of a woman attacking her imperial lover, the woman designated to share the emperor's couch was stripped naked, wrapped in a quilt, and carried into the emperor's room on the back of a eunuch.[20]

To Westerners, the single word that best captures the social life just sketched for China is *harem*, a word of Arabic origin with the meanings of "protected," "inviolate," and "sacred." Harem is the place in which women are confined, inviolate to the outside world but, of course, open to use by the master of the house. Before the triumph of Islam, Arab women enjoyed considerable freedom; following its triumph they tended to be increasingly segregated. As a social and political institution, the harem gained real importance and power under the sultans of Turkey, beginning in the fifteenth century. The harem developed into a complex world of its own in the Grand Seraglio of Istanbul. During the reign of Sulayman the Magnificent (1494–1566), it contained three hundred women, a number that rose to twelve hundred in the time of his grandson.[21] The harem, as a whole, was an austere rather than a luxurious place for most of its inhabitants. Every member had her exact duties to perform and belonged to an *oda* (court), each with its specialized function such as coffee-making, dressmaking, and accountancy. A woman might spend her entire life perfecting a skill, rising slowly but steadily in the hierarchy. Her moment of glory would come—if it ever did come—when for some reason she caught the sultan's eye. From that time on, she was "marked," separated from the rest of the girls and given an apartment and slaves to herself. Should the sultan actually express a desire to have the lucky girl in his bed, an elaborate fuss was made over her—preparing her as though she were a culinary delight. The heads of the different departments were called in to assist. First to take charge of her was the keeper of baths, who supervised her toilet with massage, shampooing, perfuming, and hair dressing. The shaving of the body, dyeing of the nails, and other such details followed. The girl then proceeded to the keeper of the lingerie, the mistress of the robes, the head of the treasury; and so on until she was at last ready for the royal bed.[22]

Should the fruit of the union be a male child, the girl was elevated to the status of *kadin* (concubine), with the possibility of one day becoming the *valideh sultan,* or queen mother, the highest and most powerful position that any woman could hope to reach. On the other hand, should she fail to produce a male child and should the ardor of the sultan wane, she would be stripped of appurtenances and privileges and returned to her former status as a worker in the harem. Although it would be inappropriate to characterize the harem as a workshop, yet most of the women there were occupied in acquiring some skill, which helped to pass the time, provide an avenue of achievement, and could lead to a satisfying and respected position of training others. Nevertheless, a woman's greatest aspiration and constant hope (up to a certain age) was to be able to crawl humbly into the bed of her lord.[23] Humiliation plumbs a poignant depth when its victim regards it as the highest form of honor.

Accounts of the enclosed women's quarters in the Moslem world, in South and East Asia, all have an air of the fabulous, however responsibly told. They seem like tales out of the Arabian Nights. We know that in the Western world women have also been segregated, but it has been difficult for us to connect them in any serious way with the foot-bound women of premodern China, with the girls behind the purdah and in the harem. Yet the link can be and has been made, notably by Eleanor Perényi, who asks us to ponder over the innocent and appealing images of "flower and garden."[24] Are these images and things so innocent? In the Western world as elsewhere, flower connotes beauty, but also a certain useless passivity and frivolity. *Du bist wie eine Blume.* You are like a flower. The "you," of course, is a woman and the comparison is meant to flatter her. A man, thus compared, would feel insulted. In the harem of the Grand Seraglio, castrated black boys were given the names of flowers such as Hyacinth, Narcissus, Rose, and Carnation. In China, that bundle of crushed flesh and splintered bones—the bound foot—was compared to the lotus. In Europe, "shy as a violet" and "clinging vine" were once intended to be commendatory. It was proper for a woman to be shy and clinging.

The enclosed garden is lovely, but if its inmates have no right to leave it at will, it serves in reality as a prison. The word *paradise,* as we all know, is derived from a Persian word for the garden. The walled-in compound is indeed a paradise for the master of the house: all its contents—flowers, shrubs, and fountains, exotic animals and lovely women—cater to his pleasure. The master of the house alone enters and leaves as he pleases; none of the other inmates enjoys such freedom. Flowers figure in varying degrees of prominence in all the inner spaces designed to accommodate primarily women, whether we think of the inner courts of the Chinese house, those of India where the purdah is strictly enforced, or the Moslem harem. In the Western world, too, the symbolism of femininity and masculinity is clear. On the one side might be the Roman atrium or some flower-filled enclosure chiefly for women, and on the other were the far more expansive pleasure grounds such as those laid out by Pliny, which he designated as for himself and his male friends. Except for violet beds he did not mention flowers and he did not mention women. In Renaissance and post-Renaissance times, the female realm was the hedged-in *giardino segreto*; beyond it stretched the vast, rather austere formal spaces—almost flowerless—designed by men in large part to reflect their own sense of grandeur and power.

Women in their sheltered and flower-strewn spaces could lead a life of comfort and even luxury. Within their own realm they might exercise undisputed authority. Given their ability to maneuver their men, the women could also exert influence over the public realm far beyond the walls within which they were sequestered. In the European Middle Ages, the noble ladies—those whom we see embroidering or playing a zither among the flowers in tapestries and illuminations—could boast a great deal more. To judge from the troubadour poetry of the period, they were able to inspire absolute allegiance from their men. Their wish, however whimsical, was obeyed; their rebukes, however unjust, were silently received. Emerging in southern France during the eleventh century was the cult of courtly love, in which the lover pledged his service to his lady as would a vassal to his lord. The lover was the lady's "man." He addressed her as *midons*, which has the meaning of "my lord" rather than "my lady." But who was the lover? Who were the men who lived for the favor of their ladies? They were not the lord of the castle: he would have viewed the lady and her damsels as his property. They were rather the male contingents of a feudal domain, "the inferior nobles, the landless knights, the squires, and the pages—haughty creatures enough in relation to the peasantry beyond the walls, but feudally inferior to the lady as to her lord—her 'men' as feudal language had it."[25] In the hard and comfort-scarce world of the castle—hard and raw in part because of the surplus of unattached males—almost all the touches of grace, beauty, good manners, and the good life flowed from the lady and her damsels. Most of the men within the castle could not aspire to marriage with these women; what they could hope for was illicit love and the few graces that emanated from the female presence. The chatelaine could indeed dominate her male social inferiors. But what was her relationship with her lord? Significantly, while the mass folly of the Crusades occupied the men for some two hundred years the chatelaine in effect took control of the absentee lord's estate and managed it well for him. She assumed a position of power and of responsibility. Nevertheless, as Perényi puts it, "she lived behind fortified walls, and it isn't hard to conjecture that her garden was in the nature of a chastity belt, locking her in until the return of her lord and master."[26]

We have looked at woman in the harem and woman in the garden and castle. Let us turn now to a third image, much closer to our time, and that is woman in a "doll's house." This last image, although it was beginning to emerge in the eighteenth century, came into sharper focus later, in the midst of the socioeconomic transformations and moral hypocrisies of the Victorian Age. The flower garden is a part of that image: we can see in our mind's eye the lady of the house wearing a large sun hat and garden gloves clipping flowers for her table. But other pictures, as vivid or more vivid, come to mind. There is the house itself, which, from the mid nineteenth century onward, took on romantic and even playful airs—a fictitious example being old Mr. Wemmick's castellated house, described by Dickens in *Great Expectations*, with its moat, its drawbridge, and its gun salutes at sunset.[27] Within the house are maids dusting the furniture and the extraordinary clutter of bibelots; the lady at her various little jobs, writing a letter, thinking what should go on the menu of Saturday's dinner, reading a novel, putting some touches on a watercolor, puttering around the flower garden (as we have seen), or playing with the children. It is a curiously cloistered world of women and small children throughout the day—a curiously dreamlike world in which so many of the activities seem more play or domestic ritual than necessity, including even the recurrent dusting and polishing of so many useless objects.

"Home, sweet home." "There is no place like home." These were still fresh sentiments at the start of the nineteenth century. At about this time too home was commonly viewed as "retreat," "haven," or "retirement." Home was a fortress—old Wemmick's castellated house—set against a hostile world of strangers, meaning by that the crowded and industrialized city. Home was also a sanctuary—a pure and inviolate world for women and children (*harem*, we remember, means "sacred" or "inviolate")—set against the male, commercial world of competition and strife.

How did the propertied men, the fathers and husbands, see their womenfolk? Whether daughter or wife, a woman was a ministering angel, a salve to the men returning from the battlefield of economic life. She was, of course, always a child to the father. To the husband, she was the "child-wife." Custom dictated that the husband be several years older than the wife: from the vantage point of maturer years and greater experience alone he could look down upon her. Before suffrage, the wife in fact had the legal status of a minor. In New England, in 1835, "a married woman had no legal existence apart from her husband's: she could not sue, contract, or even execute a will on her own; her person, estate, and wages became her husband's when she took his name."[28] The child-wife was playful. She prattled on entertainingly and dispelled the clouds that gathered around her husband's brows in the course of a workday. She had accomplishments to her credit: she could sing, do watercolors, and speak a little French. She knew enough to help educate her young children and preside graciously at the dining table, but not so much that her knowledge threatened her "sweetness." She was pure. Her thoughts were always loving, but curiously she was also amoral like a child. She did not fully appreciate the impersonal majesty of the law or the concept of honor; she obeyed rather the "laws of the heart." If pure and childlike, how could a woman also be the object of sexual desire? The sexual nature of woman was carefully hidden during daytime. When she left the house to go shopping or visiting, she went as it were in purdah— under a large hat, behind a veil, and wearing a dress that covered almost every part of her body. Yet in the evening, at a formal dinner or ball, she could appear in a provocative gown that emphasized her breasts and revealed her shoulder and arms.[29] Under certain conditions, then, the men could bring out their women and show them to be not just virtuous mothers and wives but also glittering possessions, adornments, and tantalizing sex objects.

What is sketched here is valid for only a narrow layer of society—the affluent bourgeoisie, people with enough money to have several live-in servants. In less prosperous households, the women would have to busy themselves to maintain their homes in a proper state of social respectability. In New England, leisure was even more scarce. Middle-class women there were engaged in such domestic manufactures as spinning, weaving, and candle-making until well into the second half of the nineteenth century. Obviously they could not play at being child-wife. As for the aristocracy in England and on the Continent, their women had tradition-ally enjoyed greater freedom of movement and of manners than had their sisters of the upper bourgeoisie, who were constrained by more stringent notions of morality and domestic virtue.

A classic statement of the upper-middle-class woman as a man's child-wife and pet is Ibsen's play A Doll's House, published in 1879.[30] We can use Ibsen's words and ideas to recapture the essence of what it means for a woman to be dominated, indeed humiliated, under the guise of affection. Standing out at the start of the first act are the differences in the way husband and wife address each other. Whereas the wife simply uses her husband's given name, Torvald, the husband calls his wife his "little lark" who twitters charmingly, his "little squirrel" busy at her nonessential tasks, and his "little sweet-tooth" who must be rebuked for secretly eating macaroons when she had promised him not to. Nora, the wife, plays so excitedly with her three young children that there seems hardly any difference in age between them. Motherhood for her is reduced to such romping in the living room and to buying presents at Christmas time, since the more serious tasks of nurturing and training the children are taken over by the nurse. Nora does possess one special talent: she can dance. She has learned the tarantella while she and her husband were in Capri. It is the wish of the husband that she dress up as a Neapolitan peasant girl and dance the tarantella at a neighbor's party. She is to be shown off; a very proper wife she is, but also a doll—a dancing doll. The plot of the play centers on Nora's attempt to save the health of her husband by sending him to a resort with money that neither of them had. She borrows the money by forging her father's signature on a document. When her deed is exposed, her husband—far from understanding her motivation of love—denounces her hypocritically for her crime, for her inability to appreciate the impersonal honor of contractual agreement and the letter of the law. Nora at last realizes that she has been living for eight years not with a husband but with a stranger in a doll's house.

Torvald: Haven't you been happy here?
Nora: No, never, I thought I was, but I wasn't really.
Torvald: Not—not happy!

Nora: No; only merry. You've always been so kind to me. But our home has never been anything but a play-room. I've been your doll-wife, just as at home I was Papa's doll-child. And the children in turn have been my dolls. I thought it was fun when you played games with me, just as they thought it fun when I played games with them. And that's been our marriage, Torvald.[31]

Nora's words capture the theme of this chapter.

8 SLAVES, DWARFS, FOOLS

Domination of one group over another is inescapable in any large and complex society. The degree of domination varies, as does the sharpness of the distinctions drawn between the groups: witness the terms *masters* and *slaves* (or *servants*), *lords* and *peasants* (or *serfs*), *Brahmans* and *Untouchables, upper class* and *under class*. Where humans have won indisputable power over nature, their use and exploitation of animals and plants no longer calls for an explanatory myth. Inequality between adults and children, because it is a temporary condition, has never required defense. Man's exercise of power over woman does call for an explanatory myth, and the one that man has traditionally used is an appeal to biology. What happens when one group dominates another without the excuse of either age or gender? Other myths emerge to make inequality acceptable, even right, to both parties.

Perhaps the most unusual and most effective of these myths is the ethical-religious explanation for the caste system of India, a system that has been maintained without major disturbance for some two thousand and three hundred years. Caste is based on birth. The institution of caste suggests that whole groups share genetic inheritances so markedly different from each other that such groups ought to hold quite different positions in society. Thus stated, the view is clearly racist, but the statement misrepresents the Hindu view. The Hindu's frame of thought does not include genetic inheritance. What an outcaste or Untouchable inherits are not genes but the misdeeds of a past life. It is legitimate to look down on an Untouchable and to assign unpleasant tasks to him because of

132

these misdeeds. On the other hand, caste status *is* transmitted down lines of biological descent, and the distinctions of caste are often recognized on grounds of physical appearance. In general, members of the lower castes are darker skinned that those of higher status. So racism and racial prejudice may indeed be a significant component of Indian caste consciousness, even though the formal justification for the system rests on a religious belief that emphasizes cycles of rebirth and the transmission of merits and demerits from previous lives.

The Indian rationale for caste is unique to India. Elsewhere it is far more common to use differences in physical appearance and in mental capacities believed to be associated with them as justification for domination and subservience.[1] Skin color is a highly visible physical trait that has often been used to separate people into distinct social layers with vast differences in power. Light and dark, or white and black, form polarities. Worldwide there is a strong tendency to attribute positive values to "white" and negative ones to "black." In Europe, particularly from the sixteenth century onward, this tendency developed into a fully articulated set of antithetical values: white and black connoted, respectively, purity and filth, virginity and sin, virtue and baseness, beauty and ugliness, beneficence and evil, God and the devil. Europeans were learning more and more about Africans from the distorted accounts of travelers and slave traders and from seeing black servants and slaves in Europe. White skin, in itself, became a mark of superiority. Interestingly, this stress was preeminent in England, where Elizabeth was queen. Elizabeth herself deliberately fostered "pale looks" as an image of beauty. When entering the capital on one occasion, "her litter was uncovered that she might shew herself to the people, clothed all in white, her face sickly pale." In the middle of her struggle with Mary Queen of Scots, Elizabeth felt it sufficiently important to ask one of Mary's courtiers who was the fairer of the two.[2]

The association of dark skin with animality or childishness is a familiar one in Western culture. The dark-skinned person, as someone barely human, is to be harnessed to toil; or, if young and comely, to be treated as an exotic pet. The dark-skinned person, as a perpetual child, is to be fed and clothed, disciplined and trained to perform menial tasks suited to his mental capacity. This well-known theme will be further explored later, but a proper perspective requires us to know that this setting up of superiority and inferiority, of domination and subordination, based on physical appearance and skin color is far from being an aberration of Western culture alone. Other civilizations and cultures share it, in varying degrees. Consider, as an illustration, the social hierarchy of Ruanda, a central African kingdom, as it pertained in the hundred years or so before the middle of the twentieth century. Three distinctive groups live in Ruanda: Twa, Hutu, and Tutsi. The Twa are a pygmoid people, hunter-gatherers who were probably the country's earliest inhabitants. The Hutu are of middle stature and are hoe-cultivators who appeared in Ruanda at about the same time as the Twa or somewhat later. The Tutsi are very slender and tall, of light brown skin color, and are herders of cattle. In Ruanda's hierarchical order, the Tutsi form an aristocracy, the Hutu are commoners, and the Twa are said, "half jokingly, by most of the other Ruanda, to be more akin to monkeys than to human beings." Added to these physical differences, objectively present but greatly exaggerated by the habit of stereotyping, are differences in moral quality as perceived by the Ruanda peoples themselves: the Tutsi are intelligent, capable of command, refined, and cruel; the Hutu are hardworking, physically strong, not very clever, extrovert, unsophisticated in manners, and obedient; the Twa, in direct antithesis to the Tutsi, are gluttonous and lazy, but they are also said to be courageous in hunting and loyal to their Tutsi masters. All three groups believe that the differences are innate rather than the result of upbringing and culture. As the top crust of society the Tutsi lead a lordly and leisurely life. When they travel, for instance, they may do so in litters carried by their Hutu and Twa subordinates. In return for labor and personal service, the Tutsi offer patronage and protection. However, it is up to the Tutsi to decide how much protection to grant. A Tutsi lord may decide to take care of the whole of the subordinate's life, treating him as a child, or he may offer only limited patronage. The subordinate, on his part, must assume a posture of inferiority and be totally compliant to the will of his lord, his only way out of this bondage being to exchange one master for another.[3]

Differences in physical appearance make it easy for society to justify orders of unequal power and prestige, but they are not by any means necessary. Humans are seldom at a loss to find innate inferiority in the people they wish to dominate. A characteristic of slavery in classical antiquity is the lack of racial distinctiveness in the enslaved class. Nevertheless, Aristotle was prepared to argue that some humans were slaves by nature. The very fact that they allowed themselves to belong to another stigmatized them. Like domestic animals, natural slaves were deficient in reason; they needed to be controlled by others and to serve others with their bodies. Indeed nature endowed them with strong bodies, in comparison with those of free men, so that they could perform the hard and necessitous tasks.[4] In the modern period, we have the example of the ease with which the English were able to treat the Irish poor as an inferior race—dirty, lazy, and irresponsible, though capable of being trained into competent servants—despite the absence of distinguishing physical marks. Of course, upper-class Europeans, including Englishmen, have habitually looked down upon their own working poor—the "lower orders" in their midst. German nobles in the eighteenth century considered themselves so far above lower-class Germans that they could not envisage equality even in heaven.[5] Because of large differences in nourishment and other living conditions, striking differences in physical appearance between rich and poor did eventually emerge. The undernourished poor in Europe were not only shorter in stature but also darker skinned, pigmented by dirt and exposure to the sun. These traits, caused by the injustices of society, could then be taken by the well-fed and well-housed as the predictable outcome of an inferior nature.[6]

Why dominate another? By far the most common reason is use. Any complex society has a large number of tedious or hard and even dangerous jobs that must be performed if society is to be maintained. Through a combination of force and indoctrination, a segment of society is made to do the unpleasant work. The people thus compelled, whatever their legal status, are treated as tools. Care is given them because tools must be kept in good order. Cato the Elder (234–149 B.C.), in his advice to his son on how to manage a farm, refers to sick slaves as unproductive and a useless burden. Plutarch speaks of Cato as someone who "never once bought a slave for more than 1,500 drachmae, since he didn't want beautiful ones, but hard workers; and he also thought that when these got older, they should be disposed of and not fed when they were no longer useful."[7] Within the house, a Greek or Roman owner found it hard to conceive how a decent human life was possible without constant, unobtrusive attendance by slaves. In a comedy, a Greek playwright tried to envisage a world without slaves. He pretended that such a world was possible only if things could move upon command. "Each object will come to him when he calls for it. Put yourself down next to me, table. That one—get yourself ready. Fill up, jug."[8]

Slaves were a part of a house's furnishings and belonged to it as did the roof, bath, and well. No self-respecting man wants to live in a house that is not fully equipped. Human appliances, however, need not have the legal status of chattels; they could be servants. Consider an upper-class Victorian household. It was filled with servants who maintained the house and catered to the innumerable demands of the family; and yet, as furnishings and appliances they were ideally invisible. Servants were segregated from the family. They had their own work areas and living quarters, connected to each other by backstairs. Should the mistress of the house encounter by chance a gardener at work, he was to dispose of himself as quickly as possible; and should she come upon a maid dusting the furniture the maid was to press herself against the wall in an effort to fade into the woodwork.

Slaves and servants were exploited primarily for their brawn, more rarely for their special skills and for their good looks. Cato, we have seen, was not concerned with the aesthetic appeal of his slaves, only with their ability to perform tasks. Yet Cato, by declaring his lack of interest in beauty, suggests that other buyers *were* concerned with it. Pederastically inclined men could buy attractive boys for immoral purposes. Both Greeks and Romans probably purchased attractive slave women with an eye to sexual congress and to using them as prostitutes.[9] Slaves were also bought for their intellectual endowment. Thus Romans purchased educated Greek slaves as guardians and tutors to their children. In comparison with the practices of classical antiquity, slavery in the modern (that is, post-1500) period was concerned almost exclusively with the needs of labor. In America, posters announcing slave sales emphasized the slaves' age, health, and strength, and in the case of women, perhaps also their "prolific generating qualities," as one Southern newspaper put it. And yet there can be little doubt that, other things being equal, a comely slave fetched a higher price than a plain one. Slave traders knew this and would do everything they could to improve the appearance of their ware. Like a dishonest car dealer who sets back the odometers of his cars, a planter selling his slaves might pluck out the gray hair of the older ones or paint them over with a blacking brush. Old marks of abuse were covered up with grease, and grease might also be used on slave bodies to make them shine. Some sellers presented their goods in fancy wrappings, fitting the females in silks and satins and the males in neatly pressed suits. Before a buyer sealed his purchase of a slave in the Old South, "he usually wanted to examine him physically. He looked at his teeth, limbs, and back, felt and poked muscles. Often buyers touched female slaves in most familiar ways." Sometimes the slaves were carried back into a small yard, where they were stripped and minutely inspected for hidden scars, signs of syphilis, and in the case of women the pelvic areas to estimate their potential as childbearers. In the carnival atmosphere of auction day, with liquor flowing freely, we can easily imagine the crude jokes, the sexual taunting and humiliation of the humans on sale.[10]

Let us focus on the noneconomic aspects of slave ownership. As chattels of value, costly to purchase and maintain, slaves added prestige to their owners. A traveling potentate in the past had to be accompanied by a long retinue of slaves and servants and perhaps exotic animals as well in order to make the appropriate impressions on his hosts and on the populace. Hellenist kings like Antiochus IV sought to overawe their subjects by organizing processions involving hundreds if not thousands of slaves; and it was a sign of extreme indignity for an exiled monarch like Ptolemy VI to arrive at Rome accompanied by just four slaves.[11] In rich, slave-owning societies, bondsmen and women formed a part of the dowry of the bride. It is recorded in the *Later Han Dynasty*, for instance, that for the wedding of a daughter of the Yuan family in Lo-yang the dowry of the bride included one hundred silk-clad girls.[12]

In slave-owning societies, farm slaves were purchased for the work they must do to make an operation economical and profitable. Household slaves in the city, on the other hand, were often multiplied far beyond the number necessary for efficiency and convenience. Just as a modern house-owner might buy a superfluity of mechanical goods in unthinking extravagance and for prestige, so in an ancient household the master might have so many slaves that he could not possibly remember all their names and functions and so was obliged to make one servitor the *nomenclator*, whose duty was to be a memory bank.[13] Because of the very large number of servitors (Tacitus mentions four hundred for a Roman urban household), their duties tended to be highly specific. In addition to the many jobs that had to be done around the house, there were others whose existence catered to the master's sense of propriety, dignity, and luxury, as, for example, those of cupbearer, entertainers in general, and in particular the educated slave assigned to read aloud while the master and his guests dined. Slaves who performed the necessary tasks soon became invisible, but slaves who served luxury needs and prestige retained the visibility of all prized objects. They were likely to win the owner's pride and capricious affection. We can imagine, for instance, a Roman aristocrat taking special pride in the melodious voice of his reader, accepting modestly the compliments paid to his slave as a modern host might accept the compliments paid to his stereo that played soothing music during dinner. Comely and talented slaves were luxury goods but because they were also human they could be thoroughly pampered or sexually abused as pets. Although Petronius in *The Satyricon* exaggerated intentionally for effect, he nevertheless caught the flavor of decadence in an obscenely wealthy household in Nero's Rome, in which pretty slaves—pretty bibelots as it were—were fondled and ravished or dispatched to a friend as a gift, as their owner's mood dictated.[14]

Remote in time and place from Imperial Rome is Czarist Russia. Yet in the organization of household life among the powerful and in the ways the masters regarded and treated their servitors, there are some remarkable similarities. By the last quarter of the eighteenth century the Russian serf was scarcely distinguishable from a chattel slave. Serfs at that time could be sold "like cattle." When Catherine II, under the beneficent influence of her mentor Voltaire, tried to ban the spectacle of auctioning humans on the block and failed, she permitted such sales but forbad the use of the hammer by the auctioneer![15] Russian nobles, by the standard of their peers in other European countries, were extravagant in the number of domestics they retained. Some of the great establishments in St. Petersburg had as many as 150 to 200 menials. One British visitor, who had access to a selection of the greatest houses of St. Petersburg and Moscow in the years 1805 to 1807, found them "filled with vassals, or servants, both male and female, who line the halls, passages, and entrances of the rooms in splendid liveries. In almost every antechamber some of these domestics are placed, ready to obey the commands of their lord or his guest." A Russian nobleman took special pride in those serfs who possessed unusual skills. They swelled his own sense of importance. Thus, when a guest complimented him "on the pastries served at his table and surmised that they came from the most fashionable *pâtisserie* in town, he could casually answer that they had been made by his own serf confectioner." A Russian lord might have his own orchestra. Piotr Kropotkin noted how proud his father Prince Alexander was of his orchestra, even though it was not of high quality because most members were part-time players serving also other needs of the household. However, the prince did buy two violinists whose sole job was to play the violin.[16] Although some serfs were prized possessions, this standing did not guarantee them against abuse. Just as a potentate might in anger or as a gesture of disdain sweep an entire set of costly glassware crashing to the floor, so he might impose capricious punishments on his serfs, and the females among them were liable to be the victims of his lechery.

Great nobles and landowners in Victorian England, although they did not have serfs, did have servants in extravagant number. These, besides performing useful functions, were also symbols of luxury and prestige. Lower servants were a part of a great house's hidden machinery; upper servants—particularly footmen—were objects of display, chosen for their height and good looks. The lords of England had the pick of the human stock, those over six feet tall, while the little fellows sank "into pot-boys, grooms, stable men, and attendants at the inns."[17] In the best households, footmen were matched in height. A pair might stand erect behind their mistress's swaying coach, splendidly liveried and often wearing padded silk stockings to make their legs look more curvaceous (fig. 19). They were trained to act in unison, marching in stately steps up "to the great doors of a London house and banging on the double knockers in perfect harmony, before they marched back again to their lady waiting in her coach." When eight members of the Kropotkin family dined, twelve men waited on them, with one man standing behind each person at the table. English eccentrics more than matched this particular example of excess. Thus William Beckford (1760–1844) was known to have ordered a magnificent dinner for twelve guests, with a dozen footmen in attendance, only to dine alone. The eighth earl of Bridgewater was famed for his extraordinary parties in his Parisian mansion. He too had his table set for twelve, with footmen in attendance, but his guests were his favorite dogs.[18] His human menials in rich livery were made to serve his animal pets, also lavishly attired. From the exalted position of the earl, servants and favorite dogs had much the same rank and he was free to play with both.

A pet is a diminished being, whether in the figurative or in the literal sense. It serves not so much the essential needs as the vanity and pleasure of its possessor. Under this broad definition, the ornamental slaves, serfs, and servants that once cluttered up the houses of the great were pets. But there is also a narrower meaning to that word. A pet is a personal belonging, an animal with charm that one can take delight in, play with, or

Fig. 19. A *Punch* cartoon showing a dignified Victorian footman having difficulty with his leg stuffings.

set aside, as one wishes. Humans can become such pets too. To illustrate, consider the role of black domestics in England from the sixteenth to the early part of the nineteenth centuries. Their status was ambiguous. Not legally chattels, they were however often treated as such. Servants they were, like other nonblack colleagues in the household, but also pets—the personal favorites and appendages of their masters or mistresses.

As early as 1569 Lord Derby employed a black servant. From about that time onward, slave-domestics from Africa figured more and more prominently in noble households. Their initial attraction lay in their exoticism and rarity. Renaissance man's curiosity toward all things fabulous and rare extended to the African, human and yet so unlike himself. Blacks lived in Elizabeth's London in sufficient number to be a source of worry to the queen: she was concerned with feeding the growing immigrant population at a time when food was scarce and famine periodically threatened. And yet the queen herself employed Africans at court: one was known to be an entertainer, and another a page. James I made the employment of Africans a fashion. He had his own troupe of black minstrels while his wife, Anne of Denmark, used black servants. In the years after the Restoration blacks were a common sight on the streets of London. By 1680 they were so much a part of London life and society that it was alleged of the lady of fashion that "she hath always two necessary implements about her; a Blackamoor and a little dog."[19]

The treatment of African domestics as curios, accoutrements, and pets is well documented in the eighteenth century. A fine-limbed boy would make a nice present for the wife of one's boss. One of Admiral Richard Boscawen's subordinates brought back a Negro boy from America as a present for the admiral's wife. Blacks were openly offered for sale in shops, warehouses, and coffeehouses. Metropolitan and provincial newspapers regularly announced their availability. One such notice, for instance, sought to dispose of "A Pretty little Negro Boy, about nine Years old, and well limb'd." London was widely known for the size of its market for black slave-domestics. Thus in 1769, when the czarina of Russia wanted a "number of the finest best made black boys," her agent came to shop in London.[20]

Young black boys occupied a special position as exotic ornaments and pets. They were the favorite attendants of noble ladies and rich courtesans, and in that capacity gained entry into drawing rooms, bedchambers, and theater boxes and enjoyed an intimacy with their mistresses that could not be countenanced for other male servants. As they did with their pet dogs and monkeys, the ladies grew genuinely fond of their black boys. Attempts were made to educate them—in part, to test the quality of African intelligence; and when for some reason they proved inconvenient to keep, sustained efforts were made to place them with other caring mistresses. The position of blacks in society was also suggested by the art of the time. In the same manner that favorite dogs appeared in contemporary paintings, so did favorite African domestics. Thus the heroine in Hogarth's *The Harlot's Progress* is attended by a black boy, and a black boy appears in the series of six pictures called *Marriage à la Mode*. Other examples are Kneller's *Duchess of Ormonde*, Zoffany's *The Family of Sir William Young*, and George Morland's *The Fruits of Early Industry*. Sir Joshua Reynolds, using his own black as a model, painted Negro servants into a number of his portraits: he took delight, it would seem, in the contrasting colors and textures of the human skin.[21] This practice was by no means confined to England. Van Dyck's portrait of Henrietta of Lorraine, painted in 1634, shows her attended by an exotically dressed, plump-faced black boy. And F. O. Shyllon notes that "in Richard Strauss's comic opera *Der Rosenkavalier*, set in Vienna in the early years of the reign of Maria Theresa, who was proclaimed Archduchess of Austria in 1740, the Marschallin had a black boy as a pet."[22]

From the start, young African domestics in noble households were fancily attired. By the eighteenth century, the ornate livery had come to be an insignia of black, as distinct from white, servitude (fig. 20). Far more telling of the true status of the domestics, however, were the collars and padlocks that the black members were sometimes made to wear. This inhuman fad was common enough to draw the attention of enterprising craftsmen. A goldsmith, for example, announced in *The London Advertiser* for 1756 that he could make "silver padlocks for Blacks or Dogs; collars, etc." A black boy, being a prized possession, might wear a gold- or silver-plated collar with the owner's coat of arms and cipher engraved on it. Or the boy's collar might bear some such inscription as, "My Lady Bromfield's black, in Lincoln's Inn Fields."[23]

Prejudice against blacks took a wide range of forms, some more crude than others. At its crudest, blacks were regarded as stupid, indolent, and subhuman. Less harsh but more insidious was the habit of praising blacks as "faithful and obedient." And they might also be characterized as childish or childlike, always happy and grinning, drawn naturally to fancy

Fig. 20. Attributed to Johann Zoffany, *Portrait of the Third Duke of Richmond out Shooting with his Servant c. 1765*. Paul Mellon Collection, Upperville, Virginia. The servant wears the distinctive red-and-black livery of the Duke's black servants.

and farce. One talent commonly attributed to Africans, and intended
ostensibly as a compliment, was an aptitude for music. Already in the
seventeenth century and continuing through the eighteenth, a myth built
up to the effect that Africans could sing and dance. Some argued for a
cultural origin of this bent, others held it to be inborn. A major contribut-
ing factor to the myth was the black minstrel show. We have noted that
James I had his black entertainers. But it was in Victorian England that the
minstrel show, performed by whites as well as blacks, became widely
popular across all layers of society. In time the picture of a grinning,
dancing, and singing person, absurdly dressed in tall hat and cotton
garments of brilliant hue, was indelibly associated in the English mind
with the black man. Toys made in the likeness of this image were sold
throughout the country, thus affecting the way children perceived. Given
this stereotype, it was difficult to take any black man seriously. He came
to be regarded as the quintessential entertainer, someone who existed to
amuse his betters. Thus even where real talent existed it could be turned
into another cause for condescension.[24] A supercilious attitude, widespread even among highly educated Victorians, was forcefully expressed
by Thomas Carlyle, who, after fulminating over the condition of the West
Indies following emancipation, continued: "Do I then hate the Negro? No;
except when the soul is killed out of him. I decidedly like poor Quashee;
and find him a pretty kind of man. With a pennyworth of oil, you can
make a handsome glossy thing of Quashee, when the soul is not killed in
him! A swift, supple fellow; a merry-hearted, grinning, dancing, singing,
affectionate kind of creature, with a great deal of melody and amenability
in his composition."[25]

Pets offer amusement by their physical appearance, their endearing
tricks and minor talents. In Europe, young African domestics were cute
playthings for their mistresses, and blacks in general had come to be seen
as entertainers. Let us turn briefly to China, where human pets certainly
existed but they belonged to the same race as their owners. In China, it
would have been most improper for a great lady to have male menials as
pets. No doubt powerful and dissolute women had kept them in their
private chambers, but such behavior received social opprobrium. It was
common, however, for the ladies of the house to treat the numerous
young female servants that swarmed over the estate as pets and playthings.
Maids, girls in their teens and younger, were employed in large numbers
to cater to the comfort and needs of young masters and mistresses. Their

duties were light. Free time was plentiful, and being young and somewhat pampered, they occasionally got themselves into trouble. Punishment could be swift and severe, including whipping. On the other hand, because they were not only servants but also pets they might be let off lightly. "These girls are here for our amusement," explained one lady of the house to another in the great eighteenth-century novel *The Story of the Stone.*

> They are like pets. You can talk to them and play with them if you feel like it, or if you don't, you can simply ignore them. It's the same when they are naughty. Just as, when your puppy-dog bites you or your kitten scratches you, you can either ignore it or have it punished, so with these girls. If they do something to offend you, you can either let it pass, or, if you don't feel able to, you can call in one of the stewardesses and have them punished. There is absolutely no need to go rushing off in person, shouting and hollering at them. It's so undignified.[26]

Pets can be doted on, but also teased and humiliated in all sorts of ways. We will now examine some of these ways as they applied to human slaves and servants. What we shall see are not instances of physical abuse but of disdain—a sadism in which pleasure is procured by diminishing another. Those who indulge in this form of sadism may not recognize the trait in themselves; it can be mild enough to be overlooked, to seem altogether natural and even right. Consider first the question of names. Human dignity requires that a person possess an appropriate name, and that he or she be addressed in a respectful manner. In ancient Rome, a master could call his slave by anything he liked. In the earlier stages of slave-owning, he was accustomed to call his human chattel by his own name, plus the suffix *por* (*puer*—"boy"): for example, Marcipor or Lucipor. Later, practical exigency required that a much wider range of names be used. The label "boy" has always been resented by the adult servitor. "What is more hateful than to be called to a drinking party with 'Boy, boy'—and that by some adolescent who hasn't grown a beard yet" complained a house slave in a Greek drama of the fourth century B.C.[27] The arrogant masters of the world have evidently found this simple verbal device to humiliate the weak a useful one, for it has retained currency through the millennia right to our time.

Giving slaves absurd names was clearly a playful way of showing contempt. In the colonies as well as in the mother country, blacks, dispossessed of power and education, were tacked with such resounding classical names as Pompey (perhaps the most popular of all), Socrates, Cato, and Scipio; or they might be called Starling, Tallow, Little Ephraim, Robin John, and Othello. When a clergyman visited a Mississippi plantation to baptize forty slave children, he could barely keep his countenance as he administered the sacrament to Alexander the Great, General Jackson, Walter Scott, Napoleon, Queen Victoria, Lady Jane Grey, Madame de Staël, among others. It transpired that the names originated in the "merry brain" of the planter's sister. All the white visitors at the ceremony were vastly amused.[28]

Slaves were not alone in being robbed of their individuality and personality in this way. In Victorian England, domestics were often addressed by names that were not their own. The best known of these is probably James, which came to be attached to the first footman. A maidservant who happened to be baptized Julia might be asked to change it into something more appropriate to her station such as Martha. In a large, traditional Chinese household, it was common practice for young servants raised there to be addressed by such fanciful pet names as (for girls) Aroma, Butterfly, Cicada, Emerald, Lotus, Felicity, and Sunset; and (for boys) Happy, Joker, Cheerful, Lively, and Rich.[29] These are words for animals and things and for qualities that are pleasant and desirable but not grand or noble in animals and things. A young mistress could have a real butterfly for a pet; "Butterfly" also happened to be how she called her personal maid. A young master, taught to be a serious scholar, could smile in condescension at his pages named Happy, Cheerful, and Lively.

To tease and humiliate another person, call him Boy or Alexander the Great, that is, either by a diminutive name or by one so grand as to be manifestly absurd given that person's chances in life. Likewise, dress a slave either in tatters or in fine livery. Planters of the Old American South seemed to be of two minds as to how their human chattels were to be clothed. Considerations of economy argued for minimal cover, a step favored moreover by the view that blacks were physical beings, near the state of nature. Field hands wore garments so torn from use that they offered little protection from either inclement weather or appraising eyes. Slaves who worked in the field were known to run and hide their seminudity when they saw visitors coming. House slaves, by comparison, wore decent garments. In a grand country estate or in a townhouse they might even be lavishly attired. On the other hand, in some good homes it was apparently not unusual for slave boys, some of them fully mature physically, to wait upon dinner tables wearing only a shirt not always long enough to conceal their private parts. Visitors observed that both master and mistress appeared to take such seminudity in their midst for granted. Socially, they could pretend to do so, fully accepting the fact that the proper attire of a houseboy was the minimal smock. Subconsciously and perhaps even consciously they must have been aware of their servitor's state of undress; it was, after all, an important part of white people's myth that blacks were heavily sexed.[30]

Slaves were frequently exposed to ridicule. Here are a few illustrations. A field slave could be asked to help out in the big house from time to time. His clumsiness might provide a source of merriment not only to the mistress but also to house menials, far better dressed and far more knowledgeable in the proprieties of civilized life. Some punishments were ingeniously designed to force the victim to feel his own complete helplessness and inferiority. "A Maryland tobacco grower," Kenneth Stampp writes, "forced a hand to eat the worms he failed to pick off the tobacco leaves. A Mississippian gave a runaway a wretched time by requiring him to sit at the table and eat his evening meal with the white family. A Louisiana planter humiliated disobedient male-hands by giving them 'woman's work' such as washing clothes, by dressing them in women's clothing, and by exhibiting them on a scaffold wearing a red flannel cap."[31]

Anyone who claims to be an individual must have some control over his or her space and time; moreover, this control must be recognized as a right by others. The *biological* needs of a pet animal are recognized. A dog, for instance, should be fed at fairly regular intervals and must be allowed space in which to exercise. However, apart from these allowances that derive directly from biological exigency the pet animal has no right to space and time of its own. The slave, whether viewed as a workhorse or as a household convenience or as a pet, is placed in a similar position. He has no space of his own. On a plantation of the Old South, slaves could not close their quarters and their cabins to visitation by their white masters and mistresses. People from the big house enjoyed visiting the quarters. It provided them with the pleasures of slumming. It made them feel superior and even kind. "We went into the Quarters and had lots of fun in Uncle

Bob's cabin.'' So people from the big house might effuse after such an excursion. Some house slaves had no privacy at all. At any time of the day or night, services could be demanded of them. They slept in the same room as their master and mistress, normally on the floor like a guard dog, sometimes on a bed of their own, and sometimes in the same bed as the master or the mistress when the couple occupied separate rooms. These personal attendants were usually youngsters, but they could be sexually mature teenagers and older.[32]

Slaves had no control over time. For field slaves the working hours might be no longer than those of their overseers or of small white farmers, but slaves had no say in the pace and schedule of work. A good master gave his hands breaks to rest or go swimming, but he could not give them the sense of controlling their own time and labor. House slaves were even worse off. Field-workers could at least return to their cabins after sunset and play with their children or putter about in their small vegetable patch, but house menials had no recognized "after hours." Slaves in the house had better access to better food but there was no set time when they could eat undisturbed. They had to snatch at food at those times when they were free to do so. They were made to feel that they were always at the disposal of others. A small but constant source of humiliation for house slaves was that they always had to stand—to assume that posture of disposability— in the presence of whites.[33]

Where one person has great power over another its exercise tends to be capricious, harsh on many occasions, indulgent on a few, and sometimes teasing. Treatment of slave children is a case in point. On a Maryland farm where Frederick Douglass was a child, at mealtime, the "corn-meal mush was placed in a large wooden tray and set down, either on the floor of the kitchen, or out of doors on the ground; and the children were called . . . and like so many pigs would come, and literally devour the mush—some with oyster shells, some with pieces of shingles, and none with spoons."[34] In vivid contrast, at a North Carolina plantation, it was the rule that every Sunday morning all the children were to be bathed, dressed, and their hair combed, and taken to the big house for breakfast, where they were doted upon by master and mistress. In general, slave-owners treated the children with indulgence as though they were cute animals. Even masters with a reputation for severity seemed to take delight in their "pickaninnies" and "little niggers," liked to spoil them with little gifts, and permitted them liberties of speech and action denied to their own children.[35] An adult slave might also acquire the ambiguous status of a pet and be allowed to behave in an outrageous manner. For example, "in Charleston a visitor went for a drive with a mistress who asked her coachman to take them down a certain street. But the coachman ignored all her pleas and took them a different way. The guest of a Georgia planter told of another coachman who suddenly stopped the carriage and reported that he had lost one of his white gloves and must go back to find it. 'As time pressed, the master in despair took off his own gloves and gave them to him. When our charioteer had deliberately put them on, we started again.'"[36]

One type of evidence frequently cited to show how a planter in the antebellum South was capable of genuine kindness toward his slaves was the enormous care he and his wife might bestow on their social events, such as weddings and balls. There could have been genuine consideration, a sincere desire on the part of master and mistress to give pleasure. On the other hand, they themselves derived pleasure, and according to Kenneth Stampp, not all that pleasure was of a wholly innocent kind. "The white family," writes Stampp, "found it a pure delight to watch a bride and groom move awkwardly through the wedding ceremony, to hear a solemn preacher mispronounce and misuse polysyllabic words, or to witness the incredible maneuvers and gyrations of a 'shakedown." [37] A planter might give his slaves a holiday for no other reason than that they should dance and have a barbecue, and thus provide a spectacle for a group of visiting white children. Slave performances were never considered high art, or even art, but amusements such as those that could be seen done by acrobats and performing animals in carnivals and circuses.

The rulers of this world have exploited their human subjects in all manner of ways, but, in contrast to the treatment imposed on pet plants and animals, they have on the whole refrained from the enormity of trying to breed humans systematically for specialized purposes. It is true that some potentates or their minions have tried to emasculate helpless people so as to make them suitable for the performance of certain services, including that of entertainment, but, fortunately, such practices have been rare. An important exception is the castration of the human male, a custom known in widely different parts of the world.

Cutting off the testicles of large and powerful animals has been a technique of domestication since protohistoric times. Castration of humans was a form of punishment known since antiquity, along with other forms of dismemberment, such as the cutting off of hands and feet and, ultimately, decapitation. Was dismemberment considered primarily a retribution or was it also a method of controlling unruly persons? It served both purposes. In the New World, slaves who ran away or otherwise showed signs of excessive spirit might be castrated. Planters who ordered this punishment and who were in the habit of regarding their slaves as livestock no doubt compared it to the step they naturally took to tame their bulls and stallions. Until well into the eighteenth century, castration persisted as a way of punishing and subduing refractory slaves, although by then it tended to be confined to punishment for one crime— that of raping white women. And here we are reminded again of the centuries-old white man's fear and envy of black man's potency. This potency, which white mythology took to be a special attribute of the black race, was to be curbed unless, of course, it served white man's purpose by producing more slaves.[38]

Punishment and control were not the only reasons for castration. Another was religion. A boy or man might submit to the knife in order to qualify for service to a Mother Goddess or God. The basic idea seemed to be this. An individual, by depriving himself of potency, could devote his whole being to the source of all potency. In the secular sphere, this source was the despot. Where despotism was combined with polygamy, eunuchs emerged as a necessary mechanism of the social structure. Deprived of their manhood, eunuchs could enter the intimate household of the despot and become the guardians of his women. Eunuchs lacked not only sexual potency but also political power—other than that which flowed directly from the despot. But because eunuchs enjoyed this direct access to the source of all power, some of them were able to acquire great power and wealth for themselves. From the despot's viewpoint, the chief appeal of the eunuchs lay in their loyalty and their usefulness. Loyalty was absolute because the welfare of these "de-natured" men depended absolutely on the favor of their master and because eunuchs, their power and wealth notwithstanding, tended to be despised by normal men and women. Usefulness was enhanced, not diminished, by castration, not only for the special purpose of guarding the harem but also for affairs of state because of the single-mindedness with which eunuchs could do their master's bidding.

The Persians provided us with the earliest historical record of castration: it was done on prisoners for the purpose of employing them to guard the harem. Other uses were also recognized. Cyrus the Great, according to Xenophon, appreciated eunuchs for their fidelity and for the skills they could dedicatedly acquire. Unlike many men, Cyrus did not see eunuchs as weaklings.

> He drew this conclusion from the case of other animals: for instance, vicious horses, when gelded, stop prancing about, but are none the less fit for service in war; and bulls, when castrated, lose somewhat of their high spirit and unruliness but are not deprived of their strength or capacity for work. . . . Similarly, men become gentler when deprived of this desire, but not less careful of that which is entrusted to them; they are not made any less efficient horsemen, or any less skilful lancers, or less ambitious men. On the contrary, they showed both in times of war and in hunting that they still preserved in their souls a spirit of rivalry; and of their fidelity they gave the best proof upon the fall of their masters, for no one ever performed acts of greater fidelity in his master's misfortunes than eunuchs do. . . . Recognizing these facts, he selected eunuchs for every post of personal service to him, from the door-keepers up.[39]

Eunuchs flourished in the Ottoman and Chinese empires. Biologically impotent, some of them were able to compensate by acquiring wealth and political influence. In the Ottoman Empire, during the sixteenth and seventeenth centuries, the number of black eunuchs employed to guard the harem of the Grand Seraglio rose to eight hundred. A service of this size had to be organized into a bureaucracy. As is characteristic of bureaucracies, most of the jobs there were humble and routine such as that of guarding the gates. However, when young, all the neutered males enjoyed a period of favored treatment. They were given a handsome allowance and robes of the finest silk. As adults, they lived in the knowledge that some, at least, could catch the eye of the sultan and rise to the top of the harem hierarchy. One of them would eventually attain the rank of the *kislar agha*, a position of enormous power. Intelligence and knowledge were qualifications for the post, and yet the black eunuch occupying it might be an ignorant and crude fellow with no skills other than those of intrigue and ingratiation.[40]

In China, eunuchs probably served in feudal courts as early as the late Chou period (ca. 500–300 B.C.). Throughout Chinese imperial history, they played an important role in the manipulation of power around the throne. This role was more prominent in some periods than in others but at no time more notable and pervasive than during the later part of the Ming dynasty. In the 1580s, for instance, close to 20,000 of them were employed, in ranks varying from that on a par with top bureaucrats down to messengers and household attendants. Castrated boys, presented to the emperor by their ambitious parents, attended the Inner Palace School at an age of no older than ten and were taught there by the best scholars of the Han-lin Academy. The exalted positions that some of them would eventually occupy were thus earned, although "it was not impossible for an illiterate eunuch who had won the emperor's favor to break into this inner circle by becoming the Director of Ceremonies." The most senior and talented of the eunuchs were given special privileges and marks of esteem. Some of them, for example, enjoyed the right to wear jackets with designs authorized by the emperor himself and could even be carried about in a sedan chair, which was the pinnacle of honor when it occurred within the palace. Nevertheless, eunuchs, in distinction to their co-workers the scholar-officials, were creatures of the emperor and had no independent base of power and virtue in the idealized Confucian view of the world. The few who managed to achieve wealth and power were thus obliged to confine their ostentation to the palace. "Their work remained anonymous; they would forever be unsung heroes within the governmental structure."[41]

One more reason for castrating the human male remains to be noted, and that is to produce singers. As water was made to jump, as plants were twisted and dogs bred and clipped for aesthetic ends, so where boys castrated. One of the more grotesque ironies of history was the role of the Church in the emasculation of children. Church choirs called for singers with high voices. Boys supplied the demand, but inadequately: just when they had learned their art their voices were starting to break. Falsettists might be used as a substitute, but their voices had an unpleasant quality and could not, in any case, reach the high soprano range. Women, endowed by nature to fulfill the role, were nonetheless forbidden to sing in church on no less an authority than Saint Paul.

Supplying good voices became a more urgent problem from the middle of the fifteenth century onward. The increasing popularity of the *cappella* style, elaborate and calling for a higher degree of virtuosity than anything that had gone before, made the efforts of the choirboys and falsettists manifestly inadequate. The services of the castrati were in rising demand.

Ambitious but poor parents, with boys who showed even the least musical talent, sought to meet it. During the peak period of the castrato's art, in the seventeenth and eighteenth centuries, castrated boys went to colleges of music for long years of training alongside their unoperated peers. The young castrati were considered delicate and were given better food and warmer rooms than the others. They were also dressed in distinctive costumes. Nevertheless, their life in the college must have been exceptionally difficult. No doubt they were teased mercilessly by fellow students. Some ran away, a step that the other students apparently never took. In the adult world, the successful castrati received wealth and adulation, but an underlying contempt for their kind was indicated by the Church's rule prohibiting them to marry, even when they ardently desired it.

The secular opera attained immense popularity in eighteenth-century Italy; likewise the castrati who had exceptional talent, especially if vocal virtuosity was combined with youth and good looks. Such a person was Farinelli (1705–82). His career was a triumph from beginning to end. He sang in the major cities of Italy, in Vienna and London, and everywhere he was showered by acclaim and handsome fees. He died in old age, with honor and dignity. There was, however, a famous episode in his life that illustrates the ambivalent status of a castrato, no matter how favored. This was when he gave up acclaim in the opera houses to enter the private service of Philip V of Spain. The king at that time suffered from profound and incurable melancholia. It transpired that one of the few things in this world that could provide him with a measure of relief was the miraculous voice of Farinelli. And so, over a number of years, Farinelli was paid a royal sum for one duty, namely, to sing four songs every night before the king. He was the royal songbird, a personal entertainer to one mortal, a humbling position for any human person to occupy. On the other hand, Farinelli's talent was real and commanded ungrudging admiration. Moreover, he possessed a generous character which enabled him to rise above the sordid jealousies that afflicted his profession. Finally, Farinelli was exceptional among the castrati in being nobly born, a fact which no doubt helped to shield him against the taunting of his colleagues, especially in the early training periods of his career.[42]

Human pets are people whom their self-designated superiors regard as powerless, not fully human, and in some ways entertainingly peculiar. We have seen that children, women, certain household slaves and servants, and castrated males qualified for this status. We now turn to another class of human pets—dwarfs and fools. Concerning dwarfs, the first question we might raise is a horrifying one, namely, were they deliberately created? Throughout history, humans have tried to control nature by reducing its scale. Wilderness miniaturized becomes bonsai. Large animals have been made smaller in the initial processes of domestication; largish canines have been turned into lapdogs. Were there attempts to stunt human growth or breed small people for their aesthetic and entertainment value? The answer would seem to be yes. For example, in the Greek language there is the word *gloottokoma*, which refers to the chests used to lock up little children with the aim of opening up for them a lucrative career as dwarfs. In his essay *On the Sublime*, Longinus (ca. first century A.D.) mentions the practice of keeping people in cages so as to impede their growth. Romans who sank to the depth of disfiguring children to make them into more pathetic and effective beggars would not have abjured techniques of stunting them so that as dwarfs they could seek careers in entertainment. One technique the Romans used was dietary deprivation. Depriving children of "lime-salts" would cause rickets, the Romans thought.[43] Did the ancients try to breed dwarfs? Probably. We do know that the princes of the Italian Renaissance made such attempts, but the results often failed to conform to their wishes: the offspring of dwarfs need not be dwarfs at all.

The earliest record of a person of subnormal stature employed because he could "divert the court and rejoice the heart of the King" dates back to Fifth Dynasty Egypt (ca. 2500 B.C.). A pygmy in the service of Pharaoh Dadkeri-Assi had been purchased in Puanit, a country to the south of Egypt described by Egyptians as "ten leagues beyond man's life" and inhabited by ghosts and talking serpents. No doubt a part of the pygmy's value to the pharaoh and his court lay in the aura of mystery associated with his land of origin. To judge by the evidence of the tombstones, pharaohs other than Assi also loved to surround themselves with dwarfs who, acting the buffoon, provided entertainment, although a few of them might have been given responsible office such as superintendent of the royal linen.[44]

The custom of keeping dwarfs and fools as entertainers and pets is ancient and recurrent. It appears in some civilizations but not in others, in some periods of history but not in others. Dwarfs and fools abounded in the court of the Ptolemies but played little role in the life of the Greeks. In the Roman Empire, jaded men of wealth kept half-wits and deformed slaves in their houses, not so much out of compassion as for the distraction and amusement they could provide. To give pleasure to aristocratic Roman ladies, dwarfs ran about naked or were decked in jewels. Clement of Alexandria reports that delicately reared young ladies liked to play with deformed jesters at their table. Martial paints an even more bizarre picture of the uses to which they could be put. "Labulla has discovered how to kiss her lover in the presence of her husband. She gives repeated kisses to her dwarf-fool (*Morio*); this creature slobbered with many kisses, the lover at once pounces upon, fills him up with his own kisses, and hands him back to the smiling lady."[45]

Dwarfs figured prominently in the consciousness of princely and aristocratic Europe for some two hundred years, roughly from 1500 to 1700 (fig. 21). The flippant manner with which they could be treated is indicated by the following incidents, which all suggest that somehow stunted people were delicious and amusing—part of the fare that might be offered at a feast. In 1580, Lucrezia Borgia gave a banquet at which two dwarfs, Ledardino and Francatripp, were served up with the fruit to amuse the ladies. Jeffery Hudson, a handsome midget and a favorite of Charles I and his queen, Henrietta Maria, was once sent to the queen hidden in the crust of a huge pie. Packing people into pies was still deemed clever entertainment in the backward courts of eighteenth-century Russia: on one occasion two such pies were delivered to a banquet table, and out of them emerged a male and a female dwarf, who then danced a minuet.[46]

Slave pets, we have seen, were sometimes given absurdly inappropriate names; likewise dwarf-fools. Those at Renaissance courts were often addressed as King. Queen Elizabeth had an Italian jester whom she called Monarch, explaining in a teasing manner that he was such a great lord that he had no need of land. Philip IV named Christobal da Pernia "Barbarossa," after the pirate king. In Mantua, a dwarf was called "the first born" (primogenitus), and he presumed the right to address Federigo Gonzaga, heir to the throne, as his younger brother. At the Milanese court, the quarters for dwarfs and jesters were known as the "Giants' House." Lodovico il Moro called one dwarf "il Signore"—*il signore* being Sultan Mohamet II, a fact known to everyone.

During the seventeenth century, a remarkable number of distinguished

Finito sacro officio. Dux D. Cosmus Medices Magni Ducis corona insignitus magna pompa ad pallatium reducitur clangentibus varijs musices artis instrumentis nec non tympanis et tubarum clangoribus.

Fig. 21. Dwarfs in the court of Cosimo Medici; engraved by Jan van Straet, after 1575.

artists—including Rubens, Velásquez, and Van Dyck—painted dwarfs alongside either a dog or a monkey (fig. 22). Dwarfs, dogs, and monkeys were all a part of the menagerie of a noble lord or lady. Dogs were valued pets at this time, as we have seen, but not quite in the sentimental manner of the Victorian period. As for monkeys, their fascination lay in their position just below that of humanity in the great chain of being. The literature of the period took rather for granted that the blacks of West Africa and the monkeys of the same region were closely related species and capable of interbreeding. Now, when an artist painted a dwarf next to a monkey, the message was conveyed that they too somehow belonged together, that although both bore a striking resemblance to normal people they were nevertheless subhuman. Officially, however, dwarfs were counted as fully human, dressed—sometimes resplendently—as people, baptized as Christians, and usually treated rather well. In pictures where a dwarf appears with a dog or a monkey, the patronizing hand of a master or mistress is always placed on the head of the animal and not on that of the dwarf. Was this a contradiction? Yes, perhaps, but humans have rarely been consistent.[47]

The ambiguous status of the dwarf is illustrated by the attitudes and actions of the Gonzaga household at Mantua in the sixteenth century. The Gonzagas had introduced dwarfs into their court and had ordered built, in their own residence, a suite of miniature rooms that had become famous. Like their masters, the short people were dressed in lush cloth of silver and gold. They were the privileged servitors of a household and yet also, in subtle ways, counted among the nonhuman members of a menagerie. Something of this ambivalence is suggested in the following passage from historian Lauro Martines's account of Renaissance life. "When in November 1515 the Venetian ambassadors to Milan passed through Mantua, they found the Marquis Francesco, disabled by syphilis, lying on a couch in a richly adorned room. His favorite dwarf, attired in gold brocade, attended him. Three pages stood nearby, as well as three of his pet greyhounds. Some of his falcons, reined by leashes, were also in the room; and the walls were hung with pictures of his favorite dogs and horses."[48]

Dwarfs often acted the fool so as to entertain their owners. They went by the label of dwarf-fools. However, not all fools were dwarfs. Indeed fools or buffoons could be perfectly normal people pretending to be half-wits in order to earn a livelihood. In ancient Greece and Rome, such

Fig. 22. *Queen Henrietta Maria with Her Dwarf* (Jeffery Hudson) by Sir Anthony Van Dyck. Note the position of the queen's hand over the monkey rather than over Hudson. (National Gallery of Art, Washington; Samuel H. Kress Collection)

people were known as "parasites," or laughter-makers; they peddled a skill and traveled from place to place rather than settling down with one master. A similar profession existed in late medieval and Renaissance times. The buffoons plied their trade aggressively in market squares and in the halls of residences. While most of their jokes and tricks pleased, despite their impudence, some were so deeply offensive that, as punishment, the fake fools were made to *be* fools.

As early as the twelfth century, the distinction between artificial and natural fools was clearly recognized. Natural fools were either born with some mental defect or had become that way for causes beyond their control. These persons could find shelter and employment in the households of the powerful and wealthy, where they were given over to the care of keepers who probably had the additional job of training their charges, enabling them to say and do things that evinced a witless wisdom. Natural fools, like dwarfs, seem to have been treated well. Some of them indeed became great pets, their value so recognized that they were sent from one potentate to another on loan or as outright gifts. Enid Welsford writes:

> In 1498 Alfonso d'Este fell seriously ill, and Isabella sent her favourite fool to cheer him. His success was amazing. Alfonso writes of Matello in most enthusiastic terms, saying that he made him forget the severity of his illness. His appreciation indeed took an inconvenient form, for he was so unwilling to return him, that a courtier had to be sent to fetch him away. Later on, when Alfonso once more fell ill, his sister sent to him Matello and another buffoon, a gift which her brother declared was more welcome to him than the gift of a beautiful castle would have been.[49]

The fact that fools could be sent away on loan or as a gift and that this was indeed a common practice among Italian and German princes demonstrates that fools, however highly valued, were a personal property and disposable as other possessions—precious goods and animals—were disposable. Moreover, some masters were cruel and perverse and abused their fools by encouraging them to engage in acts of obscenity of which they in their befogged minds were not fully aware.

Why did the potentates find deformity and dementia amusing rather than sad, reassuring rather than threatening? Although potentate and dwarf-fool lived in close physical proximity, there did exist the buffer of social distance which was just sufficient, it would appear, to provide the potentate with pleasing charitable feelings tinged by amusement: a little closer and the potentate would have found the deformity painful, a little farther apart and the potentate might lose that measure of sympathy which made both the charitable impulse and amusement possible. Having a half-wit or two, a dwarf or two, in court as objects of compassion, as charms and playthings, though a bit bizarre by the blander standards of modern taste, is still understandable. What strains our comprehension is the large number of such retainers in a few great households. Thus in 1566, Cardinal Vitelli gave a banquet in Rome at which no fewer than thirty-four dwarfs served. In seventeenth-century Paris, Monsieur and Madame Rambouillet were well known for the large number of fools they kept in their household. It was suggested that they chose their servants not for efficiency but for that tincture of absurd in their constitution. The aristocracy of that period, for all their ability to enjoy the subtleties of a Racine or a Fénelon, also appreciated crude humor and brutal practical jokes. In eighteenth-century Russia, Peter the Great kept many fools: no fewer than one hundred might assemble in the hall for feeding. Dwarfs, equally numerous, were married to one another to keep up the supply. One such wedding was attended by the czar himself and culminated in a ball, at which the members of court sat along the edges of the room so that they could enjoy an unimpeded view of the feasting and comical capers of the dwarfs. At the end of the ceremony and diversions, the newly married couple were carried to the czar's palace and bedded in his own bedchamber.

Many of the fools in the court of Peter the Great were not, however, half-witted at all. They were normal people made to act the fool as a peculiarly humiliating form of punishment. The czar's plan was to send young men abroad for their education, but should they fail to benefit from the experience in ways the czar considered appropriate, they would be transformed into court fools upon their return. Anna, the czarina of Russia (1730–40), displayed a similar taste. She had the power to exercise it on whomever she pleased; not even noblemen were safe. In 1739, she celebrated a great feast on the occasion of the marriage of her court fool to a disreputable woman. She emphasized the absurdity of the affair by collecting guests from all the races of the Russian Empire, placing them in sledges drawn by every kind of animal, and making them dance their various national dances. The whole point of the affair centered on the fact that the court fool was perfectly sound of mind. He was a middle-aged nobleman forced into the humiliating role for crossing the empress on points of religion.[50]

"So-and-so is a fool!" We have all pronounced such judgments in moments of anger, knowing full well that their sole effect is to make us feel better. Despots of the past, however, had the power of forcing their victim to conform to the label. Whatever they declared became, to all outward appearances, true.

9 DOMINANCE AND AFFECTION: CONCLUSIONS

 Pets are visible and precious. By contrast, "hands" or manpower and resources (so long as these are abundant) are invisible and have little value. Thus, while entire forests are cleared without a thought, a few treasured twigs may be saved, put in a basin to simulate a forest, and be much admired. Animals are slaughtered for food and clothing without a twinge of conscience. A few specimens and species, however, catch the fancy of people in a playful mood and are made into pampered pets or fervently supported causes. Humans are grossly exploited as hands and chattels with barely a thought. Some, however, are adopted as pets and given capricious attention.

Attention is highly selective and bestows value. What prompts one to attend? The act may be prompted by lust, as in the case of the planter for his comely slave. It may be the result of an aesthetic taste joined to the prestige of having such taste: for instance, the gardener's pleasure in his bonsai, the dog owner's pleasure in his pure breed, and the eighteenth-century European lady's pleasure in her Chinese domestic. And the attention may be the result of genuine affection, which is the flow of warmth and protective love from the strong to the weak, from the superior to the inferior: thus parents love their young children, the mistress grows fond of her personal maid, a man becomes attached to his dog, and the proud mind patronizes the body.

Pets are a part of one's personal entourage. They are physically and emotionally close to their owner. They can be taken for granted and yet are never out of their owner's mind for long. Relationship to pets is intimate. What does intimacy imply? Gestures of physical intimacy may express equality and brotherhood: picture two friends with their arms around each other's shoulder. On the other hand, more often and (I believe) more deeply, they presuppose inequality: picture a mother hugging her child, a horsewoman patting the flank of her steed, or think of such historical bonds as that between a knight and his squire, a man and his valet. Intimacy has declined in modern times. A modern woman can still be intimate with her dog, allowing it to sleep at the foot of her bed, but she no longer has a maid to patronize, and even if she has, the maid can hardly share her bed, as was done in Europe even in the eighteenth century. A modern man may claim intimacy with nature—with wilderness itself. But this sense of ease in wilderness is possible only because wild animals and forests are no longer threatening. Wilderness, although not yet a pet to the degree that the garden and certainly the miniature garden is a pet, nonetheless is widely perceived by modern society to be a fragile existence that needs its care and protection.

Equality presupposes a certain distance—the distance of respect as between two sovereign individuals. Friends can rarely be intimate with each other in ways that husband and wife can, not only because most societies maintain a state of inequality between man and woman but also because the married couple, by living together, encounter many occasions in which one member needs and receives the care of the other (as in sickness), thus introducing temporary bonds of inequality that nurture affection. Modern democratic society decries inequality between adults. Patronage and dependency draw such disapproval that even sickness may be felt as troubling because it puts one person under the authority of another. Familiarity, which is possible only when respect is curtailed, breeds affection—and, as the saying goes, contempt. That blend of affection and condescension (if not also a hint of contempt) is a characteristic attitude toward the pet. Modern society, by frowning upon permanent states of dependency, has weakened the ties of affection but it has simultaneously undercut opportunities for the development of sadomasochistic bondage between the powerful and the powerless.

In intimate and unequal relationships, how is affection to be distinguished from teasing playfulness, patronage from condescension, or cruelty from love? The word *play* provides a key to these questions. Play is the quintessential activity of children. Through play children learn to master a world. In a world of play, fantasy easily becomes reality. A child gains confidence and a sense of power as he manipulates the things around him. Sticks and stones, toy soldiers and teddy bears, kittens and pups are all his subjects, pliant to his imagination and obedient to his command. When a doll or a pup turns recalcitrant, it can be punished. This power to dominate another—including the power to inflict pain and humiliation on another—is vaguely pleasurable. And yet there is also deep attachment. A child is attached to his toys as extensions of himself. They are his possessions; their worth reflects his worth; praise for them is praise for him. Of course, genuine affection also exists. In the unequal relationship with toys and small animals, the child can develop feelings of protectiveness and nurture—feelings that interpenetrate with his awareness of superiority and power.

In the adult's world, play often has to yield to necessity. There is still time for play, but under restrained circumstances and with a sort of lid placed on the élan of imagination. In the world of primitive hunters and gatherers, mothers play with young children, and children, like the young everywhere, play with whatever is at hand, including small animals. Adults too may adopt animals and treat them as playthings. One example. Certain aboriginal tribes in Australia have domesticated the dog for a number of reasons, the practical among them, but they also keep other animals simply as pets. Wallabies, opossums, bandicoots, rats, even frogs and young birds are tied up in the camp to provide periodic amusement for their captors. The animals are fed and cared for in a capricious manner, and most of them soon die.[1] In the egalitarian society of simple hunters and gatherers, human adults can treat animals as pets; they cannot, however, treat one another as pets. A teasing bond may exist, and such teasing implies a need to dominate—to convert another person into a clumsy object of fun. But the teaser is teased back as in a game between equals, and no permanent order of superiority and inferiority is established.[2]

Rituals and ceremonies, often incorporating song and dance, are an important part of many primitive societies, both agricultural and nonagricultural. These activities are not, however, play. They may have moments of fun and even of farce, but their fundamental purpose is the serious business of maintaining their world by ensuring the adequacy and timeliness of rain and harvest. In a ritual, participants feel that they are operating under rules and constraints not of their own making. What they do is necessary and not an uninhibited assertion of power and will. Rituals and ceremonials attained peaks of splendor in premodern high cultures. They were needed because even in high cultures food supply was uncertain, and the course of nature on which livelihood depended must be assured by ritualistic as well as material and technological means. However, high cultures have normally been able to support an elite, members of which enjoy a surplus of resources and of power that they can use freely in play. In other words, the elite are in the position of children whose fantasies and whims are catered to by the wealth and power at their command.

At the top of the elite is the monarch, who would like to rule a kingdom that responds to his wish and will in every way. Ideally the kingdom runs with the ease and majesty of the cosmos: all things in it move around the throne, under the guiding hands of the ruler, as heavenly bodies move around the polestar or the sun. In reality, not even the most powerful monarch could create in his own realm an order of plenitude and of obedience that approximated his dreams. What he could aspire to was to construct dreamworlds on a much smaller scale. Call these dreamworlds works of art or playgrounds. Whatever we choose to call them now, they satisfied the longings of the potentate for the tangible as well as psychological assurance of luxury, for power and the deference it could command, and for the pleasure—sexually tinted—of being able to play freely (that is, more or less irresponsibly) with the comely creatures of the earth.

What, in actuality, were these playgrounds? Palaces represented one type. An Oriental despot, unable to transform a whole realm to his taste, could at least build a palace to his liking and fill it with things that responded to his needs and whims; and all that he could see was ruled directly by him with the help of eunuchs who were his creatures. Another type of playground was the theater. As Stephen Orgel has shown, the Royal Spectacle was a substitute for the perfect realm that potentates in Renaissance Europe could not command. Only in the extravagant masques and plays could the potentates make themselves believe that their power was absolute and that they lived at the center of a well-ordered universe in which all people and nature itself deferred to their wish.[3] But, perhaps the most universal of these playgrounds was the garden. Some of these gardens, we have noted, were built on the most lavish scale and packed with things for the delectation of their owners who, in the garden, could believe themselves divine.

Take another look at the garden built in A.D. 607 for the Sui emperor. How was it furnished? Besides artifical mountains and lakes, which an army of laborers had constructed, the emperor had packed his garden with every variety of plant, including not only flowers and herbs but full-grown forest trees, every kind of animal, including not only fishes and frogs but also "golden gibbons and green deer," and, in addition, palaces and concubines. Of the concubines, history records that "all were beautiful, respectful, virtuous and lovely of face. Each group was chosen in turn by the emperor as the recipient of his imperial favors."[4] Of course, great gardens in other cultures and times differed—perhaps in every detail—from that created for the Sui emperor. Nevertheless, all of them, European as well as Oriental, signified some proud man's yearning for a tangible world that matched his imagination, a world in which everything—rock, water, plant, manservant, or maid—deferred to his will and truckled to his pleasure. Within the confines of a garden, the constraints of nature and society are largely removed: a man there is sovereign among subjects, a child among toys.

Palaces, theaters, and gardens are the playgrounds of the powerful and the rich. Note that they often interpenetrate, being parts of one idealized, semi-illusory world. Thus, palaces contain gardens and may themselves be located in large parks; both the palace and the garden, in China as well as in Renaissance and baroque Europe, are known to provide spaces for dramatic and musical performances. Note, moreover, that a palace is not just a playground. People live in it and servants work in it as well. Conversely, every large house that belongs to a person of power and wealth is not merely a place to live in, but also an idealized world and a sort of playground for the owner and his family. What are the evidences of power and play? What natural objects have been transformed, domesticated, and often reduced in size so as to become suitable decorations, toys, and pets in a great house? The answer would differ, of course, depending on time and place. In Europe, before 1700, the halls of a great house tended to be rather empty, with but few pieces of furniture, few decorations and knick-knacks. Perhaps the most prominent playthings in such a house were all animate—the large number of servants and hangers-on, possibly a dwarf or a fool, dogs of all sizes and breeds, monkeys, and exotic birds. After 1700, rooms tended to be increasingly cluttered with inanimate possessions, not only furniture but also bibelots and wall decorations. Nature was permitted to enter the house as landscape paintings and county maps, and, during the nineteenth century, as an exuberance of potted plants. The number and variety of animal pets declined. A few well-trained hounds, a toy dog or two for the mistress were favored. The domestic staff might still be large, but many servants became merely a part of the machinery of the house and were, in no sense of the word, pets. In addition to the "invisible" staff, a household also maintained liveried footmen. Conspicuous in attire and in such ceremonial acts as the announcement of dinner, footmen were in other situations trained to stand in the background and anticipate their employer's every wish with quiet, machinelike precision.[5]

The psychology of dominance and affection has its ambivalences and paradoxes. These have already been noted in earlier chapters, but we are now in a position to assemble them and offer some general conclusions. People who exploit nature for pleasure and for aesthetic and symbolic reasons seldom realize that they are doing harm to the plants and animals, distorting them into shapes they are not meant to have and, in the case of animals, forcing them into behavior that is not natural to them. People who exploit other humans for profit or pleasure have, by contrast, an uneasy conscience. The masters do not feel entirely comfortable in their positions of superiority and power. They need some kind of justification. One kind is the distinction between culture and nature, or between mind and body. Culture and mind have the right to dominate nature and body. In the second category are included not only plants and animals but children, women, slaves, and members of the lower class, especially if they are distinguishable from the masters by skin color or some other physical trait. Dominance normally takes the form of straight exploitation. When it takes the form of condescending playfulness, it expresses the belief that women and slaves, fools and blacks are immature and naive, animal-like, and sexual. Men of power, arrogating to themselves the attributes of mind and culture, find it pleasing to have around them humans of a lesser breed—closer to nature—on whose head they may lay an indulgent hand.

And yet the relationship of culture to superiority and of nature to inferiority is neither clear nor firm. Culture, for instance, may be identified with effeminacy, frivolity, or decadence; nature with male power that is as often destructive as constructive. Culture can be the label of inconsequential activities—acts of refinement that are little more than bodily maintenance and acts of creativity that are little more than childlike games. Nature, by contrast, is an irresistible force capable of destroying or creating a world. The masters, then, assume the role of nature and patronize culture from a lordly distance, making an occasional appearance at the church bazaar or ballet. They see themselves as the true creators, the others—women mostly, and men engaged in occupations closely linked to women's world—as refiners and decorators. From the viewpoint of the masters, culture (thus perceived) is a glittering plaything that they can pick up and amuse themselves with as they wish.

Note how women can also arrogate to themselves the superior role of nature and assign the inferior role of culture to men. Women, in this model, are a natural force, sometimes destructive, more often creative. They are the ones who create and sustain life and world at the fundamental level, while the children play with toys or conduct little agonistic games at their feet; and in this the women's view, men remain boys all their lives—they never quite outgrow their childish pride in their manufactures and games. Men who constantly need to show off what they can do and what they can make are boastful but endearing pets who, however, need to be put firmly in their place with a cutting retort or with a raised eyebrow from time to time.

Power is the ability to overcome resistance. While there is pleasure in having resistances that can then be overcome, resistances that must be overcome repeatedly detract from the dignity of power. This is a probable reason for the deep ambivalence of potentates toward animate nature. Plants, animals, and human subjects all seem to have wills of their own. The delight of power is to make these wills submit to one's own will. Plants cannot be allowed to grow as their natures dictate. In a garden they are clipped and trimmed to conform to human aesthetic ideals. Moreover, as we have seen in chapters 3 and 4, minor alterations have not always proven sufficiently satisfying. Historically, in Europe as well as in the Orient, plants have been not only trimmed but grotesquely twisted and stunted, as though the garden-designers, drunk with power, want to know how far they can proceed in converting living things into artifacts. Twisted and stunted, plants still grow. Their submission is not complete until they have become inorganic. This curious desire for the inorganic is manifest in such ways as forcing plants to look like brick walls and stone pillars, substituting colored pebbles and paint for shrubs and flowers in parterres, and making mineral trees and fruits.

Plants are at least rooted in place. Animals move and are far more difficult to control. They can be put into pits and cages but these purely physical devices are admissions of failure. In medieval and Renaissance images of the garden, animals other than birds are rarely shown. Chinese gardens boast birds and fishes, but rarely large mammals except in imperial parks. To foster an illusion of animal life, gardeners have cut hedges into the shapes of animals, sculpted menageries of stone or wooden beasts, and (in China) set up deeply corroded rocks that bear a resemblance to wild fauna and monsters. Certain European gardens contain ingenious mechanical animals, such as the singing birds and owl at the Villa d'Este and the domestic animals of the highly contrived picturesque garden (*Le Rocher*) at Lunéville. These toys may break down, but otherwise they do not thwart the human will. Power over animals can be satisfyingly exerted in other ways. After all, with skill and application animals can be thoroughly tamed. Even a lion can be turned into a deferential pet and made to "kneel" upon command. Moreover, people are able to breed animals into the shapes and characteristics they desire. Success in these endeavors gives people a godlike sense of power over life. This power they have used and abused. Breeders have created, we have seen, goldfish with bulging eyes and dogs that are genetically defective, and dogs of exceptional ugliness such as the *shar-pei*, which has corrugated skins that fold over like an unmade bed (fig. 23).

Finally, there are the human pets, most difficult of all to control and train. Despite marked physical differences in appearance, people are still too much alike for one group to dominate another with ease and a clear conscience. How can the dominated be made to seem more obviously inferior so as to justify perpetual patronage? Nature itself has obliged by producing misshapen specimens and half-wits. Roman potentates and European princes of the Renaissance period found a ready source of amusement in them; and, indeed, to judge by the popularity of freak shows past and present, dwarfs and fools have a widespread appeal that transcends the perverted taste of a particular class.

One reason why freaks enjoyed the patronage of the powerful is that they seemed fascinatingly *un*natural, not only in the sense of departing strikingly from the norms of nature but also because they seemed, like extravagant artifacts, the products of an unbridled and cruel imagination. Potentates who saw themselves as free and whole persons saw their fools and dwarfs as partial and specialized beings, like animals and artifacts that could not be other than what they were. All human pets shared this limitation. Eunuchs and castrati, for example, were artifacts to the extent that they were made that way by surgery for narrow ends. And we have

Fig. 23. Fawn II, a one-year-old Chinese *shar-pei*, took top prize at the Ugly Dog Contest (August 1981) in Petaluma, California. The judges voted Fawn, who looked not unlike an unmade bed, the "ugliest by any standard." (Drawing by Wayne Howell)

noted how in large aristocratic and upper-class households, the human potential of domestics could be narrowed down to one or two lines of specialized work—that, for instance, of a cupbearer, a reciter of poems at the dinner table, a decorative and decorous footman, and (in medieval China) a painter of orchids, a zither player, a trainer of insects, an imitator of animal noises, and an amusing poser of riddles.[6] Humans so specialized seemed hardly human, and it was not surprising that potentates periodically failed to see their full humanity and exchanged them as curios and gifts as they did with other valued possessions. Note, furthermore, that the wearing of livery, the expressionless face and stiff posture when standing, and the disciplined, semimilitary, semiballetic steps when marching all served to highlight the artifactitious, puppetlike character of the valued servant.

Plants make easy pets. They are attractive to look at, easy to maintain, and do not rebel except by dying. While making only minimal demands on the owner, they give him a sense of power and of virtue—the power of enabling a thing to grow and the virtue of care. Animals make more difficult pets, although much depends on size and temperament. Goldfish, for example, do not have to be taken for a walk or to the veterinarian. Their world—a bowl—is as narrowly circumscribed as that of a potted plant. Like plants, goldfish can be used almost purely as decoration, placed on a dining table next to a bed of cut flowers. In modern, affluent Western societies, dogs and cats can and do make large demands on their owners, not only in time and money but also in attention and personal care. It has sometimes been said that the owners have become domesticated and enslaved by their pets, so much work do they put in to keep their pets healthy and happy. But these services, commendable as they are as acts of devotion, also have the effect of emphasizing the animal's total dependence. Moreover, a relationship of dominance—of superior to inferior—is not in doubt so long as the owners feel free to bend down to pat their dog or cat on the head or run their hand down its coat. These are gestures of affection. They are bestowed by the superior on the inferior and can never be used between equals.

Humans make intractable pets. Although they can be taught to accept their peculiar status through a combination of indoctrination and the threat of physical force, from the viewpoint of the masters success is never guaranteed. Human pets can always withhold love and rebel; they can also acquire power and wealth for themselves by subtle means. All these paths are open to them because, unlike an exploited farm slave or factory hand, the pet is by definition an object of value, to which attention is paid, however condescendingly or capriciously. Between master and personal slave there exists an intimacy of physical contact and regard that is closer than that between master and household servant and far closer than that between employer and worker in a capitalist society. Human pets, if they wish, can skillfully exploit this intimacy for their own benefit. In a patriarchal society, for example, powerful men may have for their enjoyment and prestige concubines or slave women. History, however, is full of stories of how some of these women, despite their lowly station, have managed to dominate their masters and acquire enormous riches and influence for themselves. Another well-known example is from the history of eunuchs. Humiliatingly deprived of their full manhood in order to serve as guardians of a potentate's women, some of them were nonetheless able to exploit their positions—including that of formal powerlessness—to become, paradoxically, potentates themselves with nearly all the attributes and prerogatives of such persons except that of independence. A third example might be the mammy of the Old South. The basis of her power, like that of all privileged subordinates, lay in her access to and intimacy with the private and tender world of the powerful. Mammy raised her mistress's children and bound them to her with unbreakable ties of affection. She was the confidante not only of the children and the mistress but sometimes even of the master. A symbol of her authority was the whip, which she used on black and white servants alike when they thwarted her will. In moments of righteous anger, even the master and the mistress might not escape her tongue-lashing.[7] But these prerogatives were hers only on condition of unquestioning loyalty. Concubine, eunuch, and mammy—all must show, if not feel, total devotion. Moreover, they knew (as all those around them knew) that their standing derived wholly from conditions of intimacy with another, sovereign source of power.

Dominance is the theme of this book. Now that we approach its end, we need to round out the picture by turning briefly to the converse of dominance—dependency and obedience, the widespread and seemingly easy acceptance of the status of pethood. The question of acceptance does not arise with respect to plants and comes to a head with respect to humans; and it is to the problem of human submission that we now turn. Why submit? First and foremost among the reasons is discrepancy in power. Consider this discrepancy as it exists between nature and people. Until the modern period, nature was perceived by most people in the world as overwhelmingly powerful. At different times and in different cultures, people have humbly regarded themselves as "children" and nature as "parent." Nature was a sovereign power that must not be crossed. It provided sustenance but also, often inexplicably, inflicted punishment. Whether the one or the other, humans chose to believe that nature showed parental concern and that it was their obligation to respond to this concern with respect and love.[8] So completely did humans feel nature's dominance and their own helplessness that they frequently denied the initiatives they were able to take. They tended to minimize their role as creators and shapers of reality, despite all the evidences that stretched before them—fields and villages and (in the case of civilizations) cities of great size and splendor. Civilizations, after all, could emerge only through the mastery of nature. It is remarkable how consistently people in the past have thought it expedient to suppress this fact. From time to time there were boasts of progress and of subduing nature, but not often. Far more pervasive were the fears of offending the gods, of nature's revenge in the form of famine and pestilence, and of living in a world unbounded by externally imposed limits. Before the modern period, even in high civilizations, submission to nature and acceptance of a permanent state of childhood were the common posture.

At a microscale, a vast discrepancy of power exists between parent and child. Childhood dependency is exceptionally long among humans, and childhood is pethood. Parents and other grownups play with young children as though they were kids or pups or dolls to be clothed and unclothed. Children have to be trained in special skills and are praised as they acquire them. Children are patted on the head for being "good," and usually for being "good *at*" something. Children learn to place value less on who they are than on what they can do, on the more or less specialized tasks and roles they can perform. They are pleased when they have won the approval of an adult for what they can do. And, of course, they look up to adults for protection, guidance, and affection.

In a hierarchical society, members of the lower class are treated as perpetual minors to be shaped and patronized all their lives. The elite perceive and present paternalism as a natural order. It is natural for some to rule, provided the rule is benevolent, and it is natural for others to obey—and obey not grudgingly but as would filial children to their parents. Given the fact that most people have had the experience of submitting to nature and to human parents, it is not hard to understand why this paternalistic model of the social order should seem reasonable, especially when it is backed up—as it inevitably is—by irresistible force. We do know that this model has won acceptance in a remarkably wide range of social and historical contexts: think, for example, of the Chinese magistrate (the "father-official") and his charges, the feudal lord and his vassals, the shepherd-bishop and his flock, the Old South planter and his household, the German factory owner and his workers, among others.[9]

Inequality of power in society and acceptance by the dominated members of their status as a mere skill or even thing are suggested by the names that people assume. In Europe, whereas a nobleman is known by his title and his geographical base (for example, the duke of Bedford and the marquis de Rambouillet), the common man is usually known by his given (Christian) name, which may be altered to become a pet name, and sometimes also by his occupation, for example, Jim Baker. Title and geographical base define the power of a lord: some titles and geographical bases signify more power than do others. That is the extent of the lord's limitation. Otherwise, he is free—and he *is*, that is, he does not have to define himself further by a line of work. The common man, by contrast, clings to an identity given by a line of work. Skill is the source of his pride. He is baker. He makes things, and he himself is a sort of thing—a fine tool that makes fine things. His master praises him not for what he is but for his having learned something and thereby become someone (or thing).

The poet William Butler Yeats wrote: "Never shall a young man, / Thrown into despair / By those great honey-coloured ramparts at your ear, / Love you for yourself alone / And not for your yellow hair." Actually, the idea of being loved for "oneself alone" is a highly individualistic, romantic, and abstract idea that could not have been widely held in any society. Most people are content to be appreciated for whatever quality or skill they may possess. To be categorized as someone with adorable ramparts at the ear or as an amusing poser of riddles does imply that severe limits have been put on what that person can be and do, but few people would in fact object. To be noticed at all is rewarding. *What* is being noticed matters relatively little. Most people—most of us—do not object to being a "thing," provided it is an appreciated thing. There is, moreover, comfort in being a thing the value of which, being externally fixed, does not depend on internal striving.

Passivity is an integral part of human experience and may well lie at the psychic core of our being. Historically, humans have had to be passive in the face of nature; then, with the grip of nature more or less broken, they have had to be passive in the face of the powers of society. Furthermore, every individual was once a child, passive to the initiative and rule of parents. It is far from true that humans, collectively or individually, have always felt the state of passivity to be a great burden and the product of oppression. After all, the Golden Age is placed in the past, when nature ruled with a benevolent hand; or when priest-kings ruled with a firm hand but also provided security; or when parents dominated but also cared. In retrospection, the status of being a child, a minor, or even a pet can have a certain appeal on account of the accompanying feelings of safety and passivity. At the level of individual experience, even a "shaker of the world" yearns to be dictated to at the marginal areas of his life, and no matter how great the thirst for life and activity, every person still welcomes nightfall and the pleasures of yielding to drowsiness and sleep.

Given the long history of nature's dominance, it is not surprising that humans have learned to see merit in the submissive posture. Given the horrors of death and destruction and of enslavement to harsh labor that despots, throughout history, have fitfully inflicted on their fellow creatures, it is understandable why the status of pet, plaything, or adornment in some despot's household should seem bearable, even desirable. There is sweetness in yielding and pleasure in being dominated, especially if along with that domination come intimacy with power and tangible rewards, not the least of which are power's gestures of affection.

While passivity is both necessary and desirable, the ability to dominate is even more necessary and desirable because it is a vital sign of life. Children everywhere begin their careers of power by playing first with inanimate toys, then with small, crawling things. Adults weakened and disoriented by disease or age may regain a sense of life by, first, playing with plants; then, as their conditions improve they take on the greater challenge of playing with tame animals. Play, in these instances, ideally mixes dominance with affection, control with nurturing care. In actuality, however, the toys are broken and the animals are emasculated, discarded, or dead, as the children grow up to occupy larger stages of action and as adult patients, to the extent that their sense of power is restored, resume the more difficult task of ordering other people.

Human relation with nature is seldom pure. Whether we use plants and animals for economic or playful and aesthetic ends, we *use* them; we do not attend to them for their own good, except in fables. As to our relation with other people, exploitation to some degree is unavoidable in any hierarchical society. In all civilizations it can be extremely harsh, even in the creation of seemingly harmless cultural artifacts such as the pleasure garden. The exercise of power, in itself, can give pleasure; perhaps that is one reason why exploitation is so pervasive. However, there is pleasure of a special sadoerotic kind when power is used to reduce other humans to the status of pets. Whereas a child can order toy soldiers and dolls around as though they were real people, a potentate has the satisfaction of playing with real people as though they were stuffed toys.

In human relations, power is not inevitably abused. A parent or a teacher, for instance, may indeed try to control a child but only so that he or she may grow and prosper. Friends can use the power at their disposal to generate for each other, to use Roland Barthes's phrase, "spaces that resonate." In each case, virtue goes out of the donor, leaving behind at least a temporary sense of depletion; simultaneously, the recipient gains a new expanse of life. What transpires is an act so rare as to escape the coarse observational net of social science; it is power as creative attention, or love.

NOTES

CHAPTER 1. INTRODUCTION

1. Pitrim A. Sorokin, *The Ways and Power of Love* (Boston: Beacon Press, 1954).
2. Lewis Mumford, *The Myth of the Machine: Technics and Human Development* (New York: Harcourt, Brace and World, 1967).

CHAPTER 2. POWER AND DOMINANCE

1. George Santayana, *Reason in Society*, vol. 2 of *The Life of Reason* (1905; reprint, New York: Dover Publications, 1980), 81.
2. Colin Wilson, *Origins of the Sexual Impulse* (London: Arthur Baker, 1963), 167.
3. Wilhelm von Humboldt, *Humanist Without Portfolio* (Detroit: Wayne State University Press, 1963), 383–84.
4. John Updike, *Picked-Up Pieces* (New York: Knopf, 1975), 89.
5. J. Glenn Gray, *The Warriors: Reflections on Man in Battle* (New York: Harper Torchbooks, 1967), 51.
6. Daniel David Luckenbill, *The Annals of Sennacherib* (Chicago: University of Chicago Press, 1924), 17.
7. S. N. Kramer, *The Sumerians: Their History, Culture, and Character* (Chicago: University of Chicago Press, 1963), 125.
8. Quoted by Theodor Adorno, *Minima Moralia: Reflections from Damaged Life* (London: NLB, 1978), 78.
9. Ernest Becker, *Escape from Evil* (New York: Free Press, 1975), 1–2.
10. Quoted by F. L. Lucas, *The Drama of Chekhov, Synge, Yeats, and Pirandello* (London: Cassell, 1965), 13.
11. W. N. P. Barbellion, *Enjoying Life and Other Literary Remains* (London: Chatto and Windus, 1919), 107.
12. Seneca, *Letters from a Stoic*, trans. Robin Campbell (Harmondsworth, Middlesex: Penguin Books, 1969), 146.
13. Peter Laslett, *The World We Have Lost* (New York: Scribner's, 1971), 65.
14. Roy Perrott, *The Aristocrats: A Portrait of Britain's Nobility and Their Way of Life Today* (London: Weidenfeld and Nicolson, 1968), 202.
15. Bertrand de Jouvenal, *On Power: Its Nature and the History of Its Growth* (New York: Viking, 1949), 101.

16. Wolfram Eberhard, *Conquerors and Rulers: Social Forces in Medieval China* (Leiden: E. J. Brill, 1965), 122–23.

17. Arthur F. Wright, *The Sui Dynasty* (New York: Knopf, 1978), 49–50.

18. Gilette Ziegler, *The Court of Versailles in the Reign of Louis XIV* (London: George Allen and Unwin, 1966), 30.

19. Karl Wittfogel, *Oriental Despotism* (New Haven: Yale University Press, 1957), 152–53.

20. Elias Canetti, *Crowds and Power* (New York: Seabury Press, 1978), 389–90.

21. Malcolm Muggeridge, *Things Past* (New York: Morrow, 1978), 71.

22. Desmond Morris, *Intimate Behavior* (New York: Random House, 1971), 158.

23. Jean-Paul Sartre, *Saint Genet* (New York: Braziller, 1963), 360–61.

24. David McCullough, *Mornings on Horseback* (New York: Simon and Schuster, 1981), 88.

25. Jacques le Goff, *Time, Work, and Culture in the Middle Ages* (Chicago: University of Chicago Press, 1982), 49.

26. See the short stories of Harvey Swados in *On the Line* (Boston: Little, Brown, 1957).

27. P. Kropotkin, *Memoirs of a Revolutionist* (1899; reprint, New York: Horizon Press, 1968), 10.

28. Joseph Needham, *Science and Civilisation in China*, vol. 4, pt. 2: "Mechanical Engineering" (Cambridge at the University Press, 1965), 132, 160.

CHAPTER 3. GARDENS OF POWER AND OF CAPRICE

1. Cicero, *De natura deorum*, trans. H. Rackham (New York: Putnam's, 1933), 271.

2. Mencius, *The Four Books*, trans. James Legge (New York: Paragon Book Reprint Corp., 1966), bk. 3, pt. 2, 674–75.

3. Miles Hadfield, *The Art of the Garden* (New York: Dutton, 1965), 93.

4. Lucy Norton, comp. and trans., *Saint-Simon at Versailles* (London: Hamish Hamilton, 1958), 265.

5. Loraine Kuck, *The World of the Japanese Garden* (New York and Tokyo: Walker/Weatherhill, 1968), 138.

6. Quoted in Sheila Haywood, "The Indian Background—The Emperors and Their Gardens," in *The Gardens of Mughul India: A History and A Guide*, ed. Sylvia Crowe et al. (London: Thames and Hudson, 1972), 93.

7. Axel Boethius, *The Golden House of Nero: Some Aspects of Roman Architecture* (Ann Arbor: University of Michigan Press, 1960), 108–09; Suetonius, *The Twelve Caesars*, trans. Robert Graves (Baltimore: Penguin Books, 1957), 224–25; Tacitus *Annals* 15.42.

8. S. Lang, "The Genesis of the English Landscape Garden," in *The Picturesque Garden and Its Influence Outside the British Isles*, ed. Nikolaus Pevsner (Washington, D.C.: Dumbarton Oaks, 1974), 20, 23; Margaret Jourdain, *The Work of William Kent: Artist, Painter, Designer and Landscape Gardener*

(London: Country Life Limited, 1948), 76.

9. Dora Wiebenson, *The Picturesque Garden in France* (Princeton: Princeton University Press, 1978), 11-12.

10. Robert and Monica Beckinsale, *The English Heartland* (London: Duckworth, 1980), 186; Edward Malins, *English Landscaping and Literature 1660-1840* (London: Oxford University Press, 1966), 99.

11. Maggie Keswick, *The Chinese Garden: History, Art and Architecture* (New York: Rizzoli, 1978), 53. Likewise in Renaissance Italy. "Borso d'Este, lord of Ferrara, decided to have a mountain built on the flat Ferrarese landscape, in January 1471. All the peasants of the region were put under a decree of forced labor; ships, wagons, and carts were employed to haul earth and rocks to the site . . ." Lauro Martines, *Power and Imagination: City-States in Renaissance Italy* (New York: Vintage Books, 1980), 267.

12. Teresa McLean, *Medieval English Gardens* (New York: Viking, 1980), 106.

13. William Howard Adams, *The French Garden 1500-1800* (New York: Braziller, 1979), 40, 47.

14. Bernard Palissy, *The Delectable Garden*, trans. Helen M. Fox (Peekskill, N.Y.: Watch Hill Press, 1931), 22-25.

15. The advice of a late Ming dynasty work on the garden, the *Yuan Yeh* (1634). See Osvald Sirén, *Gardens of China* (New York: Ronald Press, 1949), 22.

16. A. Richard Turner, *The Vision of Landscape in Renaissance Italy* (Princeton: Princeton University Press, 1966), 197-98.

17. Helen M. Fox, *André le Nôtre: Garden Architect to Kings* (New York: Crown, 1962), 31, 33, 35.

18. Edward Norgate, *Miniatura: or The Art of Limning*, MS written between 1648 and 1650, ed. Martin Hardie, (Oxford at the Clarendon Press, 1919), 43.

19. Derek Clifford, *A History of Garden Design* (London: Faber and Faber, 1962), 140.

20. Nan Fairbrother, *Men and Gardens* (New York: Knopf, 1956), 94.

21. Pierre de Nolhac, *The Trianon of Marie-Antoinette* (New York: Brentano's, n.d.), 203-04.

22. Quoted by Wiebenson, *Picturesque Garden in France*, 97-98.

23. Donald N. Wilber, *Persian Gardens and Garden Pavilions* (Washington, D.C.: Dumbarton Oaks, 1979), 14.

24. *Hung Lu Meng* (The Story of the Stone), chap. 17, trans. H. B. Joly (1892).

25. Sirén, *Gardens of China*, 19.

26. Ibid., 63.

27. Keswick, *Chinese Garden*, 119.

28. Chuin Tung, "Chinese Gardens: Contrasts, Designs," in *Chinese Houses and Gardens*, ed. Henry Inn and S. C. Lee (New York: Hastings House, 1950), 28.

29. *The Story of the Stone*, chap. 17, trans. David Hawkes (Harmondsworth, Middlesex: Penguin Books, 1973), 346.

30. Fox, *André le Nôtre*, 90.

31. Adams, *The French Garden*, 84.

CHAPTER 4. FOUNTAINS AND PLANTS

1. Mencius, *The Four Books*, bk. 6, pt. 1, 852.

2. Jacques Gernet, *Daily Life in China on the Eve of the Mongol Invasion 1250-1276* (London: George Allen and Unwin, 1962), 51-52; A. C. Moule, *Quinsai* (London: Cambridge University Press, 1957), 29-30.

3. Needham, *Science and Civilisation in China*, 133-34.

4. Wilber, *Persian Gardens*, 15.

5. Crowe et al., *The Gardens of Mughul India*, 45, 140, 148, 158; Jonas Lehrman, *Earthly Paradise: Garden and Courtyard in Islam* (Berkeley and Los Angeles: University of California Press, 1980), 113.

6. Pierre Grimal, *Les Jardins Romains* (Paris: Presses Universitaires de France, 1969), 293.

7. Helen H. Tanzer, *The Villas of Pliny the Younger* (New York: Columbia University Press, 1924), 23.

8. Eleanor Clark, *Rome and A Villa* (Garden City, N.Y.: Doubleday, 1952), 148.

9. Hunter Rouse and Simon Ince, *History of Hydraulics* (New York: Dover, 1963), 32. "Another popular belief is that the aqueducts were an efficient triumph of Roman engineering genius, whereas it is clear from Frontinus that they all leaked like sieves." See H. C. V. Morton, *The Waters of Rome* (London: Connoisseur and Joseph, 1966), 35.

10. David R. Coffin, *The Villa d'Este at Tivoli* (Princeton: Princeton University Press, 1960), 38.

11. Georgina Masson, *Italian Gardens* (New York: Abrams, 1961), 136.

12. Morton, *Waters of Rome*, 288.

13. Quoted in Peter Coats, *Great Gardens of the Western World* (New York: Putnam, 1963), 87.

14. Norton, *Saint-Simon at Versailles*, 262.

15. Adams, *The French Garden*, 88.

16. Fox, *André le Nôtre*, 101-02.

17. Adams, *The French Garden*, 88.

18. Fairbrother, *Men and Gardens*, 96; George F. Hervey and Jack Hems, *The Book of the Garden Pond* (London: Faber and Faber, 1970), 27; Needham, *Science and Civilisation in China*, 157; Coffin, *Villa d'Este*, 28.

19. *The Complete Works of Michael de Montaigne*, "Montaigne's Journey into Italy," William Hazlitt, trans. (New York: Worthington, 1889), 591.

20. Montaigne, *Complete Works*, 612.

21. William Cowper, *Poetry and Prose*, comp. Brian Spiller (London: Rupert Hart-Davis, 1968), 462.

22. Masson, *Italian Gardens*, 148.

23. Francis Bacon, *Sylva Sylvarum or a Natural History* (first published in 1627), in *The Works of Francis Bacon* (Boston: Brown and Taggard, 1862), 5:392.

24. John Parkinson, *Paradisi in Sole Paradisus Terrestris* (1629; reprint, Amsterdam: Theatrum Orbis Terrarum, 1975), 22, 245, 338-39.

25. Eleanor Perényi, *Green Thoughts: A Writer in the Garden* (New York: Random House, 1981), 33.
26. Tanzer, *Villas of Pliny*, 18, 22–23.
27. McLean, *Medieval English Gardens*, 100.
28. Giovanni Rucellai, *Ed Il Suo Zibaldone*, ed. Alessandro Perosa (London: The Warburg Institute, University of London, 1960), 21.
29. Quoted in Marie Luise Gothein, *A History of Garden Art*, trans. Mrs. Archer-Hind (New York: Dutton, 1928), 1:212–13.
30. Hadfield, *The Art of the Garden*, 19.
31. Franklin Hamilton Hazlehurst, *Jacques Boyceau and the French Formal Garden* (Athens: University of Georgia Press, 1966), 39.
32. Francis Bacon, *Of Gardens* (1625; reprint, Northampton, Mass.: Gehenna Press, 1959).
33. *The Journeys of Celia Fiennes, or Through England on a Side Saddle in the Time of William and Mary 1685–1697*, ed. Christopher Morris (London: Cresset Press, 1947), 341.
34. Alexander Pope in *The Guardian*, September 29, 1713, no. 173; quoted in Malins, *English Landscaping and Literature*, 23–24.
35. Ronald Blythe, *Akenfield: Portrait of An English Village* (New York: Pantheon Books, 1969), 107.
36. *Twin Cities Reader*, April 30, May 7, 1981.
37. Rolf Stein, "Jardin en Miniature d'Extrême-Orient," *Bulletin de l'Ecole Française d'Extrême-Orient* 42 (1942): 1–104 (Hanoi).
38. Arthur de Carle Sowerby, *Nature in Chinese Art* (New York: John Day, 1940), 156.
39. See E. Chavannes, *Le T'ai Shan* (Paris: Ernest Leroux, 1910); Keswick, *Chinese Garden*, 37.
40. Stein, "Jardin en Miniature," 28.
41. Perényi, *Green Thoughts*, 76–78.
42. Keswick, *Chinese Garden*, 38.
43. Stein, "Jardin en Miniature," 8; Keswick, *Chinese Garden*, 49.
44. For instance, Doug Hall and Don Black, *The South African Bonsai Book* (Capetown: Howard Timmins, 1976), 20.
45. Keswick, *Chinese Garden*, 49.
46. Wilber, *Persian Gardens*, 8–9.
47. Gothein, *History of Garden Art*, 148–49.
48. Ibid., 190–91.
49. Martin H. Krieger, "What's Wrong with Plastic Trees?" *Science* 179 (1973): 446–55.

CHAPTER 5. ANIMALS: FROM POWERS TO PETS

1. *The Letters of Evelyn Underhill*, Charles Williams, ed. (London: Longmans, Green, 1943), 301–02.
2. Walker D. Wyman, *Mythical Creatures of the North Country* (River Falls,

Wis.: State University Press, 1969).

3. Edward H. Schafer, *The Vermilion Bird: T'ang Images of the South* (Berkeley and Los Angeles: University of California Press, 1967), 206-07.

4. Martin P. Nilsson, *Greek Popular Religion* (New York: Columbia University Press, 1940), 10-14.

5. Gustave Loisel, *Histoire des ménageries: de l'antiquité à nos jours* (Paris: Henri Laurens, 1912), 1:18-19; M. Oldfield Howey, *The Cat in the Mysteries of Religion and Magic* (London: Rider, 1931), 145.

6. Zofia Ameisenowa, "Animal-headed Gods, Evangelists, Saints and Righteous Men," *Journal of the Warburg and Courtauld Institutes* 12 (1949): 21-45.

7. Francis Klingender, *Animals in Art and Thought to the End of the Middle Ages*, ed. Evelyn Antal and John Harthan (Cambridge: MIT Press, 1971), 302-03; Wera von Blankenburg, *Heilige und dämonische Tiere: die Symbolsprache der deutsch Ornamentik im frühen Mittelalter* (Leipzig: Koehler & Amerlang, 1943).

8. Charles Diehl, *Manuel d'art Byzantin* (Paris: Librairie Auguste Picard, 1925), 1:368.

9. *The Travels of Marco Polo*, R. E. Latham, trans. (Harmondsworth, Middlesex: Penguin Books, 1958), 111-12.

10. George Jennison, *Animals for Show and Pleasure in Ancient Rome* (Manchester: Manchester University Press, 1937), 30-35.

11. *Pliny Natural History*, bk. 8, H. Rackham, trans. (London: Heinemann, 1940), 3:5, 127.

12. *Seneca's Letters to Lucilius* (no. 85), E. Phillips Barker, trans. (Oxford at the Clarendon Press, 1932), 2:41-42.

13. Jennison, *Animals for Show*, 65, 71-72, 90.

14. Loisel, *Histoire des ménageries*, 84-89; Jennison, *Animals for Show*, 123-24.

15. Heini Hediger, *Man and Animal in the Zoo* (London: Routledge and Kegan Paul, 1970), 11.

16. James Fischer, *Zoos of the World* (London: Aldus Books, 1966), 23-43.

17. E. R. Hughes, *Two Chinese Poets: Vignettes of Han Life and Thought* (Princeton: Princeton University Press, 1960), 27.

18. Edward A. Armstrong, *Saint Francis: Nature Mystic* (Berkeley and Los Angeles: University of California Press, 1976), 7; Loisel, *Histoire des ménageries*, 163.

19. Klingender, *Animals in Art*, 447-49.

20. "Cortes's Account of the City of Mexico; from his Second Letter to the Emperor Charles V," *Old South Leaflets* (Boston: Directors of the Old South Work, n.d.), vol. 2, no. 35, pp. 9-10.

21. Neil Harris, *Humbug: The Art of P. T. Barnum* (Chicago: University of Chicago Press, 1973), 52-53.

22. Richard D. Altick, *The Shows of London* (Cambridge: Harvard University Press, 1978), 22-33; Harris, *Art of Barnum*, 33.

23. Altick, *Shows of London*, 317-19; James Turner, *Reckoning with the Beast:*

Animals, Pain and Humanity in the Victorian Mind (Baltimore: Johns Hopkins University Press, 1980), 54, 63.

24. William Mann, *Wild Animals in and out of the Zoo* (New York: Smithsonian Scientific Series, 1930), 45.

25. Hediger, *Man and Animal*, 116.

26. Ibid., 121-23.

27. Vera Hegi, *Les Captifs du zoo* (Lausanne: Spes, 1942), 8, 13; quoted in Henri F. Ellenberger, "The Mental Hospital and the Zoological Garden," in *Animals and Man in Historical Perspective*, ed. Joseph and Barrie Klaits (New York: Harper and Row, 1974), 69.

28. Robert R. Reed, Jr., *Bedlam on the Jacobean Stage* (Cambridge: Harvard University Press, 1952), 25.

29. Albert Deutsch, *The Mentally Ill in America*, 2d ed. (New York: Columbia University Press, 1949), 64-65.

30. John Prest, *The Garden of Eden: The Botanic Garden and the Re-Creation of Paradise* (New Haven and London: Yale University Press, 1981), 25-26, 51, 54, pl. 39.

31. Ibid., 84.

32. Adams, *The French Garden*, 18.

33. Prest, *Garden of Eden*, 44-45.

34. Keswick, *Chinese Garden*, 148.

35. Tzu-hsui, *Record of Hua Yang Palace*, trans. Grace Wan; quoted in Keswick, *Chinese Garden*, 54.

36. Fairbrother, *Men and Gardens*, 92.

CHAPTER 6. ANIMAL PETS: CRUELTY AND AFFECTION

1. Kathleen Szasz, *Petishism: Pets and Their People in the Western World* (New York: Holt, Rinehart and Winston, 1969), p. xiii.

2. Glenn Radde, personal communication. See Robert H. Wilbur, "Pets, Pet Ownership and Animal Control: Social and Psychological Attitudes," *The National Conference on Dog and Cat Control* (1975), Denver, *Proceedings* (1976), 21-34.

3. On castrating instruments, see *Omaha Vaccine Company Summer Catalog 1983*.

4. Elizabeth Marshall Thomas, *The Harmless People* (New York: Vintage Books, 1965), 51-52.

5. Ibid., 53.

6. Edward Moffat Weyer, *The Eskimos: Their Environment and Folkways* (New Haven: Yale University Press, 1932), 73.

7. Knud Rasmussen, "Intellectual Life of the Iglulik Eskimos," *Report of the Fifth Thule Expedition 1921-24*, The Danish Expedition to Arctic North America, vol. 7, no. 1, 1929 (Copenhagen), p. 74.

8. Ibid., 56.

9. E. E. Evans-Pritchard, *The Nuer* (Oxford at the Clarendon Press, 1940), 37.

10. Ibid., 27.
11. George Santayana, *Dominations and Powers* (New York: Scribner's, 1951), 75.
12. Quoted in Margaret Titcomb, *Dog and Man in the Ancient Pacific* (Honolulu: Bernice P. Bishop Museum Special Publication 59, 1969), 3-4.
13. Photograph in Adolph H. Schultz, "Some Factors Influencing the Social Life of Primates in General and of Early Man in Particular," in *Social Life of Early Man*, ed. S. L. Washburn (Chicago: Aldine, 1961), 72.
14. Titcomb, *Dog and Man*, 9-10.
15. S. L. Washburn, "Speculations of the Interrelations of the History of Tools and Biological Evolution," in *The Evolution of Man's Capacity for Culture*, ed. J. N. Spuhler (Detroit: Wayne State University Press, 1959); S. L. Washburn and C. S. Lancaster, "The Evolution of Hunting," in *Man the Hunter*, ed. R. B. Lee and I. DeVore (Chicago: Aldine, 1968), 293-303, esp. 293, 300.
16. George F. Hervey and Jack Hems, *The Goldfish* (London: Faber and Faber, 1968), 248-49. I have depended on this work for the section on goldfish.
17. *Japanese Goldfish: Their Varieties and Cultivation* (Washington, D.C.: W. F. Roberts, 1909), 37.
18. Quoted by Hervey and Hems, *Goldfish*, 77.
19. George Hervey, *The Goldfish of China in the Eighteenth Century* (London: The China Society, 1950), 33.
20. Ibid., 26.
21. Hervey and Hems, *Goldfish*, 228.
22. Ibid., 240.
23. H. H. Scullard, *The Elephant in the Greek and Roman World* (Ithaca: Cornell University Press, 1974), 250-59.
24. Frederick E. Zeuner, *A History of Domesticated Animals* (New York: Harper and Row, 1963), 36-43, 46-49, 51-63.
25. Juliet Clutton-Brock, *Domesticated Animals from Early Times* (Austin: University of Texas Press, 1981), 22-24.
26. Konrad Lorenz, *Man Meets Dog* (Harmondsworth, Middlesex: Penguin Books, 1964), 24.
27. John Paul Scott and John L. Fuller, *Genetics and the Social Behavior of the Dog* (Chicago: University of Chicago Press, 1965), 29.
28. M. Hilzheimer, *Animal Remains from Tell Asmar*, Studies in Ancient Oriental Civilization, no. 20 (Chicago: University of Chicago Press, 1941); P. E. Newberry, Beni Hasan, part I, in F. L. Griffeth, ed., *Archaeological Survey of Egypt*, Egypt Exploration Fund (London: Kegan Paul, Trübner Co., 1893).
29. G. M. Trevelyan, *English Social History* (London: Longman, Green, 1942), 22-23.
30. Richard Blome, *The Gentlemans Recreation* (London: S. Roycroft, 1686), quoted in Scott and Fuller, *Social Behavior of the Dog*, 46-47.
31. Grace E. L. Boyd, "Poodle," in *The Book of the Dog*, ed. Brian Vesey-Fitzgerald (London: Nicholson and Watson, 1948), 598-99.

32. V. W. F. Collier, *Dogs of China and Japan in Nature and Art* (New York: Fredrick A. Stokes, 1921); Annie Coath Dixey, *The Lion Dog of Peking* (London: Peter Davies, 1931); Clifford L. B. Hubbard, "Pekinese," in Vesey-Fitzgerald, *Book of the Dog*, 583-86.

33. Rumer Godden, *The Butterfly Lions: The Pekinese in History, Legend and Art* (New York: Viking, 1978), 137.

34. Collier, *Dogs of China and Japan*, 53-54.

35. Lorenz, *Man Meets Dog*, 88-90.

36. Godden, *Butterfly Lions*, 159.

37. Nicholas Cox, *The Gentleman's Recreation* (1677; reprint, East Ardsley, 1973); quoted in Keith Thomas, *Man and the Natural World: A History of Modern Sensibility* (New York: Pantheon Books, 1983), 60.

38. W. L. McCandlish, "Breeding for Show," in Vesey-Fitzgerald, *Book of the Dog*, 84.

39. Winnie Barber, "The Canine Cult," in ibid., 105.

40. J. R. Ackerley, *My Dog Tulip* (New York: Fleet, 1965), 68, 77, 84.

41. A. Croxton-Smith, "The Dog in History," in Vesey-Fitzgerald, *Book of the Dog*, 24.

42. *Pliny's Natural History in Philemon Holland's Translation*, P. Turner, ed. (London: Centaur Press, 1962), 316.

43. "Alcibiades," in *Plutarch's Lives* (New York: Modern Library, n.d.), 238.

44. Gladys Scott Thomson, *Life in a Noble Household 1641-1700* (London: Jonathan Cape, 1937), 234.

45. Thomas de Grey, *The Compleat Horse-Man*, 3d ed. 1656; quoted in K. Thomas, *Man and the Natural World*, 100; see Trevelyan, *English Social History*, 280-81, 406-07.

46. Brian Vesey-Fitzgerald, *The Domestic Dog: An Introduction to Its History* (London: Routledge and Kegan Paul, 1957), 67.

47. Turner, *Reckoning with the Beast*, 19.

48. Mary Renault, *The Nature of Alexander* (Harmondsworth, Middlesex: Penguin Books, 1983), 158, 168; Norton, *Saint-Simon at Versailles*, 260; Thomas Carlyle, *History of Friedrich II of Prussia called Frederick the Great*, ed. John Clive (Chicago: University of Chicago Press, 1969), 469.

49. Sylvia Townsend Warner, *T. H. White* (London: Jonathan Cape, 1967), 72, 211-13.

50. Lorenz, *Man Meets Dog*, 138-39, 194-95.

CHAPTER 7. CHILDREN AND WOMEN

1. Nancy F. Cott, *The Bonds of Womanhood: "Woman's Sphere" in New England 1750-1835* (New Haven and London: Yale University Press, 1977), 47.

2. Jules Henry, *Jungle People: A Kaingáng Tribe of the Highlands of Brazil* (J. J. Augustin, 1941), 18.

3. Lloyd deMause, "The Evolution of Childhood," in *The History of Childhood*, ed. Lloyd deMause (New York: Harper Torchbook, 1975), 21.

4. Ibid., 31.
5. Hans Licht, *Sexual Life in Ancient Greece* (London: Routledge and Kegan Paul, 1932), 438; Cora E. Lutz, "Musonius Rufus, 'The Roman Socrates,'" in Alfred R. Bellinger, ed., *Yale Classical Studies*, vol. 10 (1947), 101; Pierre Grimal, *Love in Ancient Rome* (New York: Crown, 1967), 106-07; Suetonius, *The Twelve Caesars*, 131; Petronius, *The Satyricon*, trans. William Arrowsmith (New York: Mentor Books, 1960).
6. E. Soulié and E. de Barthélemy, eds., *Journal de Jean Héroard sur l'enfance et la jeunesse de Louis XIII, 1601-1610* (Paris: Firmin Didot Frères, 1868), 1: 34, 35, 45; Philippe Ariès, *Centuries of Childhood* (New York: Vintage Books, 1965), 101.
7. Ariès, *Centuries of Childhood*, 47, 130-31.
8. In New England, "as early as the 1760s school districts began the practice of hiring women rather than men as teachers for summer sessions, which were for very young children and older girls, who were excluded from winter terms." Cott, *Bonds of Womanhood*, 30.
9. Ariès, *Centuries of Childhood*, 103.
10. Philip E. Slater, *The Glory of Hera: Greek Mythology and the Greek Family* (Boston: Beacon Press, 1968), 30-31.
11. Erich Neumann, *The Great Mother: An Analysis of the Archetype* (Princeton: Princeton University Press, 1972), 148-49.
12. Peggy Reeves Sanday, *Female Power and Male Dominance: On the Origins of Sexual Inequality* (Cambridge: Cambridge University Press, 1981), 115.
13. J. J. Rousseau, "Sur la femme," *Oeuvres complètes* (Paris: Hachette), 6: 28; quoted in Susan Moller Okin, *Women in Western Political Thought* (Princeton: Princeton University Press, 1979), 149.
14. Annette Kolodny, *The Lay of the Land: Metaphor as Experience and History in American Life and Letters* (Chapel Hill: University of North Carolina Press, 1975), 15.
15. The idea of women's speech as blunt, lacking the subtlety of men's, appears among the Merinda tribe in Madagascar. See Michele Zimbalist Rosaldo, "A Theoretical Overview," in *Women, Culture, and Society*, ed. Michele Zimbalist Rosaldo and Louise Lamphere (Stanford: Stanford University Press, 1974), 20.
16. Robert Hans van Gulik, *Sexual Life in Ancient China* (Leiden: E. J. Brill, 1961), 17.
17. Quoted in ibid., 224.
18. Ibid., 184.
19. Ray Huang, *1587: A Year of No Significance: The Ming Dynasty in Decline* (New Haven and London: Yale University Press, 1981), 28-29.
20. Gulik, *Sexual Life in Ancient China*, 189-90.
21. Barnette Miller, *Beyond the Sublime Gate: The Grand Seraglio of Stambul* (New Haven: Yale University Press, 1931), 96.
22. N. M. Penzer, *The Harēm: An Account of the Institution as It Existed in the Palace of the Turkish Sultans with a History of the Grand Seraglio from the Foundation to*

the Present Time (London: George G. Harrap, 1936), 179.

23. Despite Lady Mary Worley Montagu's dismissal of this custom as myth, Penzer believes that it has some basis in fact. Ibid.

24. Perényi, *Green Thoughts*, 259-70.

25. C. S. Lewis, *The Allegory of Love: A Study in Medieval Tradition* (London: Oxford University Press, 1958), 12.

26. Perényi, *Green Thoughts*, 263.

27. See Lewis Mumford on the "romantic suburb" in *The City in History: Its Origins, Its Transformations, and Its Prospects* (New York: Harcourt, Brace and World, 1961), 491.

28. Cott, *Bonds of Womanhood*, 5.

29. Quentin Bell, *On Human Finery*, rev. ed. (New York: Schocken Books, 1978), 142; see also Richard Sennett, *The Fall of Public Man* (Cambridge: Cambridge University Press, 1977), 169

30. Other characterizations occur in the novels of Thackeray, Dickens, and Disraeli.

31. Henrik Ibsen, "A Doll's House," in *Six Plays*, trans. Eva Le Gallienne (New York: Modern Library, 1953), 76.

CHAPTER 8. SLAVES, DWARFS, FOOLS

1. Philip Mason, *Patterns of Dominance* (London: Oxford University Press, 1971); Barrington Moore, Jr., *Injustice: The Social Basis of Obedience and Revolt* (New York: M. E. Sharpe, 1978).

2. W. C. Curry, *The Middle English Ideal of Personal Beauty* (Baltimore: J. H. Furst, 1916); J. E. Neale, *Queen Elizabeth I* (Harmondsworth, Middlesex: Penguin Books, 1961), 42.

3. Jacques J. Maquet, *The Premise of Inequality in Ruanda: A Study of Political Relations in a Central African Kingdom* (London: Oxford University Press, 1961).

4. *The Politics of Aristotle*, bk. 1, chap. 5, trans. Ernest Barker (London: Oxford University Press, 1958), 13-14.

5. W. H. Bruford, *Germany in the Eighteenth Century: The Social Background of the Literary Revival* (Cambridge at the University Press, 1939), 58.

6. "Lord Curzon, seeing British troops bathing in India, reflected how strange it was that the poor should have such white skin." In Philip Mason, *Prospero's Magic: Some Thoughts on Class and Race* (London: Oxford University Press, 1962), 1.

7. Marcus Porcius Cato, *On Agriculture*, trans. W. D. Hooper and H. B. Ash (London: Heinemann, 1934), 9; *Plutarch's Lives*, trans. John Dryden and revised by Arthur Hugh Clough (New York: Modern Library, n.d.), 414.

8. Crates (5th century B.C.) in *The Beasts*. Quoted by Thomas Wiedemann, *Greek and Roman Slavery* (Baltimore: Johns Hopkins University Press, 1981), 87-88.

9. Hans Licht, *Sexual Life in Ancient Greece*; William L. Westermann, *The Slave*

System of Greek and Roman Antiquity (Philadelphia: American Philosophical Society, 1955), 118.

10. Leslie Howard Owens, *This Species of Property: Slave Life and Culture in the Old South* (New York: Oxford University Press, 1976), 186-90.

11. Wiedemann, *Greek and Roman Slavery*, 78-79.

12. Yang Lien-sheng, "Great Families of Eastern Han," in *Chinese Social History*, ed. E-Tu Zen Sun, trans. John DeFrancis (Washington, D.C.: American Council of Learned Societies, 1956), 115.

13. *The Natural History of Pliny*, bk. 33, chap. 6, John Bostock and H. T. Riley, trans. (London: Henry G. Bohn, 1858), 6: 81.

14. Petronius, *The Satyricon*.

15. Jerome Blum, *Lord and Peasant in Russia: From the Ninth to the Nineteenth Century* (Princeton: Princeton University Press, 1971), 424.

16. Ibid., 456-57; Kropotkin, *Memoirs of a Revolutionist*, 28-29.

17. James Fenimore Cooper's observation when he was in London. Quoted by Frank E. Huggett, *Life Below Stairs: Domestic Servants in England from Victorian Times* (London: John Murray, 1977), 27.

18. Ibid., 13.

19. James Walvin, *Black and White: The Negro and English Society 1555-1945* (London: Allen Lane The Penguin Press, 1973), 7-11.

20. J. Jean Hecht, "Continental and Colonial Servants in Eighteenth-Century England," *Smith College Studies in History*, 40, (1954): 34, 37; Walvin, *Black and White*, 48.

21. Hecht, "Continental and Colonial Servants," 36n.

22. F. O. Shyllon, *Black Slaves in Britain* (London: Oxford University Press, 1974), 11.

23. Ibid., 9.

24. Douglas A. Lorimer, *Colour, Class and the Victorians* (Leicester: Leicester University Press, 1978), 86-89.

25. Thomas Carlyle, "The Nigger Question, 1849," in *Critical and Miscellaneous Essays* (London: Chapman and Hall, 1837-66), 4: 357-58.

26. Cao Xueqin, *The Story of the Stone*, vol. 3, "The Warning Voice," 157.

27. *Natural History of Pliny*, 81; Wiedemann, *Greek and Roman Slavery*, 34, 80.

28. Walvin, *Black and White*, 66; J. H. Ingraham, ed., *The Sunny South; or The Southerner at Home* (1860; reprint, New York: Negro Universities Press, 1968), 69-70; see also Orlando Patterson, *Slavery and Social Death* (Cambridge: Harvard University Press, 1982), 54-58.

29. See the names of servants in Cao Xueqin, *Story of the Stone*.

30. Winthrop D. Jordan, *White Over Black: American Attitudes Toward the Negro 1550-1812* (Chapel Hill: University of North Carolina Press, 1968), 161-62.

31. Kenneth M. Stampp, *The Peculiar Institution: Slavery in the Ante-Bellum South* (New York: Knopf, 1956), 172.

32. Eugene D. Genovese, *Roll, Jordan, Roll: The World the Slaves Made* (New York: Pantheon Books, 1974), 336.

33. Ibid., 61, 332, 334.
34. Frederick Douglass, *My Bondage and My Freedom* (1855; reprint, New York: Arno Press and The New York Times, 1968), 132-33.
35. Genovese, *Roll, Jordan, Roll*, 512-13.
36. Stampp, *Peculiar Institution*, 326-27.
37. Ibid., 329.
38. Jordan, *White Over Black*, 154-56.
39. Xenophon, *Cyropaedia* 7.5. 60-65, trans. W. Miller, vol. 2 (1914), The Loeb Classical Library.
40. N. M. Panzer, *The Harēm* (London: Harrap, 1936), 132-33.
41. Huang, *1587: A Year of No Significance*, 13, 19-21.
42. Sacheverell Sitwell, *Southern Baroque Revisited* (London: Weidenfeld and Nicolson, 1967), 224-39; Angus Heriot, *The Castrati in Opera* (London: Secker and Warburg, 1956).
43. E. Tietze-Conrat, *Dwarfs and Jesters in Art* (London: Phaidon Press, 1957), 7, 14; Leslie Fiedler, *Freaks: Myths and Images of the Secret Self* (New York: Simon and Schuster, 1978), 50-51.
44. Tietze-Conrat, *Dwarfs and Jesters*, 9.
45. Enid Welsford, *The Fool: His Social and Literary History* (London: Faber and Faber, n.d.), 59-60.
46. Ibid., 135; Tietze-Conrat, *Dwarfs and Jesters*, 80.
47. Tietze-Conrat, *Dwarfs and Jesters*.
48. Martines, *Power and Imagination*, 231.
49. Welsford, *The Fool*, 132-33.
50. Ibid., 182-83.

CHAPTER 9. DOMINANCE AND AFFECTION: CONCLUSIONS

1. Zeuner, *History of Domesticated Animals*, 39.
2. Colin M. Turnbull, *The Forest People: A Study of the Pygmies of the Congo* (Garden City, N.Y.: Anchor Books, 1962), 113.
3. Stephen Orgel, *The Illusion of Power: Political Theater in the English Renaissance* (Berkeley and Los Angeles: University of California Press, 1975).
4. *Sui Yang Ti Hai Shan Chi* (Sea and Mountain Records of Sui Yang-ti), in the *T'ang Sung Ch'uan Ch'i Chi* (Collection of Fictional Works of the T'ang and Sung Dynasties), trans. Alexander Soper. See Kuck, *World of the Japanese Garden*, 19-20.
5. Yi-Fu Tuan, *Segmented Worlds and Self: Group Life and Individual Consciousness* (Minneapolis: University of Minnesota Press, 1982), 52-85.
6. Gernet, *Daily Life in China*, 93.
7. Genovese, *Roll, Jordan, Roll*, 355-57.
8. Yi-Fu Tuan, "Geopiety: A Theme in Man's Attachment to Nature and to Place," in *Geographies of the Mind*, ed. David Lowenthal and Martyn J. Bowden (New York: Oxford University Press, 1976), 11-39.
9. On German factory worker docility, see Moore, *Injustice*, 258-59.

INDEX

Affection: distinguished from other feelings, 1–2, 5; pastoralists for their stock, 91–92; for dogs, 109–14; for children, 115, 116, 118–19; and inequality, 162–64

Alexander the Great (356–323 B.C.): his pets Bucephalus and Peritas, 112–13

Animal deities, 70–72

Animals in the garden: of rock and wood, 33, 34, 55, 56, 86, 87, 169; mechanical, 46–47, 67, 169; made of plants, 53, 57, 62–63; stuffed, 85

Artificial plants: medieval European, 52–53; Chinese, 66; Islamic, Persian, and Byzantine, 66–67, 72; modern home and city, 67–68

Bacon, Francis (1561–1626): on altering the shape of fruits, 50–51; topiary fantasies, 55

Becker, Ernest: on incorporation (eating), 9

Birds: mechanical, 46–47, 67; in parks and gardens, 76, 84–85; falconry, 77

Blacks: eunuchs, 126, 151; servants, 141; pets (boys), 141–42; entertainers, 144, 149; humiliation of, 146–48; indulgence toward, 148–49

Bonsai, 61–63, 76, 77, 154

Brown, Lancelot (1716–83), 20, 23–24, 49, 87

Canetti, Elias: on the dignity of sitting, 13

Carlyle, Thomas (1795–1881): his racism, 144

Castration: animals, 88–89; humans, 126, 149–53

Castrato, 152–53

Cato the Elder (234–149 B.C.): on slaves, 135, 136

China: and nomads, 11–12; size of labor teams, 12, 20; kowtow, 13; Sui Yang-ti's toys, 17; gardens, 19, 24, 25, 27, 29–36, 38, 60–63, 66, 86, 165–66; fountains, 38–39; hunting preserve, 76, 86; goldfish, 95–99; dogs, 104–06; harem, 123–25, 166

Cicero (106–43 B.C.): on dominance of nature, 18

Circus and museums, 74, 78–79

Civilization: extravagance of, 10–11; luxury and sweat, 14; menagerie and cosmos, 75–76; hunting as sport, 103–04, 111; and harshness, 176

Cosmos, 18, 75, 85, 165

Cruelty: unselfawareness of, 2; sadistic taunting, 15, 80, 121 (see humiliation); toward laborers, 21; toward plants, 28, 62–63; toward the insane, 83–84; among hunter-gatherers, 89–90; toward animals, 106, 108–09, 110, 111; toward children (see sexual abuse); in rage, 121

Dependency and obedience, 172–75

Destruction: in relation to power and creation, 7–10; of villages and old gardens, 19–20; as steps in learning and healing, 175–76

Dogs: percentage destroyed, 88; neutering of, 88–89; loved and eaten, 93; domestication and training of, 102–09; affection for, 109–14

Domestication, 99–109, 164

Douglass, Frederick (1817?–1895): on black children as pets, 148

Eden (paradise), 63, 84–87, 126–27

Elephants: performing tricks, 74, 75; tameability, 100